Water

a shared responsibility

The United Nations World Water Development Report 2

World **Water**
Assessment Programme

UNESCO
United Nations
Educational, Scientific and
Cultural Organization

BERGHAHN BOOKS

UN WATER

Published in 2006 jointly by the
**United Nations Educational, Scientific
and Cultural Organization (UNESCO)**
7, place de Fontenoy, 75007 Paris, France,
and **Berghahn Books**, 150 Broadway, Suite 812, New
York, NY 10038, United States of America.

This Report has been published on behalf of the partners
of the United Nations World Water Assessment Programme
(WWAP) with the support of the following countries and
organizations:

Argentina, Bolivia, Brazil, Denmark, Estonia, Ethiopia,
France, Germany, International Commission for the
Protection of the Danube River Basin (ICPDR) in
cooperation with the countries of the Danube River Basin
District, Japan, Kenya, Mali, Mexico, Mongolia, Paraguay,
Peru, Russian Federation, South Africa, Spain, Sri Lanka,
Thailand, Turkey, Uganda, Uruguay, United Kingdom.

United Nations Funds and Programmes
United Nations Centre for Human Settlements (UN-
HABITAT)
United Nations Children's Fund (UNICEF)
United Nations Department of Economic and Social Affairs
(UNDESA)
United Nations Development Programme (UNDP)
United Nations Environment Programme (UNEP)
United Nations High Commissioner for Refugees (UNHCR)
United Nations University (UNU)

Specialized UN Agencies
Food and Agriculture Organization (FAO)
International Atomic Energy Agency (IAEA)
International Bank for Reconstruction and Development
(World Bank)
World Health Organization (WHO)
World Meteorological Organization (WMO)
United Nations Educational, Scientific and Cultural
Organization (UNESCO)
International Fund for Agricultural Development (IFAD)
United Nations Industrial Development Organization
(UNIDO)

United Nations Regional Commissions
Economic Commission for Europe (ECE)
Economic and Social Commission for Asia and the Pacific
(ESCAP)
Economic Commission for Africa (ECA)
Economic Commission for Latin America and the Caribbean
(ECLAC)
Economic Commission for Western Asia (ESCWA)

**Secretariat of United Nations Conventions
and Decades**
Secretariat of the Convention to Combat Desertification
(CCD)
Secretariat of the Convention on Biological Diversity (CBD)
Secretariat of the United Nations Framework Convention
on Climate Change (CCC)
Secretariat of the International Strategy for Disaster
Reduction (ISDR)

Library of Congress Cataloging-in-Publication Data
A catalogue record for this book is available from the
Library of Congress.

British Library Cataloguing in Publication Data
A catalogue record for this book is available from the
Library of Congress.

ISBN UNESCO: 92-3-104006-5
ISBN Berghahn: 1-84545-177-5

The designations employed and the presentation of
material throughout this publication do not imply the
expression of any opinion whatsoever on the part of
UNESCO and WWAP concerning the legal status of any
country, territory, city or area or of its authorities, or the
delimitation of its frontiers or boundaries.

UNESCO Publishing: http://upo.unesco.org/
Berghahn Books: www.berghahnbooks.com

Printed in Barcelona.

Design & production
Andrew Esson, Baseline Arts Ltd, Oxford, UK

All websites accessed in February 2006.

Contents

*Water distribution during
a drought in Mandera,
Kenya*

Foreword

Water is an essential life-sustaining element. It pervades our lives and is deeply embedded in our cultural backgrounds. The basic human needs of a secure food supply and freedom from disease depend on it. Social development – endeavours such as the smooth functioning of hospitals – likewise relies on the availability of clean water. Economic development requires energy resources and industrial activities, and both are in turn water-dependent. The provision of sanitation for girls in schools offers yet another example of water's broader links – it has positive effects on hygiene and health, keeps girls in school, and helps to safeguard the natural environment. For these reasons and many more, access to safe drinking water and sanitation is both a development target in its own right and integrally linked to achieving all the Millennium Development Goals.

The United Nations *World Water Development Report* is the flagship publication of UN-Water, the inter-agency mechanism established to coordinate the activities of all United Nations agencies and entities working in the area of freshwater resources. First published in 2003 as a contribution to the International Year of Freshwater, the Report is produced by UN-Water's World Water Assessment Programme (WWAP). Working closely with governments, non-governmental organizations, civil society groups and the private sector, WWAP monitors water problems, provides recommendations for meeting future demand, and develops case studies in order to promote informed discussion of freshwater issues.

This second edition of the *World Water Development Report – Water, A Shared Responsibility –* shows that collective responsibility is essential for assessing and monitoring progress and for meeting internationally-agreed targets and goals. As we move further into the International Decade for Action, 'Water for Life' (2005–2015), I urge all partners to work more closely together to promote respect for the natural ecosystems on which we depend, and to ensure that all people enjoy access to safe water and the benefits it makes possible.

Kofi A. Annan
UN Secretary General

*Fishing on the Mekong
River in Viet Nam*

Prologue

In March 2003, at the Third World Water Forum held in Kyoto, Japan, I had the pleasure of introducing the first *World Water Development Report*, which is now being used as an educational tool and as a guide for decision-makers in many countries around the world. Its impact was such that it created a momentum at the international level for the creation of the International Decade for Action, 'Water for Life' (2005-2015).

It gives me great pleasure, therefore, to introduce the second in this series of World Water Development Reports – *Water, A Shared Responsibility*. Its publication is most timely, coming just one year after the launch of the Decade and in time for the fourth World Water Forum in Mexico City in March 2006. Subsequent editions of the Report are scheduled for production in 2009, 2012 and 2015, and will provide substantive content for the Decade's agenda. They will assist in monitoring progress towards achieving the targets set at the Millennium Summit and the World Summit for Sustainable Development, many of which have timelines culminating in 2015.

Water, of course, is everyone's business. Hardly a day goes by when we do not hear of another flood, another drought or another pollution spill into surface waters or groundwaters. Each of these issues has a direct or indirect impact not only on human security but also on livelihoods and development. The issues involved range from those of basic human well-being (food security and health), to those of economic development (industry and energy), to essential questions about the preservation of natural ecosystems on which ultimately we all depend. These issues are inter-related and have to be considered together in a holistic manner.

It is thus entirely appropriate that some twenty-four agencies and entities within the United Nations system are involved, with a shared purpose, in producing a comprehensive and objective global report on water issues and the measures being taken to address the related challenges that beset humanity worldwide.

I am very proud that UNESCO, by housing the Secretariat for the World Water Assessment Programme and providing a trust fund to help underwrite the costs of the production of the Report, is facilitating the process of bringing the UN agencies together in common cause. I firmly believe that understanding the many systems that underlie water issues – scientific and cultural, economic and social – will enhance our ability to better manage this precious resource and will help lead to poverty elimination and world peace.

Koïchiro Matsuura
UNESCO Director General

*Perito Moreno glacier,
Argentina*

Preface

In the three years since the launch of the first *World Water Development Report* at the Third World Water Forum in Kyoto (March 2003), the world has witnessed considerable change. There have been many instances of major water-related disasters: the 2004 Indian Ocean tsunami; the 2004 and 2005 hurricanes in the Caribbean, the west Pacific and the United States; the 2005 floods in central and eastern Europe as well as in many other regions; and the extensive droughts in Niger, Mali, Spain and Portugal. These are a constant reminder of both the destructive power of water and the misery deriving from lack of it in so many regions of the world.

These extreme events are the most prominent illustrations of fundamental changes that are affecting water resources worldwide. In many cases, this evolution is most probably linked to slow but persistent changes in the global climate, a phenomenon supported by a growing body of evidence. The combination of lower precipitation and higher evaporation in many regions is diminishing water quantities in rivers, lakes and groundwater storage, while increased pollution is damaging ecosystems and the health, lives and livelihoods of those without access to adequate, safe drinking water and basic sanitation.

Major demographic changes are also seriously affecting the quality and quantity of available freshwater on the planet. While the more developed countries enjoy relatively stable populations, the less-developed regions of the world are generally experiencing rapid growth and population shifts, particularly in towns, small cities and mega-cities. In many rapidly growing urban areas, it is proving difficult to build the infrastructure necessary to deliver water supply and sanitation facilities to service the population, leading to poor health, low quality of life and, in many cases, to social unrest. To the urban demands for water must be added the increasing demands on water for food production, energy creation and industrial uses.

Large shifts in the geographic distribution of populations occur in various contexts, often adding to water supply problems and social tension. In areas, such as Darfur, there are both internally displaced persons and transboundary refugees. Legal and illegal economic migrants are swelling populations in parts of the United States, and Western Europe, as elsewhere. Increasing tourism to many holiday destinations often exerts a strain on the water supplies of these regions. Whether the result of continued unrest and warfare, terrorist activities or economic instability, population movement is a factor that has a substantial impact on water availability in the world.

It is against these changes in the global situation – some rapid and very noticeable, others insidious and yet persistent – that the governance of water resources must be assessed. This second Report, *Water, A Shared Responsibility*, sets water issues against this evolving background and places greater emphasis on governance issues.

It is proving extremely difficult for many governments to effectively confront the many intertwined issues concerning water. Not only is it difficult for departments within national governments to collaborate effectively, but problems are compounded when many management decisions have to be taken at sub-national and community levels, as the linkage and cooperation between different levels of government is often tenuous at best. The challenges for government agencies to link to NGOs and the private sector for resolving water issues further complicate management and decision-making. The task of managing water becomes even more complex when rivers flow from one country to another. The building of cooperative upstream-downstream relationships is becoming increasingly important with close to half of the world's people living in river basins or above aquifers that cross international borders.

An important goal of the World Water Assessment Programme – founded in 2000 at the request of governments within the Commission on Sustainable Development – is therefore to assist governments in developing their national water management plans. Thus, a number of case studies have been developed and included in the Report. In the first Report, 7 case studies involving 12 countries were included to illustrate the variety of circumstances in different regions of the world. Since then, the number of case studies has grown to 17 involving 41 countries. In a single volume, it is not possible to describe all case studies in detail. Thus we choose to summarize the case studies in the Report and publish the details of each study on our website. This strategy also allows us to make all the necessary updates as new data and information become available.

As we move through the International Decade for Action, 'Water for Life', 2005-2015, the World Water Development Reports will provide a series of assessments that will facilitate the monitoring of change in the water sector, both on a global basis and within a growing number of case study countries and river basins. The purpose of the Decade is to focus on the implementation of water-related programmes and projects, while striving to ensure cooperation at all levels, including the participation of women, to achieve the internationally-agreed water-related goals.

A number of issues identified by UN-Water as priorities for the Decade include coping with water scarcity, access to drinking water, sanitation and hygiene, and disaster risk reduction, particularly in Africa. The Decade aims to support countries in addressing the challenges and achieving the water-related goals of Agenda 21, the UN Millennium Declaration and the Johannesburg Plan of Implementation, as well as those of the 12th and 13th sessions of the Commission on Sustainable Development.

The triennial World Water Development Reports will provide substantive content for the Decade's agenda (subsequent editions of the Report are scheduled for production in 2009, 2012 and 2015) and lay the foundation for a continuous, global monitoring system, pooling the unique perspectives and expertise of the 24 UN agencies that comprise UN-Water, in partnership with governments and other entities concerned with freshwater issues.

We trust that you will find this Report both informative and stimulating.

Gordon Young
WWAP Coordinator

Acknowledgements

This report would not have been possible without the generous and varied contributions of many individuals and organizations from around the world. In addition to the twenty-four agencies that make up UN-Water, numerous other UN organizations, universities, institutes, NGOs and national governments have contributed invaluable input. We would especially like to thank the Government of Japan for its generous support and the publishers, Berghahn Books and UNESCO Publishing.

Team for the preparation of WWDR2: *Water, A Shared Responsibility*

WWAP coordination

Gordon Young	*Coordinator*
Carlos Fernández-Jáuregui	*Deputy coordinator*

WWAP editorial team

Engin Koncagül	*Programme officer, case studies*
Deanna Donovan	*Programme officer, indicators*
Janine Treves-Habar	*Editor-in-chief*
Sean Lee	*Editor*
Isabelle Brugnon	*Photo editor*
Kristin Pittman	*Editorial assistant and CD preparation*
Alejandra Núñez-Luna	*Research assistant*
Casey Walther	*Publicity and editorial support*
Alia Hassan	*Assistant*

WWAP communications and administration

Cornelia Hauke	*Assistant project coordinator*
Georgette Gobina	*Programme secretary*
Pilar González Meyaui	*Communications officer*
Saskia Castelein	*Project officer*
Toshihiro Sonoda	*Liaison officer*
Maria Rosa Cárdenas	*Communications assistant*
Mustapha Boutegrabet	*Technical assistant*

External Contributors

Tony Milburn	*Scientific editor*
Marie-Aude Bodin	*Proofreader*
David McDonald	*Assistant editor*

Baseline Arts

Andrew Esson	*Design, typography and layout*
Nicki Averill and Shirley Bolton	*Design, illustration and layout*
Sue Bushell	*Typesetter*

Berghahn Books

Mark Stanton and Jen Cottrill	*Proofreaders*
Caroline Richards	*Proofreader*
Jim Henderson	*Indexer*

Chapter 1: Living in a Changing World

This chapter was drafted by Tony Milburn (consultant) and the WWAP editorial team, with contributions from UN-ECE and IOC.

Chapter 2: The Challenges of Governance

This chapter was coordinated and drafted by Håkan Tropp (UNDP Water Governance Facility, Stockholm International Water Institute).

The following individuals contributed as authors, reviewers, editors, working group members and/or workshop and meeting participants: Nighisty Ghezae, Karin Krchnak, Joakim Harlin, Melvyn Kay, Alan Hall, Sebastian Silva Leander, David Trouba, Rudolph Cleveringa and Thord Palmlund.

Chapter 3: Water and Human Settlements in an Urbanizing World

This chapter draws from the second issue of UN-HABITAT's Water and Sanitation in the World's Cities (2006), which is currently under print, to be published by Earthscan Publications, London. UN-HABITAT gratefully acknowledges the contribution of David Satterthwaite of IIED, London, and UN-HCR for their contribution on refugees.

Chapter 4: The State of the Resource

This chapter was drafted by Keith Kennedy (consultant) and supervised by Alice Aureli (UNESCO) and Avinash Tyagi (WMO).

The following individuals contributed to the chapter either as working group members and/or workshop and meeting participants, authors, reviewers or editors: Tommaso Abrate, Pradeep Aggarwal, Bo Appelgren, Roger Barry, Åse Eliasson, Andy Fraser, Regula Frauenfelder, Lindsey Higgs, Hege Hisdal, Regine Hock, Jippe Hoogeveen, Kshitij Kulkarni, Annukka Lipponen, Jean Margat, Datius Rutashobya, Joop Steenvoorden, Mohammed Tawfik, Jac van der Gun, Jaroslav Vrba, Bruce Webb and Gary Wright.

Chapter 5: Coastal and Freshwater Ecosystems

The chapter was coordinated by S. Diop and P. M'mayi (UNEP) and drafted by C. Revenga (The Nature Conservancy-TNC), R. D. Robarts (UNEP-GEMS /Water) and C. Zöckler (UNEP-WCMC).

The following individuals contributed to the chapter either as working group members and/or workshop and meeting participants, authors, reviewers or editors: M. Adriaanse, K. Ambrose, N. Ash, S. Barker, C. Bene, S. Butchart, W. Darwall, N. Davidson, R. Davis, M. Diamond, N. Dudley, P. Dugan, M. Dyhr-Nielsen, J. M. Faures, M. Finlayson, D. Gerten, M. Hatziolos, R. Hirji, H. Hoff, N. Holmes, C. Lacambra, B. Lankford, C. Leveque, E. McManus, Muchina-Kreutzberg, C. Nilsson, S. Oppenheimer, C. A. Reidy, M. Schomaker, K. Schuyt, D. Stroud and S. Tomkins. The following individuals contributed to the chapter as reviewers, contributors and/or participants in meetings: A. Calcagno, G. Carr, M. Cheatle, N. Cox, D. Daler, H. Drammeh, T. Goverse, J. Heppeler, K. Hodgson, R. Johnstone (Editor), E. Khaka, S. Koeppel, H. M. Lindblom, P. Manyara, F. Masai, C. Ouma, W. Rast, M. Scheffer, D. Smith, K. Vervuurt and R. G. Witt.

Chapter 6: Protecting and Promoting Human Health

This chapter was coordinated by Robert Bos (WHO) and drafted by Wim van der Hoek (IWMI) and Rolf Luyendijk (UNICEF).

Chapter 7: Water for Food, Agriculture and Rural Livelihoods

This chapter was coordinated and drafted by Wulf Klohn and Jean-Marc Faurès (FAO).

The following individuals contributed as authors, reviewers, editors, working group members and/or workshop and meeting participants: Melvyn Kay, Karen Frenken, Rudolph Cleveringa, Cécile Brugère, Jake Burke, Carlos Garces, Paul van Hofwegen, Sasha Koo-Oshima, Audrey Nepveu de Villemarceau, Åse Eliasson, David Molden, Daniel Renault, Uwe Barg, Leon Hermans, Pasquale Steduto and Michael Wales.

Chapter 8: Water and Industry

This chapter was coordinated and drafted by Ania Grobicki (consultant) on behalf of UNIDO.

The following individuals contributed as authors, reviewers, editors, working group members and/or workshop and meeting participants: Pablo Huidobro, Susanna Galloni, Takashi Asano and Karen Franz Delgau.

Chapter 9: Water and Energy

This chapter was drafted by Ania Grobicki (consultant) and coordinated by Robert Williams (UNIDO).

The following individuals contributed as authors, reviewers, editors, working group members and/or workshop and meeting participants: Richard Taylor, Pravin Karki, Margaret McMorrow, Vestal Tutterow, Michael Brown, Tong Jiandong, Lucille Langlois, Ferenc Toth, John Topper, Gordon Couch and Drona Upadhyay.

Chapter 10: Managing Risks: Securing the Gains of Development

This chapter was coordinated and drafted by Bastien Affeltranger (UNU-EHS).

The following individuals contributed as working group members: Wolfgang Grabs (WMO) and Yuichi Ono (UN-ISDR). And the following individuals contributed as authors or reviewers: Mohammed Abchir, Reid Basher, Janos Bogardi, Salvano Briceno, Xiaotao Cheng, Ken Davidson, John Harding, Tarek Merabtene, Tony Milburn, Buruhani Nyenzi, Pascal Peduzzi, Erich Plate, Rajib Shaw, Slobodan Simonovic, Caroline Sullivan, Mohamed Tawfik, Avinash Tyagi and Junichi Yoshitani.

Chapter 11: Sharing Water

This chapter was drafted by Evan Vlachos (Colorado State University) and coordinated by Léna Salamé (UNESCO).

The following individuals contributed as authors, reviewers, editors, working group members and/or workshop and meeting participants: Shammy Puri, P. B. Anand, Aaron T. Wolf, Joshua T. Newton, Houria Tazi Sadeq, Raya Stefan, Volker Böge, Lars Wirkus, Arjen Y. Hoekestra, Dipak Gyawali, Bruce Hooper, Monica Porto, Eugene Stakhiv, and Waleed El Zubeiri, Bozena Blix, András Szöllösi-Nagy, Alberto Tejada-Guibert and Alice Aureli.

Chapter 12: Valuing and Charging for Water

This chapter was drafted by Robert A. Young (consultant) and M. Aslam Chaudhry (UNDESA) and coordinated by M. Aslam Chaudhry (UNDESA).

The following individuals contributed as reviewers: Manuel Dengo, Claude Sauveplane, Jean-Michel Chene and Leon Hermans. The following individuals provided background material and reports: Marcia Brewster and Jacob Burke.

Chapter 13: Enhancing Knowledge and Capacity

This chapter was coordinated and drafted by Jan Luijendijk, Roland Price and Kyle Robertson (UNESCO-IHE).

The following individuals contributed as authors, reviewers, editors, working group members and/or workshop and meeting participants: Diego Mejia-Velez, Guy J. F. R. Alaerts, Paul W. J. van Hofwegen, Saba Bokhari, Claudio Caponi, Ralph Daley, Jac van der Gun, Keith Kennedy, Kees Leendertse, Wouter Lincklaen Arriens, Annukka Lipponen, Paul Taylor, Alexey Volynets, Charles Vörösmarty and Jan Yap.

Chapter 14: Case Studies: Moving Towards an Integrated Approach

This chapter was coordinated by Engin Koncagül. Jean-Marie Barrat contributed to the African case studies, and the chapter is based on information provided by the following case study partners:

The Autonomous Community of the Basque Country
Ana Isabel Oregi Bastarrika, Tomas Epalza Solano, José María Sanz de Galdeano Equiza, Iñaki Arrate Jorrín, Jasone Unzueta, Mikel Mancisidor and Iñaki Urrutia Garayo.

The Danube River Basin
Ursula Schmedtje, Igor Liska and Michaela Popovici.

Ethiopia
Abera Mekonen, Teshome Workie, Tesfaye Woldemihret, Michael Abebe, Mesfin Amare, Zeleke Chafamo and Teshome Afrassa.

France
The Water Directorate at the French Ministry of Ecology and Sustainable Development, its regional services and the French Water Agencies.

Japan
Kouji Ikeuchi, Masaru Kunitomo, Satoru Ohtani, Takashi Nimura, Hiroki Ishikawa, Junichi Yoshitani, Tarek Merabtene, Daisuke Kuribayashi, Masato Toyama, Katsutoshi Koga and Ken Yoneyama.

Kenya
George O. Krhoda, Simeon Ochieng, George K. Chesang, Samuel Mureithi Kioni, Patrick Opondo Oloo, Zablon N. Isaboke Oonge, Francis J. Edalia, Bernard Imbambi Kasabuli, Andy Tola Maro, Josiah W. Kaara, Peterson Nyaga Njiru, Evelyn M. Mbatia, Simon Kariuki Mugera, Peter Musuva, Patrick O. Hayombe, Daniel M. Mbithi, John Gachuki Kariuki and Helen Musyoki.

Lake Peipsi/Chudskoe-Pskovskoe Basin
Estonia: Ago Jaani, Harry Liiv, Margus Korsjukov.
Russian Federation: Natalia P. Alexeeva, Vladimir F. Budarin, Alla A. Sedova.

Lake Titicaca
Alberto Crespo Milliet, Jorge Molina Carpio and Julio Sanjinez-Goytia.

Mali
Malick Alhousseni, Adama Tiémoko Diarra, Sidi Toure, Housseini Maiga and Karaba Traore.

State of Mexico
Enrique Peña Nieto, Benjamín Fournier Espinosa, José Manuel Camacho Salmón, Edgardo Castañeda Espinosa, José Raúl Millán López, Mario Gerardo Macay Lim, José Luis Luege Tamargo and Mónica Salazar Balderrama.

Mongolia
Dr. Basandorj, G. Davaa, N. Jadambaa, N. Batsukh, Z. Batbayar and Ramasamy Jayakumar.

La Plata
Victor Pochat, Silvia González, Elena Benítez, Carlos Díaz, Miguel Giraut, Julio Thadeu Kettelhut, Luis Loureiro, Ana Mugetti, Silvia Rafaelli, Roberto Torres, Helio de Macedo Soares and the technical and administrative staff of Comité Intergubernamental Coordinador de los Países de la Cuenca del Plata.

South Africa
Fred Van Zyl and Eberhard Braune.

Sri Lanka
Maithripala Sirisena, B.V.R. Punyawardane, Ananda Wijesuriya, B.J.P. Mendis, K.S.R. de Silva, M.H. Abeygunawardane, A.P.R. Jayasinghe, W.A.N. Somaweera, Amara Satharasinghe, Badra Kamaladasa, T.J. Meegastenne, T.M. Abayawickrama, Tissa Warnasuriya, A.D.S. Gunawardane, H.P.S. Somasiri, B.M.S. Samarasekara, K.Athukorale, M.S. Wickramarachchi, U.S. Imbulana, M. Wickramage, Dayantha S. Wijeyesekara, Malik Ranasinghe, L.T. Wijesuriya, P.P.G. Dias, C.R. Panabokke, A.P.G.R.L. Perera, H.M. Jayatillake, L. Chandrapala, B.R.S.B. Basnayake, G.H.P. Dharmaratne, R.S.C. George, K.W. Nimal Rohana, C.K. Shanmugarajah, S.L. Weerasena, A.R.M. Mahrouf, N.Senanayake, G.A.M.S. Emitiyagoda, K.D.N. Weerasinghe, M.P. de Silva, U. Wickramasinghe, R.N. Karunaratne, B.K.C.C. Seneviratne, T.D. Handagama, S. Senaratne, U.R. Ratnayake, G. Herath, M.M. Ariyabandu, B.M.S. Batagoda, N.K. Atapattu, R.W.F. Ratnayake, N.T.S. Wijesekara and B.R. Neupane.

Thailand
Department of Water Resources, Surapol Pattanee and Sukontha Aekaraj.

Uganda
Patrick Kahangire, Nsubuga Senfuma, Sottie Bomukama, Fred Kimaite, Justin Ecaat, Henry Bidasala, Disan Ssozi, Mohammed Badaza, Abushen Majugu, Joseph Epitu, Nicholas Azza, Joyce Ikwaput, Joel Okonga, Callist Tindimugaya, Patrick Okuni and Ben Torach.

Chapter 15: Conclusions and Recommendations for Action

This chapter was drafted by the WWAP editorial team.

SECTION 1
Changing Contexts

The key challenges of water management can only be understood within the context of water's role in the world today. Many of the world's socio-economic systems are becoming linked at an unprecedented rate. Fast developing communications and transportation systems – including television, Internet and mobile phones – enable many of us to see first hand, and often in real time, what is happening in the world and even take us there should we wish. We are witnessing the impact of extreme climates in floods and drought conditions as well as that of poverty, warfare and disease, which still bedevil so many people of the world, often in increasingly crowded urban conditions.

It is within this setting that the world's water managers have to manage what is an increasingly scarce resource. The pressures and complexity that they face, in what is often a fast changing setting where the available resources can vary greatly in time and space, are huge. This section gives an overview of this and the increasingly refined techniques necessary to secure the equitable management of one of the planet's most precious resources.

Global Map 1: *Index of Non-sustainable Water Use*
Global Map 2: *Urban Population Growth*

Chapter 1 – **Living in a Changing World**

Emphasizing the central role of water use and allocation in poverty alleviation and socio-economic development, this chapter discusses some of the many ways in which demographic and technological change, globalization and trade, climate variability, HIV/AIDS, warfare, etc., affect and are impacted by water. Key concepts of water management, sustainability and equity are introduced, as is the pivotal role of the many activities of the UN system in the water sector.

Chapter 2 – **The Challenges of Governance** (UNDP with IFAD)

Recognizing that the water crisis is largely a crisis of governance, this chapter outlines many of the leading obstacles to sound and sustainable water management: sector fragmentation, poverty, corruption, stagnated budgets, declining levels of development assistance and investment in the water sector, inadequate institutions and limited stakeholder participation. While the progress towards reforming water governance remains slow, this chapter provides recommendations for balancing the social, economic, political and environmental dimensions of water.

Chapter 3 – **Water and Human Settlements in an Urbanizing World** (UN-HABITAT)

Increasing population growth is creating major problems worldwide. Growing urban water supply and sanitation needs, particularly in lower- and middle-income countries, face increasing competition with other sectors. Rising incomes in other portions of the world population fuel demand for manufactured goods and environmental services and amenities, all of which require water. This chapter emphasizes the scale of the growing urban water challenges, pointing out that nearly one-third of urban dwellers worldwide live in slums.

Index of Non-sustainable Water Use

In general, human society has positioned itself in areas with locally sustainable water supplies, in the form of runoff, and/or river and stream flows (Postel et al., 1996; Vörösmarty et al., 2005b). This map illustrates where human water use (domestic, industrial and agricultural) exceeds average water supplies annually. Areas of high water overuse (highlighted in red to brown tones) tend to occur in regions that are highly dependent on irrigated agriculture, such as the Indo-Gangetic Plain in South Asia, the North China Plain and the High Plains in North America. Urban concentration of water demand adds a highly localized dimension to these broader geographic trends. Where water use exceeds local supplies society is dependent on infrastructure that transports water over long distances (i.e., pipelines and canals) or on groundwater extraction – an unsustainable practice over the long-term. Both the map and the graph below understate the problem, as the impact of seasonal shortages are not reflected. The consequences of overuse include diminished river flow, depletion of groundwater reserves, reduction of environmental flows needed to sustain aquatic ecosystems, and potential societal conflict.

Water use in excess of natural supply (average annual)

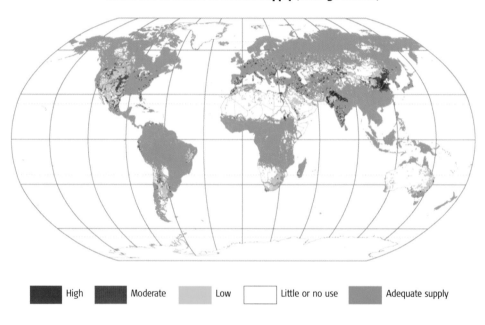

| | High | | Moderate | | Low | | Little or no use | | Adequate supply |

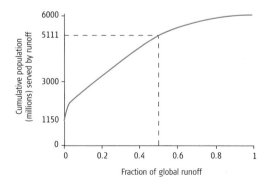

The graph (left) shows that in 2000, of the world's total population 20% had no appreciable natural water supply, 65% (85% minus the 20% with no appreciable water supply mentioned above) shared low-to-moderate supplies (≤50% of global runoff) and only 15% enjoyed relative abundance (>50% of global runoff).

Source: Water Systems Analysis Group, University of New Hampshire. Datasets available for download at http://wwdrii.sr.unh.edu/

Urban Population Growth

In 1950, the world's population was about 2.5 billion people; by 2000, global population was just over 6 billion, an increase of nearly 150 percent in only 50 years. During this time, the proportion of the global population living in urban areas increased from 29 to 47 percent and it is estimated that by 2010, more than 50 percent of the global population will be urban dwellers (UN, 2003).

In less developed regions of the world, this increase has been even more dramatic: in Africa and Asia the fraction of urban population has nearly tripled in the last 50 years (see graph below). Between 2000 and 2030, most population growth is expected to occur within the urban areas of less developed countries, while overall, rural population is expected to decline slightly.

Global Population Density, 2000

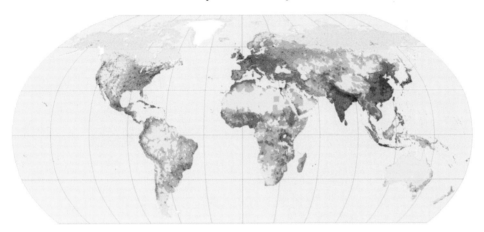

Global Rural Urban Mapping Project (GRUMP) alpha Centre for International Earth Science Information Network (CIESIN) Columbia University in the City of New York

Persons per square km

<1   1–4   5–24   25–249   250–999   1000+   No data

Proportion of total population that resides in urban areas by region

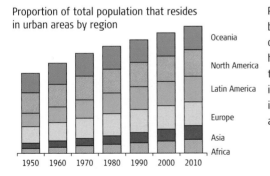

Oceania
North America
Latin America
Europe
Asia
Africa

1950 1960 1970 1980 1990 2000 2010

Roughly 3% of the earth's land surface is occupied by urban areas, with the highest concentrations occurring along the coasts and waterways. The historical importance of water as a means of transport as well as a resource has meant that inland water and river corridors have been important in determining the spatial organization and distribution of human settlements.

Sources: Center for International Earth Science Information Network, Columbia University, Water Systems Analysis Group, University of New Hampshire
Data available for download at http://wwdrii.sr.unh.edu/

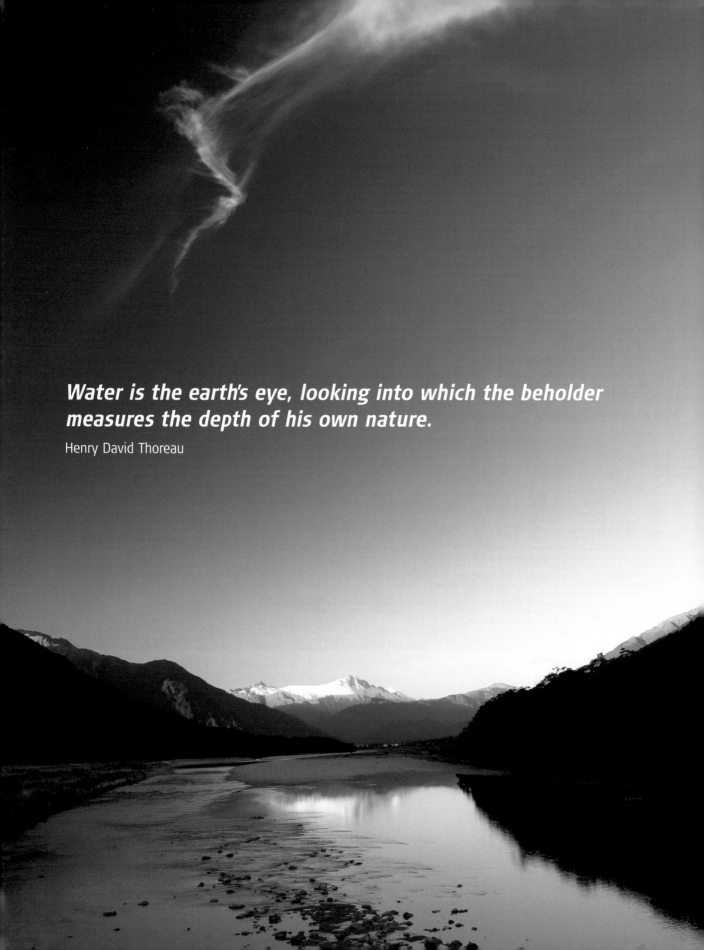

Water is the earth's eye, looking into which the beholder measures the depth of his own nature.

Henry David Thoreau

CHAPTER 1

Living in a Changing World

The confluence of two rivers, New Zealand

Key messages:

At present, our society has not yet attained a level of sustainability whereby humanity honours and respects life upon this planet and uses fairly and equitably the resources it provides. The UN system has taken on a lead role in addressing this challenge through the setting of the Millennium Development Goals and water has a crucial role to play in this. Forty percent of the world's population live in situations of extreme poverty and efforts are underway to lift them out of the poverty trap and to offer greater protection from the natural hazards that still prevail. This introductory chapter will give a flavour of some of the critical challenges involved in managing freshwater to enable poverty alleviation and socio-economic development, within an environmentally-sound integrated framework.

■ Water is the primary life-giving resource. Its availability is an essential component in socio-economic development and poverty reduction. Today, a number of significant factors have an impact both on this resource and on managing water in an integrated, sustainable and equitable manner. These include widespread poverty, malnutrition, the dramatic impacts of demographic change, growing urbanization, the effects of globalization – with the threats and opportunities this brings – and the recent manifestations of climate change. All these factors impinge on the water sector in increasingly complex ways.

■ The defining characteristic of today's world is change. In almost every sector, including the natural world, the pace of change is unprecedented in recent history. Technological change, especially in information and communications technology, facilitates 'globalization', which in turn affects virtually all aspects of our lives as physical and cultural products move ever more easily around the world. As internationalization and rapid economic growth in many societies alter traditional socio-economic structures, it is clear that change, although virtually pervasive, is not entirely positive. Many people, especially in the developing world and especially those on urban margins and in rural areas, are left behind in poverty and mired in preventable disease. All the chapters in this Report address this issue in one form or another.

■ Exacerbating the challenge of economic development is the issue of climate change, which strongly influences the hydrological cycle. Droughts and floods, intensified by climate change, can lead to famine, loss of resources and contamination of water supplies. Population pressure on forest resources can accelerate land degradation and compromise watershed functions, increasing the vulnerability of the poorest communities. Warming temperatures, rising sea levels, uncertain effects on ecosystems, and increased climatic variability are just some of the changes expected to have a disproportionate and significant impact on developing countries. While climate may reduce poor people's assets, increased climate variability will increase their vulnerability and undermine their resilience and coping ability. Thus, climate variability and change present a fundamental challenge to the long-term development prospects of many developing countries, and will make it difficult to meet and sustain the Millennium Development Goals (MDGs).

■ In short, water is fundamental to our way of life, at whatever point in the socio-economic spectrum a community may be situated. It is likewise crucial to the preservation of the essential ecosystems upon which our lives depend. Whatever development initiatives are proposed over and above the provision of secure access to water – and such initiatives are many and varied – unless the requisite water services are secured and provided, these initiatives will not succeed. Access to secure water supplies is essential. This seems self-evident. Yet, as this Report shows, it is clear that the central role of water in development is neither well understood nor appreciated. Much more needs to be done by the water sector to educate the world at large and decision-makers in particular.

Part 1. Changing Socio-economic Contexts

Poverty impinges on individual households and families. In aggregate it affects approximately 1 billion people worldwide. This represents one-sixth of the total world population who, through sickness, hunger, thirst, destitution and marginalization, find it nearly impossible to climb out of the pit of extreme poverty. Very poor people struggle to pay for adequate food and water, for housing, for medicines and drugs to treat sick family members, for transport to get to places of work or carry sick family members to treatment centres, and for the education of their children.

The rural poor are often at the end of irrigation systems, and at the whim of richer upstream users for water...

1a. Poverty, water and development

The extreme poor live hand to mouth – what they earn, in an urban area on a good day, will buy food and water for the family for that day. Very often, the quantity of water needed for good personal and domestic hygiene is too expensive to buy from street water vendors, too far to carry in the case of distant water sources, and often necessitates the use of polluted water from nearby, heavily used, rivers and streams. Rarely do they have access to improved sanitation and, where this may be available from a public facility in towns and cities, the cost to the whole family may be prohibitive (see **Chapter 6**). Many poor families occupy land over which they have no formal legal rights – in a squatter community or slum, often with little flood protection infrastructure (see **Chapters 3** and **10**). Many also farm on marginal lands owned by others with limited access to reliable water (see **Chapter 7**). Drainage systems for urban rain and storm water are frequently inadequate, no formal systems for solid waste collection are provided, and there is a lack of paved areas, such as footpaths and roads. The latter are important and not just for movement; they also provide a location for the installation and ready operation and maintenance of network utility services such as water, drainage and electricity. The payment structure for many utility services (e.g. water, electricity), with their up-front connection charges and monthly consumption charges (see **Chapter 12**), are often too high for the poor to pay them. On top of all of this, debt frequently adds to the burdens of poor households.

In rural areas, the food and water needed by families will be taken largely from the natural environment. Water is carried from a distant spring or pool, some

not very nutritious food may be grown on marginally productive land, or collected from forests and is most often insufficient to satisfy hunger and provide needed nourishment. The rural poor are often at the end of irrigation systems, and at the whim of richer upstream users for water, or pushed out onto land dependent totally on what may be, with growing climate variability, increasingly erratic rainfall. Deep well water abstractions by richer farmers and water-using industries can lower water tables to the extent that poorer families and communities cannot then access the groundwater. Untreated municipal and industrial effluents also pollute the surface and groundwater sources relied on by the poor for their water supplies, without redress.

Unbridled competition from richer farmers and industry, productive land, agriculture and fisheries often puts the poor at a serious disadvantage. The implementation of national food policies (through subsidies, taxes, tariffs, food aid etc.) can distort markets and marginalize the rural poor; and inadequately organized and non pro-poor international trade liberalization can exacerbate this. Because of the difficulties poor families face in accumulating any surpluses – food or financial – they find it difficult to maintain consumption when their incomes are interrupted or their crops fail. The poor are excluded from many life-saving and livelihood opportunities, either because of inadequate provision of basic community services by local authorities – health care, transport, education and training, emergency services (e.g. fire-fighting) and law enforcement – or their inability to pay for these services.

Perhaps at no stage in the poverty relief process is water and sanitation more critical than at the

BOX 1.1: THE PARTICULAR PROBLEMS OF AFRICA

Africa is subject to famine, beset by disease and mostly isolated from contemporary international trade. Bad governance and rapid population growth add to the problems. Its very narrow range of exports, restricted to agricultural commodities, some mineral resources and hydrocarbons – all of which are subject to the price vagaries of international markets – further restricts economic development. Africa is not dissimilar to Asia around forty years ago. In Asia, however, high-yield staple crops (rice and wheat), introduced during the Asian green revolution, enabled food production to grow rapidly as the continent's vast plains were well suited to irrigation. Agricultural income grew rapidly, and production diversified. Surplus labour migrated to the cities, leading to rapid urbanization and industrialization. However, Africa does not have the same sort of irrigation potential as Asia. Malaria and the growing AIDs crisis have added to its burdens. Unlike Asia, which hosts coastal cities with good access to ports and sea routes, most African people live inland, too far from ports to enable growth from industrial exports. Road, rail and inland water transport infrastructure are poor and air travel is cumbersome between African countries.

Source: Sachs, 2005.

Child carrying water across an open drain, Ghana

beginning of movement out of abject poverty. Access to a reliable nearby source of water provides relief from the burden of carrying water from distant springs and wells, freeing up time for livelihood activities and, in the case of girls, for school attendance. Having enough water to cover drinking and domestic hygiene needs promotes better health and well-being. Sanitation facilities help to ensure the safe disposal of human waste and reduce disease and death. Adequate water supplies improve the prospects of new livelihood activities, which are otherwise denied, and are often a key step out of poverty. In many lower-income countries, large parts of the population depend on agriculture for their basic livelihood. Others, living in great poverty on marginal land, struggle just to survive. Access to reliable water sources, under the control of the people concerned, reduces crop-loss risks and leads to the possibility of accumulating surpluses and the chance to invest in more intensive agriculture (Moench et al., 2003). Diversification into other activities becomes possible, education opportunities for children grow and, maybe, transition out of agriculture to more profitable enterprises. Industry at all scales needs reliable water resources to prosper and encourage investment in industrial growth. Available water resources and freedom from water-related disease also encourage inward foreign investment.

1b. Demographic changes

The present global population is around 6.4 billion and growing at some 70 million per year, mostly in low-income countries. What has been called the global demographic transition, from populations with short life expectancy and large families, to longer life expectation and smaller families, is very far from complete. Approximately one-third of all countries are still in the early stages of the process, all of which are low-income countries. In fact, of the projected population growth to 8.1 billion by 2030 and some 8.9 billion by 2050, almost all will be in low-income countries (Browne, 2005).

A growing problem, as covered in Section 3 of the Report, is the increasing competition for freshwater between agriculture and urban and industrial uses, causing tension between rural and urban areas and possibly threatening regional or national food security. In fact nearly all malnutrition and low food yield problems are found in low-income countries in the tropics, where water scarcity in relation to food, people and the environment are at their greatest. The four principal demographic risk factors currently challenging humanity – (1) the increasing percentages of young adults, (2) rapid urbanization, (3) reduced availability of freshwater and cropland for food production, (4) HIV/AIDs – rarely occur singly. More usually they occur in combination and coupled with other obstacles, such as weak institutions, unresponsive governments and historic ethnic tensions. The resulting challenges to the leadership of governments can reduce the ability of countries to function effectively (Worldwatch Institute, 2005), as explored in **Chapter 2**.

A particular problem of recent rapid population growth is the so-called 'youth bulge', where young people between the ages of 15 and 30 represent over 40 percent of the total adult population. Many people in this age group have no jobs and even the educated can struggle to find meaningful work. As things stand now, 85 percent of the world's young people are in low-income countries and the average unemployment rate is four times the overall adult rate. The potential consequences of this situation are significant social and political unrest.

The problem is often worst in rural areas where young men cannot inherit land because plot sizes, subdivided through successive generations of inheritance to large families, have become so small that they are no longer viable. Thus, the men lack a secure livelihood and reduced prospects of marriage – a socially destabilizing situation. While the youth bulge will decline as fertility rates continue to fall, some countries (in sub-Saharan Africa and the Middle East) are still experiencing rapid growth in young adult populations. It is likely that these countries will pose a challenge to the development of their region and to international security (Worldwatch Institute, 2005).

Population growth and urbanization

Back in 1970, about two-thirds of the total world population lived in rural areas. By 2001, this had dropped to just over 50 percent. On current predictions, by 2020 this will have fallen to 44 percent with 56 percent of the population living in urban areas. Until recently, Africa was considered the least urbanized continent. This has changed. By 2020, Africa's urban population is estimated to reach 500 million – up from 138 million in 1990. Malawi is the current fastest urbanizing nation due to population flight from severe flooding. Nigeria has also seen tremendous urban growth while huge slums are found in Johannesburg and Nairobi (Worldwatch Institute, 2005).[1]

Kibera slum, Nairobi, Kenya

Urbanization can be a force for good, in terms of economic growth and global integration. However, some of the factors that helped to create wealth in industrialized countries, such as youthful populations, a middle class, nearness to political power and ethnic/religious diversity, can be potential sources of conflict in fast-growing but

1. www.worldwatch.org

BOX 1.2: ENVIRONMENTAL REFUGEES

It is estimated that there are presently some 30 million environmental refuges and a further 17 million other refugees and displaced persons from wars, persecution and other causes. The former have fled from resource scarcity, from deforestation and environmental degradation, climate change impacts, overpopulation, displacement by development projects, etc. Large displacements of population can cause instability or conflict in the host country, country of origin, or within a region. They entail depletion of scarce resources, overcrowding, shortage of potable water and unsanitary conditions that can lead to disease epidemics.

It has been suggested that the number of environmental refugees could rise to 150 million by 2050 as one of the results of climate change.

Source: Worldwatch Institute, 2005.

An increasing number of low-income countries have actively promoted a large increase in tourism activities to foster their economic development. While there are clear economic benefits, there is also a downside. Problems of excessive water consumption in tourist complexes in water-scarce areas, especially where golf courses are involved, an increase in marine pollution in coastal areas from inadequate wastewater treatment and loss of crucial marine biodiversity, including coral reef destruction, have all occurred. Competition by tourism for scarce water supplies has led to instances of water diversion from farmers, effectively driving them out of agriculture and their livelihoods.

Source: www.uneptie.org/pc/tourism/ sust-tourism/env-3main.htm

Otash camp for Internally Displaced Persons (IDP), Sudan

poor cities in developing countries. Statistics show that countries with urban growth exceeding 4 percent per year are twice as likely as others to experience civil disturbances (Population Action International, 2003). **Chapter 3** looks at the issues of urbanization and human settlements in much more detail, especially the challenges of providing water and sanitation to improve both health and livelihood activities. The food and water implications related to demographic change and urbanization are reviewed in **Chapter 7.**

1c. Political and economic changes

We are living in a period of rapid and significant geopolitical change. Previously established empires and countries have broken up (e.g. the Soviet Union and Yugoslavia) while neighbouring groups of countries seek closer economic collaboration or consolidation (e.g. the European Union). The former centrally controlled economy of the Soviet Union is now a collection of nation states trying to enter the global economy, without the experience or institutions to cope effectively. Ethnic tensions suppressed under former political systems within the former Yugoslavia have erupted into armed conflict in the Balkans. New nation states, wary of sharing the water resources of transboundary rivers and aquifers, become very defensive about their perceived sovereignty over such resources, especially as resources are pressured by increased demand and deteriorating water quality.

Warfare and conflicts

The Post Conflict Assessment Unit of the United Nations Environment Programme (UNEP) has shown that conflicts are almost always followed by environmental crises: chemicals leaching into waterways, damage to irrigation systems, deforestation, the destruction of infrastructure and

collapses of governance systems – local and national. Rebuilding economies, damaged lives, shattered infrastructure including water and power systems, rebuilding and restoring damaged irrigation systems, removing landmines in post-conflict situations, absorb 27 percent of all Overseas Development Assistance (Worldwatch Institute, 2005). The Convention on the Prohibition of Military or any Other Hostile Use of Environmental Modification Techniques (ENMOD Convention)[2] seeks to prohibit acts such as weather modification and harmful flood creation. The threat posed by the release of toxic chemicals into the environment has further prompted calls for a new convention. It is no coincidence that many of the countries yet to make progress on debt relief are those recently emerged from conflict situations (World in 2005). **Chapters 2, 3** and **11** cover these and other issues of warfare and refugees, and point to the need for introduction of agreements and conventions to address these problems.

Globalization

At present, the world is going through an unprecedented process of integrating finance, trade, communication and technology. By eliminating tariffs and other barriers to trade, the world's economy is becoming increasingly interlinked. This has advantages. Transaction costs and investment risks can be reduced and greater investment encouraged. The increased competition encouraged by regional integration fosters competition and innovation. Reduced costs in telecommunications and energy infrastructure are possible. For water, globalization enables economies of scale through access to bigger markets, facilitates improved cooperation over international waters, and allows a benefits-based approach towards regional water-resource systems and inter-country collaboration on water knowledge and skills

2. www.unep.org/ Documents.Multilingual/ Default.asp?DocumentID= 65&ArticleID=1291&l=en

BOX 1.4: **MOBILE PHONES AND THE WATER SECTOR**

Current available evidence suggests that promoting a widespread use of mobile phones (cell phones) may be a sensible way to encourage bottom-up development. Mobile phones help to raise long-term growth rates – an extra ten phones per 100 people in a typical lower-income country has been shown to raise GDP growth by 0.6 percentage points. Mobile phones help reduce transaction costs, widen trade networks and do away with the need for intensive travelling. In terms of the water sector, in low-income countries they are used by fishers and farmers to obtain the best prices for their produce, to help provide early warnings to communities of floods, to get information and help in treating water-related diseases and many more. The UN has set a target of access by 50 percent of the world population, although some three-quarters of that population already live within range of a mobile telephone network.

Source: *Economist*, March 2005.

transfer. Disadvantages, however, may include increased water scarcity and pollution, if water demand and pollution control are not carefully managed (World Development Report, 2005). Countries with poor or weakly enforced environmental regulations which allow pollution (air or water) to flow across international boundaries are of great concern (World Bank, 2005).

In some countries, there are moves to divert water from the production of low-value staple crops to higher-value cash crops such as vegetables, fruit and flowers. As exporting grows, there are concerns that the rules of the North American Free Trade Agreement (NAFTA) and the World Trade Organization (WTO) increase environmental risk due to their restrictions on the use of the precautionary principle.[3] Several critics of these organizations' rules argue that WTO, for example, has always put the interests of commerce before environmental protection. This may lead to countries bound by these trade rules to agree to bulk exports of water to other countries against their wishes (Figueres, 2003).

One of the consequences of globalization and the increase of market-based economics is that rights markets have been widely advocated as the way to manage natural resources. **Chapter 12** looks at economic valuation techniques for water.

Technological innovations and water

Technology can offer significant opportunities for the water sector. In water treatment, membrane technology is an example. Membranes are manufactured filtration systems that can separate a wide and growing range of substances – both organic and inorganic – which are present in water, from the water itself. They can be used for industrial and drinking water treatment, wastewater treatment, desalination of salt water and brackish water, and so on. The previous high costs are being reduced substantially and the technology is now increasingly available worldwide. The use of ultra-violet irradiation of waters for drinking water, in industrial water treatment, and for reducing the polluting burden of wastewater effluents, is spreading. New understanding is emerging of on-site wastewater treatment and recycling and small water and wastewater systems. This offers lower overall costs for water supply and sanitation systems and nutrient recovery options, as well as reducing the complexity of large centralized systems (Mathew and Ho, 2005). There is potential for using these technological applications and others in extending the provision of water supply and sanitation services to communities, as is covered in most chapters of the Report.

Much has been made of the digital divide, the uneven distribution worldwide of communications technology and access to, and use of, information. The UN has responded to this by creating the 'Digital Solidarity Fund' in March 2005, intended to enable people and countries presently excluded from the information society to gain access to it. Initiatives proposed include the construction and operation of regional telecentres where people have access to computers, the internet, telephones, and so on. Over and above this, the many applications of satellite surveillance and modelling can have substantial potential in water resources monitoring in lower-income countries, as described in **Chapters 4** and **13**. At the same time, focus needs to placed on basic knowledge and capacity-building, which can be more easily shared in this world of increased communications.

3. The Precautionary Principle, adopted by the UN Conference on the Environment and Development (1992), states that in order to protect the environment, a precautionary approach should be widely applied, meaning that where there are threats of serious or irreversible damage to the environment, lack of full scientific certainty should not be used as a reason for postponing cost-effective measures to prevent environmental degradation (from European Environmental Agency website glossary.eea.eu.int/EEAGlossary/P/precautionary_principle)

Part 2. Governing Water: A Shared Responsibility

...water managers around the world agree that the only way forward is through an inclusive and integrated approach to water resources management...

In simple terms, the great challenge of this century is to find the means to develop human capital (socio-economically, culturally and equitably), while at the same time preserving and protecting natural capital. It is necessary to acknowledge that for far too long, the headlong pursuit of material prosperity for the few has *excluded* far too many poor people from well-being, health, food and environmental security; has *excluded* the interests of the natural environment; and has *excluded* adequate consideration of the interests of future generations. We have come to realize that adopting an *inclusive* approach is essential to securing the sustainability of all forms of life.

WWDR1 (2003) concluded that governance issues form the central obstruction to sound and equitable water sharing and management worldwide. Sharing is at the heart of the governance issue and the title of this Report reflects this. Given the complexity, uncertainty and increasing vulnerability of both natural and human systems, water managers around the world agree that the only way forward is through an inclusive and integrated approach to water resources management (IWRM), which recognizes the need to ensure a holistic protection

system. **Chapter 2** on water governance leads off this discussion by looking in greater detail at obstacles connected to implementing an integrated approach to water resources management, thereafter taken up by most chapters of the Report.

Countries have to shift to a more inclusive set of values in the overall interests of the entire planet. Few have so far done so. Many of the richer countries have used redistributive taxation, education, equal opportunities and social welfare

Figure 1.1: The reiterative policy-making process

Step 1:
Identify principal stakeholders and participants

Step 2:
Situation analysis, define problem and basic principles

Socio-Cultural Institutions

Government Agencies

Water Users

Media

Private Interests

Scientific Community

NGOs

Other

Round Table

Step 9: Refine

Step 3:
Agree on and prioritize
1. goals
2. strategy
3. targets
4. criteria
5. indicators

Step 10: Review

Step 4:
Assess and modify legal, institutional and policy environment

Step 11: Revise

Step 5:
Develop management plans and secure funding

Step 8:
Review results

Step 13: Re-evaluate

Step 12: Adjust

Step 7:
Monitor & evaluate progress

Step 6:
Implement plan activities

Source: Derived from Gutrich et. al., 2005.

BOX 1.5: THE EU AND SOUTH AFRICA: INCLUSIVE WATER MANAGEMENT

In the European Union (EU), redistributive taxation has transferred wealth from the richer northern countries to the poorer south and is now beginning to do so to the new accession states to the east, significantly raising their standards of living. The bigger market and increased competition are driving wealth generation. At the same time, one of the most comprehensive environmental protection regimes in the world is being put in place in the EU, which will greatly enhance environmental protection and improved water management.

At the other end of the world, driven by South Africa's reforming government, significant changes are occurring in the southern African region in both attitudes and techniques of water management. The biggest changes are in South Africa itself but their ideas are spreading to adjacent countries. There are some limited parallels with the EU in that change is being driven by a wealthier core nation with strong institutions and clearly articulated equitable values, and is rippling out from there. In both the EU and southern Africa, the process of change is underpinned by institutional values that emphasize inclusiveness of both the whole

population and the needs of the natural environment. The water laws and regulations of both of these regions, especially at the core of them, are characterized by commitment to equality of access to water for all and to environmental protection of a more sophisticated nature (relatively speaking in each case) than almost anywhere else on the planet. Given the present strong trend towards regional economic cooperation, reported later in this chapter, the experiences of these two regions are significant. To what extent their inclusive approach will spread remains to be seen.

programmes to release the wealth-generating, creative and upwardly mobile-potential of their citizens. They have put in place extensive environmental protection/rehabilitation measures. They have entrenched human and property rights and established the clear rule of law. Multinational companies based in these countries and aware of the precious nature of their corporate reputations, have shown an increased inclination to take environmental and employment concerns seriously when operating in lower-income countries. The wealthier countries have produced cadres of educated, competent people in relatively sound (though by no means perfect) institutions and organizations for water management, such as in the European Union (EU), but such an overall pattern of development is also observable in South Africa, for example (see **Box 1.5**).

2a. An integrated approach – IWRM

Reference has already been made to the need for an integrated and holistic approach to water resources management. Fundamentally, this is a response to the much-criticized, sector-by-sector approach to water management (irrigation, municipal, energy, etc.), highlighting instead the benefits that an integrated, overall approach to water management, on a catchment or basin basis, can deliver.

Integrated Water Resources Management (IWRM) promotes not only cross-sectoral cooperation, but the coordinated management and development of land, water (both surface water and groundwater) and other related resources, so as to maximize the resulting social and economic benefits in an equitable manner, without compromising ecosystem sustainability. It is not only the watershed or basin that must be considered in the IWRM approach, but any adjacent coastal and marine environments, as well as both upstream and downstream interests in the basin (see **Chapters 4, 5** and **11**).

The socio-economic dimension, with its focus on human concerns, is a crucial component of the approach, taking full account of:

- stakeholders having input in the planning and management of the resource, ensuring especially that the interests of women and the poor are fully represented

- the multiple uses of water and the range of people's needs

- integrating water plans and strategies into the national planning process and water concerns into all government policies and priorities, as well as considering the water resource implications of these actions

Girl collecting water from a community supply, Abidjan, Côte d'Ivoire

Replacing old water fittings with new, more efficient ones can produce good results in domestic and industrial water systems

■ the compatibility of water-related decisions taken at a local level with a country's national objectives

■ the water quantity and quality needs of essential ecosystems so that they are properly protected (GWP, 2004).

The 2002 World Summit on Sustainable Development (WSSD) sought to move the water sector worldwide towards more sustainable approaches to water management, building ecosystem considerations into overall IWRM management paradigms and calling all countries to produce IWRM and water-efficiency plans by 2005. **Chapter 2** reports that some progress on this is being made, but that many countries still have much to do. As the organizing principle of water management, IWRM is covered in most of the chapters of the Report. **Chapter 2** examines water governance, while **Chapters 8** and **9** examine how an integrated approach to water and industrial energy management respectively can provide big savings in all. **Chapter 10** stresses how disaster risk reduction has to be a key component of IWRM, while **Chapter 12** looks at the use of economic valuation techniques and pricing of water – important tools for IWRM.

2b. Demand management

Traditionally, the responses to pressures on water availability were solved by increasing supply: developing new sources and expanding and increasing abstractions from existing ones. As this is not sustainable, attention is switching rapidly towards more efficient and equitable approaches. The process of using water more efficiently and fairly, improving the balance between present supplies and demand, and reducing excessive use, is known collectively as demand management.

Consumer attitudes and behaviours (wrongful and wasteful use included) are a problem in which information campaigns and consumer education programmes can play important roles. **Chapter 13** discusses some of these. Economic incentives, in the form of water-use metering and the application of tariff systems that discourage wasteful use can be used to good effect, although allowances have to be made to ensure the poor are not disadvantaged (see **Chapter 12**). Replacing old water fittings with new, more efficient ones can produce good results in domestic and industrial water systems. Fixing the leaks in urban water distribution systems, where up to 60 percent or more of the water supplied can be lost through unrepaired leaks, offers much potential (see

---

BOX 1.6: THIRTEEN KEY IWRM CHANGE AREAS

The Global Water Partnership (GWP) has identified 13 key IWRM change areas within overall water governance, which together form the process of moving towards a more integrated water management approach. These key change areas are contained within a framework divided into the enabling environment, institutional roles and management instruments.

Enabling environment

1. Policies – setting goals for water use, protection and conservation
2. Legislative framework – defining the rules needed to achieve policies and goals
3. Financing and incentive structures – allocating financial resources to meet water needs.

Institutional structure

4. Creating an organizational framework – understanding resources and needs
5. Institutional capacity-building – developing human resources.

Management instruments

6. Water resources assessment – understanding resources and needs
7. Plans for IWRM – combining development options, resource use and human interaction
8. Demand management – using water more efficiently
9. Social change instruments – encouraging a water-oriented civil society
10. Conflict resolution – managing disputes and ensuring the sharing of water

11. Regulatory instruments – determining equitable allocations and water use limits
12. Economic instruments – valuing and pricing water for efficiency and equity
13. Information management and exchange – improving knowledge for better water management.

Source: GWP, 2004.

Chapter 3). In agriculture, changing cropping patterns, moving to more water-efficient crops, precision application of irrigation water (see **Chapter 7**), and improving the performance of water delivery and distribution systems can collectively produce improved water productivity. **Chapter 8** offers a detailed look at how industry has access to a growing range of cost-effective methods of optimizing water-use productivity and minimizing harmful industrial emissions. Combinations of all of these, as appropriate, can be very effective (GWP, 2004).

A big expansion in water harvesting, at domestic and community levels, is ongoing, particularly in Asia. Water recycling and reuse, already very prevalent in dry areas, is set to grow. Improvement in knowledge and understanding of treatment at different levels of sophistication is increasing, which will help to minimize risks to workers and consumers involved in the many different applications of wastewater reuse. The world has substantial deposits of brackish water, often in underground aquifers. As the cost of desalination is falling, because of technology improvements and lower energy costs, the prospects of desalinating brackish water – and also seawater in the case of coastal communities – are becoming more attractive.

Allocative efficiency – seeking to ensure that water is allocated to the highest value uses, while ensuring the interests of the poor and ecosystems are not neglected – may be sought through water rights, water markets and appropriate cost-benefit analyses (see **Chapters 2** and **12**). In low-income countries, it is essential that the role of water in poverty alleviation is fully factored in and that crucial environmental flows are maintained (GWP, 2004).

2c. Subsidiarity
There is an increasing trend towards delegation of water management responsibility to local authorities and water user groups, thereby promoting the principle of subsidiarity.

Devolution or decentralization of power from national governments and agencies to regional and/or local government authorities and organizations –including responsibility for water – is ongoing in many parts of the world. Examples of

this trend include new river basin management arrangements; transfer of responsibility for water supply and sanitation to municipal authorities, NGOs or community groups; and irrigation management transfer (IMT) to farmer/user groups (see **Chapter 7**). The potential benefits are good, as local management should better understand the needs, resources and demands of the situation. A degree of competition between local authorities can stimulate innovation while cooperation between stakeholders can be improved (World Bank, 2005).

The downside in practice is that many governments transfer water management responsibilities to a range of subnational entities that lack the capacity and resources to cope. Also there are larger-scale issues in water management that cannot readily be dealt with at the local level – allocations, pollution control, storage and others. Administrative areas may not coincide with river basins and watersheds. They may overlap adjacent basins, or several administrative units may share a basin. Some communities undergoing rapid socio-economic development involving significant upward and regional social mobility may find that membership of community management arrangements is unpopular, as people see no long-term advantage in participating (Moench et al, 2003). **Chapter 2** goes deeper into many of the problems associated with devolving responsibility for water management from central government to other entities and organizations and **Chapter 11** addresses the issue of moving water and resolving conflicts between countries, sectors, communities and other stakeholders.

2d. Gender mainstreaming
Of the 1.3 billion people living in abject poverty, the majority are women and children. They also happen to be the largest group systematically under-represented in water management arrangements. Water management is often gender specific at its different scales, reflecting the different ways men and women take responsibility. Generally, men take care of longer-term needs. Women, on the other hand, are mostly responsible for household hygiene, food and water. Often, this involves women and girls walking long distances to obtain water. Not only is the heavy burden of the water physically harmful, but the time lost means

A big expansion in water harvesting, at domestic and community levels, is ongoing, particularly in Asia. Water recycling and reuse, already very prevalent in dry areas, is set to grow

...women possess a lot of knowledge and experience of management and conservation of natural resources...

This community in Rajapur village, western Bangladesh, holds monthly meetings to discuss primary school attendance and other important issues

less available time for more productive purposes, such as livelihood activities and enhanced childcare. Ecosystems are frequently important food sources for poorer families and it is generally women who are involved in gathering food from them. Thus, ecosystem damage and species loss hit poor families and women particularly hard.

The pressing need of women for water supply and sanitation for their families gives them in a key role in community water service provision. Since many of the farming activities in poor communities are carried out by women, their needs for crop water are essential for family nutrition. Women, children and the elderly are also the most at risk from water-related hazards. Yet, all too often, women are excluded from important planning and decision-making in water management. This exclusion inevitably makes water service provision, in its many forms, less responsive to real need. Moreover, as Agenda 21 noted, women possess a lot of knowledge and experience of management and conservation of natural resources – including local water sources – as well as good water management skills. However, significant barriers to their participation in this role have arisen from a variety of causes – legal, constitutional, social, behavioural,

cultural and economic. In some societies, men have deep-seated insecurity about the idea of women owning property, including land or water rights for farming (Vyas, 2001).

Greater involvement of women in water matters enables better demand responsiveness to water provision and prevention of pollution. By ensuring their voices are fully heard in the water planning process, the effects on their subsistence and their development needs can be acknowledged and their interests protected. However, a number of issues have to be considered. The different status of men and women has to be acknowledged in its entirety; they have different needs and priorities and their life courses differ considerably. Equal treatment will not necessarily produce equal results and a gender equity approach is needed, requiring a good understanding of the frequently complicated relationships between domestic water use and its use in agriculture, industry and energy. Men and women often approach different decision-making differently. In addition, the institutional structures of general governance and water management determine the roles, rights and responsibilities of each sex in relation to control over and access to resources. Gender equity also requires that both sexes receive equitable benefits from any decentralized management structures and from new and improved infrastructure.

Gender issues in water management are well understood at the international level and, as a result, most guidelines produced by governments, designs for new projects, and programme policies now take account of gender issues. Gender mainstreaming (including gender equity matters in policies, programmes and procedures), gender budgeting (analysing all projects and policies to ensure equitable benefits for all), and affirmative action (to secure fully equitable participation in water planning and management), are all acknowledged as essential for greater gender equity and better water governance. However, much still remains to be done at the local level, a long-term task that will require persistence, capacity development and high-level political commitment. Despite all this, there is reason for cautious optimism, as progress is being made (Guerquin et al., 2003).

Part 3. Changing Natural Systems

The past twenty-five to thirty years have seen a substantial focus on the environmental impacts of water resources infrastructure development. Rather less attention has been paid to assessing the environmental impacts of water resource strategy. Recently, cooperation between ecologists and water managers has led to attempts to integrate an ecosystem approach into Integrated Water Resources Management (IWRM), although this is at an early stage. The task has been to conceptualize a catchment- or basin-based holistic approach, which recognizes the multiple roles of water both in ecosystems and human socio-economic systems. This involves consideration of terrestrial and aquatic ecosystems and the water links between them. Water managers are challenged with increasing their understanding of the biotic linkages between freshwater circulation and ecosystems. The process of photosynthesis (which consumes vast quantities of water resources) and the very significant changes in runoff from major land use changes, need to be better appreciated, as indicated in Chapters 4 and 5.

In a very short space of time, in planetary terms, we have sought to redesign and impose a new order on natural planetary systems built over aeons of time

3a. Human intervention

Humanity has embarked on a huge global ecological engineering project, with little or no preconception, or indeed full present knowledge, of the consequences. In a very short space of time, in planetary terms, we have sought to redesign and impose a new order on natural planetary systems built over aeons of time. In the water sector, securing reliable and secure water supplies for health and food, the needs of industrial and energy production processes, and the development of rights markets for both land and water have hugely changed the natural order of many rivers worldwide (see **Sections 3** and **4** of Report). There is a vast range of interactions between the biosphere and landscapes, as a result of which great variability results at a range of scales, and novel and unexpected properties of the system emerge. This variability is critical for the way ecosystems function, sustain themselves and evolve, and we never cease interfering with these natural systems. Land-use changes, urban development, dam construction and other river diversions all disrupt the natural pattern and rhythm of natural processes, without attention to the consequences and the negative effects on biodiversity.

Threatened environmental resilience

Left undisturbed, natural ecosystems have great resilience but a minimum composition of species must be maintained to ensure that the relations between the primary producers, consumers and decomposers can be sustained. Only thus can they continue the mediation of energy flow, the cycling of elements, and the spatial and temporal patterns of vegetation. Resilience is a buffer against disturbances and this buffer is best provided through maintaining biological diversity.

However, human impacts on the quantity and quality of available water seriously inhibit this resilience, leading to the risk of a retreat to a more vulnerable state. Pollution from agriculture, industry and domestic wastewater is making water resources, both surface water and groundwater, increasingly scarce and decreasingly poor in quality.

Loss of biodiversity is an important indicator of lowered resilience and the current deterioration in freshwater biodiversity (greater than either marine or terrestrial systems) is of great concern, as discussed in **Chapter 5**. Human reactions to environmental changes are less direct than for other species, because we are slow to become aware of changes before responding. Human resilience rests in the coping capacity of society and its institutions. As any resilience declines, whether social or ecological, it takes progressively smaller external changes to cause big problems. Reduced ecological resilience, from land degradation and drought, can increase social and environmental vulnerability, leading to the loss of livelihood and creating tension and conflict over freshwater and food. The key challenge facing water managers, now and in the future, is to try to optimize ecosystem resilience in response to human and

...land-use management and property ownership fragment the natural landscape in a totally different way from natural ecosystem processes

natural disturbances and protect this resilience with catchment-level life-support systems – in particular essential productivity functions (GWP, 2003).

3b. Climate variability and change

There is frequent confusion between climate change and climate variability. Climate change is associated with global warming and is a long-term change with its origins in natural factors and, as is now accepted, human activities. Climate variability, on the other hand, has always been part of the Earth's climate system, although it has so far received surprisingly little attention from the water sector. It affects water resources by way of floods, droughts, waterborne disease, and so on. It is not just the extremes of climate variability that are of concern to the water sector: the increasing and extreme variability in the hydrological cycle and climate systems, as is shown in **Chapter 4**, together with the dynamic processes that lie behind it, impact on countries' water resources and can make it difficult to meet the MDGs (Lenton, 2004).

Managing climate variability and the impacts of climate extremes is one of the challenges of sustainable development. In fact, the skills and knowledge obtained in dealing with these variability problems will be invaluable in confronting the longer-term challenges of climate change, as specifically discussed in **Chapters 10** and **13**. As ever, it is the poor who are at greatest risk. Thus climate effects have to be built into poverty reduction activities and included in national development plans and national water resources policies, using the IWRM approach. Both water managers and decision-makers have to be encouraged to engage in greater dialogue with climate and development specialists to better understand the climate-related challenges and how to deal with them. At the same time, but on a broader front, although there is a clear need to learn to adapt to the challenges of climate variability and change, all actions to mitigate the anthropological impacts of this must continue.[4]

On the broader issue of climate change several concerns are apparent. The yields of staple crop production (e.g. rice, corn and wheat) are sensitive to temperature increase, the most vulnerable period being during pollination, just before seed formation.

It had been thought that increased CO_2 levels would lead to higher grain yields, but the view is now that negative effects of temperature increase will outweigh this. **Chapter 7** examines key issues connected with the potential for climate effects to alter food production patterns. Warming over land will be greater than warming over the seas and this effect will be greater in the higher latitudes, affecting continental interiors more than coastal regions. This has major implications for grain-producing regions. The headwaters of many large Asian rivers originate in the Himalayas. The large amount of freshwater traditionally stored in the glaciers there is being reduced as glaciers shrink. This will likely alter seasonal runoff patterns, increasing flood extremes and affecting availability of critical irrigation waters (Lenton, 2003).

Chapter 8 points out the growing risk of what it calls 'Natech' disasters, where extreme climate events can severely damage industrial installations, reducing not only economic activity but also releasing gross pollution into the environment. Given the fact that much energy generation is located in fossil-fuel-powered electricity generating stations and that the very large greenhouse gas emissions from these are believed to have a big impact on climate, **Chapter 9** looks at the issues involved in connection with more sustainable energy provision as related to water.

3c. Ecological water management

As discussed, land-use management and property ownership fragment the natural landscape in a totally different way from natural ecosystem processes. Financial markets and global and national business cycles have their own patterns and cycles and the capitalistic approach needs market advantage and security of tenure, which is at variance with natural patterns and cycles. As a result, much policy is made within overly simple settings and fails to recognize the complexity of these different cycles and their interactions. The critical challenge is to recognize that the spatial and temporal scales of variability within ecosystems, society and the economy are strongly linked, but are not congruent.

Global development must be equitable and inclusive not only of the interests of humanity but also of

4. For more information on the Dialogue on Water and Climate see www.waterandclimate.org

BOX 1.7: THE PARTICULAR PROBLEMS OF TROPICAL COUNTRIES

Climate impacts are particularly severe in low-income countries in the tropics, which generally include those countries having the greatest difficulties working towards the MDGs. The problem is exacerbated by rainflow and streamflow, which are concentrated over a short period of a few months. Very significant seasonal and annual fluctuations around long-term historical averages are reflected in long dry periods and recurrent droughts and floods. Since these countries often rely substantially on natural resources, the impact of floods and droughts on development is amplified. Climate variability can also increase vector-borne disease outbreaks (e.g. malaria) and the incidence of diarrhoeal disease in the rainy season.

In addition, climate uncertainties lead to greater risk aversion by farmers in crop selection, planting and fertilization, as well as problems for reservoir managers responsible for irrigation and hydroelectrical production. Thus, the challenge is to greatly increase water storage to minimize the impact of climate variability, while trying to avoid the environmental and social disruption of large dams. Balancing the high demand for irrigation water against other uses adds to the challenge of obtaining greater water productivity from irrigation waters ('more crop per drop'). These storage and water productivity issues require further substantial research and development work (Lenton, 2004) See **Chapter 7** for more on the issue of storage.

Source: Lenton, 2004.

---

the natural planetary ecosystems that support us. The task of water managers is therefore far from easy. They must satisfy socio-economic needs, minimize the pollution burden and accept the consumptive use involved, including a better understanding of the limits of the self-cleansing capacities of ecosystems. Minimum ecological criteria have to be met.

Catchments have to be viewed as socio-eco-hydrological systems in which trade-offs are needed or will have to be made socially acceptable by appropriate institutions, regulations and finance. A key entry point is defining minimum criteria or 'bottom lines' for terrestrial ecosystems. In order to balance upstream and downstream interests, work has to start downstream, identifying bottom lines for the different components of the aquatic ecosystems, for example, uncommitted environmental flows and minimum water quality. Thereafter the process is carried on upstream, section by section, constantly seeking to identify resilience determinants to avoid ecosystem collapse. Agricultural water management and food production as major water users have to be very sensitive to ecosystem considerations to ensure sustainability.

Skills will have to be developed to achieve all of this – to negotiate trade-offs and define ecological bottom lines and sustainability, based on a fuller understanding of both ecosystem and societal resilience. Increased cooperation between ecologists, water managers and social scientists is needed to make clear the water linkages connecting terrestrial ecosystems, human communities and resilience. Concepts of vulnerability and resilience, coupled with a better appreciation of the crucial and central role of both terrestrial and aquatic ecosystems to humanity, must be understood by all parties – technical specialists and other stakeholders alike, including the water consumer base. The ways in which these skills can be better developed are covered in **Chapter 13**. The subsequent attitude and behaviour changes that would follow such improved understanding would go a long way to furthering social, economic and environmental sustainability and enhance the effectiveness of IWRM (GWP, 2003). While IWRM is undoubtedly the essential approach to effective and optimum water management, implementing it can present its own challenges.

Global development must be equitable and inclusive...

Fishermen fixing a net, India

There are more than 1 million deaths each year from malaria, with between 300 and 500 million cases in total...

Part 4. Challenges for Well-being and Development

Balancing the increasing competition among the diverse and different water-using sectors – irrigation, municipalities, industry, environmental flows – including the demands of upstream and downstream users, is a challenge facing watersheds worldwide. Decisions on water allocations have to be made at different scales and a wide range of transboundary and other regulatory instruments and water and pollution management techniques need to be developed and shared: local scale in particular catchments, full-river basin scale where the geographical extent of the basin may well encompass several domestic political boundaries, national level to ensure that the potential of water to stimulate socio-economic development is realized, and at international level in the case of transboundary waters (Stockholm, 2002).

4a. Water and health: Reducing infectious diseases

In terms of threats to human security from premature death, infectious disease ranks at number one, being responsible for 26 percent of all premature deaths. The top five communicable diseases worldwide in 2002, in rank order, in terms of early mortality, were:

- Respiratory infections caused around 4 million deaths

- HIV/AIDs with some 2.8 million deaths

- Diarrhoea causing 1.8 million deaths

- Tuberculosis, causing 1.6 million deaths

- Malaria, accounting for 1.3 million deaths.

Although not all of these can be directly related to water issues, they are closely connected with water supply, sanitation and habitat challenges, which as noted earlier, the Commission on Sustainable Development wishes to be considered together in future. As discussed in **Chapter 6**, it is increasingly widely recognized that diarrhoea, the leading cause of deaths in children of developing countries, could be controlled by improving access to safe drinking water and sanitation. There are more than 1 million deaths each year from malaria, with between 300 and 500 million cases in total, affecting populations in tropical regions of Africa, Asia and the Americas. Approximately 40 percent of the total world population is at risk of infection,

particularly pregnant women, unborn babies and children under 5 (Concern/Guardian, 2005).

Every year, around 10.8 million children die before their fifth birthday and, of these, 4 million die before they reach 1 month old. Some 92 percent of all deaths of under-5 children occur in just forty-two lower-income countries. It is estimated that 63 percent of all deaths of under-5 children can be prevented using current knowledge and methods including oral rehydration for diarrhoea, antibiotics for pneumonia, mosquito nets and anti-malaria drugs for malaria, better water supply sanitation and domestic hygiene. The links between childhood sickness and death and inadequate water and sanitation availability, unsatisfactory hygiene, lack of better water management practices are clear.

4b. Water and food: Facing growing demand and competition

Over the last fifty years, agriculture has been facing the great challenge of providing food to a global population doubling in size. This has resulted in water withdrawals that largely exceed those of any other sector. However, 13 percent of the human population is still underfed, the majority living in rural areas of developing countries – the countries most likely to support the biggest share of demographic growth in the years to come. Increased competition for water and the need to integrate environmental issues threatens water for food and is an issue that cannot be tackled through a narrow sectoral approach. New forms of water management in agriculture, including irrigation management, must continue to be explored and implemented with focus on livelihoods as well as on productivity, as discussed in **Chapter 7**.

In agriculture, changing cropping patterns to lower water use crops, precision application of irrigation water at the critical point of the crop growing cycle, and better water delivery and distribution systems can collectively produce improved water productivity. Improved irrigation water application technologies enable a more precise and timely application of water at critical points in the plant life-cycle, improving irrigation water productivity and efficiency. These technologies are well known and widely applied by better resourced farmers. However, innovations in micro-irrigation techniques mean that these can now be made affordable to poor farmers. Very low-cost drip irrigation systems and treadle pumps allied to low-cost double walled plastic water storage tanks, which rest in easily dug earthen trenches, have now been developed. This combination costs one-fifth of the price of conventional ferro-cement tanks. These new methods, when applied to the increasingly smaller plots, enable them to produce a range of higher-value cash crops and significantly improve their income prospect (Polak, 2004). In the growing competition for increasingly scarce water resources, policy-makers are looking to the value generated by water use. As reforms to agriculture are forced to compete with industry and service sector developments, crop production has shifted from low-value staple crops to high-value horticultural crops.

4c. Water for industry and energy: Aiming for sustainability

Though not explicitly included in the MDGs, industry and energy are both water-related issues vital to socio-economic development. The World Summit on Sustainable Development held in Johannesburg in 2002 proposed a Plan of Implementation that makes a strong link between the related goals of industrial development, improved access to energy services, and poverty eradication and sustainable natural resource management. Industry is a significant engine of growth, accelerating particularly in highly indebted countries, and making up the bulk of the economy in East Asia and the Pacific. But to be sustainable, economic development also needs an adequate and steady supply of energy, for which water is a key resource – whether through hydropower, nuclear-based energy generation, coal slurry technology, small-scale hydels or other sources, as discussed in **Chapter 8**.

Both industrial growth and increased energy production are demanding an enlarged share of water resources. Currently, the total water withdrawal by industry is much greater than the water actually consumed. Industries have a dramatic effect on the state of the world's freshwater resources, both by the quantity of water they consume and their potential to pollute the water environment by their discharge. Industrial discharge returned without treatment has high organic content, leading to rapid growth of algae, bacteria and slime, oxygen-depleted water, and thermal pollution. Discharge can affect a relatively large volume of water and have numerous impacts on human health. Polluted water may affect fishing grounds, irrigated lands, municipalities located downstream and even bathing water. It is also recognized that water pollution can have significant transboundary effects.

Energy-intensive water delivery systems can also have dire impacts for areas with scarce water and energy resources. Some sources of water supply are more energy intensive than others, such as thermal desalination, which requires more energy than wastewater recycling. Pumping water is a major cost element everywhere, and consumes significant energy resources worldwide. Reducing the inefficiencies that occur in energy production (e.g. during electricity generation, transmissions, distribution and usage) will reduce electric power requirements, leading to higher water savings, as discussed in **Chapter 9**. In addition, changing environmental contexts demand that a greater investment be made in renewable energies.

Improving environmental governance is central to limiting industrial pollution and reducing the inefficiencies that occur within energy production and distribution systems. In industry, governance initiatives now exist at international and national levels, as well as at the level of industrial sectors and individual companies. The Basel Convention on the Control of Transboundary Movements of

Polluted water may affect fishing grounds, irrigated lands, municipalities located downstream and even bathing water

This self-propelled, centre-pivot irrigation machine drills for water 30 to 400 m below the surface in Ma'an, Jordan. A pivoting pipeline with sprinklers irrigates 78 hectares of land. Production of 1 ton of grain requires about 1,000 tons of water. At the current rate of use in Jordan, subterranean water reserves could dry up before 2010

BOX 1.8: INLAND WATER TRANSPORT: A TOOL FOR PROMOTING ECONOMIC AND SUSTAINABLE DEVELOPMENT

A well-functioning transport system is crucial to the development of a strong and vibrant economy, enabling ready access to both raw materials and markets. In the twentieth century, road transport has come to be regarded as a particularly effective mode of transport. Yet inland water transport (IWT), using rivers, canals and lakes, has been historically important in economic development worldwide and offers important environmental, economic and other practical benefits that make it one of the most advantageous modes of transport even today.

In Europe, where more than 35,000 kilometres (km) of waterways connect hundreds of cities and industrial regions, 125 billion ton-kilometres of freight were transported by inland waterways in 2003 alone. In the United States, where more than 25,000 km of inland, coastal and intracoastal waterways exist, water traffic represented 656 million tons in 2000. In fact, many well-known and prosperous cities, such as Paris, San Francisco, Rotterdam, Shanghai and London, developed as a result of their position as water transport hubs. Building on the natural advantages of geographic location and navigable waterways, developing countries may find IWT a cost-effective and sustainable way of developing transport infrastructure where constraints of land availability and cost inhibit the expansion of rail and road infrastructure.

The environmental benefits of water transport, when compared to other modes, are also apparent. Whereas road transport consumes large amounts of non-renewable energy and contributes significantly to air pollution, water transport is more energy efficient and environment-friendly. Energy consumption for water transport per ton-kilometre is half of that of rail and one-sixth that of road, while carbon dioxide emissions from IWT are approximately one-thirteenth of those of road freight transport. Additionally, while vehicular transport contributes to noise pollution and exacerbates land congestion and road accidents, water

transport can relieve pressure on overloaded road systems in densely populated regions, thus reducing both traffic accidents and noise levels.

The financial and environmental advantages of water transport make it a smart investment for many regions. The Asian and Pacific region, for example, has at least 280,000 km of navigable waterways, more than 340,000 large vessels and millions of traditional craft, carrying over 1 billion tons of cargo and a half billion passengers each year. In some countries, such as China, water transport is already well developed. China has more than 5,600 navigable rivers, with a total navigable length of 119,000 km, including the Yangtze River, which alone comprises 50 percent of the national total. The annual volume of IWT freight in China was about 690 million tons in 2000, the large majority of which moved along the Yangtze. Despite possessing vast IWT potential, other countries in the region have been slow in putting it to use. Such is the case of India, which has an extensive river system, including 14,500 km of navigable waterways, only 37 percent of which is currently utilized for motorized transport. In 2001/02, IWT accounted for a mere 0.1 percent of India's total domestic surface transport (compared to 68 percent for road and 30 percent for rail).

IWT is important in other regions as well. In Latin America, the Paraguay-Parana Waterway Project was proposed in the late 1980s as a means to promote the economic development and integration of countries within the La Plata Basin. The Paraguay and Paraná rivers are natural north–south transport corridors, extending through four countries (Argentina, Bolivia, Brazil and Paraguay) and accessible to a fifth (Uruguay), thus connecting the heart of South America to the Atlantic Ocean. Designed to expand navigation possibilities, the Project is meant to reduce the cost of transport within the region, improve links between commercial centres and provide an outlet to the sea for the

landlocked countries of Bolivia and Paraguay. Though the project is still in the planning stages, its legal framework was approved by all associated riparian countries in 1996.

Although IWT development is picking up speed on a global scale (particularly in Asia), vast lengths of navigable water remain underdeveloped. In some areas, the potential of IWT may be greatly limited by natural constraints. Where long and harsh dry seasons diminish water levels, IWT may be considered an unreliable mode of transport. In Bangladesh, for example, where an inland navigation network spans 24,000 km, the dry season (from December to May) limits access to the system to vessels of 100 deadweight tons or below. Throughout Africa, seasonal climate variation and unpredictable water depths limit the number of inland water bodies that are navigable. There are only three rivers classified as international waterways in Africa: the Congo, Nile and Zambezi rivers. Hydraulic work could, however, increase the number of potentially navigable rivers on the continent. Nigeria, for example, is estimated to have over 3,000 km of potentially navigable inland waterways were they to be developed.

Factors limiting the development of IWT systems include the poor recognition of IWT potential, lack of technology, limited financial resources, exclusion of IWT from Integrated Water Resources Management (IWRM) planning, insufficient institutional capacity, inadequate legal instruments, an absence of policies, limited information sharing and poor public awareness.

Despite the numerous advantages of water transport, it is not without negative environmental impacts. Hydraulic work undertaken to make rivers more navigable (e.g. constructing dikes, straightening canals, destroying rapids, dredging and sometimes even adding artificial waterways), can prove harmful to an ecosystem's balance and local biodiversity.

BOX 1.8: *continued*

For example, over the past 150 years, regulation work on the Danube River Basin has significantly damaged historical floodplains (see **Chapter 14**). Large dikes and disconnected meanders in this area were found to suppress the linkage between surface water and groundwater, reducing the recharge of aquifers important for local drinking water supplies. Concern has also been raised over the impact of navigation channel repairs on wetlands and biodiversity in the Niger Delta.

In order to promote efficient and sustainable waterway projects, it is essential that IWT be integrated into overall IWRM plans. Although inland transport may carry some environmental risks, overall IWT accounts for comparatively less environmental externalities than other modes of transport. In addition, Environmental Impact Assessments of IWT projects can greatly help to identify areas at risk so that mitigation measures can be undertaken. There is an urgent need for research as we need to find more environmentally friendly means to maintain the navigability of watercourses in addition to learning more about how the world's water resources may be impacted by new environmental challenges, such as climate change. Overall, IWT remains one of the most economically and environmentally sustainable modes of transportation, and when integrated with other transport development in the context of IWRM planning, it can help to re-establish a balance between the various modes of transport, making the transportation industry as a whole more responsive to broader societal goals.

Sources: EUROPA, 2005; US Army Corps of Engineers, 2004; ADB, 2003; River Bureau of the Ministry of Land, Infrastructure and Transport of Japan, 2003; UNECA, 2002; UNESCAP, 2003 and 2004.

Hazardous Wastes and their Disposal is a recent example of an international mechanism aimed at addressing issues of waste generation, movement, management and disposal. Yet, as discussed in **Chapter 8**, to be truly effective, efforts to curb industrial water pollution require that such agreements be translated into action through national policies and at the industry/sectoral level. Stepped water tariffs, subsidies for industries implementing innovative environmental technologies, and financial and advisory support for new research are just a few examples of measures that can be taken.

Environmental concerns, particularly over climate change and nuclear waste disposal, as well as safety and security of supply, are prompting governments to introduce policies aimed at accelerating the use of renewable energy and Combined Heat and Power (CHP). Total worldwide investment in renewable energy rose from $6 billion in 1995 to approximately $22 billion in 2003, and is increasing rapidly. This trend of investment in renewable energies can not only help to increase the production of more efficient energy, but is critical to our ability to face future challenges posed by environmental uncertainties.

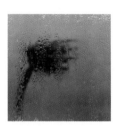

Part 5. Management Responses and Stewardship

Over the last century, there has been a significant rise in water-related disasters, affecting an increasing number of people, particularly those living in developing countries. Resulting damages to property and losses of life and livelihoods compromise the gains of development.

5a. Managing risks: Dealing with increasing frequency

It is quite possible that climate change will not only cause rises in global temperature, but also lead to changes in the frequency of floods, droughts, storms, fires – bringing about more and greater unexpected effects. One example is the headwaters of many large Asian rivers originating in the Himalayas. The large amount of freshwater traditionally stored in the glaciers there is being reduced as glaciers shrink. This will likely alter seasonal runoff patterns, increasing flood extremes and affecting availability of critical irrigation waters (Lenton, 2003).

Over the past decade, progress has been made in risk management, thanks to scientific advancements and the recognition of the various dimensions of risk, including political, social and cultural issues. As discussed in **Chapter 10**, however, technical and organizational constraints remain high and slow down the design and implementation of efficient risk reduction.

5b. Sharing water: Facing increased competition

Over 260 of the international or transboundary basins, with over 50 percent of Earth's surface and 40 percent of the global population, are shared by one or more countries worldwide. Opinions vary as to the likelihood of cooperation rather than conflict, but experience has shown that cooperation is more likely, despite that fact that wars over natural resources – oil, minerals, metals, diamonds, timber, water, and so on – have been a feature of almost a quarter of recent wars. Given the importance of international or transboundary water resources and their potential for cooperation in development, plus the need to avoid conflict, **Chapter 11** explores in more detail the cooperation possibilities, which can produce benefits way beyond the water sector as covered in **Chapter 2**.

Cooperation may arise spontaneously from perceived threats or opportunities by riparian states, or from without by concerned intermediaries, for example, multilateral agencies and respected statesmen. Threats may be associated with increasing extremes of climate variability, while opportunities could relate to the socio-economic development potential of a cooperative approach. Once the principle of cooperation is established, trust-building measures such as cooperative research, joint data collection, knowledge and information sharing are important for building the basis for collaborative planning and management.

There are compelling arguments that riparian countries collect compatible data, which is analysed and shared to facilitate efficient use of shared water resources (Moench, 2003). Experience has shown that, with shared water resources, the greater the capacity to collect, process, interpret and accept data, the greater the range of policy options that can be generated – and the less likelihood there is of disagreement and conflict between riparian users. Data gathering may be best delegated to a trusted neutral organization, as suggested above. Alternatively, riparian states might set up data collection arrangements under their joint control. It is now widely accepted that jointly controlled data generation and analysis is an essential early step in building long-term riparian cooperation over shared water resources.

Perceptions of fairness for all parties are essential and it is important to recognize different riparian views of the benefits on offer. Trust is a *sine qua non* – riparian states need to move from their pre-cooperation positions over the water itself to fostering an interest in the benefits to be gained from cooperation. Unequal capacity between riparian states complicates negotiations. Self-financing institutions for basin cooperation are vital to pave the way for needed investment. The trade-offs between environmental, political and economic challenges have to be balanced. This is no easy task, and the key to resolving it lies in the choice of process and subsequent commitment to it. A small but growing body of needed expertise is now becoming available and the prospects of furthering the benefits-based approach set out above are improving (Grey, 2002).

5c. Enhancing knowledge and capacity: At all levels

Deficiencies in some countries in data collection and information sharing pose several challenges to water resources management. There is a serious dearth of detailed hydrometeorological data. Many

hydrometeorological measuring stations are degraded as a result of both lack of maintenance and skilled operating staff. Many of the instruments are out of date and poorly calibrated. Network characteristics and measured variables vary from country to country. Systems for storing, processing and managing data for water resources are often rudimentary. To try to cope with these deficiencies, a growing range of satellite-based remote sensing systems are under development, as explored in **Chapters 4** and **13,** although without a sound and accessible knowledge base and capacity-building efforts, these systems will not benefit the areas most in need of attention. Indeed, there is the matter of who collects the data, how it is to be interpreted, and who has access to it, other than the collection agency, and how people in lower-income countries can access the vast and growing literature and knowledge on solving problems that is accumulating in agencies, archives and organizations around the world.

Hydrological conditions are highly variable from season to season and year to year. Since much hydrometeorological data is in such short supply, the combination of these two factors means that the nature of many emerging water problems and the possible responses are often uncertain. Much hydrometeorological information in some parts of the world is held by hierarchically structured government departments functioning in specific water-using sectors, for example irrigation or water supply. The way information is generated, analysed, controlled and disseminated sets up the context in which perspectives are formed and solutions generated. Different organizations collect and analyse the information that supports their paradigm relating to the part of the water sector in which they operate. Thus, there are arguments to ensure that primary baseline information should be produced by organizations that are institutionally separated from executive functions in water.

As discussed earlier, there is an increasing trend towards delegation of water management responsibility to local authorities and water user groups. They must, therefore, have access to baseline data on water needs and availability. But data itself is useless without the capacity to interpret and analyse it meaningfully. A vast amount

There is an increasing trend towards delegation of water management responsibility to local authorities and water user groups

*Charging is but
one policy
option, full-cost
subsidy is
another*

of information is now available on solutions to many of the world's water problems. It seems increasingly that, someone, somewhere, has an answer with a potentially wide application. However, this information is not well analysed, collated and disseminated. It has been alleged that twenty years is the average period of time for a new idea to enter mainstream consciousness and understanding – this certainly seems true of many techniques developed for different parts of the water sector. Much more could usefully be done to collect and collate good international practice on key aspects of water use and management and disseminate it more widely, especially in lower-income countries. **Chapter 13** explores many of these issues and challenges. As the problem of data scarcity is widespread across all sectors of water, all the chapters point to the additional challenges that this poses, not only to water managers but also to international, national and local monitoring and policy-making.

5d. Valuing and charging for water: Market vs. non-market values

The water sector requires reform if the MDGs are to be met. Policy-makers must reform institutions, reformulate water policies, and initiate new ways of organizing water supply and sanitation. To select among the different policy options and programme initiatives on the table, policy-makers must have a means of determining which are likely to bring results that best meet society's goals, recognizing the many values of water.

*Metering and charging
for water consumption
contribute to the
sustainable utilization of
water resources*

The common method used for public policy analysis, that is, to differentiate the various options, is *benefit-cost analysis* (BCA). This method totals up the pluses and minuses of each option so that the net benefits of the different options may be considered, and the trade-offs (the different level of advantages and disadvantages associated with various sub-elements of the programmes/projects) between the different options may be clearly seen.

In preparing a BCA one needs to make an *economic valuation* (calculate in monetary terms) of the benefits and costs associated with each option. A problem emerges when the benefits or costs associated with a particular activity are not subject to any market transaction, which in turn means that

there is no market price by which to measure it. In such cases, economists have developed a variety of *non-market valuation techniques* that can be used to estimate surrogate (or shadow) prices that may be used to value the goods and services in question.

Many of the goods or services that must be evaluated in assessing alternative water policies are secondary effects or externalities of the policy or project in question and include social and environmental impacts. In certain cases, some members of the community may be resistant to (even offended by) the attempts to put a monetary value on certain social or environmental effects. In such cases, BCA must be complemented by public discourse open to all stakeholders and political negotiations in order to reach consensus on the most suitable policy/programme.

Charging for water is but one policy option (full-cost subsidy is another). It serves several objectives, including cost recovery, revenue raising, and demand management, all of which contribute to the ultimate objective of sustainable utilization of water resources respecting the societal principles of social equity, environmental preservation and economic efficiency. Determining the tariff structure – form and level – is essentially a political decision, which may also draw on the techniques of economic valuation and BCA to elucidate the net result of various options. Benefit capture analysis, that is, more focused attention on *who benefits* and *who bears the costs* is increasingly applied in order to understand more clearly the distributional aspects as well as the financial implications of various policy options.

Private-public partnerships, payment for environmental services and trade policies revised to reflect the concept 'virtual water' are all policy responses that recognize directly or indirectly the increasing value of water, and in which the valuation techniques described above would have been employed to determine their suitability to a particular situation. **Chapter 12** examines all the issues related to valuing and charging for water in greater detail.

BOX 1.11: POLICY-MAKING AND SCIENTIFIC INTEGRITY

Responsible water resources management in particular and good governance in general rely on sound policy decisions, which require the objective collection and analysis of data and information. As scientific knowledge becomes simultaneously wider in breadth and more specialized in depth, governments, and the people these governments represent, rely increasingly on the expert knowledge of scientists.

Today, however, the world is seeing a strong politicization of natural and social science, which is detrimental to both good governance and scientific inquiry. Political interference manifests itself through corruption; conflicts of interest; cronyism; the political vetting of scientific appointments; and governmental censorship, suppression and distortion of scientific findings.

These problems manifest themselves to varying degrees in many countries (both developed and developing) and can be found across the spectrum of scientific endeavour, including climate change, AIDS prevention, agricultural science, reproductive health, environmental protection, military intelligence, etc.

Due to the rapid pace of scientific advancement, a layman's education is no longer sufficient to evaluate many aspects of public policy, which means that the general public is increasingly dependent on the integrity of scientists and the institutions for which these scientists work.

Transparency and scientific integrity are critical for good, democratic governance. Policy-makers and the electorate need accessible information in order to make informed decisions about public

policy. Scientists, both in the private and public sectors, must be independent and not subject to political, financial or physical retribution in response to scientific findings that do not fall in line with a government's or corporation's policies and ideology. And in the case of publicly funded research, findings should be transparent and not subject to political manipulation or suppression. Scientists must maintain their integrity by resisting pressure from corporations, governments or other interested parties to compromise their research.

For more information, see UNESCO's Ethics of Science and Technology Programme (www.unesco.org/shs/est); the Union of Concerned Scientists (http://www.ucsusa.org/) and the International Council for Science (www.icsu.org).

Part 6. Water and Global Targets: Where Do We Stand?

Within the UN system, a clear wish has emerged to take a lead role in finding ways to share the world's available resources more equitably. Here we review some of the global targets involved in the UN's aspirations for poverty relief as they relate to water and WWAP's mandate, as the flagship programme of UN-Water – to undertake and report on assessment processes and refine the thinking behind better-adapted monitoring tools and indicator rationale for the water sector.

6a. The Millennium Development Goals (MDGs)

Long experience has shown that setting targets is vitally important for focusing attention and providing incentives to mobilize action on key issues of development. Recognizing the need to speed up poverty alleviation and socio-economic development, the 2000 UN General Assembly Millennium Meeting established eight Millennium Development Goals (MDGs), with targets, to be achieved by 2015, from a baseline of 1990 and with a major review in 2005. The role played by water in achieving the goals is summarized in **Box 1.12**.

The major UN conferences and other international water meetings (e.g. the World Water Forums, see WWDR1, 2003) have a history of global target setting.[5] However, all too frequently, these have not included detailed enough implementation plans or the necessary financial resources. As a result, although good progress was made on some early targets, they were rarely met in full. Global targets are just that—global ambitions that can only be met via the aggregate of local actions in communities worldwide. Without local commitment and the needed resources, targets will never be met in full.

5. http://www.unesco.org/ water/wwap/index.shtml

BOX 1.12 WATER AND THE MILLENNIUM DEVELOPMENT GOALS

GOAL 1. ERADICATE EXTREME POVERTY AND HUNGER*

Water is a factor of production in virtually all enterprise, including agriculture, industry and the services sector. Improved nutrition and food security reduces susceptibility to diseases, including HIV/AIDS, malaria among others. Access to electricity is key to improving quality of life in the modern age. Competition between the various sectors must be balanced by policies that recognize the ability and responsibility of all sectors to address the issues of poverty and hunger.

Targets:
- Halve, between 1990 and 2015, the proportion of people whose income is less than $1 a day
- Halve, between 1990 and 2015, the proportion of people who suffer from hunger

WWDR2 Water-related Indicators:
- Percentage of undernourished people
- Percentage of poor people living in rural areas
- Relative importance of agriculture
- Irrigated land as percentage of cultivated land
- Relative importance of agriculture water withdrawals in water balance
- Extent of land salinized by irrigation
- Importance of groundwater in irrigation
- Dietary Energy Supply (DES)

See Chapter 7: *Water for Food, Agriculture and Rural Livelihoods*

- Trends in industrial water use
- Water use by sector
- Organic pollution emissions by industrial sector
- Industrial water productivity
- Trends in ISO 14001 certification, 1997-2002
- Access to electricity and domestic use
- Electricity generation by fuel, 1971-2001
- Capability for hydropower generation, 2002
- Total primary energy supply by fuel
- Carbon intensity of electricity production, 2002
- Volume of desalinated water produced

See Chapter 8: *Water and Industry* and Chapter 9: *Water and Energy*

GOAL 2. ACHIEVE UNIVERSAL PRIMARY EDUCATION

Promotion of a healthy school environment is an essential element of ensuring universal access to education, and school enrolment, attendance, retention and performance are improved; teacher placement is improved. In this respect access to adequate drinking water and sanitation is key.

Target:
- Ensure that, by 2015, children everywhere, boys and girls alike, will be able to complete a full course of primary schooling

WWDR2 Water-related Indicator:
- Knowledge Index

See Chapter 13: *Enhancing Knowledge and Capacity*

GOAL 3. PROMOTE GENDER EQUALITY AND EMPOWER WOMEN

Educating women and girls will permit them to fulfil their potential as full partners in the development effort.

Target:
- Eliminate gender disparity in primary and secondary education, preferably by 2015 and in all levels of education no later than 2015

WWDR2 Water-related Indicator:
- Access to information, participation and justice in water decisions

See Chapter 2: *Challenges of Governance*

GOAL 4. REDUCE CHILD MORTALITY

Improvements in access to safe drinking water and adequate sanitation will help prevent diarrhoea, and lay a foundation for the control of soil-transmitted helminths and schistosomiasis among other pathogens.

Target:
- Reduce by two-thirds, between 1990 and 2015, the under-five mortality rate

WWDR2 Water-related Indicators:
- Mortality in children < 5 yrs
- Prevalence of underweight children < 5 yrs
- Prevalence of stunting among children < 5 yrs

See Chapter 6: *Protecting and Promoting Human Health*

GOAL 5. IMPROVE MATERNAL HEALTH

Improved health and nutrition reduce susceptibility to anaemia and other conditions that affect maternal mortality. Sufficient quantities of clean water for washing pre-and-post birth cut down on life-threatening infection.

Target:
- Reduce by three-quarters, between 1990 and 2015, the maternal mortality rate

WWDR2 Water-related Indicator:
- DALY (Disability Adjusted Life Year)

See Chapter 6: *Protecting and Promoting Human Health*

GOAL 6. COMBAT HIV, AIDS, MALARIA AND OTHER DISEASES

Improved water supply and sanitation reduces susceptibility to/severity of HIV/AIDS and other major diseases.

Targets:
- Have halted by 2015 and begun to reverse the spread of HIV/AIDS
- Have halted by 2015 and begun to reverse the incidence of malaria and other major diseases

WWDR2 Water-related Indicator:
- DALY (Disability Adjusted Life Year)

See Chapter 6: *Protecting and Promoting Human Health*

BOX 1.12: *continued*

GOAL 7. ENSURE ENVIRONMENTAL SUSTAINABILITY

Healthy ecosystems are essential for the maintenance of biodiversity and human well-being. We depend upon them for our drinking water, food security and a wide range of environmental goods and services.

Target:

■ Integrate the principles of sustainable development into country policies and programmes and reverse the loss of environmental resources

WWDR2 Water-related Indicators:

■ Water Stress Index
■ Groundwater development
■ Precipitation annually
■ TARWR volume (total annual renewable water resources)
■ TARWR per capita
■ Surface water (SW) as a % TARWR
■ Groundwater (GW) as a % of TARWR
■ Overlap % TARWR
■ Inflow % TARWR
■ Outflow % TARWR
■ Total Use as % TARWR

See Chapter 4: *The State of the Resource*

■ Fragmentation and flow regulation of rivers
■ Dissolved nitrogen ($NO_3 + NO_2$)
■ Trends in freshwater habitat protection
■ Trends in freshwater species
■ Biological Oxygen Demand (BOD)

See Chapter 5: *Coastal and Freshwater Ecosystems*

Targets:

■ Halve by 2015 the proportion of people without sustainable access to safe drinking water and basic sanitation
■ By 2020, to have achieved a significant improvement in the lives of at least 100 million slum dwellers

WWDR2 Water-related Indicators:

■ Urban Water and Sanitation Governance Index
■ Index of Performance of Water Utilities

See Chapter 3: *Water and Human Settlements in an Urbanizing World*

■ Access to safe drinking water
■ Access to basic sanitation

See Chapter 6: *Protecting and Promoting Human Health*

GOAL 8. DEVELOP A GLOBAL PARTNERSHIP FOR DEVELOPMENT*

Water has a range of values that must be recognized in selecting governance strategies. Valuation techniques inform decision-making for water allocation, which promote sustainable social, environmental and economic development as well as transparency and accountability in governance. Development agendas and partnerships should recognize the fundamental role that safe drinking water and basic sanitation play in economic and social development.

Targets:

■ Develop further an open trading and financial system that is rule-based, predictable and non-discriminatory, includes a commitment to good governance, development and poverty reduction – nationally and internationally
■ Address the special needs of landlocked and small island developing states

WWDR2 Water-related Indicators:

■ Water sector share in total public spending
■ Ratio of actual to desired level of public investment in water supply
■ Rate of cost recovery
■ Water charges as a percent of household income

See Chapter 12: *Valuing and Charging for Water*

■ Water interdependency indicator
■ Cooperation indicator
■ Vulnerability indicator
■ Fragility indicator
■ Development indicator

See Chapter 11: *Sharing Water*

■ Disaster Risk Index
■ Risk and Policy Assessment Index
■ Climate Vulnerability Index

See Chapter 10: *Managing Risks*

■ Progress toward implementing IWRM

See Chapter 2: *Challenges of Governance*

* Only the most relevant targets have been listed for this goal.

Taking precautions at household level to prevent water-related disease through sound domestic hygiene practices is a challenge to the individual family

Extending the provision of water supply and sanitation facilities is a challenge to individual communities. Making more effective use of modern communications technology to speed up warnings to communities at risk of flooding and other water-related hazards must be tackled by individual governments and their agencies within particular river basins. Expanding water use productivity in both rainfed and irrigated croplands has to be done by individual farmers, irrigation managers and water user associations. Taking precautions at household level to prevent water-related disease through sound domestic hygiene practices is a challenge to the individual family. Yet it is the aggregate of all these many millions of actions which help to realize the MDGs. Governments and NGOs must help through the provision of needed resources, including education and training, to improve knowledge and skill and thus foster the development of the self-sufficiency and resilience needed to meet the MDGs.

Recognizing these problems, the UN has established a number of initiatives to help meet the MDG targets, as well as others. One such initiative is the Millennium Research Project – an independent advisory body set up by the UN Secretary General to propose the best strategies to meet the MDGs. In turn, the Project established ten Millennium Task Forces, charged with identifying what was needed to reach the MDG targets. One of these, Millennium Task Force 7, covers water supply and sanitation, and highlights from its latest findings can be found in **Chapter 6**. **Chapter 10** reviews the linkages between the Millennium Development Goals and disaster risk reduction. The UN has instigated Millennium Campaigns across the world, encouraging industrialized countries to increase support through aid, trade and debt relief. For lower-income countries, the Campaigns focus on engaging support for urgent action on the MDGs.

Progress on global goals and targets
Progress on the MDGs is monitored via the Millennium Development Goal Reports, which build on the national Human Development Reports,[6] and the UN Secretary General's reports to the General Assembly. The latest of these shows that, with only ten years to go on the MDGs, progress has been patchy and slow.

The 13th Commission on Sustainable Development (CSD) sessions in April 2005 set out a number of priority policy options designed to accelerate progress towards achieving the MDGs on water and sanitation and human settlements. It confirmed that, in future, water, sanitation and human settlements should be dealt with in an integrated manner. This is logical since the challenge for the poor is essentially one of securing acceptable habitation of which water, sanitation and shelter are key components.

It recommended also that countries should identify or establish an institutional base for sanitation and prioritize investment for it where needs are greatest and the impacts likely to be most substantial – in health centres, schools and workplaces. Both financial and human resources are required, as discussed in **Chapters 12** and **13**. Greater resources are needed for sanitation, together with more community involvement and an emphasis on low-cost technology options. Issues of strengthening national and local authority capacity to deliver and maintain water supply and sanitation systems, the contentious subject of cost recovery, approaches to the provision of wastewater systems, use of debt relief to mobilize resources for water and sanitation, and the greater use of grant aid, were also covered. A notable feature of the April meeting of the Commission was the announcement by Mikhail Gorbachev of Green Cross International, that he and others are promoting an initiative for a global convention on the right to water (Water 21, 2005).

The September 2005 meeting of the UN General Assembly was set to review progress and to agree an agenda for the next stage. This last point is crucial since it is widely agreed that 2005 is regarded as a make or break year for getting the MDG project on course to deliver the targets. Professor Jeffrey Sachs, director of the Millennium Project, has submitted to the Secretary General a plan showing how the MDGs can still be met. The plan sets out a coordinated programme of proposed investments in infrastructure, health and education in low-income countries, plus additional overseas development assistance (ODA) from the richer countries and progress in the Doha negotiations of the World Trade Organization (Sachs, 2005). Importantly, the September meeting of the UN General Assembly was able to reach agreement on

6. hdr.undp.org/

a commitment by countries to prepare, by 2006, comprehensive national development strategies designed to reach internationally agreed development goals and objectives, which include among them the MDGs.

Elsewhere, the UN Millennium Task Force 7 on Water and Sanitation has indicated that the targets for water and sanitation will not be met worldwide at present rates of progress. Good progress is being made with water supply but sanitation is lagging substantially behind. The Task Force has set out five guiding principles and ten critical actions (see **Box 1.13** below). These are vital to achieving the water and sanitation MDGs and ensuring that sound management and development of water resources are a fundamental component of the whole MDG programme. The slow progress on sanitation is of particular concern, since poor sanitation is implicated in much-water related disease, as is shown in **Chapter 6.**

6b. Indicator development and the World Water Assessment Programme (WWAP)

In order to check on progress towards meeting goals and targets, regular and reliable monitoring is required. In recognition of this and the critical role of water in poverty alleviation and socio-economic development, WWAP was established in 2000 under the auspices of the UN and charged with the responsibility to monitor and report on water around the world – its availability, condition and use, and the world's progress towards water-related targets and goals. The identification of the most crucial issues to monitor is a key part of the process as is the development of indicators relevant to the data and trends, goals and targets being monitored in areas where freshwater plays a key role.[7]

Experience in many sectors has shown that, done correctly, development and testing of indicators is a lengthy process. Indicators have to meet well-defined criteria and be selected through a carefully planned and implemented process, including stakeholder involvement. Understanding causal relationships in complex, dynamic systems requires information that is not always readily available. Indicator production can involve time-consuming collection, collation and systematization of large amounts of data. Because

the same indicator may need to satisfy often conflicting but equally important social, political, financial and scientific goals and objectives, deriving indicators becomes an objective-maximization exercise constrained by available time, resources and partnership arrangements.

One critical challenge is to identify or develop indicators applicable to as many situations as possible so that cross-country and inter-regional comparisons can be made. With data gathered according to commonly agreed and standardized norms, it could be possible to derive 'lessons' that are relevant across many locations. Data plotted over time can reveal developing trends, while country-specific data collected in a common format facilitate inter-area comparison. Inter-country and inter-regional analyses illuminate success as well as stagnation and enable decision-makers to discern areas in need of attention. Selected to address the key concerns of decision-makers, indicators provide critical data for policy analysis, programme design and fiscal planning. Thus, prepared from carefully selected data, distilled into authoritative information and presented clearly and concisely in a user-friendly format, indicators play a key role in documenting global trends that are crucial to sustainable development. A balance has to be struck between the 'ideal' – indicators that are consistent with theoretical definitions – and the 'practical' or feasibly measurable variables that provide acceptable approximations to the ideal. Striking a balance is critically important in determining cost-efficient and cost-effective data collection.

Indicator development within WWAP focuses on utilizing and adapting existing knowledge, datasets and indicators to formulate and develop easy-to-use, easy-to-understand, yet robust and reliable indicators. These promote better water resource management by:

■ providing a clear assessment of the state of water resources

■ identifying the emergence of critical water resources issues

■ monitoring progress towards achieving water policy objectives.

Data plotted over time can reveal developing trends, while country-specific data collected in a common format facilitates inter-area comparison

7. The first edition of the WWDR (WWDR1, 2003) provided an assessment of the world's progress in meeting critical water needs since the UNCED in Rio de Janeiro in 1992. WWDR1 identified challenges in eleven areas: meeting basic needs, securing the food supply; protecting ecosystems; sharing water resources; managing risks; valuing water, water governance; water use in industry and energy production; providing water for cities; and ensuring the water knowledge base.

...political relevance and quantifiable data are key features in indicator selection...

Table 1.1: Proposed WWDR2 indicators by challenge area

Challenge Area	Indicators[1]	DPSIR aspect[2]	Status[3]
Global	Index of non-sustainable water use	R	K
	Urban and rural population	D	B
	Relative Water Stress Index	S/P	K
	Domestic and Industrial Water Use	D	B
	Water Pollution Index	P	K
	Sediment Trapping Efficiency Index	P	K
	Climate Moisture Index (CMI)	D	K
	Water Reuse Index (WRI)	P	K
Governance	Access to information, participation and justice	R	D
	Progress toward implementing IWRM	R	K
Settlements	Index of Performance of Water Utilities	S	D
	Urban Water and Sanitation governance index	S	D
	Slum Profile in Human Settlements	P	D
Resources	Precipitation annually	D	B
	TARWR volume (total actual renewable water resources)	S	K
	TARWR per capita	S	D
	Surface water (SW) as a % of TARWR	S	D
	Groundwater development (GW % of TARWR)	S	K
	Overlap %TARWR	S	D
	Inflow as % TARWR	S	D
	Outflow as % TARWR	S	D
	Total use as % TARWR	S	D
Ecosystems	Fragmentation and flow regulation of rivers	S/I	K
	Dissolved nitrogen ($NO_3 + NO_2$)	S	K
	Trends in freshwater habitat protection	S/R	K
	Trends in freshwater species populations	S	K
	Biological Oxygen Demand (BOD)	S	K
Health	DALY (Disability Adjusted Life Year)	I	K
	Prevalence of underweight children < 5 years old	I	D
	Prevalence of stunting in children < 5 years old	I	D
	Mortality in children < 5 years old	I	D
	Access to safe drinking water	S	K
	Access to basic sanitation	S	K
Agriculture	Percentage of undernourished people	S	K
	Percentage of poor people living in rural areas	S	K
	Relative importance of agriculture in the economy	S	K
	Irrigated land as a percentage of cultivated land	S/P	K
	Relative importance of agriculture water withdrawals in water balance	P	K
	Extent of land salinized by irrigation	S	K
	Importance of groundwater in irrigation	S/P	K
Industry	Trends in industrial water use	P	K
	Water use by sector	S	K
	Organic pollution emissions by industrial sector	I	K
	Industrial water productivity	R	K
	Trends in ISO 14001 certification, 1997-2002	R	K
Energy	Capability for hydropower generation, 2002	S	K
	Access to electricity and water for domestic use	S	K
	Electricity generation by fuel, 1971-2001	S	K
	Total primary energy supply by fuel, 2001	S	K
	Carbon intensity of electricity production, 2002	S	K
	Volume of desalinated water produced	R	K
Risk	Disaster Risk Index	S	K
	Climate Vulnerability Index (CVI)	P	K
	Risk and Policy Assessment Index	R	K

Table 1.1: *continued*

Challenge Area	Indicators[1]	DPSIR aspect[2]	Status[3]
Sharing[4]	Water interdependency indicator	S	C
	Cooperation indicator	S	C
	Vulnerability indicator	S	C
	Fragility indicator	S	C
	Development indicator	S	C
Valuing	Water sector share in total public spending	S	D
	Ratio of actual to desired level of public investment in water supply	P	D
	Rate of cost recovery	S	D
	Water charges as percent of household income	P	D
Knowledge	Knowledge Index	S	D

Notes:

1. Indicator Profile Sheet provides detailed definition and information on computation of indicator, and can be found on the accompanying CD.
2. DPSIR is the UNECE analytical framework employed in the assessment of the challenge areas, specifically **D**riving force, **P**ressure, **S**tate, **I**mpact and **R**esponse.
3. Level of development, highest to lowest: B = basic indicator; K = key indicator, for which there is an Indicator Profile Sheet and statistical data ; D = developing indicators for which there is an Indicator Profile Sheet* but not yet statistical presentation, and C = conceptual indicator for which there is conceptual discussion only.
4. A total of 25 potential indicators were proposed as the basis for discussion at the 'Indicators of Water Conflict and Cooperation Workshop' convened in Paris, November 2004, by UNESCO; here we present the few central indicators proposed for testing.

■ *Key indicators*, well defined and validated, have global coverage, and are linked directly to policy goals and convey important messages of the present Report

■ *Developing indicators* are in a formative stage and may evolve into key indicators, following refinement of methodological issues or data development and testing

■ *Conceptual indicators* require considerable methodological advancement, resolution of data issues and fieldwork before evolving into key indicators.

Bringing all of this together, WWAP has produced a catalogue of the indicator work done to date (see **Table 1.1** and the **CD-ROM**).

Each chapter of the present Report focuses only on the policy-relevant indicators most directly associated with their challenge area. Depending on the particular nature of the challenge areas, some chapters have more indicators than others. Since political relevance and quantifiable data are key features in indicator selection, it is easier to identify quantifiable variables in health, agriculture, industry

and energy. Where institutional change is more relevant than infrastructure development – for example, in water governance, risk management, sharing and valuing water – identifying qualitative indicators that provide a meaningful measure of progress towards sectoral goals and objectives is more difficult. However, since qualitative aspects can be the deciding factor as to whether goals are achieved – despite being more challenging and costly to monitor – development work on them needs to continue. Furthermore, since indicator development is an ongoing process, not all indicators presented in the following chapters are elaborated to the same degree.

Experience has shown that the WWAP indicator development process has not only facilitated countries' utilization and testing of existing indicators but has also helped them to develop their own indicators. It is clear that both the product (the information produced) and the process (developing indicators and analysing the resulting data) contribute to building needed individual as well as organizational capacity.

As water management grows increasingly complex, well-designed indicators will enable complex

...well-designed indicators will enable complex information to be presented in a meaningful and under-standable way both for decision-makers and the public

information to be presented in a meaningful and understandable way both for decision-makers and the public. Indicators have an especially important role to play in IWRM, which requires information not only on water resources but also a variety of socio-economic factors and their impact on water systems. Appropriate indicators, by simplifying complex information, can provide better communication and cooperation between stakeholders. The organization of this second WWDR is such that its core chapters address the challenge areas recognized to be critical for effective IWRM.

6c. The crucial role of case studies

One of WWAP's significant features is a range of seventeen case studies in forty-one countries. Collectively, these illustrate the many different types of problems and challenges faced by policy-makers and water managers. **Chapter 14** introduces the case studies (and much more detail can be found on the WWAP website) and highlights their key features. Virtually all of the many factors influencing water resources management raised in this introductory chapter, can be observed, in one form or another, in the various case studies.

The case studies include profiles of highly developed countries, such as Japan, and some of the poorest countries in the world, such as Ethiopia. The studies also reflect the challenges in major transboundary river basins such as the Danube River Basin, the second largest in Europe, and the La Plata River Basin, the fifth largest basin in the world. Almost all the case study partners from WWDR1 have continued developing their pilot projects and have contributed to WWDR2 with national-scale case studies. In addition, five case studies have been developed in Africa to highlight the range of water challenges confronting the continent. The Mongolian case study has helped to provide a more complete picture of water problems in Asia. Efforts towards attaining global coverage will continue in subsequent editions of the WWDR as additional case study partners are sought.

The WWAP case studies clearly show that the approach towards sustainable utilization of water resources is evolving globally in the direction of IWRM. Integrating surface water and groundwater

resources within a basin and balancing competing sectoral interests with the needs of ecosystems within the integrity of the hydrological unit are becoming mainstream values that are increasingly accepted around the globe. However, political boundaries, which do not necessarily coincide with the natural borders of basins, make cooperation a necessity – cooperation not only in the international context, but also at national, sub-national and local levels. The WWAP case studies are in fact an instrument for promoting and enhancing cooperation among all relevant stakeholders, including NGOs, IGOs, research institutions, universities and water users themselves. Case study-related national meetings often bring all relevant agencies together, breaking the standard approach whereby each organization works in isolation. This process has helped WWAP's case study partners identify problems and reach consensus on the challenges to be addressed in the water sector.

The WWAP case studies also serve to benchmark the current situation and thus provide a basis on which to analyse change (positive or negative) in the water sector. They have facilitated the testing of the indicators suggested in WWDR1, which are critical to monitoring the impact of policy and programmes.

The case studies clearly highlight the diversity of circumstances and various challenges and priorities facing different regions. For example, in the Danube River Basin, homogeneous implementation of the Water Framework Directive among EU Members and non-EU Member countries is a priority, whereas in the La Plata Basin, poverty alleviation and curbing the health burden of increasing environmental pollution is high on the agenda. In Japan, thanks to the adoption of proper waste management techniques, water-borne diseases are no longer considered a major threat, whereas in Africa, water-related illnesses are common and still claim a great number of lives every year. In South Africa, due to the limited availability of surface water, hydro-power is minimal, and coal is the country's major source of energy production, whereas in the La Plata River Basin, the production of hydropower is a regional priority (over 90 percent of all energy used by Brazil comes from hydropower).

Perhaps one of the most important aspects of case studies is how they illustrate the importance of vertical integration. In other words, how the policies developed at national and sub-national levels are translated into action at the community level, and how decisions taken at the local level affect the decisions of higher management. For example, in Mongolia, lack of public involvement at the local level has limited the effectiveness of many policies and programmes. Facilitating the involvement of water users and stakeholders in managing water resources remains a challenge in many developing countries. Meanwhile, in countries such as Estonia, where the Water Framework Directive is being implemented, it is widely recognized that water management must respond to local actions and needs. A strong public information and consultation component is therefore a prerequisite for the preparation of river basin management plans.

The attainment of the MDGs remains high on the global agenda. Although global progress is being made, at present not all countries are on track. In countries such as South Africa, where the water and sanitation-related MDGs have already been attained, the governments are trying to further improve the livelihoods of their people. In other areas, for example in the Lake Titicaca Basin, many people are struggling with poverty and lack of access to safe water and sanitation. As with WWDR1, the WWDR2 continues to be an important advocacy tool for water supply and sanitation concerns. The WWAP case studies demonstrate the close link between inadequacies in the provision of water and sanitation facilities and a lack of financial and human resources. Low capacity in the water sector can be identified as the main reason behind the failure of countries to utilize water resources to contribute significantly to socio-economic development.

6d. Looking ahead: WWAP in the medium term

Harmonizing indicators at a global level requires considerable effort. Indicators developed for one location may not be applicable worldwide or suitable for scaling-up to a regional or global level. High-quality data may not be available for a theoretically relevant indicator. In fact data availability is a serious limitation for some indicators and some regions. For reasons reported in WWDR1 and re-emphasized here in **Chapter 13**, there is an ongoing deterioration in the systems of collecting

hydrometeorological data. Thus WWAP is tasked to develop simple objective indicators that can be supported by available data or data that is relatively easy to collect. WWAP will also refrain from the trend elsewhere of merging variables into ostensibly more comprehensive, yet, by their nature, more subjective and complex indices. Developing good, usable indicators is a slow, painstaking process.

The following specific areas are those on which WWAP intends to concentrate in the next few years:

Cooperation with participating countries in testing and evaluating indicators, improving data sets and developing monitoring programmes with indicators. Government officials, and all users and stakeholders need to be represented in the development process so that indicators accurately reflect experience on the ground. Indicator sets must be linked to national- and local-level strategies for water resource management and the targets and objectives from which these emanate. WWAP's intention is to work to improve the involvement of UN member countries in supplying data to the UN agencies and in working with WWAP to help the world improve the management of water resources.

Development of methods to enhance stakeholder participation at all levels in indicator development, assessment and monitoring. Emphasizing the need for stakeholder involvement in indicator development, WWAP will seek to tackle the problems of commitment to information production, reporting and application to decision-making. Encouraging countries to view indicator development within the wider context of planning and management, WWAP will seek to demonstrate how indicators are an important management tool to identify and minimize damage from environmental hazards.

Working with scientists to define and develop indicators proposed by our partner agencies and cooperating countries and identifying research needed to clarify linkages and provide the information needed to refine computer models. WWAP is aware of initiatives by a number of organizations – NGOs, institutes and universities – whose work it will endeavour to incorporate as applicable within the indicator development process.

The WWAP case studies demonstrate the close link between inadequacies in the provision of water and sanitation facilities and a lack of financial and human resources

Moving forward with developing geo-referenced data and mapping capability for the analysis of water-related challenges among member countries. The advent of spatially discrete, high-resolution earth system data sets is poised to enable a truly global picture of progressive changes to inland water systems to be produced, monitoring of water availability worldwide to be facilitated, and a consistent, 'political boundary-free' view of the main elements of the terrestrial water cycle to be produced. WWAP has responded by commencing assessment of the relevance of potentially useful data sets that these new systems will generate. Integrating the newly available information into its indicator development programme will provide a central challenge for WWAP, one which will require extensive investment in GIS technology and training.

Working with UN partner agencies to develop a corporate database and reconciling inconsistencies and incompatibilities of current data sets. UN-Water has identified the need to develop a user-friendly, uniform and consistent UN corporate database containing the key water indicators – a process which has begun.

It has become increasingly clear throughout the preparation of this Report that water resource issues are extremely complex and transcend the water sector. With the targets of the Millennium Development Goals facing today's water managers, it is urgent that we extend the horizon of concern to embrace the major social, cultural and economic issues that are fundamental to the forces driving the fast-paced change characteristic of our world today. Given the magnitude of the challenges we face if we will only meet the MDGs we recognize that managing water is a shared responsibility. Thus, we stress the importance of bringing together all parties to address key governance issues raised in this Report so that all may secure a better quality of life not only in the short to medium term but through sustainable development of water resources over the long term.

Wastewater treatment at a bottling factory, Indonesia

References and Websites

AGI (American Geological Institute). 2005. Summary of hearings on Hurricane Katrina. www.agiweb.org/gap/legis109/katrina_hearings.html#sep14.

Asian Development Bank (ADB). 2003. Inland Water Transport Development In India –the Role of the ADB. www.adb.org/Documents/Speeches/2003/sp2003008.pdf.

Braga, B. P. F. 2003. The role of regulatory agencies in multiple water use. Water Science Technology, Vol. 47, No. 6, London, IWA Publishing.

Braga, B. and Granit, J. 2003. Criteria for priorities between competing water interests in a catchment. Water Science and Technology, Vol. 47, No. 6, London, IWA Publishing.

Browne, L. 2005. Outgrowing the Earth: the Food Security Challenge in an Era of Falling Water Tables and Rising Temperatures. London, Earthscan.

Cincotta, R. P., Engelman, R. and Anastasion, D., 2003. The Security Demographic: Population and Civil Conflict after the Cold War. Washington DC, Population action International.

Concern Worldwide. 2005. Concern Worldwide and hunger: a briefing paper prepared for the UN World Summit. September. London, Concern Worldwide.

——. 2005. Looking into the future: a review of progress on the MDGs, prepared for the September 2005 UN World Summit. The Guardian, Manchester.

Costantino, C., Falcitelli, F., Femia, A. and Tudini, A. 2003. Integrated environmental and economic accounting in Italy. Paper. Workshop on Accounting Frameworks to Measure Sustainable Development, 14-16 May 2003. Paris, OECD.

Department of Homeland Security. 2004. Catastrophic Incident Annex. National Response Plan. Washington DC.

Economist. 2005. The real digital divide. The Economist, 12 March 2005. London, 2005.

——. 2004. World in 2005: a survey of key issues and likely trends worldwide in 2005. The Economist, London.

EUROPA. 2005. Inland Water Transport. European Commission. europa.eu.int/comm/transport/iw/index_en.htm.

European Commission. 2005. Opening the Door to Development: Developing Country Access to EU Markets 1999-2003. Brussels, European Commission.

FEMA (Federal Emergency Management Agency). 2006. By the numbers: FEMA recovery update in Louisiana. Press release, 11 January. Washington DC.

——. 2005. First responders urged not to respond to hurricane impact areas unless dispatched by state, local authorities. Press release, 29 August 2005. Washington DC.

——. 2004. Hurricane Pam exercise concludes. Press release, 23 July 2004. Washington DC.

Figueres, C., Tortajada, C. and Rockstrom, J. 2003. Rethinking Water Management: Innovative Approaches to Contemporary Issues. London, Earthscan.

Grey, D. and Sadoff, C. 2003. Beyond the River: the Benefits of Cooperation on International Rivers. Water Science and Technology, Vol. 47, No. 6. London, IWA Publishing.

——. 2002. Water Resources and Poverty in Africa: Essential Economic and Political Responses. Working paper prepared by the World Bank for the African Regional Ministerial Conference on Water (ARMCOW). Washington DC, World Bank.

Guerquin, F., Ahmed, T., Mi Hua Ikeda, T., Ozbilen, V. and Schuttelaar, M. 2003. World Water Actions: Making Water Flow for All, World Water Council, Water Actions Unit. London, Earthscan.

Gutrich J., Donovan D., Finucane M., Focht W., Hitzhusen F., Manopimoke S., McCauley D., Norton B., Sabatier P., Salzman J., Sasmitawidjaja V. 2005. Science in the public process of ecosystem management: lessons from Hawaii, Southeast Asia, Africa and the US Mainland. Journal of Environmental Management Vol. 76, No.3, pp.197-209.

GWP (Global Water Resources). 2004. Catalyzing Change: A Handbook for Developing Integrated Water Resources Management (IWRM) and Water Efficiency Strategies. Stockholm, GWP Technical Committee.

——. 2003. Water Management and Ecosystems: Living with Change. Draft document, Stockholm, GWP.

Harrald, J. R. 2005. Back to the drawing board: A first look at lessons learned from Katrina. Testimony for the House Committee on Government Reform Hearings, September 15, 2005. Washington DC. reform.house.gov/GovReform/Hearings/EventSingle.aspx?EventID=33985

Harris, G. 2002. Ensuring Sustainability: Paradigm Shifts and Big Hairy Goals, opening speech for the Enviro 2002 joint conference of the International Water Association and Australian Water and Wastewater Association, Melbourne.

Hawken, P., Lovins, A. B., and Lovins, L. H. 1999. Natural Capitalism: the Next Industrial Revolution. London, Earthscan.

Henderson, M. 2005. Rice genome is key to ending hunger. The Times, London, 11 August 2005.

Knabb, R. D., Rhome, R. J. and Brown, D. P. 2005. Tropical Cyclone Report: Hurricane Katrina – 23-30 August 2005. National Hurricane Center. www.nhc.noaa.gov/pdf/TCR-AL122005_Katrina.pdf

Lenton, R. 2004. Water and climate variability: development impacts and coping strategies. Water Science and Technology, Vol. 49, No. 7. London, IWA Publishing.

Mathew, K. and Ho, G. (eds). 2005. Onsite wastewater treatment, recycling and small water and wastewater systems. Water Science and Technology, Vol. 51, No. 8, London, IWA Publishing.

Mbeki, M. 2005. Eye Witness; Sunday Times, 3 July 2005, London.

Moench, M., Dixit, A., Janakarajan, S., Rathotre, M. S. and Mudrakarthe, S. 2003. The Fluid Mosaic: Water Governance in the Context of Variability, Uncertainty and Change. A Synthesis Paper; Institute of Development Studies (IDS), Institute for Social And Development Transition (ISET), Madras Institute of Development Studies (MIDS), Nepal Water Conservation Foundation (NWCF), Vikram Sarabhai Centre for Development Interaction (VIKSAT); NWCF, Kathmandu, Nepal and ISCT, Boulder, Colorado, USA.

Polak, P. Water and the other three revolutions needed to end rural poverty. Water Science and Technology, Vol. 51, No. 8, London, IWA Publishing.

River Bureau of the Ministry of Land, Infrastructure and Transport of Japan. 2003. Water and Transport Theme, Statement, Third World Water Forum. www.rfc.or.jp/IWT/PDF/Statement%20_adE_.pdf.

Sachs, J. 2005. The End of Poverty: How We Can Make it Happen in Our Lifetime. London, Penguin Books.

——. 2005. The African challenge: the mission. Sunday Times, London, 3 July 2005.

Smith, D. 2005. Can the politicians do it? Sunday Times, London, 3 July 2005.

State of Louisiana. 2005. State of Emergency – Hurricane Katrina. Proclamation No. 48 KBB 2005. Baton Rouge, State of Louisiana Executive Department.

Takahashi, K. 2004. Keynote address for the Stockholm Water Symposium. Water Science and Technology Vol. 51, No. 8, London, IWA Publishing.

——. 2001. Globalization and its challenges for water management in the developing world. Water Science and Technology, Vol. 45, No. 8, London, IWA Publishing.

Times-Picayune, The. 2002. Washing away. Five part series, 23-27 July 2002.

United Nations (UN) & World Water Assessment Programme. 2003. UN World Water Development Report: Water for People, Water for Life. Paris, New York and Oxford, UNESCO and Berghahn Books.

United Nations Economic and Social Commission for Asia and the Pacific (UNESCAP). 2004. Manual on Modernization of Inland Water Transport for Integration within a Multimodal Transport System. United Nations Publication, Bangkok. Available Online at: www.unescap.org/ttdw/Publications/TFS_pubs/Pub_2285/pub_2285_Ch5.pdf.

——. 2003. Review of Developments in Transport in the ESCAP Region. United Nations Publications, New York. Available Online at: www.unescap.org/ttdw/Publications/TPTS_pubs/pub_2307/pub_2307_ch11.pdf.

United Nations Economic Commission for Africa (UNECA). 2002. The Way Forward. www.uneca.org/eca_programmes/trade_and_regional_integration/THE%2520WAY%2520FORWARD-FINAL.doc

United States Census Bureau. 2005. Income, Poverty, and Health Insurance Coverage in the United States: 2004. Washington DC, United States Department of Commerce, Economics and Statistics Administration.

United States Senate Committee on Homeland Security and Government Affairs. 2005. Hurricane Katrina: Why did the levees fail? United States Senate Hearing, Washington DC.

US Army Corps of Engineers. 2004. Inland Waterway Navigation Value to the Nation. www.mvr.usace.army.mil/Brochures/InlandWaterwayNavigation.asp.

van Heeden, I. 2004/5. Storm that drowned a city. Interviews with Nova Science programming on National Public Radio. 19 October 2004, 10 September and 5 October 2005. www.pbs.org/wgbh/nova/orleans/vanheerden.html

——. 2004. Coastal land loss: Hurricanes and New Orleans. Baton Rouge, Center for the Study of Public Health Impacts of Hurricanes Louisiana State University Hurricane Center.

Vyas, JN. 2001. Dams environment and regional development: harnessing the elixir of life: water. Water Science and Technology Vol. 45, No. 8, London, IWA Publishing.

Water 21, 2005 – taken from articles in Water21, the magazine of the International Water Association, issue June 2005; publ. IWA Publishing, London, 2005.

White House. 2005. Statement on federal emergency assistance for Louisiana. White House press release, 27 August 2005. Washington DC, Office of the Press Secretary.

World Bank. 2004. World Development Report 2005: A Better Investment Climate for Everyone. Washington DC, World Bank.

Worldwatch Institute. 2005. The State of the World 2005: Global Security. London, Earthscan.

If the misery of our poor be caused not by the laws of nature, but by our institutions, great is our sin.

Charles Darwin

CHAPTER 2

The Challenges of Water Governance

By

UNDP

(United Nations Development Programme)

With

IFAD

(International Fund for Agricultural Development)

Line of buckets waiting to be filled by a slow tap at a water distribution point in Kansay, near Ngorongoro, Tanzania. People will carry these buckets of water up to 3 miles each way to and from their homes

Key messages:

In many countries water governance is in a state of confusion: in some countries there is a total lack of water institutions, and others display fragmented institutional structures or conflicting decision-making structures. In many places conflicting upstream and downstream interests regarding riparian rights and access to water resources are pressing issues that need immediate attention; in many other cases there are strong tendencies to divert public resources for personal gain, or unpredictability in the use of laws and regulations and licensing practices impede markets and voluntary action and encourage corruption.

■ Good water governance is a complex process, influenced by a given country's overall standard of governance, its customs, mores, and politics and conditions, events within and around it (e.g. conflict) and by developments in the global economy. There is no blueprint for good water governance.

■ Reforms of water governance are being driven by internal pressures on water resources and environmental threats, growing population and the focus of the international community on poverty alleviation and socio-economic development (e.g. Millennium Development Goals). However the rate of reform is patchy and slow.

■ There are significant and serious gaps in developing countries between land and water use policies and governance *and* between policy-making and its implementation, often due to institutional resistance to change, corruption, etc.

■ In the water sector, as worldwide, corruption is pervasive, though shortage of information about its extent in the water sector prevents a full picture from being obtained. It has had little attention to date in the water sector and much remains to be done.

■ Increasing recognition is accorded to the right to water, in terms of a human right to a supply of safe water, the role of water rights in helping to deal with local competition for water and in dealing with social, economic and environmental problems.

■ The privatization of water services displays uneven results. Many multinational water companies are currently decreasing their activities in developing countries. The potential of local small-scale companies and civil society organizations to help improve water services has largely been overlooked by governments and donors.

■ Many governments recognize the need to localize water management but fail to delegate adequate powers and resources to make it work. Local groups and individuals are often without access to information, are excluded from water decision-making, and thus lack a capacity to act.

Top: Hydraulic drilling stations, equipped with manual pumps, are gradually replacing the less sanitary, traditional village wells, as seen here in northern Côte d'Ivoire.

Above: Pipeline in the outskirts of Gangtok, Sikkim, India

Below: Fishermen preparing their nets for fishing on Surma River, Bangladesh

Part 1. Water Governance Today

A basic insight – which has not yet garnered enough attention – is that the insufficiency of water (particularly for drinking water supply and sanitation), is primarily driven by an inefficient supply of services rather than by water shortages. Lack of basic services is often due to mismanagement, corruption, lack of appropriate institutions, bureaucratic inertia and a shortage of new investments in building human capacity, as well as physical infrastructure. Water supply and sanitation have recently received more international attention than water for food production, despite the fact that in most developing countries agriculture accounts for 80 percent of total water use. It is increasingly agreed in development circles that water shortages and increasing pollution are to a large extent socially and politically induced challenges, which means that there are issues that can be addressed by changes in water demand and use and through increased awareness, education and water policy reforms. The water crisis is thus increasingly about how we, as individuals, and as part of a collective society, govern the access to and control over water resources and their benefits.

In many places of the world, a staggering 30 to 40 percent of water or more goes unaccounted for due to water leakages in pipes and canals and illegal tapping

Water governance is an overarching theme of the World Water Development Report. This chapter will present the state of and trends in key governance variables, such as ongoing water reform work and its implementation, the impacts of corruption on water development and water governance from below. Citizens and organized interests are demanding much more transparency and influence in water decision-making.

It will also illustrate that very complex and dynamic events and processes external to the water sector define how we relate to water. Changes in water use patterns are continuously redefined through such things as culture, macroeconomic and development trends, processes of democratization and social and political stability or unrest. This chapter will also look at how water governance is undertaken in practice and discuss and analyse various settings related to water and power politics. Examples are provided that point at complex urban and rural water use dynamics, the increasing need for integrated approaches to water, the range of international targets for local actions and the multitude of stakeholder interests. Finally, some overarching challenges are identified, which are taken up by the ensuing chapters and relate to specific water governance issues, challenges and potential solutions with respect to their fields.

1a. The water–poverty link

How societies choose to govern their water resources has profound impacts on people's lives and their ability to prosper, as well as on environmental sustainability. On the ground, this means that some groups or individuals will benefit while others will lose out when water allocation changes are made. Having a fair water provision can, for many people, be a matter of daily survival. How and for whom water is being governed has impacts on river flows, groundwater tables and pollution levels, affecting both upstream and tail-end water users. The capacity of countries to pursue poverty reduction strategies and Integrated Water Resources Management (IWRM) plans, meet new demands and manage conflicts and risks depends to a large extent on their ability to promote and put into place sound and effective governance systems.

Improved governance is essentially about improving people's livelihood opportunities, while providing the backbone for governments worldwide to alleviate poverty and increase the chances of sustainable development. **Box 2.1** provides an example of how governance, development and livelihood opportunities can be linked in practice.

One of the most striking features of the link between water and poverty is that each year, thousands of African and Asian children die from water- and sanitation-related diseases (see **Chapter 6**). In the poorest countries, one out of every five children fails to reach his or her fifth birthday, mainly due to infectious and environmental diseases that arise from poor water quality. Over the last two decades, the number and scale of water-related disasters – either too much water (floods) or too little (droughts) – have increased greatly because of changing climate patterns (see **Chapters 4** and **10**). Many countries in sub-Saharan Africa and the Indian and Pacific oceans, along with low-lying Small Island States, are the most vulnerable to climate change, because widespread poverty limits their capabilities to adapt to climate variability. Too often, those affected by such disasters are the poor, who do not have the means to escape poverty traps.

1b. The four dimensions of water governance

The conceptual development of water management has paved the way for an IWRM approach (see **Figure 2.1**), which is considered by many as an appropriate vehicle to resolve the world's water challenges. As defined by the Global Water Partnership (GWP), IWRM is 'a process which promotes the co-ordinated development and management of water, land and related resources in order to maximize the resultant economic and social welfare in an equitable manner without compromising the sustainability of vital ecosystems' (GWP, 2000). IWRM should be seen as a comprehensive approach to the development and management of water, addressing its management both as a resource and the framework for provision of water services (see also **Chapter 1**).

■ The social dimension points to the equitable use of water resources. Apart from being unevenly distributed in time and space, water is also unevenly distributed among various socio-economic strata of society in both rural and urban settlements. How water quality and quantity and related services are allocated and distributed have direct impacts on people's health as well as on their livelihood opportunities. It is estimated that daily water use per inhabitant totals 600 L in residential areas of North America and Japan and between 250 L and 350 L in Europe, while daily water use per inhabitant in sub-Saharan Africa averages just 10 L to 20 L. Currently, 1.1 billion people lack sufficient access to safe drinking water, and 2.6 billion people lack access to basic sanitation (see **Chapter 6**). People in slums have very limited access to safe water for household uses. A slum dweller may only have 5 L to 10 L per day at his or her disposal (see **Chapter 3**). A middle- or high-income household in the same city, however, may use some 50 L to 150 L per day, if not more. Similarly, water for food production often benefits large-scale farmers to the detriment of small-scale and landless farmers (see **Chapter 7**).

■ The economic dimension draws attention to the efficient use of water resources and the role of water in overall economic growth (see **Chapter 12**). Prospects for aggressive poverty reduction and economic growth remain highly dependent on water and other natural resources. Studies have illustrated that per capita incomes and the quality of governance

Over the last two decades, the number and scale of water-related disasters (either too much water or too little) has greatly increased due to changing climate patterns

are strongly positively correlated across countries. Better governance exerts a powerful effect on per capita incomes. As recently as 200 years ago, per capita incomes were not very different across countries. Today's wide income gaps across countries reflect the fact that countries that are currently rich have grown rapidly over the past two centuries, while those that are poor have not. It has been suggested that a substantial fraction of these vast income gaps is due to 'deep historical differences in institutional quality' (Kaufmann and Kraay, 2003). Water use efficiency in developing countries is very low in both urban and rural areas, and there is great room for improving the water situation through improved water distribution and management.

■ The political empowerment dimension points at granting water stakeholders and citizens at large equal democratic opportunities to influence and monitor political processes and outcomes. At both national and international levels, marginalized citizens, such as indigenous people, women, slum dwellers, etc., are rarely recognized as legitimate stakeholders in water-related decision-making, and typically lack voices, institutions and capacities for promoting their water interests to the outside world (see **Chapter 13**). Empowering women, as well as other socially, economically and politically weak groups, is critical to achieving more focused and effective water management and actions to ensure greater equity.

■ The environmental sustainability dimension shows that improved governance allows for enhanced sustainable use of water resources and ecosystem integrity (see

Figure 2.1: Dimensions of water governance

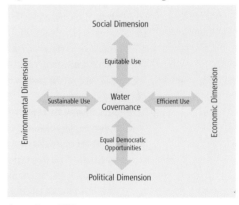

Source: Tropp, 2005.

BOX 2.1: GENDER, POVERTY, IMPROVED GOVERNANCE AND WATER ACCESS IN PUNJAB, PAKISTAN

In Punjab, women and children are often the most affected by the lack of access to water. The Government of Pakistan has implemented the Punjab Rural Water Supply and Sanitation Sector Project. The project has provided safe drinking water and drainage facilities to about 800,000 people by using a community-based, demand-driven approach, wherein the local people participated from planning through construction and eventually became fully responsible for operation and maintenance work. The project also implied strict implementation of water fees. Both men and women formed and were part of community-based organizations to implement the water-related activities and promote other development and livelihood activities. The main impact of the project was to free women and children from the hard labour of carrying water. Other positive impacts included increased household income by an average of 24 percent. It was reported that 45 percent of the time saved from carrying water is spent on income-generating activities. In addition, there is a reported 90 percent decrease in water-related diseases and as much as an 80 percent increase in the enrolment of school children in some communities. The Punjab project demonstrates that it is possible to combine an efficient and large-scale extension of services with actions to improve governance and that it is critical for any development effort to involve both women and men.

Source: Soussan, 2003.

Chapter 5). The sufficient flow of quality water is critical to maintaining ecosystem functions and services and sustaining groundwater aquifers, wetlands, and other wildlife habitats. A worrisome sign is that water quality appears to have declined worldwide in most regions with intensive agriculture and large urban and industrial areas (see **Chapters 7** and **8**). With the reduction and pollution of natural habitats, the diversity of freshwater flora and fauna is becoming increasingly threatened. Poor people's livelihood opportunities, in particular, depend directly upon sustained access to natural resources, including water – especially since they tend to live in marginalized areas that are prone to pollution, droughts and floods. The essential role of water for maintaining a healthy environment is being increasingly emphasized in the change of attitudes towards wetlands, which is an encouraging sign.

Decisions about water are being made by the minute around the world within urban and rural households, neighbourhoods, small businesses, corporate boardrooms, and in the offices of local, state and national governments, as well as on the international scale. The particular settings vary, as do the people and groups involved.

Water decisions are anchored in governance systems across three levels: government, civil society and the private sector. Facilitating dynamic interactions among them is critical for developed and developing countries alike.[1] The water sector is a part of a broader society and its politics and is thus affected by decisions that lie outside of the water sector. The governance of water in particular can be said to be made up of the range of political, social, economic and administrative systems that are in place, which directly or indirectly affect the use, development and management of water resources and the delivery of water services at different levels of society. Governance systems determine who gets what water, when and how and decide who has the right to water and related services and their benefits. The representation of various interests in water decision-making and the role of politics are important components in addressing governance dynamics.

Water is power, and those who control the flow of water in time and space can exercise this power in various ways. It is often claimed that clean water tends to gravitate towards the rich and wastewater towards the poor. Sandra Postel has aptly noted that 'water grabs and power plays are legendary in the western United States'. The water tensions of the American west have been captured in popular movies such as *Chinatown*, where farmers were being 'sucked dry' by Los Angeles (Postel, 1999). As water demands and uses increase at exponential rates due to population growth, stakes rise in many parts of the world. As opportunities to expand water supplies decrease, competition over current supplies escalate, creating the need for improved governance (see **Chapter 11**).

The way in which societies govern their water resources has profound impacts on settlements, livelihoods and environmental sustainability, yet governance has traditionally not received the same attention as technical issues. Any water governance system must be able to allocate water to ensure food and security but also be

Water is power, and those who control the flow of water in time and space can exercise this power in various ways

1. The United Nations Development Programme (UNDP) defines governance as 'the exercise of economic, political and administrative authority to manage a country's affairs at all levels. It comprises the mechanisms, processes and institutions, through which citizens and groups articulate their interests, exercise their legal rights, meet their obligations and mediate their differences'.

able to assess for whom and what purposes water is provided. In practice, trade-offs have to be made and the allocation of benefits and costs clarified. In short, governance is about making choices, decisions and trade-offs. Governance addresses the relationship between organizations and social groups involved in water decision-making, both horizontally, across sectors and between urban and rural areas, and vertically, from local to international levels. Operating principles include downward and upward accountability, transparency, participation, equity, rule of law, ethics and responsiveness (see **Box 2.2**). Governance is therefore *not* limited to 'government' but includes the roles of the private sector and civil society. The character of relationships (and the formal and informal rules and regulations guiding such relationships) and the nature of information flow between different social actors and organizations are both key features of governance (Rogers and Hall, 2003; GWP, 2003).

Water governance is sometimes equated with the actual water policy in place, but governance is more; it is about the exercise of power in policy-making and whether or not to implement particular policies. Which actors were involved in influencing the policy in question? Was the policy developed in a participatory and transparent fashion? Can revenues and public and bureaucratic support be raised to implement the policy? These are just some of the important questions involved, but they indicate that governance is about the process of decision-making, its content and the likelihood of policies and decisions to be implemented. To be able to understand why water is allocated in different ways, it is necessary to look into the dynamics of policy and decision-making, informal and formal legislation, collective action, negotiation and consensus-building and how these interact with other institutions.

1c. Privatization, conflicts and democratization

The past decades have witnessed tremendous social, political and economic changes. The end of the cold war and the process of decolonization continue to shape current societal events. Globalization and the increasing speed of information exchange have had tremendous impacts on societies. Terrorism has also had a major impact on how countries interact with each other and on how governments interact with their citizens. Some commentators worry that we are heading towards a more closed 'barbed-wire' society in an effort to keep out

threats, while others feel that our new means of communication and economic growth make for more open societies (see **Chapter 1**).

The way we perceive and govern our water resources is also rooted in culture. But although water is considered by most cultures to be something critical for all life, with a prominent place in cultural and religious beliefs, it is something of a paradox that water is often taken for granted and is increasingly polluted, with many people having limited access to clean drinking water and water for productive activities.

The development of governance and management systems within the water sector is closely related to overall development trends in which the role of the state has shifted from the provider to the enabler of development and welfare (the 'rolling back of the state'). By 2000, national, provincial and local governments in ninety-three countries had begun to privatize drinking water and wastewater services. Between 1995 and 1999, governments around the world privatized an average of thirty-six water supply or wastewater treatment systems annually (WRI, 2003). Despite the push for increased privatization, the water-services sector remains one of the last public 'bastions'. Water still remains an area that is generally heavily dependent on public investment and regulations in developed and developing countries alike.

War and social and political unrest demolish people's lives and livelihood, as well as destroy important water resources, disrupting water services and impacting negatively on governance. Between 1990 and 2000, 118 armed conflicts worldwide claimed approximately 6 million lives. War will have long-term effects and will continue to affect people's livelihood opportunities and access to natural resources and public services many years after the actual conflict has ended. In 2001 it was estimated that some 12 million refugees and 5 million 'internally displaced persons' were forced to settle in resource-scarce areas, putting further pressure on people, water and the environment (WRI, 2003). Recent conflicts in Kosovo, Afghanistan and Iraq have led to the destruction of economically vital water infrastructures, and many people are deprived of safe drinking water and basic sanitation as well as sufficient water for productive uses (WRI, 2003; see also **Chapters 1**, **3** and **11**).

The resolution of conflict and social and political instability can sometimes yield unexpected opportunities

Annually, between 1995 and 1999, governments around the world privatized an average of thirty-six water supply or wastewater treatment systems

---

BOX 2.2: CRITERIA FOR EFFECTIVE GOVERNANCE

■ Participation: all citizens, both men and women, should have a voice, directly or through intermediary organizations representing their interests, throughout the processes of policy- and decision-making. Broad-based participation hinges upon national and local governments following an inclusive approach.

■ Transparency: information should flow freely in society. Processes, institutions and information must be directly accessible to those concerned.

■ Equity: all groups in society, both men and women, should have the opportunities to improve their well-being.

■ Effectiveness and efficiency: processes and institutions should produce results that meet needs while making the best use of resources.

■ Rule of law: legal frameworks should be fair and enforced impartially, especially laws on human rights.

■ Accountability: governments, the private sector and civil society organizations should be accountable to the public or the interests they are representing.

■ Coherency: taking into account the increasing complexity of water resources issues, appropriate policies and actions must be coherent, consistent and easily understood.

■ Responsiveness: institutions and processes should serve all stakeholders and respond properly to changes in demand and preferences, or other new circumstances.

■ Integration: water governance should enhance and promote integrated and holistic approaches.

■ Ethical considerations: water governance has to be based on the ethical principles of the societies in which it functions, for example, by respecting traditional water rights.

Source: UN, 2003.

---

for fundamental changes in society that can lead to improved policy-making, which in turn can benefit a nation's water prospects (see **Chapter 14**). The political changes in South Africa in the early 1990s and the emergence of a democratic system have allowed for reform of the water sector in the areas of policy, organizational structure, water rights and legislation. South African water reform is a very comprehensive and innovative approach to water management, allowing for more holistic, people-centred and ecological approaches to the governance of water. It also aims at redistributing water resources to the benefit of poor people.

Democratization, macroeconomic changes, population growth and other demographic changes, and social and political instability often have much greater impacts on water use and demands than any water policy itself. Global market conditions and trade regimes are factors that affect crop choices and thus also have serious implications for water use and demands in agriculture. Market liberalization can contribute to improving the water situation for many people but can also increase pressures to overexploit water and the environment. The importance for water professionals to increase their understanding of social, economic and political conditions external to the water sector that have both

direct and indirect impacts on how water is being used and governed is highlighted in Waterbury's study of cooperation among the Nile Basin countries (2002; see also **Chapter 11**).

Improved governance and water shortages: A double challenge

Increasing water demands will lead to a decline of per capita supply in the future. Currently, an estimated twenty-six countries with a combined population of more than 350 million people are located in regions with severe water scarcity where the available water resources seem to be sufficient to meet reasonable water needs for development activities, *but* only if these countries take appropriate water demand and supply management measures. In many countries, there will also be additional, sometimes severe, local water scarcities, even within countries that have sufficient aggregate water resources, such as within the US and India.

A comparison of water shortages and governance challenges shows that many countries, particularly in the Middle East and North Africa, are facing a double challenge. It is also evident that countries that have bountiful water resources are facing governance challenges to provide water and sanitation services *and*

10 percent – or some US $300 million – of the total aid in the water sector is directed to support the development of water policy, planning and programmes

increasingly viewed as an integral part of water crises and thus as a part of resolving them (see **Box 2.3**).

An important part of the work of bilateral and multilateral organizations has been to support the enhancement of capacities to strengthen national and local water agendas and policies, investment priorities, while providing useful examples for scaling up activities. Despite these efforts, water is not considered a main priority in most countries. Investment in the water sector is still at a very low level in developing countries, and despite promises of action-oriented outcomes by the world's governments at the WSSD, much remains to be done about water governance issues in donor budgets.

According to statistics from the Organisation for Economic Co-operation and Development (OECD), total aid to the water sector during recent years has averaged approximately US $3 billion a year. An additional US $1 to 1.5 billion a year is allocated to the water sector in the form of non-concessional lending, mainly by the World Bank.

Over three-quarters of the aid to the water sector is allocated to water supply and sanitation. The bulk of the aid for water supply and sanitation is allocated to a handful of large projects undertaken in urban areas. While such support is, of course, much needed and desired, it is disheartening from a governance point of view that only about 10 percent – or some US $300 million – of the total aid in the water sector is directed to support the development of water policy, planning and programmes.

The statistics also show that many countries where a large portion of the population have insufficient access to safe water received very little of the aid. Only 12 percent of total aid to the water sector in 2000-01 went to countries where less than 60 percent of the population has access to an improved water source, which includes most of the least developed countries. On the positive side, aid allocated to various types of low-cost and small-scale technologies (for example, treadle pumps, gravity-fed systems, rainwater harvesting, sustainable small-scale sanitation, etc.) seems to be increasing (OECD, 2002).

In 1999, the World Bank and the International Monetary Fund (IMF) started to develop a new framework for giving low-interest loans and debt relief to forty-two of the poorest countries in the world. The poor countries that want to be a part of this must formulate and put in place what is called a Poverty Reduction Strategy Paper (PRSP). The strategy is supposed to indicate how a government will use the funds for targeted poverty reduction in their country. The process leading to a PRSP is also supposed to be based on broad multi-stakeholder and participatory processes for their design, implementation and monitoring. It is seen as critical that PRSPs are driven and owned by the forty-two countries in question. In essence, the PRSPs represent a means of securing resources for development priorities and serve as countries' long-term development strategy. Both multi- and bilateral donors are increasingly using PRSPs to coordinate their development cooperation and to achieve coherence in development objectives with recipient governments. Considering the fact that PRSPs represent long-term development strategies, it is worrisome that water resources issues and related services have so far received very low priority in their design. Two PRSP assessments show that the key initial planning and resource commitments needed to achieve water-related targets are not being met. Water targets are not linked to key strategies that prioritize and fund action (see **Box 2.4**).

Within the water sector, there is a widespread belief that we now have most of the needed principles in place in order to make a lasting improvement to the world's water resources situation, which will also make a major contribution to the overall work of alleviating poverty. What is lacking today are the concerted actions and the means for effective implementation of various water policies and development programmes. The implementation of countries' existing water policies would go a long way in meeting the MDGs and the water targets set in Johannesburg.

Life on the Mekong River, Viet Nam

BOX 2.4: WATER IN POVERTY REDUCTION STRATEGY PAPERS (PRSPs)

A recent study by the Overseas Development Institute (ODI) and WaterAid on the extent to which water supply and sanitation (WSS) was given priority in PRSPs in sub-Saharan Africa concluded: 'WSS had been inadequately reflected both in terms of the process of PRSP preparation and the content of emerging PRSPs'. In total, seventeen African PRSPs were examined, and of these, only Uganda showed a high level of priority to water supply and sanitation (see **Chapter 14**). This is surprising, given the international prominence given to these issues through the MDG on water and sanitation and a strong demand from rural and urban communities to urgently improve water-related services. There are several reasons that can explain this, including a limited understanding of the social and economic benefits of improved water and sanitation, weak poverty diagnosis and limited dialogue and interaction between central ministries, local

governments and local communities within the sector. In other words, water supply and sanitation issues are under-represented in PRSPs, partly because the water sector has failed to articulate the needs and potential impacts on poverty of investments in this sector and partly due to critical national decision-makers' limited understanding of the issues.

A water resources assessment of nine Asian PRSPs found similar results. In the Asian cases, water resource issues, such as floods and droughts, as well as water supply and sanitation and irrigation, were frequently present in the analysis of issues in the PRSPs but were more rarely reflected in the programmes for action or priorities for investment. The failure of key water advocates and decision-makers has again been cited as the main reason for this. However, it is important not to forget key economic decision-makers outside the water sector, as well as their

failure to fully appreciate the importance of improved water resources management and water supply and sanitation for social and economic development. A wider assessment of forty interim and full PRSPs by the World Bank confirms this. The assessment showed that natural resources management and environmental protection were only included in limited ways. There were some exceptions, however, like in Mozambique where the protection and management of environmental and natural resources was seen as being prioritized. The assessment also indicated that the result for full or final PRSPs was slightly better than for the interim version, suggesting that priority issues of natural resources and environment improved as consultations were wider and more thorough.

Sources: Frans and Soussan, 2003; Bojö and Reddy, 2002; Slaymaker and Newborne, 2004.

Training around a new water pump with an instructor during water and sanitation programme in Budari, Uganda

Meeting the Johannesburg target on IWRM plans

Putting into place strategic and well-planned water projects will help countries to set the right priorities and undertake actions required to meet the Johannesburg target. These plans can thus become critical instruments for achieving domestic political targets as well as targets agreed on in the international arena, like the MDGs or regional transboundary water cooperation agreements. If we take the status of the recent Johannesburg target to 'develop integrated water resource management and water efficiency plans by 2005, with support to developing countries' as a proxy for improved reform and governance in the water sector, it reveals that progress is taking place but that much remains to be done.

At the end of 2003, an 'informal stakeholder baseline survey' was conducted by the GWP on the status of water sector reform processes in various countries of the world. The survey was conducted in 108 countries[2] and provides a number of qualitative elements allowing an assessment of countries' readiness to meet the 2005 Johannesburg implementation plan target on IWRM Plan preparation. In this respect, the level of awareness, political support and the countries' capacity to build on past and ongoing processes relating to water-related reforms and rely on existing multi-stakeholder platforms were some of the components that were assessed.

The survey provides a snapshot of where countries stand in terms of adapting and reforming their water management systems towards more sustainable water management practices. The pilot results show that of the 108 countries surveyed to date, about 10 percent have made good progress towards more integrated approaches and 50 percent have taken some steps in this direction but need to increase their efforts, while the remaining 40 percent remain at the initial stages of the process (see **Table 2.1**).

Several countries have begun, or have already been through, the process of putting into place IWRM elements. South Africa, Uganda and Burkina Faso have, with international assistance, gone through multi-year IWRM planning processes resulting in new national policies, strategies and laws for their water resources development and management. Other countries in Africa have also been identified as having good opportunities to advance their water agenda. For example, water legislation is being prepared in Congo-Brazzaville and Malawi, where the opportunity can be seized to promote

integrated approaches towards water management. Similar opportunities exist in Asia, such as with China's water policy work, and the water reform processes in countries like Sri Lanka and Pakistan. Development has also been rapid in Central Asia, where, for example, Kazakhstan and Kyrgyzstan have made headway towards developing IWRM approaches. In Latin America, Brazil's wastewater reform is an example of IWRM processes. Many of these are now in or on the verge of the implementation stage. Other countries in Latin America have also made headway (see **Chapter 14**). There are, for example, favourable political and institutional conditions in Honduras where the multi-stakeholder Water Platform (Plataforma del Agua de Honduras) provides momentum to advance IWRM approaches and other water-related issues.

This qualitative assessment does not, however, allow for regional or country comparisons, as exemplified by the cases of Viet Nam and Sierra Leone, which have both been classified as in the initial stages of developing IWRM approaches. Sierra Leone is a conflict-ridden country where the main focus is on building peace and stability and reconstructing basic services such as water supply and sanitation; it is thus far from engaging in developing IWRM approaches. Viet Nam, on the other hand, has showed progress in recent years. In 1988, it adopted a national water act and a National Water Resources Council, and three river basin organizations were established in 2000 and 2001. It is clear that water is fairly high on the political agenda and Viet Nam is in a good position to advance implementation as well as incorporation of IWRM approaches.

The assessment indicated that the countries that have made the most progress in adapting and reforming their water management systems towards more sustainable water management practices have often started by focusing on specific water challenges, such as coping with perennial droughts or finding ways to increase water for agriculture while still ensuring access to domestic water in burgeoning urban areas. South Africa, for example, developed comprehensive policies, legislation and strategies starting in 1994, focusing outward from drinking water (and later on sanitation) to give expression to the political, economic and social aspirations and values of the new democratic political paradigm.

Recently, there have also been other IWRM plan assessments initiated to measure how much progress

2. Forty-five in Africa, forty-one in Asia and the Pacific and twenty-two in Latin America. For more information on this assessment see: www.gwpforum.org

Table 2.1: Country readiness to meet the Johannesburg target on IWRM planning by 2005

Region	Number of countries surveyed	Good progress	Some steps	Initial stage
Africa				
Central Africa	7		3	4
Eastern Africa	5	1	2	2
Med (North Africa)	5	1	3	1
Southern Africa	12	2	5	5
West Africa	16	2	4	10
Total	*45*	*6*	*17*	*22*
Asia and Pacific				
Central Asia	8	2	4	2
China	1	1		
South Asia	6		4	2
Southeast Asia	8		4	4
Pacific	18	2	8	8
Total	*41*	*5*	*20*	*16*
Latin America and the Caribbean				
Caribbean	6		6	
Central America	7	2	3	2
South America	9	1	5	3
Total	*22*	*3*	*14*	*5*
Total	**108**	**14**	**51**	**43**

Source: GWP, 2003.

countries have made towards adopting and implementing IWRM. A 2005 study of the status of IWRM plans in the Arab States indicated that progress is very uneven in the region. Some places, such as Jordan, Egypt, the Palestinian Autonomous Territories, Yemen and Tunisia, have national water policies, plans or strategies in place that incorporate many elements of IWRM. Eleven out of the twenty-two countries included in the study need major water policy enhancements to put IWRM plans in place. For most of these eleven countries, the study identified ambition and ongoing efforts to further progress of developing IWRM plans. For six of the countries included in the study the situation seems to be less progressive, with some of the countries even lacking ongoing efforts to develop IWRM plans (Arab Water Council, 2005).

It is important to stress that, even though many countries lack IWRM elements in their water reform attempts and aspirations, this should not refrain them from acting. It is more realistic to implement reforms incrementally than to await the 'perfect' policy document that may never get past the drawing board. **Box 2.6** highlights the fact that making and implementing water policy can take very different paths.

Water policies, politics and resistance

No reform is stronger than its weakest link, which is to say, implementation. Recent years have seen the development of sophisticated water policies and plans in many parts of the world, such as in South Africa, in Europe with the EU Water Framework Directive and in Chile with water privatization. Some of the reforms in developing countries have been assisted by the international community and have frequently been motivated, at least in part, by the active international debate on these issues. These achievements also need to be balanced, however, by a recognition that policy changes at the national level have often only been imperfectly followed through to effective implementation. A recent example is Zimbabwe, where the actual content of water reform is considered progressive, but where reform has stalled due to recent political instability and weak implementation capacity.

There is a tendency to separate policy-making processes from implementation. The notion is that policy-making is ascribed to decision-makers, while implementation is linked to administrative capacity. This kind of thinking is too rigid and fails to acknowledge that policies are often modified as they move through public administrations and

It is more realistic to implement reforms incrementally than to await the 'perfect' policy document that may never get past the drawing board

The limited funding opportunities in low-income countries expose domestic decision-makers and policy development to pressure from international lending institutes and donors

failure, it is critical to address three key strategic issues: keeping the scope of change narrow, limiting the role of aid donors and giving reform firm leadership while simultaneously allowing for line management discretion (Polidano, 2001).

Some critical issues for overcoming policy obstacles are outlined below:

■ **Acknowledge the role of politics and develop strategies accordingly:** Even though most reforms require technical input the process itself is essentially political and thus involves political compromises, bargaining and negotiated outcomes. In most cases, the proper packaging, sequencing, alliance building and communication of reform can lead to more tolerable reform content that can be more easily implemented. The power balance between critical political, social and economic actors will have a significant impact on reform outcomes.

■ **Secure high-level political support and commitment:** Without high-level political commitment to undertake reform, it will be very difficult to go from policy formulation to implementation. The whole government needs to be involved to ensure that sufficient resources and capacities are provided to achieve the reform objectives.

■ **Focus on process and seize the moment:** Management of the policy process, which has so far received very little attention, is just as important. Some policy studies suggest that the process is even more important than the actual policy content. The timing of a reform is important. According to the 'crisis hypothesis', a perceived or real crisis due to floods and droughts is needed to create conditions under which it is politically possible to undertake the reform. The 'honeymoon hypothesis' suggests that it is easier to implement a reform immediately after a government takes office (Williamson, 1994).

■ **Participation and inclusiveness:** Effective policy formulation and implementation requires transparency and inclusiveness. For example, does media and civil society advocacy representing the needs and interests of vulnerable groups, such as indigenous people, women and children and threatened ecosystems, influence the timing and content of decisions on policy changes? Inclusiveness and active engagement do not

only refer to civil society but also to different government agencies at various levels.

■ **National ownership of policy process and content:** The limited funding opportunities in low-income countries expose domestic decision-makers and policy development to pressure from international lending institutes and donors. If a country does not develop a certain 'internationally' required policy, it may face difficulties attracting international loans and development project funds. It is not uncommon in many low-income countries that due to external pressure they are required to put into place policies, plans and development programmes that lack 'national ownership' and have little chance of actually being implemented.

■ **Allow for incremental change and proper time for successful reform:** Reforms should be well prepared, because once they are in place, they are often difficult to modify. If possible, keep the reform as simple as possible and avoid addressing many reform objectives at the same time. Reform is an incremental process, which sometimes can be painstakingly slow, and managing policy processes is laborious and time-consuming and should not be underestimated. Although policy reform is an ongoing process and modification occurs over time, it is important that the main thrust of the policy can be sustained over time.

■ **Compensate policy reform losers:** Adequate compensation mechanisms, negotiated with stakeholders, are an important part of a reform. Those who are losing out considerably in a reform should be adequately compensated: paying a fair amount of compensation is important for building support and avoiding social and political clashes that can jeopardize or slow down the reform. In the case of water pricing reforms, several groups or issues, such as the poor, or the environment, may need to be specifically addressed. For example, addressing the needs of poor people may mean including a differentiated tariff structure.

■ **Improve coordination:** Uncoordinated donor activities increase the risk of overloading the capacity of governments and slow down reform work. Donors should also allow greater flexibility in the design and implementation of reforms and allow for more experimentation by governments. Different forms of tension and competition among various government agencies are common. It is thus critical that the political leadership of reform is intact to allow for an effective coordination and a broad buy-in from central government agencies down to local regional and local administrations.

■ **Monitor implementation and impacts:** The monitoring of policy reform and implementation is an area often neglected by governments. Some attempts have been made towards more systematic monitoring of the progress and impact of water reform, but there still remains much work to be done in this area in order to actually examine if claimed progress in water reform also impacts positively on sustainable water resource use and improved water services. Effective monitoring will also imply that policies can be fine-tuned, allowing for financial reallocation between reform priorities.

2b. Water rights

Ownership or the right to use a resource means power and control. While it may seem simple, water rights and ownership often have a complex relationship with water governance. How property rights are defined, who benefits from these rights and how they are enforced are all central issues that need further clarification in current water policies and legislation. Insecurity of water rights, mismatches between formal legislation and informal customary water rights, and an unequal distribution of water rights are frequent sources of conflict that can lead to poor decisions on efficient water resource use and equitable allocation. Also, the problem of managing dwindling groundwater supplies or fish stocks – which many times lack clear user rights – is a problematic water governance challenge.

Water rights can be defined as 'authorized demands to use (part of) a flow of surface water and groundwater. Including certain privileges, restrictions, obligations and sanctions accompanying this authorization, among which a key element is the power to take part in collective decision-making about system management and direction' (Beccar et al., 2002). Water rights are inextricably linked to property.

Well-defined and coherent water rights are fundamental to dealing with situations of increased competition between water users, an important issue, which is addressed in more detail in **Chapter 11**. Water management is a complex activity; it is a mobile resource

that is attached to many different and sometimes competing, economic, social and environmental values. While water users compete for the same resource and struggle for increasing control, they also need to cooperate if they want to make effective use of water and sustain the water's quantity and quality in the long run. This often occurs in 'pluralistic' legal contexts, where formal and informal normative systems sometimes clash. For example, in South Africa, water management moved from a pre-colonial collective activity to a publicly regulated resource under Roman-Dutch law. It was then transformed under Anglo-Saxon jurisprudence when it was captured as a private resource to the benefit of a small minority. A main objective of the current 1998 Water Act in South Africa is to redistribute water rights by granting water permits to sections of society that were previously discriminated against.[3] The minimization and resolution of water conflicts and disputes require clear and coherent water rights that contain management principles and strategies that can cooperate with fluctuations of water supply and demand.

It has been noted, for example, that water rights provide the backbone of water management strategies in small-scale agriculture and in many local contexts basing their water use on customary traditions. Water rights define who has access to water and in what ways the user can take part in local water decision-making. They also specify roles and responsibilities regarding operation, maintenance, monitoring and policing. In this sense, water rights manifest social relationships and local power structures of who is included or excluded from the benefits of water and what the various rights and responsibilities include. Water management practices in the Andes, for example, have shown that social and political inequalities can prevent successful collective action. However, this also showed that collective management of water can lead to more equitable water distribution, in addition to strengthening the bargaining position of weaker stakeholders (Boelens and Hoogendam, 2002). The critical importance of water rights is not unique to small-scale agriculture or indigenous systems but is equally relevant to society at large.

From a formal legal point of view, water is considered a property that belongs to the state in many countries. Many governments have largely ignored informal customary or traditional water rights. This oversight was initiated during colonialism and continued under state-led

While it may seem simple, water rights and ownership often have a complex relationship with water governance

3. See www.thewaterpage.com/ leestemaker.htm

Table 2.3: Quality and accessibility of water data, selected countries

Country	Quality of information[1]	Accessibility
Hungary[2]	Intermediate	Weak
India	Intermediate	Weak
Indonesia[3]	Weak	Weak
Mexico[4]	Strong	Weak
South Africa	Intermediate	Intermediate
Thailand	Weak	Weak
Uganda	Weak	Weak
United States: California	Intermediate	Strong

1. Systems score weak when only a few parameters on quality of water are collected.
2. Data from almost all 12 inspectorates and from 7 of 19 public health offices in four weeks; 7 of the 19 offices responded on drinking water.
3. Indonesia submitted a single value for both air and water quality information.
4. Mexico disseminates drinking water information at the state level but not by individual water supply.

Source: The Access Initiative, National Team Reports, 2004.

■ Detailed information on drinking and surface water quality, on the other hand, is difficult to obtain in all but two of the pilot countries: the United States and South Africa. Under the 1996 amendments to the Safe Drinking Water Act, the United States requires water suppliers to provide customers with annual reports. These reports are usually mailed with bills; many are also posted on the Internet. Teams in five countries (Hungary, India, Mexico, Thailand and Uganda) found no active dissemination of data on drinking water quality for the public on the Internet or in the press. In Mexico and Uganda, teams could not obtain the data at all; in India, data could be obtained only through a personal contact.

In short, there are considerable differences in the performance of government agencies in providing information to the public about drinking or surface water quality. Collectively, performance scores in providing water quality information are weak. This should be contrasted to the assessment of information disclosure and public participation with regard to air quality that the assessment found to be strong.

Men fishing at sunset with square nets in Dhaka, Bangladesh

Part 4. Water Governance Ahead

In the past decade, water and its governance have featured prominently on the international political agenda and will continue to be an international priority through 2015 within the Decade on Water for Life. International efforts to foster water institutional reform have included recommendations on good water management practice, and the setting of goals and targets for improved water service provision to the poor and for greater environmental sustainability via the MDG structure. High hopes and expectations are now vested in recent international water targets from the Millennium Summit and the WSSD to improve the water situation for billions of people. It is a paradox that while various international fora have intensified their work towards improving the world's water situation and implementing time-bound water targets, the actual funding to the water sector in developing countries is diminishing, or stagnating at best. Funding from donors remains stagnant, and additional investments from multinational water companies to improve water governance and access to water are currently decreasing. There is very little evidence that governments in developing countries are strengthening their water budgets.

It has been demonstrated that water governance is nested in the setting of overall national governance and is correspondingly influenced, for better or for worse, by that, by the national culture, and by events local to the country and its surrounds (e.g., conflict) and developments in the global economy. Some of the trends of water governance include the following:

- As a response to internal pressures and to pressures from the international community and regional organizations such as the EU, a widespread process of reform of water governance is now underway. Progress is patchy but generally slow, as evidenced by the limited achievements in the production of national IWRM plans and the weak coverage of water in PRSPs. In developing countries there are often significant and serious gaps between policy-making and its implementation, not least because of institutional resistance by public sector water organizations.

- Progress is being made in water rights – in recognizing their importance in dealing with social and economic problems, in recognizing the importance of local traditions and customs, in facilitating the management of local competition for water and in recognition of human rights to safe water.

- Corruption is a major issue in the water sector, as in many other sectors, but the impact of it is not well quantified because of a lack of detailed information. It is one of the least addressed challenges in the sector and much remains to be done.

- Privatization of water services in developing countries has not been able to meet the high expectations on improved and extended water supply and sanitation services. Much of the privatization debate has had a biased focus on multinational water companies. Local and small-scale water companies are mushrooming in both urban and rural settings and their potential to improve water supply and sanitation largely remains unexplored. There is thus a need to refocus privatization to more systematically explore how local water enterprises, including both water companies and civil society organizations, can contribute to improved water services. It is also high time to bring the government back in and re-emphasize its importance in raising and stimulating adequate investment funds, as well as its critical role in regulatory and other governance functions.

- Recent moves by governments in lower-income countries to delegate responsibility for water management to lower levels of administration have had limited success. Progress is slow, governments are not delegating the needed powers and resources and have in some cases taken back the delegated responsibility. Often local governments do not have the capacity to do what is required. Local groups and individuals are hampered by lack of access to key information and frequently by exclusion from participating in water decision-making. There should also be a more sober view on decentralization itself and what types of decentralization are useful for improved water resources management and services provision.

In developing countries there are often significant and serious gaps between policy-making and its implementation, not least because of institutional resistance by public sector water organizations

The sewer is the conscience of the city

Victor Hugo, *Les Misérables*

CHAPTER 3

Water and Human Settlements in an Urbanizing World

By
UN-HABITAT
(United Nations Human Settlements Programme)

Low-income neighbourhood built on a hill in Mexico City

In principle, sound water governance should be open and transparent, inclusive and communicative, coherent and integrative, and equitable and ethical

Opposite: A favela (slum housing) in Rio de Janeiro, Brazil

Particularly challenging issues include:

- meeting water, sanitation and wastewater management needs in the largest and fastest growing cities, especially on their peripheries

- changing water management systems to cope with the more decentralized patterns of urban development evident in most high-income nations and many middle-income nations and low-density sprawl around urban centres

- improving provision in large villages and small towns, especially to the high proportion of the population with very limited capacity to pay

- recognizing the importance of regular and convenient water supplies for the livelihoods of low-income households, as well as for health, including urban agriculture, for instance, which makes up an important part of the livelihoods of tens of millions of urban households (Smit et al., 1996) and for household enterprises.

Few valid generalizations can be made as to what approach should be taken, because the most effective means of addressing these provision deficiencies varies so much from urban centre to urban centre. However, in most instances, the following is true:

- Provision deficiencies are not a problem that either the private sector or the public sector can solve alone.

- In many nations, at least in the next five to ten years, it will not be possible for the provision deficiencies in most urban areas to be addressed by the conventional model of a (public or private) water utility extending piped water supplies and sewers to individual households.

- It will be impossible to meet the MDG targets in urban areas, unless there are policies for improving water and sanitation provision for low-income households and community organizations, including brokering agreements for those living in illegal settlements.

- What is normally considered part of water and sanitation provision must be expanded to include slum and squatter upgrading programmes and provisions for housing finance, as these play important complementary roles.

- Whether formal provision for water and sanitation is undertaken by public or private utilities, city and municipal governments have a critical role to play in water governance, both in terms of ensuring provision for water, sanitation and wastewater removal and in improving sustainable water management within their boundaries.

- The MDG targets for water and sanitation will not be met without better urban governance. These also need to be embedded within regional water governance arrangements that often require agreements developed with freshwater users upstream of the city and more attention to reducing the impact of water pollution and urban runoff on water quality for users downstream of the city (see, for instance, Guadalajara in von Bertraub, 2003).

BOX 3.1: WATER SUPPLY INADEQUACIES WEIGH HEAVIEST ON WOMEN

There is no water to wash our hands when we use the nearby bushes, plastic bags or the only public toilet available some distance from our homes. There is always fighting on who will be next, although there is a queue. Everyone watches. There are no doors for privacy. How long are we going to live this way? It is affecting our pride and dignity. ... Sometimes we have to go to the back of our house to defecate in a plastic bag and throw it in nearby bushes or in the gully - this is called 'kitting'. The problem gets worse during menstruation both for us and our daughters - they too can't attend school as there is nowhere at school for them to clean themselves, and we the mothers don't have enough water to wash our bodies and to feel clean.
 - *Charlene, living in a slum in the Caribbean*

We have been in this settlement (in Kothrud, in the western part of Pune) for more than twelve years, since we worked as labourers on the construction of these apartment blocks that you see all around here. Nearly 700 families live here now. When the construction work was in progress, we got water at our work sites. But now we face acute shortage of water. We have public standposts in the settlement, but the water is available for only two to three hours a day. In such a short period of time, it is not possible for all of us to fill water. There is always a long queue and frequent fights. Women come to blows because some try to fill many *handaas* (small water containers) or jump the queue. Those who do not get their turn before the water is turned off have to walk 20 to 30

minutes to fetch water. Some pay up to five rupees for one *handaa* of water. Some collect the water that keeps percolating in a small ditch by the side of the path near the water taps. As you can see the water is turbid. We cannot drink it, but we can use it for washing. For a few weeks before the municipal elections, one of the candidates who lives just on the other side of this hill used to supply water to us in long hosepipes from taps in his house. After the elections, the hosepipes disappeared and our water supply stopped. Now if we go to him to ask for water he drives us away as if we are beggars. It is so humiliating!
 - *from interviews with women in Laxminagar, Pune, India.*

Sources: UN-HABITAT, 2004, as quoted in Millennium Project 2005a (for the Caribbean); Bapat and Agarwal, 2003 (for India).

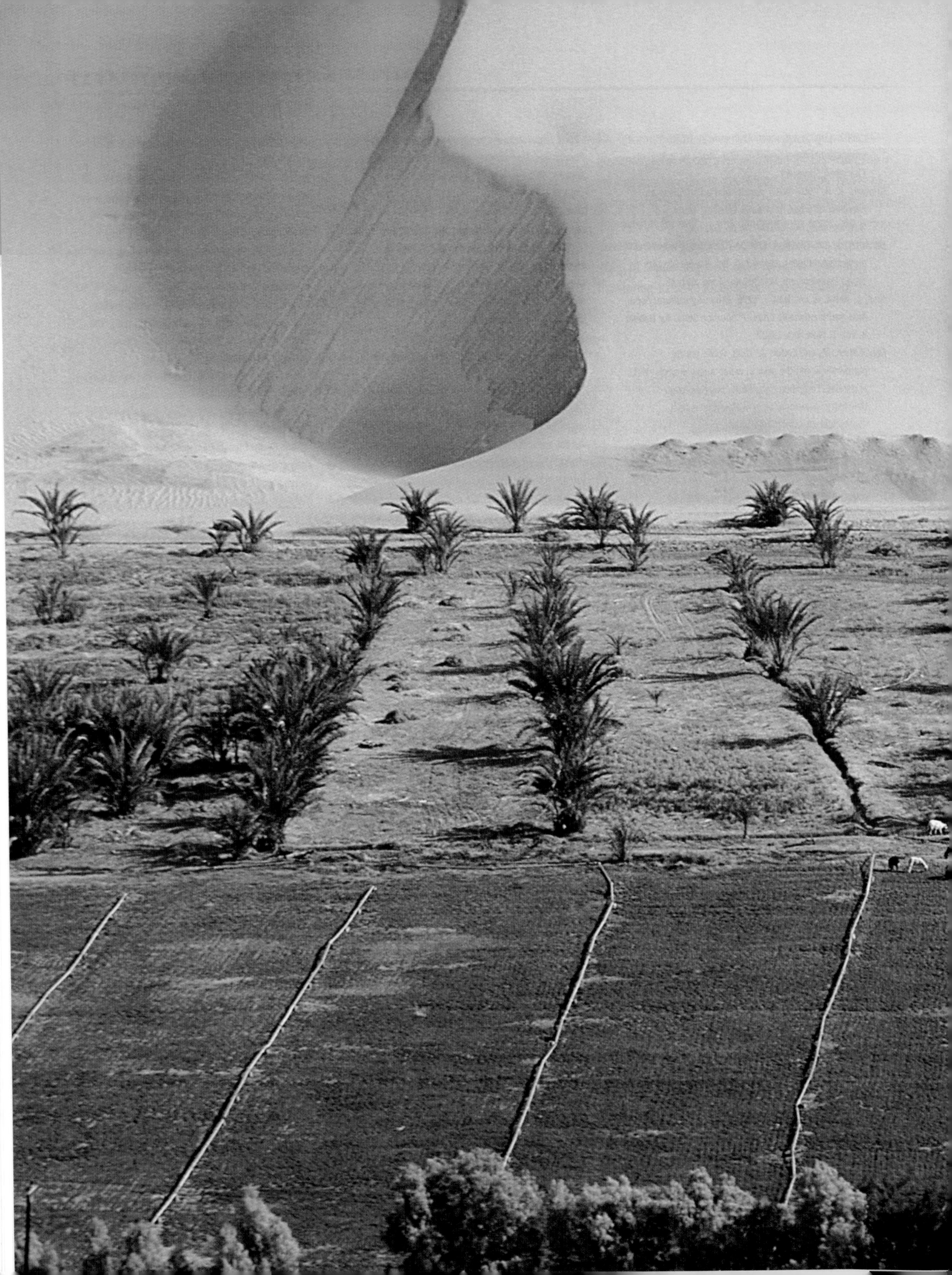

SECTION 2
Changing Natural Systems

Both naturally occurring conditions and human impacts are asserting strong pressure on our water resources today, in the form of warming temperatures, rising sea levels, ecosystems damage and increased climatic variability, among others. Human influence is arguably becoming more important than natural factors. The construction of dams and diversions continue to affect river regimes, fragmenting and modifying aquatic habitats, altering the flow of matter and energy, and establishing barriers to the movement of migratory species. Deforestation, increasing areas of farmland, urbanization, pollutants in both surface and sub-surface water bodies and so on, all influence the timing and quantities of flows and are having a huge impact on the quality and quantity of freshwater.

It is against this background that we must assess the state of the water resources. Assessment is a critical and necessary first step to ensuring that the dual goals of water for environmental and human needs are met. This section presents an overview of the state of water resources and ecosystems and explores current assessment techniques and approaches to Integrated Water Resources Management (IWRM).

Global Map 3: *Relative Water Stress Index*
Global Map 4: *Sources of Contemporary Nitrogen Loading*

I would feel more optimistic about a bright future for man if he spent less time proving he can outwit Nature and more time tasting her sweetness and respecting her seniority.

CHAPTER 4

The State of the Resource

By

UNESCO
(United Nations Educational, Scientific and Cultural Organization)

WMO
(World Meteorological Organization)

IAEA
(International Atomic Energy Agency)

Most renewable groundwater is of a high quality, is adequate for domestic use, irrigation and other uses, and does not require treatment

Table 4.2: Selected large aquifer systems with non-renewable groundwater resources

Countries	Aquifer system	Area (km²)	Estimated total volume (km³)	Estimated exploitable volume (km³)	Estimated annual recharge (km³)	Estimated annual abstraction (km³)
Egypt, Libya, Sudan, Chad	Nubian Sandstone Aquifer System	2,200,000	150,000 to 457,000	> 6,500	13	1.6
Algeria, Libya, Tunisia	NW Sahara Aquifer System	1,000,000	60,000	1,280	14	2.5
Algeria, Libya, Niger	Murzuk Basin	450,000	> 4,800	> 60 to 80	n.a.	1.75
Mali, Niger, Nigeria	Iullemeden Aquifer System	500,000	10,000 to 15,000	250 to 550	50 to 80	n.a.
Niger, Nigeria, Chad, Cameroon	Chad Basin Aquifer	600,000	n.a.	>170 to 350	n.a.	n.a.
S.Arabia, UAR, Bahrain, Qatar	Multilayer Aquifer Arabian Platform	250,000	n.a.	500?	30	13.9
Australia	Great Artesian Basin	1,700,000	20,000	170	50	0.6
Russia	West Siberian Artesian Basin	3,200,000	1,000,000	n.a.	55	n.a.

Source: Jean Margat, personal communication, 2004.
(Adapted from the UNESCO Working Group on Non-Renewable Groundwater Resources, 2004).

several international organizations that are addressing sustainable management strategies which would enable shared socio-economic development of such aquifers. At present, the UNESCO Internationally Shared Aquifer Resources Management (ISARM) project is compiling an inventory of transboundary aquifers.

Natural groundwater quality

Most renewable groundwater is of a high quality, is adequate for domestic use, irrigation and other uses, and does not require treatment. However, it should be noted that uncontrolled development of groundwater resources, without analysis of the chemical and biological content, is an unacceptable practice that can (as in the example of fluoride and arsenic problems in Southeast Asia) lead to serious health problems. Some waters have beneficial uses owing to naturally high temperatures and levels of minerals and gas. This is the case for thermal waters where these properties have been created by high geothermal gradients, volcanic settings or natural radioactive decay. In most cases, these groundwaters are highly developed and used for health and recreation (spa) and geothermal energy services.

Groundwater monitoring networks

Groundwater monitoring networks, as with surface water systems, operate differently at national, regional and local levels. Groundwater levels constitute the most

observed parameter, whereas widespread and continuous water quality and natural groundwater discharge and abstraction networks are operational in only a few countries (Jousma and Roelofson, 2003). Several large-scale efforts are underway to upgrade monitoring and networks, for example, in Europe (Proposal for new Directive on Groundwater Protection [EC 2003] and in India [World Bank, 2005]). However, groundwater assessment, monitoring and data management activities are for the most part minimal or ineffective in many developing countries and are being downsized and reduced in many developed counties (see **Chapter 13**). Lack of data and institutional capacity is endemic, making adequate groundwater development and management difficult. GEMS/Water (a UNEP programme) is currently adding national groundwater data to its international water quality database (described in Part 3). This will supplement the current global knowledge of groundwater quality information collected and displayed by IGRAC on its website, which includes special reports on both arsenic and fluorides in groundwater (IGRAC, 2005a, 2005b).

2g. Water availability

Efforts to characterize the volume of water available to a given nation have been ongoing for several decades. The primary input for many of these estimates is an information database (AQUASTAT) that has historically been developed and maintained by FAO. It is based on data related to the quantity of water resources and uses a water-balance approach for each nation (FAO, 2003a). This database has become a common reference tool used to estimate each nation's renewable water resources. FAO has compiled an Index of Total Actual Renewable Water Resources (TARWR). The details of how the TARWR Index

and its national Per Capita Equivalent of 'Availability' (PCA) are determined and some of the considerations that should be taken into account when using the database index are explained in **Box 4.1**. The TARWR and PCA results for most nations from the latest 2005 update of the FAO AQUASTAT database are found in **Table 4.3**.

BOX 4.1: INDEX OF WATER RESOURCES AVAILABILITY – TOTAL ACTUAL RENEWABLE WATER RESOURCES (TARWR)

Total Actual Renewable Water Resources (TARWR) is an index that reflects the water resources theoretically available for development from all sources within a country. It is a calculated volume expressed in km^3/year. Divided by the nation's population and adjusted to m^3/yr, it is expressed as a per capita volume more readily allowing a relative evaluation of the resource available to its inhabitants. It estimates the total available water resources per person in each nation taking into account a number of individual component indicators by:

■ adding all internally generated surface water annual runoff and groundwater recharge derived from precipitation falling within the nation's boundaries,

■ adding external flow entering from other nations which contributes to both surface water and groundwater,

■ subtracting any potential resource volumes shared by the same water which comes from surface and groundwater system interactions, and

■ subtracting, where one or more treaty exists, any flow volume required by that treaty to leave the country.

It gives the maximum theoretical amount of water actually available for the country on a per

capita basis. Beginning in about 1989, TARWR has been used to make evaluations of water scarcity and water stress.

Considerations related to availability in the TARWR index

It is important to note that the FAO estimates are maximum theoretical volumes of water renewed annually as surface water runoff and groundwater recharge, taking into consideration what is shared in both the surface and groundwater settings. These volumes, however, do not factor in the socio-economic criteria that are potentially and differentially applied by societies, nations or regions to develop those resources. Costs can vary considerably when developing different water sources. Therefore, whatever the reported 'actual' renewable volume of water, it is a theoretical maximum, and the extent to which it can be developed will be less for a variety of economic and technical reasons. For example, Falkenmark and Rockstrom (2004) point out that, globally, approximately 27 percent of the world's surface water runoff occurs as floods. That is not considered a usable water resource even though it would be counted as part of the annual renewable surface water runoff component of TARWR. Therefore, the usable volumes available as resources to meet societal demands will be considerably less than the maximum number given as a nation's TARWR.

Four additional limitations are inherent in the TARWR information. First, seasonal variability in precipitation, runoff and recharge, which is important to regional and basin-level decision making and water storage strategies, is not well reflected in annualized quantities. Second, many large countries have several climatic settings as well as highly disparate population concentrations and the TARWR does not reflect the ranges that can occur within nations. The recently developed small-scale Relative Stress Index Map (Vörösmarty) could assist in overcoming this oversight. Third, there is no data in TARWR that identifies the volumes of 'green' water that sustain ecosystems – the volumes that provide water resources for direct rain-fed agriculture, grazing, grasslands and forests – nor does it account for the volumes of water that are potentially available from non-conventional sources (reuse, desalination, non-renewable groundwater). Finally, while the accounting-based method for a nation's TARWR adds all water that enters from upstream countries, it does not subtract any part of the water that leaves the nation in the TARWR number although estimates of those volumes are available for each country from the database.

Source: FAO, 2003a; FAO-AQUASTAT, 2005.

Table 4.3: *continued*

Country	Population (1,000,000s)	Precip Rate[1] (mm/yr)	TARWR Volume 2005 (km²/yr)	TARWR Per Capita 2000 (m³/yr)	TARWR Per Capita 2005 (m³/yr)	Surface water % TARWR	Ground-water % TARWR	Overlap[2] % TARWR	Incoming Waters % TARWR	Outgoing[3] Waters % TARWR	Total Use % TARWR
189 Viet Nam	82,481	1,800	891	11,406	10,810	40%	5%	4%	59%	4%	8%
190 Palestine Territories	2,386		0.8		320	10%	90%	0%	0%	28%	
191 Yemen	20,733	200	4	223	198	98%	37%	34%	0%	0%	162%
192 Zambia	10,924	1,000	105	10,095	9,630	76%	45%	45%	24%	100%	2%
193 Zimbabwe	12,932	700	20	1,584	1,550	66%	25%	20%	39%	71%	13%

Source: FAO-AQUASTAT, 2005.

Notes:
1. Average precipitation (1961–90 from IPCC (mm/year). As in the FAO-AQUASTAT Database, for some countries large discrepancies exist between national and IPCC data on rainfall average. In these cases, IPCC data were modified to ensure consistency with water resources data.
2. Overlap is the water that is shared by both the surface water and groundwater systems.
3. Outflow – Sep. 2004 for surface water and Aug. 2005 for groundwater.

Part 3. Human Impacts

A number of forces continue to seriously affect our natural water resources. Many of these are primarily the result of human actions and include ecosystem and landscape changes, sedimentation, pollution, over-abstraction and climate change.

...each type of landscape change will have its own specific impact, usually directly on ecosystems and directly or indirectly on water resources...

The removal, destruction or impairment of natural ecosystems are among the greatest causes of critical impacts on the sustainability of our natural water resources. This issue is dealt with more broadly in **Chapter 5**. However, it should be emphasized that the ecosystems with which we interact are directly linked to the well-being of our natural water resources. Although it is difficult to integrate the intricacies of ecosystems into traditional and more hydrologically-based water assessment and management processes, this approach is being strongly advocated in some sectors and scientific domains (e.g. Falkenmark and Rockström, 2004; Figueras et al., 2003; Bergkamp et al., 2003). The basis of this approach is the recognition that each type of landscape change will have its own specific impact, usually directly on ecosystems and directly or indirectly on water resources. The magnitude of the impacts will vary according to the setting's conditions with a wide range of possible landscape changes. Changes that can occur to landscapes include: forest clearance, crop- or grazing lands replacing grasslands or other natural terrestrial ecosystems, urbanization (leading to changes in infiltration and runoff patterns as well to pollution), wetlands removal or reduction, new roadwork for transportation, and mining in quarries or large-scale open pits.

3a. Sedimentation

Sediments occur in water bodies both naturally and as a result of various human actions. When they occur excessively, they can dramatically change our water resources. Sediments occur in water mainly as a direct response to land-use changes and agricultural practices, although sediment loads can occur naturally in poorly vegetated terrains and most commonly in arid and semi-arid climates following high intensity rainfall. **Table 4.4** summarizes the principal sources of excessive sediment loads and identifies the major impacts that this degree of sediment loading can have on aquatic systems and the services that water resources can provide. A recently documented and increasing source of high sediment loads is the construction of new roads in developing countries where little consideration is given to the impacts of such actions on aquatic systems and downstream water supplies. Globally, the effects of excessive sedimentation commonly extend beyond our freshwater systems and threaten coastal habitats, wetlands, fish and coral reefs in marine environments (see **Chapter 5**). The importance of sediment control should be an integral consideration in any water resources development and protection strategy. UNESCO's International Sediment Initiative (ISI) project will attempt to improve the understanding of sediment phenomena, and provide better protection of the aquatic and terrestrial environments.

3b. Pollution

Humans have long used air, land and water resources as 'sinks' into which we dispose of the wastes we generate. These disposal practices leave most wastes inadequately treated, thereby causing pollution. This in turn affects precipitation (**Box 4.2**), surface waters (**Box 4.3**), and groundwater (**Box 4.4**), as well as degrading ecosystems (see **Chapter 5**). The sources of pollution that impact our water resources can develop at different scales (local, regional and global) but can generally be categorized (**Table 4.5**) according to nine types. Identification of source types and level of pollution is a prerequisite to assessing the risk of the pollution being created to both

Table 4.4: Major principal sources and impacts of sedimentation

Pertinence	Sector	Action or mechanism	Impacts
SOURCES			
Agriculture areas, downstream catchments	Agriculture	■ poor farming with excessive soil loss	■ increase soil erosion ■ add toxic chemicals to the environment ■ sediment and pollutants are added to streams ■ irrigation systems maintenance cost increased ■ increase natural water runoff
Forest and development access areas, downstream catchments	Forestry, Road Building, Construction, Construction, Mining	■ extensive tree cutting ■ lack of terrain reforestation ■ lack of runoff control in steep terrain	■ accelerated soil erosion creating more sediment
MAJOR IMPACTS			
Major rivers and navigable waterways	Navigation	■ deposition in rivers or lakes ■ dredging (streams, reservoirs, lakes or harbors)	■ decreases water depth making navigation difficult or impossible. ■ releases toxic chemicals into the aquatic or land environment.
Aquatic ecosystems	Fisheries / Aquatic habitat	■ decreased light penetration ■ higher suspended solids concentrations ■ absorbed solar energy increases water temperature ■ carrying toxic agricultural and industrial compounds ■ settling and settled sediment	■ affects fish feeding and schooling practices; can reduce fish survival ■ irritate gills of fish, can cause death, destroy protective mucous covering on fish eyes and scales ■ dislodge plants, invertebrates, and insects in stream beds affecting fish food sources resulting in smaller and fewer fish, increased infection and disease susceptibility ■ stress to some fish species ■ release to habitat causes fish abnormalities or death ■ buries and suffocates eggs ■ reduces reproduction
Lakes, rivers, reservoirs as water supplies	Water supply	■ increased pump/turbine wear ■ reduced water supply usability for certain purposes ■ additional treatment for usability required	■ affects water delivery, increases maintenance costs ■ reduces water resource value and volume ■ increased costs
Hydroelectric facilities	Hydropower	■ dams trap sediment carried downstream ■ increased pump/turbine wear	■ diminished reservoir capacity ■ shortened power generation lifecycle ■ higher maintenance, capital costs.
All waterways and their ecosystems	Toxic chemicals	■ become attached or adsorbed to sediment particles	■ transported to and deposited in, other areas ■ later release into the environment.

Source: Adapted from Environment Canada (2005a), www.atl.ec.gc.ca/udo/mem.html

Note: Water transforms landscapes and moves large amounts of soil and fine-grained materials in the form of *sediment*.
Sediment is: 1) eroded from the landscape, 2) transported by river systems and eventually 3) deposited in a riverbed, wetland, lake, reservoir or the ocean. Particles or fragments are eroded naturally by water, wind, glaciers, or plant and animal activities with geological (natural) erosion taking place slowly over centuries or millennia. Human activity may accelerate the erosion. Material dislodged is transported when exposed to fluvial erosion in streams and rivers. Deposition occurs as on flood plains, bars and islands in channels and deltas while considerable amounts end up in lakes, reservoirs and deep river beds.

BOX 4.4: IMPACTS TO GROUNDWATER QUALITY FROM HUMAN ACTIVITY

Protection of groundwater sources is becoming a more widespread global concern as typified by the recent European Commission directive which focuses on preventing rather than cleaning up pollution (EC 2003). Incidents of groundwater pollution arising from human actions, particularly in developing nations, remain relatively widespread and its impacts in terms of degraded water quality are summarized in Zektser and Everett (2004). Throughout the world, most countries' practices of urbanization, industrial development, agricultural activities and mining enterprises have caused groundwater contamination and its most typical sources are illustrated in **Figure 4.8**. A 2002 joint World Bank, GWP, WHO and UNESCO online guidance document (Foster et al. 2002) states '*There is growing evidence of increasing pollution threats to groundwater and some well documented cases of irreversible damage to important aquifers, following many years of widespread public policy neglect*'. This guide is supplemented by recommendations in a 2003 joint FAO, UNDESA, IAEA and UNESCO report directly addressing the universal changes needed

in groundwater management practice (FAO 2003b) to arrive at more sustainable water development and use.

Groundwater pollution contrasts markedly in terms of the activities and compounds that most commonly cause surface water pollution. In addition, there are completely different controls that govern the contaminant mobility and persistence in the two water systems' settings. Foster and Kemper (2004), UNEP (2003), FAO (2003b) and Burke and Moench (2000) point out that groundwater management commonly involves a wide range of instruments and measures (technical, process, incentive, legal and enforcement actions/sanctions and awareness raising) to deal with resources that are less visible than those in our surface water bodies.

Mapping groundwater vulnerability

Groundwater is less vulnerable to human impacts than surface water. However, once polluted, cleaning it up (remediation) takes a relatively long time (years), is more technically

demanding, and can be much more costly. While this has been recognized for several decades (Vrba 1985), this important message has not been adequately or consistently conveyed to the policy-makers or the public. To address this gap, groundwater vulnerability assessment methods are being developed. These emerging 'vulnerability maps' have historically been applied to other risks such as flooding and landslides and they can now be used as direct input to water resources and land planning (Vrba and Zaporozek 1994). Results of such studies are absolutely critical where aquifers are used for water supplies and have sensitive ecosystem dependencies. In conjunction with other environmental input, they have become effective instruments used to regulate, manage and take decisions related to impacts from existing and proposed changes in land use, ecosystems and sources of water supplies. Large-scale groundwater vulnerability maps (e.g. France, Germany, Spain, Italy, The Czech Republic, Poland, Russia and Australia) serve as guidelines for land use zoning at national or regional levels.

Figure 4.8: Primary sources of groundwater pollution

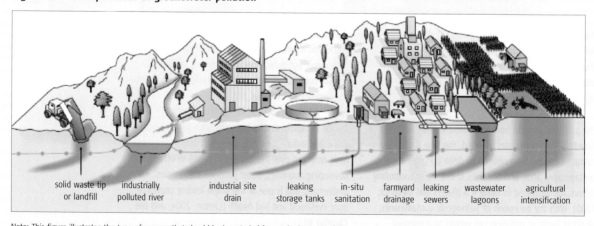

| solid waste tip or landfill | industrially polluted river | industrial site drain | leaking storage tanks | in-situ sanitation | farmyard drainage | leaking sewers | wastewater lagoons | agricultural intensification |

Note: This figure illustrates the type of sources that should be inventoried for cataloging potential sources of groundwater contamination.

Source: Foster et al., 2002.

Table 4.5: Freshwater pollution sources, effects and constituents of concern

Pollution type	Primary sources	Effects[1]	Constituents of concern[2]
1 Organic matter	Industrial wastewater and domestic sewage.	Depletion of oxygen from the water column as it decomposes, stress or suffocating aquatic life.	Biological Oxygen Demand (BOD), Dissolved Organic Carbon (DOC), Dissolved Oxygen (DO)
2 Pathogens and microbial contaminants	Domestic sewage, cattle and other livestock, natural sources.	Spreads infectious diseases through contaminated drinking water supplies leading to diarrhoeal disease and intestinal parasites, increased childhood mortality in developing countries.	Shigella, Salmonella, Cryptosporidium, Fecal coliform (Coliform), Escherichia coli (mammal faeces – E. Coli)
3 Nutrients	Principally runoff from agricultural lands and urban areas but also from some industrial discharge.	Over-stimulates growth of algae (eutrophication) which then decomposes, robbing water of oxygen and harming aquatic life. High levels of nitrate in drinking water lead to illness in humans.	Total N (organic + inorganic), total P (organic + inorganic) For eutrophication: (Dissolved Oxygen, Individual N species (NH4, NO2, NO3, Organic N), Orthophosphate)
4 Salinization	Leached from alkaline soils by over irrigation or by over-pumping coastal aquifers resulting in saltwater intrusion.	Salt build-up in soils which kills crops or reduces yields. Renders freshwater supplies undrinkable.	Electrical conductivity, Chloride (followed, post characterization by full suite of major cations (Ca, Mg), anions
5 Acidification (precipitation or runoff)	Sulphur, Nitrogen oxides and particulates from electric power generation, industrial stack and auto/truck emissions (wet and dry deposition). Acid mine drainage from tailings as well as mines.	Acidifies lakes and streams which negatively impacts aquatic organisms and leaches heavy metals such as aluminium from soils into water bodies.	pH
6 Heavy metals	Industries and mining sites.	Persists in freshwater environments such as river sediments and wetlands for long periods. Accumulates in the tissues of fish and shellfish. Can be toxic to both aquatic organisms and humans who consume them.	Pb, Cd, Zn, Cu, Ni, Cr, Hg, As (particularly groundwater)
7 Toxic organic compounds and micro-organic pollutants.[3]	Wide variety of sources from industrial sites, automobiles, farmers, home gardeners, municipal wastewaters.	A range of toxic effects in aquatic fauna and humans from mild immune suppression to acute poisoning or reproductive failure.	PAHs, PCBs, pesticides (lindane, DDT, PCP, Aldrin, Dieldrin, Endrin, Isodrin, hexachlorobenzene)
8 Thermal	Fragmentation of rivers by dams and reservoirs slowing water and allowing it to warm. Industry from cooling towers and other end-of-pipe above-ambient temperature discharges	Changes in oxygen levels and decomposition rate of organic matter in the water column. May shift the species composition of the receiving water body.	Temperature
9 Silt and suspended particles	Natural soil erosion, agriculture, road building, deforestation, construction and other land use changes.	Reduces water quality for drinking and recreation and degrades aquatic habitats by smothering them with silt, disrupting spawning and interfering with feeding.	Total suspended solids, turbidity

Other pollutants include Radioactivity, Fluoride, Selenium.

Sources and notes:

1 Principally from Revenga and Mock, 2000. Their compilation from Taylor and Smith, 1997; Shiklomanov, 1997; UNEP/GEMS, 1995.

2 From R. Peters, W. Beck, personal communication, 2004.

3 Micro-organic pollutant list now includes a suite of endocrin disrupters, antioxidants, plasticizers, fire retardants, insect repellents, solvents, insecticides, herbicides, fragrances, food additives, prescription drugs and pharmaceuticals (e.g., birth control, antibiotics, etc.), non-prescription drugs (e.g., caffeine, nicotine and derivatives, stimulants).

...the major hydrological challenge will be to achieve more equilibrium between the stored volumes needed to meet users' demands and the incoming and outgoing flow...

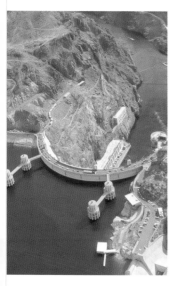

Waste from a water desalination plant in the sea of Al-Doha, Kuwait. Several seawater desalination plants produce 75% of the country's water supply

Storing water in reservoirs

The construction of dams to create reservoirs has frequently been our response to growing demands for water to provide hydropower, irrigation, potable supplies, fishing and recreation, as well as to lower the impacts and risks to our well-being from high-intensity events such as floods and droughts. These facilities collect natural runoff, frequently quite variable in its location, duration and magnitude, and store it so that its availability is more constant and reliable. Good information on the number and capacity of dams is essential to assess impacts and responses at the local, national and regional levels in order to optimize water resources management, but it is also needed to address issues related to global climate and water availability scenarios (see **Chapter 5**).

Though the creation of reservoirs enables higher water availability when and where it is needed, the construction of these facilities has had a considerable impact, both positive and negative, on the Earth's ecosystems and landscapes and has resulted in modifications to the interactions among the components of the hydrological cycle. Despite increased benefits derived from the services reservoirs provide, there is ongoing debate about how to prevent and reduce the social and environmental consequences that come from building dams and creating reservoirs. Following considerable media attention and local actions some practices are changing. Large dam construction rates have slowed, at least temporarily, and there have been advances in the reconsideration of alternatives and design criteria. Some existing dams that no longer provide extensive services have been decommissioned. Lastly, existing reservoir operations and structures have been modified to allow releases. A balance between what enters and what is released is required to have a site's upstream and downstream hydrological settings and supporting ecosystems sustained. When such a balance is achieved, the results are substantial. There are both added benefits and potential further value to the role of reservoirs in development scenarios.

Transferring water among basins

The transfer of water from one river or aquifer basin to another basin has long been used as a way to meet water demands, particularly in arid and semi-arid regions. It occurs often when large populations or, more commonly, agricultural demands have outstripped existing water resources. Even in advanced national development stages, some basins can have surplus water resources while others face shortages. Major long-distance schemes exist in many nations and new ones are in development. Linking the Ganga-Brahmaputra-Meghna system with other rivers in India is part of the solution being offered to counteract extensive recurring droughts and floods. For example, Shao et al. (2003) present the situation in China where there are seven existing major transfers and seven more planned or under consideration. They describe a large-scale south-to-north basin transfer involving the Yangtze and Yellow Rivers' basins which, when completed, would divert 450 km^3/yr. They also point out some of the impacts of such a large scheme. Multi-disciplinary approaches allow evaluation of the feasibility and sustainability of transfer schemes. Global experience has shown that although the transfer of water among basins has been identified as a hydraulically and technically feasible response, before proceeding with such potential changes, broad social and environmental considerations must be taken into account.

4c. Water reuse

Asano and Levine (2004) recently summarized the more important challenges associated with water reclamation and reuse. They noted that the technique of water reuse is being applied in many countries including the United States, Mexico, Germany, Mediterranean and Middle Eastern countries, South Africa, Australia, Japan, China and Singapore. Its increased application is being facilitated by modern wastewater treatment processes, which advanced substantially during the twentieth century. These processes can now effectively remove biodegradable material, nutrients and pathogens so the treated waters have a wide range of potential applications (**Table 4.7**). On a global scale, non-potable water reuse is currently the dominant means of supplementing supplies for irrigation, industrial cooling, river flows and other applications (Asano, 1998). The reuse of potable waters has been an accepted global practice for centuries. Settlements downstream produced their potable water from rivers and groundwater that had circulated upstream through multiple cycles of withdrawal, treatment and discharge (Steenvorden and Endreny, 2004; Asano and Cotruvo, 2004; GW MATE, 2003). San Diego gets 90 percent of its current municipal water supply from a wholesale water provider but in future that amount will decrease to 60 percent with the supplementary supply coming from reclaimed water and desalination (USGS, 2005). Similar programmes are emerging in many other large urban centres worldwide where there are limited or less readily available freshwater supplies. Similarly, riverbeds or percolation ponds have been used to artificially recharge underlying groundwater aquifers mainly with wastewater.

Recent documents from WHO (Aertgeerts and Angelakis, 2003) and the US EPA (2004) address the state-of-the-art aspects and future trends in water use, both of which predict increased development and use of the above-mentioned practice to augment water supply sources in order to meet demands. The WHO guidelines for wastewater reuse first published in 1995 are being updated with a planned release date of 2006 (WHO, 2005). According to water reuse surveys (Lazarova, 2001; Mantovani et al., 2001), the best water reuse projects in terms of economic viability and public acceptance are those that substitute reclaimed water in lieu of potable water for use in irrigation, environmental restoration, cleaning, toilet flushing and industrial uses.

The annual reclaimed water volumes total about 2.2 billion m³, based on 2000 and 2001 figures from the World Bank. Recent projections indicate that Israel, Australia and Tunisia will use reclaimed water to satisfy 25 percent, 11 percent and 10 percent, respectively, of their total water demand within the next few years (Lazarova et al., 2001). In Jordan, reclaimed water volumes are predicted to increase more than four times by 2010 if demands are to be met. By 2012, Spain will need to increase its reclaimed water use by 150 percent and, by 2025, Egypt will need to increase its usage by more than ten times. A number of Middle Eastern countries are planning significant increases

in water reuse to meet an ultimate objective of 50 to 70 percent reuse of total wastewater volume. The growing trend of water reuse is not only occurring in water-deficient areas (Mediterranean region, Middle East and Latin America), but also in highly populated countries in temperate regions (Japan, Australia, Canada, north China, Belgium, England and Germany). This method of augmenting natural water sources is becoming an integral component to many water resources management plans and future use policies.

4d. Demand management

Conserving available water and reducing demand is a necessary measure in water-short regions, especially those in arid climates. Programmes of conservation and demand reduction are referred to as water demand management (WDM). This approach differs from the traditional supply-driven method, which makes all existing water available. WDM applies selective economic incentives to promote efficient and equitable water use. It also identifies water conservation measures that are aimed at raising society's awareness of the scarcity and finite nature of the resource.

Conservation measures have not been readily implemented, particularly where water was perceived as abundant. However, the benefits in the extended useful life of water supply and treatment plants and in the operating efficiency and duration of sewage disposal systems can be considerable in terms of higher economic return on investment. On the environmental front, conservation

At inland locations or where desalination is too costly, reclaimed water can now significantly contribute to the overall water supply used for irrigation or industry...

Table 4.7: Potential applications for reclaimed water

Application settings	Examples
Urban use	
Unrestricted	Landscape irrigation (parks, playgrounds, school yards), fire protection, construction, ornamental fountains, recreational impoundments, in-building uses (toilets, air conditioning)
Restricted-access irrigation	Irrigation of areas where public access is infrequent and controlled (golf courses, cemeteries, residential, greenbelts)
Agricultural irrigation	
Food crops	Crops grown for human consumption and consumed uncooked
Non-food crops, food crops consumed after processing	Fodder, fibre, seed crops, pastures, commercial nurseries, sod farms, commercial aquaculture
Recreational use	
Unrestricted	No limitations on body contact (lakes and ponds used for swimming, snowmaking)
Restricted	Fishing, boating, and other non-contact recreational activities
Environmental use	Artificial wetlands, enhanced natural wetlands, and sustained stream flows
Groundwater recharge	Groundwater replenishment, saltwater intrusion control, and subsidence control
Industrial reuse	Cooling system makeup water, process waters, boiler feed water, construction activities, and washdown waters
Potable reuse	Blending with municipal water supply (surface water or groundwater)

Source: Asano and Leavine, 2004.

References and Websites

Abderrahman, W. A. 2003. Should intensive use of non-renewable groundwater resources always be rejected? R. Llamas and E. Custodio (eds) *Intensive Use of Groundwater: Challenges and Opportunities.* Lisse, The Netherlands, Balkema.

Aertgeerts, R. and Angelakis, A. 2003. *Health Risks in Aquifer Recharge using Reclaimed Wastewater: State of the Art Report,* SDE/WSH/03.08. (www.who.int/water_sanitation_health/wastewater/wsh03 08/en/index.html lvOct05)

Aggarwal, P. K. and Kulkarni, K. M. 2003. *Isotope Techniques in Hydrology: Role of International Atomic Energy Agency,* Advances in Hydrology (Proc. Int. Conf. Water and Environment 2003, Bhopal, India), New Delhi, Allied Publishers Pvt. Ltd. pp. 361–69.

Aggarwal, P. K., Froehlich, K., Kulkarni, K. M. and Gourcy, L. L. 2004. *Stable Isotope Evidence for Moisture Sources in Asian Summer Monsoon under Present and Past Climate Regimes.* Geo. Res. Letters, Vol. 31.

AFP (L'Agence France-Presse). 2004. China warns of 'ecological catastrophe' from Tibet's melting glaciers, News article. *Terradaily.*

Arendt, A. A., Echelmeyer, K. A., Harrison, W. D., Lingle, C. S. and Valentine, V. B. 2002. Rapid wastage of Alaska glaciers and their contribution to rising sea level, *Science,* Vol. 297, No. 5580, pp. 382–86.

Arnell, N. W. 2004. Climate change and global water resources: SRES emissions and socio-economic scenarios, *Global Environmental Change,* Vol. 14, No. 1, pp. 31–52.

Asano, T. (ed.). 1998. Wastewater Reclamation and Reuse, *Water Quality Management Library Volume 10.* Boca Raton, Florida, CRC Press.

Asano, T. and Cotruvo, J. A. 2004. A Review: Groundwater Recharge with Reclaimed Municipal Wastewater: Health and Regulatory Considerations, *Water Research,* Vol. 38, pp. 1941–51. (www.med-reunet.com/docs/asano.pdf lvOct05)

Asano, T. and Leavine, A. D. 2004. Recovering sustainable water from wastewater. *Environmental Science and Technology,* June, pp. 201–08.

Awerbuch, L. 2004. Status of desalination in today's world. S. Nicklin (ed.) *Desalination and Water Re-use.* Leicester, UK, Wyndeham Press, pp. 9–12.

Bashkin, V and Radojevic, M. 2001. A Rain Check on Asia. *Chemistry in Britain,* No. 6. (Online at: www.chemsoc.org/chembytes/ezine/2001/ bashkin_jun01.htm lvOct05)

Bergkamp, G., Orlando, B. and Burton, I. 2003. *Change: Adaptation of water resources management to climate change.* Gland, Switzerland, IUCN.

Bhattacharya, S. K., Froehlich, K., Aggarwal, P. K. and Kulkarni, K. M. 2003. Isotopic Variation in Indian Monsoon Precipitation. Records from Bombay and New Delhi, *Geophysical Research Letters,* Vol. 30, No. 24, p. 2285.

Blomquist, W., Dinar, A. and Kemper, K. 2005. Comparison of Institutional Arrangements for River Basin Management in Eight Basins. World Bank Policy Research Working Paper 3636, June 2005. (wdsbeta.worldbank.org/external/ default/WDSContentServer/IW3P/IB/2005/06/14/ 000016406_20050614124517/Rendered/PDF/ wps3636.pdf lvOct05).

Bullock, A. and Acreman, M. 2003. The role of wetlands in the hydrologic cycle. *Hydrology and Earth System Sciences,* Vol. 7, No. 3, pp. 358–89.

Burke, J. and Moench, M. 2000. *Groundwater and Society: Resources, Tensions and Opportunities.* New York, UNDESA (United Nations Department of Economic and Social Affairs) E.99.II.A.1.

CSIRO. 2004. Returning the lifeblood to rivers. A drought experiment - environmental flows resurrect irrigation country. How healthy river habitats suffer from altered flows. Clever planning and management approaches. Where wild things are dammed, *ECOS magazine,* Issue 122, pp. 11–19, CSIRO Publishing. (www.publish.csiro.au/ ecos/index.cfm?sid=10&issue_id=4847 lvOct05)

Daughton, C. G. 2004. Non-regulated water contaminants: emerging research, *Environmental Impact Assessment Review,* Vol. 24, pp. 711–32.

Digout, D. 2002. *Variations in River Runoff by Continent through Most of the 20th Century – Deviations from Average Values.* (UNEP based on source material in Shiklomanov (1999) and UNESCO 1999 at www.unep.org/vitalwater/07.htm lvOct05).

Driscoll, C. T., Lawrence, G. B., Bulger, A. J., Butler, T. J., Cronan, C. S., Eagar, C., Lambert, K. F., Likens, G. E., Stoddard, J. L. and Weathers, K. C. 2001. *Acid Rain Revisited: Advances in scientific understanding since the passage of the 1970 and 1990 Clean Air Act Amendments,* Hubbard Brook Research Foundation. Science Links Publication, Vol. 1, No. 1. (www.hbrook.sr.unh.edu./hbfound/report.pdf lvOct05)

Dyson, M., Bergkamp, G. and Scanlon, J. (eds) 2003. *Flow. The Essentials of Environmental Flows.* Gland, Switzerland and Cambridge, UK, IUCN.

Dyurgerov, M. 2003. Mountain and subpolar glaciers show an increase in sensitivity to climate warming and intensification of the water cycle, *Journal of Hydrology,* Vol. 282, pp. 164–76.

EC (European Commission). 2003. Proposal for a Directive of the European Parliament and of the Council on the 'Protection of Groundwater against Pollution'. (europa.eu.int/eur-lex/en/ com/pdf/2003/com2003_0550en01.pdf lvOct05).

——. 2000. Directive 2000/60/EC of the European Parliament and of the Council Establishing a Framework for the Community Action in the Field of Water Policy, Brussels. (europa.eu.int/comm/environment/ water/water-framework/index_en.html lvOct05).

Entekhabi, D., Njoku, E. G., Houser, P., Spencer, M., Doiron, T., Kim, Y., Smith, J., Girard, R., Belair, S., Crow, W., Jackson, T. J., Kerr, Y.H., Kimball, J. S., Koster, R., McDonald, K. C., O'Neill, P. E., Pultz, T., Running, S. W., Shi, J., Wood, E., van Zyl, J. 2004. The Hydrosphere State (Hydros) Satellite Mission: An Earth System Pathfinder for Global Mapping of Soil Moisture and Land Freeze/Thaw. IEEE Trans. *Geoscience And Remote Sensing,* Vol. 42, No. 10, pp. 2184–95. (hydros.gsfc.nasa.gov/pdf/TGARSHydros.pdf lvOct05).

Environment Canada. 2005a. *Water – The Transporter* (www.atl.ec.gc.ca/udo/mem.html lvOct05)

——. 2005b. *The Bottom Line – Water Conservation.* (www.ec.gc.ca/water/en/manage/effic/e_bottom.htm lvOct05)

——. 2005c. Acid Rain (www.ec.gc.ca/ acidrain/ lvOct05)

Falkenmark, M. and Rockstrom, J. 2004. *Balancing Water for Humans and Nature: The New Approach in Ecohydrology,* Earthscan, UK.

FAO. 2002. *World Agriculture: Towards 2015/2030. Summary Report,* FAO, Rome. (available at: www.fao.org/ documents/show_cdr.asp?url_file=/docrep/004/y3557e/y3 557e11.htm lvOct05)

——. 2005. Geo-referenced database on African dams. (www.fao.org/ag/agl/aglw/aquastat/damsafrica/index.stm lvOct05).

——. 2004. Personal communication from FAO containing National Downstream Volumes datafile, 6 Sept 2004, FAO AQUASTAT staff, Rome. (Supplemented 18 Aug 2005 with limited groundwater data available).

——. 2003a. *Review of World Water Resources by Country.* Water Report 23. (ftp://ftp.fao.org/agl/aglw/docs/ wr23e.pdf lvOct05).

——. 2003b. *Groundwater Management: The Search for Practical Approaches,* FAO Water report 25 (ftp://ftp.fao.org/agl/aglw/docs/wr25e.pdf lvOct05)

FAO-Aquastat. 2005. (www.fao.org/ag/agl/aglw/aquastat/ main/ lvOct05). Groundwater to surface water renewal ratio calculated from total annual internally generated groundwater and surface water volumes in the Aquastat database.

Figueras, C., Tortajada, C. and Rockstrom, J. 2003. *Rethinking Water Management.* UK, Earthscan.

Foster, S., Hirata, R., Gomes, D., D'Elia, M. and Paris, M. 2002. *Groundwater Quality Protection – a guide for water utilities, municipal authorities, and environment agencies.* GWMATE in association with GWP, 112 p. (DOI: 10.1596/0-8213-4951-1) (www-wds.worldbank.org/ servlet/WDSContentServer/WDSP/IB/2002/12/14/ 000094946_02112704014826/Rendered/PDF/ multi0page.pdf lvOct05).

Foster, S. and Kemper, K. 2004. *Sustainable Groundwater Management: Concepts and Tools,* World Bank GW MATE Briefing Note Series Profile (list of all fifteen briefing notes). (siteresources.worldbank.org/INTWRD/903930- 1112347717990/20424234/BN_series_profileMay04.pdf lvOct05).

Fountain, A. and Walder, J. 1998. Water Flow through Temperate Glaciers, *Review of Geophysics*, Vol. 36, No. 3, pp. 299–328.

Frauenfelder, R., Zemp, M., Haeberli,W. and Hoelzle, M. 2005. World-Wide Glacier Mass Balance Measurements: Trends and First Results of an Extraordinary Year in Central Europe, *Ice and Climate News*, No. 6. pp. 9–10. (clic.npolar.no/newsletters/archive/ice_climate_2005_08 _no_06.pdf lvOct05)

GEMS/WATER. 2005. *2004 State of the UNEP GEMS/Water Global Network and Annual Report.* (www.gemswater.org/ common/pdfs/gems_ar_2004.pdf lvOct05)

Gleick, P. H. (ed.). 1993. *Water in Crisis: A Guide to the World's Freshwater Resources.* New York, Oxford University Press.

GLIMS (Global Land Ice Measurements from Space). 2005. *Project Description: Global Land Ice Measurements from Space* (nsidc.org/data/glims/ lvOct05).

Govt. South Africa. 1997. White Paper on Water Policy (Section B: New National Water Policy) CH 5. Water Resource Policy, Subchapter 5.2 Priorities – The Basic Needs and Environmental Reserve and International Obligations. (www.polity.org.za/html/govdocs/ white_papers/water.html#Contents lvOct05).

Govt. Western Australia. 2005. (portal.environment.wa.gov.au/ portal/page?_pageid=55,34436&_dad=portal&_schema= PORTAL lvOct05).

GRDC (Global Runoff Data Center). 2005. (grdc.bafg.de/ servlet/is/1660/, grdc.bafg.de/servlet/is/943/ lvOct05).

Greenhalgh, S. and Sauer, A. 2003. *Awakening the Dead Zone: An Investment for Agriculture, Water Quality, and Climate Change*, WRI Issue Brief. (pdf.wri.org/hypoxia.pdf lvOct05).

GWP. 2005a. *Efficiency in Water Use – Managing Demand and Supply.* (gwpforum.netmasters05.netmasters.nl/en/ content/toolcategory_453AAC8B-A128-11D5-8F08- 0002A508D0B7.html lvOct05)

——. 2005b. *Water Resources Assessment – Understanding Water Resources and Needs.* (gwpforum.netmasters05. netmasters.nl/en/content/toolcategory_5E1CD3DC-3B4A- 4D82-B476-82DEF0EE0186.html lvOct05).

GW MATE. 2003. Urban Wastewater as Groundwater Recharge: evaluating and managing the risks and benefits, Sustainable Groundwater Management: Concepts and Tools, World Bank GW Mate Briefing Series Note 12. (siteresources.worldbank.org/INTWRD/903930- 1112347717990/20424258/BriefingNote_12.pdf lvOct05)

Haider, S. S., Said, S., Kothyari, U. C. and Arora, M. K. 2004. Soil Moisture Estimation Using Ers 2 Sar Data: A Case Study in the Solani River Catchment. *Journal of Hydrological Science*, pp. 323–34. (www.extenza- eps.com/extenza/ loadPDF?objectIDValue=34832 lvOct05).

Hock, R., Jansson, P. and Braun, L. 2005. Modelling the Response of Mountain Glacier Discharge to Climate Warming. U. M. Huber, H. K. M. Bugmann and M. A. Reasoner (eds), *Global Change and Mountain Regions –*

An Overview of Current Knowledge. Series: Advances in Global Change Research. Vol. 23, Springer.

IAEA. 2002. Isotope studies in large river basins: A new global research focus. *EOS* 83, pp. 613-17.

IGRAC. 2005. Global Groundwater Information System Database. (igrac.nitg.tno.nl/ggis_map/start.html lvOct05).

——. 2005a. Arsenic in Groundwater Worldwide (igrac.nitg.tno.nl/arsmain.html lvOct05).

——. 2005b. Fluoride in Groundwater Worldwide (igrac.nitg.tno.nl/flumain.html lvOct05).

——. 2004. Global Groundwater Regions. (igrac.nitg.tno.nl/pics/region.pdf lvOct05).

IPCC. 2004. *Expert Meeting on the Science to Address UNFCCC Article 2 including Key Vulnerabilities*, Buenos Aires, Argentina 18-20 May 2004, Short Report. (www.ipcc.ch/wg2sr.pdf lvOct05).

——. (Intergovernmental Panel on Climate Change). 2001. *Third Assessment Report: Climate Change 2001.* (www.ipcc.ch/pub/reports.htm lvOct05).

IRHA (International Rainwater Harvesting Association). 2004. *How RHW benefits water resources management (unpublished)* (www.irha-h2o.org – lvOct05).

Jackson, T. 2004. How Wet's Our Planet? Scientists want to be able to measure soil moisture everywhere, every day! Agric. Res. Vol. 52, No. 3, pp. 20–22. (www.ars.usda.gov/is/ AR/archive/mar04/planet0304.htm?pf=1 lvOct05).

Jansson, P., Hock, R. and Schneider, T. 2003. The Concept of Glacier Storage – A Review. *Journal of Hydrology*, Vol. 282, Nos. 1-4, pp. 116–29.

Jousma, G. and Roelofsen, F. J. 2003. *Inventory of existing guidelines and protocols for groundwater assessment and monitoring*, IGRAC. (igrac.nitg.tno.nl/pics/ inv_report1.pdf lvOct05).

Lakenet. 2005. (www.worldlakes.org lvOct05).

Lazarova, L. 2001. *Recycled Water: Technical-Economic Challenges for its Integration as a Sustainable Alternative Resource.* Proc. UNESCO Int'l. Symp. *Les frontiéres de la gestion de l'eau urbaine: impasse ou espoir?* Marseilles, 18–20 June 2001.

Lazarova, V., Levine, B., Sack, J., Cirelli, C., Jeffrey, P., Muntau, H., Salgot, M. and Brissaud, F. 2001. Role of water reuse for enhancing integrated water management in Europe and Mediterranean countries. *Water Science and Technology*, Vol. 43, No. 10, pp, 23–33.

Lehner, B. and P. Döll. 2004. Development and validation of a global database of lakes, reservoirs and wetlands. *Journal of Hydrology*, Vol. 296, Nos. 1-4, pp. 1–22.

Lenton, R. 2004. Water and climate variability: development impacts and coping strategies, *Water Science and Technology*, Vol. 49, No. 7, pp. 17–24.

Llamas, R. and Custodio, E. (eds). 2003. *Intensive use of groundwater, Challenges and Opportunities.* Balkema.

Mahnot, S. C., Sharma, D. C., Mishra, A., Singh, P. K. and Roy, K. K. 2003. *Water Harvesting Management*, Practical Guide Series 6, V. Kaul (ed.). SDC/Intercooperation Coordination Unit. Jaipur, India.

Mantovani, P., Asano, T., Chang, A. and Okun, D. A. 2001. Management Practices for Non-potable Water Reuse. Water Environment Research Foundation Report 97-IRM-6.

Meybeck, M. 1995. Global distribution of lakes. A. Lerman, D. M. Imboden and J. R. Gat (eds), *Physics and Chemistry of Lakes*, Springer, Berlin, pp. 1–36.

Meybeck, M., Chapman, D. and Helmer, R. (eds). 1989. *Global Freshwater Quality: A First Assessment.* Blackwell Ref. Oxford, UK.

Mitchell, T. D., Hulme, M. and New, M. 2002. *Climate Data for Political Areas.* Area, Vol. 34, pp. 109–12. (www.cru.uea.ac.uk/cru/data/papers/mitchell2002a.pdf lvOct05).

Morris, B. L., Lawrence, A. R. L., Chilton, P. J. C., Adams, B., Calow, R. C. and Klinck, B. A. 2003. Groundwater and its Susceptibility to Degradation. A Global Assessment of the Problem and Options for Management. Early Warning and Assessment Report Series, RS. 03-3. United Nations Environment Programme/DEWA, Nairobi, Kenya.

NSIDC (National Snow and Ice Data Center). 1999. update 2005. World glacier inventory. World Glacier Monitoring Service and National Snow and Ice Data Center/World Data Center for Glaciology. Boulder, CO. Digital media. (nsidc.org/data/docs/noaa/g01130_glacier_inventory/ lvOct05).

New, M., Hulme, M. and Jones, P. D. 1999. Representing Twentieth Century Space-Time Climate Variability. Part 1: Development of a 1961-1990 Mean Monthly Terrestrial Climatology. *Journal of Climate*, Vol. 12, pp. 829–56. (ams.allenpress.com/amsonline/?request=get-abstract &issn=1520-0442&volume=012&issue=03&page=0829 lvOct05).

Njoku, E. 2004. *AMSR-E/Aqua Daily L3 Surface Soil Moisture, Interpretive Parms, and QC EASE-Grids V001*, March to June 2004. Boulder, CO, US: National Snow and Ice Data Center. Digital media – updated daily.

Njoku, E., Chan, T., Crosson, W. and Limaye, A. 2004. Evaluation of the AMSR-E data calibration over land. *Italian Journal of Remote Sensing*, Vol. 29, No. 4, pp. 19–37. (nsidc.org/data/docs/daac/ae_land3_l3_soil_moisture.gd.html lvOct05).

OECD.1996. Guidelines for aid agencies for improved conservation and sustainable use of tropical and sub- tropical wetland. OECD Development Assistance Committee: Guidelines on Aid and Environment. No. 9.

Pandey, D. N., Gupta, A. K. and Anderson, D. M. 2003. Rainwater harvesting as an adaptation to climate change, *Current Science*, Vol. 85, No. 1, pp. 46–59. (www.irha- h2o.org/doc/text/pandey00.pdf lvOct05).

Pereira, L., Cordery, I. and Lacovides, L. 2002. Coping with water scarcity, IHP-VI Tech. Documents in Hydrology No. 58, UNESCO.

Peters, N. E. and Meybeck, M. 2000. Water quality degradation effects on freshwater availability: Impacts of human activities, Int'l Water Res. Assoc., *Water International*, Vol. 25, No. 2, pp. 185–93.

Peters, N. E. and Webb, B. 2004. Personal communication – Water quality parameters to measure related to pollution.

Pyne, R. D. G. and Howard, J. B. 2004. Desalination/Aquifer Storage Recovery (DASR): a cost-effective combination for Corpus Christi, Texas, *Desalination*, Vol. 165, pp. 363–67. (www.desline.com/articoli/5744.pdf lvOct05).

Rees, G. and Demuth, S. 2000. The application of modern information system technology in the European FRIEND project. Moderne Hydrologische Informations Systeme. *Wasser und Boden*, Vol. 52, No. 13, pp. 9–13.

Rekacewicz, P. 2002. *Industrial and Domestic Consumption Compared with Evaporation from Reservoirs.* (UNEP based on Shiklomanov (1999) and UNESCO 1999 at www.unep.org/vitalwater/15.htm lvOct05).

Revenga, C. and Mock, G. 2000. *Dirty Water: Pollution Problems Persist.* World Resources Institute Program, Pilot Analysis of Global Ecosystems: Freshwater Systems. (earthtrends.wri.org/pdf_library/features/wat_fea_dirty.pdf lvOct05).

Reynolds, K. 2003. Pharmaceuticals in Drinking Water Supplies, *Water Conditioning and Purification Magazine*, Vol. 45(6). (www.wcp.net/column.cfm?T=T&ID=2199 lvOct05).

Robock, A. and Vinnikov, K. Y. 2005. Global Soil Moisture Data Bank (climate.envsci.rutgers.edu/soil_moisture/ lv Jul2004).

Robock, A., Vinnikov, K. Y., Srinivasan, G., Entin, J. K., Hollinger, S. E., Speranskaya, M. A., Liu, S. and Namkhai, A. 2000. The Global Soil Moisture Data Bank. *Bull. Amer. Meteorol. Soc.*, Vol. 81, pp. 1281–99.

Rodda, J.C. 1998. *Hydrological Networks Need Improving!* In: H. Zebedi (ed.), *Water: A Looming Crisis?* Proc. Int. Conf. on World Water Resources at the Beginning of the 21st century. Paris, UNESCO/IHP.

Schiffler, M. 2004. Perspectives and challenges for desalination in the 21st century. *Desalination*, Vol. 165, pp. 1–9.

Shao, X., Wang, H. and Wang, Z. 2003. Interbasin transfer projects and their implications: A China case study, *International Journal of River Basin Management*, Vol. 1, No. 1, pp. 5–14. (www.jrbm.net/pages/archives/JRBMn1/Shao.PDF lv Oct05)

Shiklomanov, I. A. 1999. World Freshwater Resources: World Water Resources and their Use. webworld.unesco.org/water/ihp/db/shiklomanov/index.shtml〉

——. 1997. *Assessment of Water Resources and Availability in the World.* In Comprehensive Assessment of the Freshwater Resources of the World. Stockholm Environment Institute.

Shiklomanov, I. A. and Rodda, J. C. 2003. *World Water Resources at the Beginning of the 21st Century.* Cambridge, UK, Cambridge University Press.

Stahl, K and Hisdal, H. 2004. Hydroclimatology. Tallaksen, L. and van Lanen, H. (eds). *Hydrological Drought - Processes and Estimation Methods for Streamflow and Groundwater.* (Developments in Water Science, 48). p. 22. New York, Elsevier. Reprinted with permission from Elsevier.

Steenvorden, J. and Endreny, T. 2004. Wastewater Re-use and Groundwater Quality, IAHS Pub. 285.

Tallaksen, L. M. and Van Lanen H. A. J. (eds), *Developments in Water Science*, 48, Elsevier, The Netherlands.

Taylor, R. and Smith, I. 1997. *State of New Zealand's Environment 1997.* Wellington, New Zealand: The Ministry for the Environment. Revenga and Mock 2000.

UNEP. 2005. *Sourcebook of Alternative Technologies for Freshwater Augmentation in Africa.* ITEC. (www.unep.or.jp/ietc/Publications/TechPublications/TechPub-8a/index.asp lvOct05).

——. 2003. *Groundwater and its Susceptibility to Degradation. A global assessment of the problems and options for management,* UNEP/DEWA, Nairobi. (www.unep.org/DEWA/water/groundwater/groundwater_report.asp lvOct05).

UNEP/GEMS (United Nations Environment Program Global Environment Monitoring System/Water). 1995. *Water Quality of World River Basins.* Nairobi, Kenya: UNEP. Revenga and Mock 2000.

UNESCO. 2004. WHYMAP. *Groundwater Resources of the World.* Map 1:50 m. Special edn, August, BGR Hanover/UNESCO, Paris.

——. 2000. *Catch the water – where it drops. Rain water harvesting and artificial recharge to ground water. A guide to follow.* IHP program document.

UNESCO and World Bank. Forthcoming 2006. Non-renewable groundwater resources, a guidebook on socially sustainable management for policy matters.

US Drought Mitigation Center. 2005. *Drought Map – April 2004.* (www.drought.unl.edu/pubs/abtdrmon.pdf lvOct05).

US EPA (United States Environmental Protection Agency). 2004. *Guidelines for Water Reuse,* EPA 625/R-04/108. (www.epa.gov/ORD/NRMRL/pubs/625r04108/625r04108.htm lvOct05).

US GS (United States Geological Survey). 2005. *Reclaimed wastewater: Using treated wastewater for other purposes.* (ga.water.usgs.gov/edu/wwreclaimed.html lvOct05).

US NRC (United States National Research Council) 2004, *Review of the desalination and water purification technology roadmap.* (www.nap.edu/books/0309091578/html/R1.html lvOct05).

——. 2000. *Issues in the Integration of Research and Operational Satellite Systems for Climate Research: Part I. Science and Design, Part 6, Soil Moisture.* pp. 68–81. Commission on Physical Sciences, Mathematics, and Applications; Space Studies Board. National Academy Press, Washington DC. (print.nap.edu/pdf/0309069858/pdf_image/68.pdf lvOct05).

——. 1998. *Issues in Potable Reuse: The Viability of Augmenting Drinking Water Supplies with Reclaimed Water.* Washington DC, National Academy Press.

Vrba, J., 1985. Impact of domestic and industrial wastes and agricultural activities on groundwater quality. *Hydrogeology in the service of man*, Vol. 18, No. 1, pp. 91–117, IAH Memoirs of the 18th Congress, Cambridge, UK.

Vrba, J. and Zaporozec, A. (eds). 1994. *Guidebook on mapping groundwater vulnerability.* Vol. 16, 131. IHP-IAH International Contribution to Hydrogeology, Verlag H. Heise, Germany.

Webb, B.W. 1999. *Water quality and pollution.* Pacione, M. (ed.) *Applied Geography: Principles and Practice,* pp. 152–71. London and New York, Routledge.

Wiegel, S., Aulinger, A., Brockmeyer, R., Harms, H., Loeffler, J., Reincke, H., Schmidt, R., Stachel, B., von Tuempling, W. and Wanke, A. 2004. Pharmaceuticals in the River Elbe and its Tributaries, *Chemosphere*, Vol. 57, pp. 107–26.

WHO. 2005. Wastewater use. (www.who.int/water_sanitation_health/wastewater/en/ lvOct05).

Wolf, A. T., Natharius, J. A., Danielson, J. J., Ward, B. S. and Pender, J. K. 2002. International river basins of the world. International Journal of Water Resources Development, Vol. 15, No. 4, pp. 387-427. www.transboundarywaters.orst.edu/publications/register/tables/IRB_table_4.html

World Bank. 2005. *India's Hydrology Project Phase II.* (web.worldbank.org/external/projects/main?pagePK=104231&piPK=73230&theSitePK=40941&menuPK=228424&Projectid=P084632 lvOct05).

WMO. 2005. Analysis of data exchange problems in global atmospheric and hydrological networks, WMO/TD No. 1255, GCOS No. 96. (www.wmo.ch/web/gcos/Publications/gcos-96.pdf lvOct05).

——. 2004. Soil Moisture – Details of Recommended Variables. (www.wmo.ch/web/gcos/terre/variable/slmois.html lv-Oct05).

WWF. 2003. *Managing Rivers Wisely – Lessons Learned from WWF's Work for Integrated River Basin Management.* (www.panda.org/about_wwf/what_we_do/freshwater/our_solutions/rivers/irbm/cases.cfm lvOct05).

Zalewski, M., Janauer, G.A. and Jolankai, G. 1997. Ecohydrology. A New Paradigm for the Sustainable Use of Aquatic Resources. IHP-V. Technical Documents in Hydrology. No. 7. UNESCO, Paris.

Zektser, I.S. and Everett, L.G. 2004. *Groundwater Resources of the World and their Use,* IHP-VI, Series on Groundwater No. 6, UNESCO. (Section 6.4 – Human Activities impact on groundwater resources and their use).

We must treat each and every swamp, river basin, river and tributary, forest and field with the greatest care, for all these things are the elements of a very complex system that serves to preserve water reservoirs – and that represents the river of life.

Mikhail Gorbachev

CHAPTER 5

Coastal and Freshwater Ecosystems

By
UNEP
(United Nations Environment Programme)

Betsiboka River, Madagascar

Section 2: CHANGING NATURAL SYSTEMS

Key messages:

Coastal and freshwater ecosystems are deteriorating in many areas and at a faster rate than any other ecosystem. Such changes are caused by intertwined factors, making it difficult to identify the problems early on. While progress in integrating these various factors in managing water and ecosystems has been made in some places, the majority of the world and its inhabitants increasingly suffers from a lack of priority given to environmental protection.

■ Humans depend upon healthy aquatic ecosystems for drinking water, food security and a wide range of environmental goods and services. Aquatic biodiversity is also extremely rich, with high levels of endemic species, and is very sensitive to environmental degradation and overexploitation.

■ Aquatic ecosystems and species are deteriorating rapidly in many areas. This is having an immediate impact on the livelihoods of some of the world's most vulnerable human communities by reducing protein sources for food, availability of clean water, and potential for income generation.

■ People in regions with highly variable climatic conditions are particularly vulnerable to droughts and floods and the resulting deteriorating condition of freshwater ecosystems. Coastal lowland areas, where population densities are usually very high and coastal habitats are fragile, are most likely to be affected by sea level rise in future.

■ The conservation of biodiversity (species, habitats and ecosystem functions) must become an integral part of all water resource management programmes. This will assist poverty reduction strategies by ensuring the sustainability of aquatic ecosystems for future generations.

■ Ecosystem approaches constitute a fundamental element of Integrated Water Resource Management (IWRM) and are essential for safeguarding and balancing the needs and requirements of water resources among different stakeholder groups and ecosystems. Ecosystem approaches are the subject of global and regional targets and policy initiatives, but they have yet to be implemented in practice. This requires awareness raising, tools and methodologies to monitor and negotiate the trade-offs involved in such broad-scale approaches.

■ Our understanding of the properties and functions of many aquatic ecosystems is seriously hampered by inadequate data. Enhanced monitoring efforts are required to provide a better assessment of the status, conditions and trends of global water ecosystems, habitats and species.

Top to bottom:
Ticti reservoir, Mexico

Franz Joseph Glacier,
New Zealand

Heavy rains in the province of Misiones, Argentina, carry off significant quantities of ferruginous earth into the River Uruguay

Part 1. Ecosystems and their Capacity to Provide Goods and Services

Human population growth and the expansion of economic activities are collectively placing huge demands on coastal and freshwater ecosystems

The majority of us live in temperate and subtropical regions centred around the coast or inland water systems. Coastal waters, rivers, lakes, wetlands, aquifers and other inland water systems such as swamps and fens have in consequnce been subjected to disproportionate human-induced pressures. These include construction along coastlines for harbours and urban expansion, alteration of river systems for navigation and water storage, drainage of wetlands to increase farmland, overexploitation of fisheries, and multiple sources of pollution. Human population growth and the expansion of economic activities are collectively placing huge demands on coastal and freshwater ecosystems. Water withdrawals, for instance, have increased sixfold since the 1900s, which is twice the rate of population growth (WMO, 1997). In addition, the quality of many water bodies is declining due to increased pollution from agriculture, industry, tourism, urban runoff and domestic sewage.

Desertification is also spreading as a consequence of the misuse of water resources, not only in Africa and Central Asia, but increasingly in other regions, such as in California and southern Europe. The dramatic shrinking of the Aral Sea in Central Asia and its consequences for biodiversity and human well-being have been well documented (UNEP, 2004b; Kreutzberg-Mukhina, 2004). There are many other water crises that have received less attention, such as the serious soil erosion and groundwater depletion occurring in parts of Spain and the eutrophication of many coastal waters as a result of intensive farming. In other regions, the problem may soon be one of too much water, threatening many low-lying coastal and floodplain areas. Predictions of the impacts of melting ice caps and increased discharge from Arctic rivers due to global warming remain uncertain, although it is clear that they will change the fragile Arctic Ocean ecosystem, with potentially devastating consequences further afield, especially along often highly populated coastlines (ACIA, 2004).

While many of the world's coastal and freshwater ecosystems are continuing to deteriorate at alarming rates, the reversal of these trends and the improvement of water quality in other areas indicate that this decline is neither inevitable nor always irreversible. The management of water and land resources requires a comprehensive understanding and careful consideration of ecosystem functions and interactions. The application of such knowledge in an integrated approach to land use and water management is often referred to as an 'ecosystem approach', and such a holistic response to the challenges facing the world's water resources is at the heart of international agreements and programmes like the Convention on Biological Diversity (CBD), the Global Programme of Action (GPA) for the Protection of the

Marine Environment from Land-based Activities and the World Summit on Sustainable Development (WSSD).

The ecosystem approach, a key element of integrated water resources management (IWRM) (GWP, 2003), is a strategy for the integrated management of land, water and living resources which promotes conservation and sustainable use in an equitable way (CBD, 2000). There is no single way to implement the ecosystem approach, as it depends upon local, provincial, national, regional and global conditions. **Box 5.1** discusses one of the many systems in which an ecosystem approach should be implemented to solve a current ecosystem crisis.

IWRM is a systematic participatory planning and implementation process for the sustainable management of water, land and coastal resources, which promotes coordinated development and is based on credible science. It involves the participation of stakeholders who determine equitable resource allocation and the sharing of economic benefits and monitoring within set objectives in order to ensure the sustainability of vital ecosystems. It is also a process that promotes the coordinated development and management of water, land and related resources in order to maximize the resultant economic and social welfare in an equitable manner without compromising the sustainability of vital ecosystems (GWP, 2000).

Integrated water resources management considers the following:

■ **The hydrological cycle in its entirety:** downstream and upstream interests are taken into account (basin-wide, also across national borders), as well as surface and groundwater sources and, most importantly, rainfall.

Table 5.1: Estimated value of selected wetlands in Africa and Asia

Location	Value in million US $/ha/year	Services	Source
Bangladesh: Hail Haor	649	Crops, fisheries, plants, flood control, recreation, transportation, water quality and supplies, existence values	Colavito, 2002
Cambodia: Koh Kong Province mangroves	2 32	Carbon sequestration Storm protection	Bann, 1997
Cambodia: Ream National Park	59	Crops, fishing, plant use, hunting	Emerton et al., 2002
Cameroon: Waza Logone floodplain	3,000	Plant resources, grazing, crops, water supplies, fisheries	IUCN, 2001
Fiji: mangroves	158 5,820	Forestry, fisheries, crops Water purification	Lal, 1990
India: Bhoj urban wetland	1,206	Water quality and supplies, resource use, amenity and recreational values, crop cultivation	Verma, 2001
Indonesia: mangroves	86	Forest products and fisheries	Burbridge and Maragos, 1985
Japan: Kushiro National Park	1,400	Recreational and amenity values	Kuriyama, 1998
Kenya: Lake Nakuru National Park	400–800	Recreational value of wildlife viewing	Navrud and Mungatana, 1994
Republic of Korea: coastal wetlands	22,000	Fishery production and habitat, waste treatment, aesthetic functions	Lee, 1998
Malawi: Lower Shire wetlands	123	Plant resources, hunting, crops, grazing	Turpie et al., 1999
Malaysia: mangroves	35	Forest products	Hamilton et al., 1989
Mozambique: Zambezi Delta coastal wetlands	9	Plant resources, hunting, crops, grazing	Turpie et al., 1999
Namibia: Chobe-Caprivi wetlands	22	Plant resources, hunting, crops, grazing	Turpie et al., 1999
Nigeria: Hadejia-Nguru floodplain	2	Doum palm utilization, firewood, potash, agriculture	Eaton and Sarch, 1997
Nigeria: Hadejia-Nguru floodplain	20	Groundwater recharge for domestic consumption	Acharya, 1998
Philippines: Pagbilao mangroves	211	Forestry and fisheries	Janssen and Padilla, 1996
Sri Lanka: Muthurajawela urban marsh	2,600	Water supplies, wastewater treatment, flood attenuation, support to downstream fisheries	Emerton and Kekulandala, 2002
Thailand mangroves	165	Coastline protection	Christensen, 1982
Thailand: Surat Thani mangroves	77	Coastline protection	Sathirathai, 1998
Uganda: Nakivubo urban wetland	2,155	Wastewater treatment	Emerton et al., 1999
Uganda: Pallisa District wetlands	485	Crops, grazing, fisheries, plant use, sand and clay, maintenance of soil fertility, water supplies and quality	Karanja et al., 2001
Zambia: Barotse floodplain	16	Plant resources, hunting, crops, grazing	Turpie et al., 1999

Below: Las Huertas, Mexico

Bottom: Anawilundawa, Sri Lanka

labourers. In the Lake Chad Basin, for example, fish provide a source of income that is reinvested in farming (Béné et al., 2003).

Much of the increase in fisheries production is the result of enhancement efforts such as fish stocking and the introduction of non-native fish species in lakes and rivers (Kura et al., 2004), although the latter can in turn create environmental problems as discussed below. In 2001, aquaculture produced 37.9 million tonnes of fishery products, or nearly 40 percent of the world's total fish consumption, valued at US $55.7 billion (FAO, 2002). Aquaculture is the fastest-growing food production sector in the world, with freshwater finfish alone accounting for over 50 percent of global production. Asia, especially China, dominates inland fishery production. China produced close to 15 million tonnes of fish (about one-quarter of the world's total catch) in 2001, mostly carp for domestic consumption. Other leading inland aquaculture-producing countries include Bangladesh, Cambodia, Egypt, India, Indonesia, Myanmar, Tanzania, Thailand and Uganda (Kura et al., 2004).

Inland fishing is almost entirely dominated by small-scale and subsistence operations. In China alone, more than 80 percent of the 12 million reported fishermen are engaged in inland capture fishing and aquaculture (Miao and Yuan, 2001). In the Lower Mekong River Basin, which covers part of Cambodia, Laos, Thailand and Viet Nam, a recent study estimated that 40 million rural farmers are also engaged in fishing, at least seasonally (Kura et al., 2004). This is also true in Africa. In the major river basins and lakes in West and Central Africa, FAO (2003) estimated that fisheries employ 227,000 fishermen, producing 569,100 tonnes of fish products per year, with a value of US $295.17 million and a potential value of nearly US $750 million (Neiland et al., 2004).

All of these benefits depend on the continuation of healthy, functioning aquatic ecosystems. Unfortunately, many hydrological systems are currently being modified and damaged, resulting in a decline in biodiversity and a consequent loss of many of the services mentioned. It should be noted, furthermore, that information on inland fishery production is notoriously poor, particularly for subsistence fisheries, since catches are often grossly underestimated by national governments (Kura et al., 2004). FAO estimates under-reporting by a factor of three or four (FAO, 1999 and 2001). Despite their key role in providing nutrition to the poorest and most vulnerable members of society, coastal and inland fisheries frequently suffer from poor management, competition from industrial fishing and degradation from land-based activities, such as deforestation, pollution and upstream development (Kura et al., 2004).

Even though inland and coastal harvests continue to increase, maintained mainly by aquaculture expansion, most coastal and freshwater systems are stressed by overfishing, habitat loss and degradation, the introduction and presence of invasive species, pollution, and the disruption of river flows by dams and other diversions (FAO, 1999 and Revenga et al., 2000). This degradation threatens not only the biodiversity of riverine and lacustrine ecosystems, but also the food security and livelihood of millions of people – particularly those of poor rural and coastal communities in the developing world. The following section provides a brief overview of the status of freshwater and coastal ecosystems around the world.

...most coastal and freshwater systems are stressed by overfishing, habitat loss and degradation, the introduction and presence of invasive species, pollution and the disruption of river flows by dams and other diversions...

School of freshwater fish in the State of Mexico, Mexico

No. 6, Phnom Penh, Cambodia, Mekong River Commission.

Thilsted, S. H., Roos, N. and Hassan, N. 1997. The role of small indigenous species in food nutrition security in Bangladesh. Paper presented at the International Consultation on Fisheries Policy Research in Developing Countries, Hirtshals, Denmark, 2–5 June 1997.

Tibbetts, J. 2004. The state of the oceans, Part 2: Delving deeper into the sea's bounty. *Environmental Health Perspectives*, Vol. 112, No. 8, June 2004.

Tischler, W. 1979. *Einführung in die Ökologie*, 2nd edn, Stuttgart and New York, Spektrum Akademischer Verlag (in German).

Turpie, J., Smith, B., Emerton, L. and Barnes, J. 1999. *Economic Valuation of the Zambezi Basin Wetlands*, Harare, Zimbabwe. IUCN-The World Conservation Union, Regional Office for Southern Africa.

Ueno, D., Takahashi, S., Tanaka, H., Subramanian, A. N., Fillmann, G., Nakata, H., Lam, P. K. S., Zheng, J., Muctar, M., Prudente, M., Chung, K. H. and Tanabe, S. 2003. Global pollution monitoring of PCBs and organochlorine pesticides using skipjack tuna as a bioindicator. *Archives of Environmental Contamination and Toxicology*, Vol. 45, pp. 378–89.

Umali, D. L. 1993. Irrigation-induced salinity: A growing problem for development and the environment. World Bank Technical Paper 215, Washington D.C. www.wds.worldbank.org/servlet/WDSContentServer/WDSP/IB/1993/08/01/000009265_3970311124344/Rendered/PDF/multi_page.pdf

Umeå University and WRI (World Resource Institute). 2004. *Fragmentation and Flow Regulation Indicator*. Umeå, Sweden, Umeå University and Washington DC, World Resources Institute.

UN-WWAP (United Nations World Water Assessment Programme). 2003. *Water for People, Water for Life*. World Water Development Report. Paris, UNESCO and London, Berghahn Books.

——. 2000. UN Millennium Development Goals, United Nations, New York. www.un.org/millenniumgoals/

——. 1992. *Report of the United Nations Conference on Environment and Development*. Resolutions Adopted by the Conference. United Nations, A/CONF.151/26/Rev.1 Vol. 1, pp. 275–314.

UNEP (United Nations Environment Programme). 2006. Marine and Coastal Ecosystems and Human Wellbeing: A Synthesis Report Based on the Findings of the Millennium Ecosystem Assessment. UNEP.

——. 2005. Assessing Coastal Vulnerability: Developing a Global Index for Measuring Risk. Nairobi, Kenya. DEWA. UNEP.

——. 2004a. *Lake Chad: Sustainable Use of Land and Water in the Sahel*. Environmental Change Analysis Series. DEWA, UNEP. Nairobi, Kenya.

——. 2004b. *GEO Yearbook 2003*. London, Earthscan Publications Ltd.

——. 2004c. Fortnam, M. P. and Oguntula, J. A. (eds), *Lake Chad Basin, GIWA regional assessment 43*. Kalmar, Sweden, University of Kalmar.

——. 2002a. *Atlas of International Freshwater Agreements*, Stevenage, England, Earthprint.

——. 2002b. *Global Environment Outlook 3: Past, present and future perspectives*. London, Earthscan Publications Ltd.

——. 2002c. *Vital Water Graphics: An Overview of the State of the World's Fresh and Marine Waters*. Nairobi, Kenya, UNEP.

UNEP/GPA (United Nations Environmental Programme/Global Programme for Action for the Protection of the Marine Environment from Land-based Activities). 2004. *Water Supply and Sanitation Coverage in UNEP Regional Seas. Need for Regional Wastewater Emission Targets (WET)*. Section III: An inventory of regional specific data and the feasibility of developing regional wastewater emission targets (WET). The Hague, the Netherlands, UNEP/GPA.

UNESCO (United Nations Educational, Scientific, and Cultural Organisation). 2000. *Water Related Vision for the Aral Sea Basin for the Year 2025*. Paris, France, UNESCO.

Verma, M. 2001. Economic valuation of Bhoj wetland for sustainable use. Report prepared for India: Environmental Management Capacity Building Technical Assistance Project, Bhopal, Indian Institute of Forest Management.

Verschurem, D., Johnson, T. C., Kling, H. J., Edgington, D. N., Leavitt, P. R., Brown, E. T., Talbot, M. R. and Hecky, R. E. 2002. History and timing of human impact on Lake Victoria, East Africa. *Proceedings of the Royal Society of London B*. Vol. 269, pp. 289–94.

Watson, B., Walker, N., Hodges, L. and Worden, A. 1996. Effectiveness of peripheral level of detail degradation when used with head-mounted displays. Technical Report 96–04, Graphics, Visualization & Usability (GVU) Center, Georgia Institute of Technology.

Welcomme, R. L. 1979. *Fisheries Ecology of Floodplain Rivers*. London, Longman.

——. 2005. Annual History of Ramsar Site Designations. www.wetlands.org/RDB/global/Designations.html and www.wetlands.org/RDB/global/AreaTrend.html

Wilson, B. A., Smith, V. H., Denoyelles, F. Jr., and Larive, C. K. 2003. Effects of three pharmaceutical and personal care products on natural freshwater algal assemblages. *Environmental Science & Technology*, Vol. 37, pp. 1713–9.

Wood, S., Sebastian, K., and Scherr, S. 2000. *Pilot Analysis of Global Ecosystems: Agroecosystems Technical Report*. Washington DC: World Resources Institute and International Food Policy Research Institute.

World Commission on Dams (WCD). 2000 *Dams and development : A new framework for decision-making*, Earthscan Publ., London, UK.

World Lake Vision Committee. 2003. *World Lake Vision: A Call to Action*. World Lake Vision Committee (International Lake Environment Committee, International Environment Technology Centre, United Nations Environment Programme and Shiga, Japan Prefectural Government).

WMO (World Meteorological Organization). 1997. *Comprehensive Assessment of the Freshwater Resources of the World*. UN, UNDP, UNEP, FAO, UNESCO, WMO, UNIDO, World Bank, SEI. WMO, Geneva, Switzerland.

——. 1992. *Dublin Statement and Report of the Conference*. International Conference on Water and the Environment: Development Issues for the 21st Century. Geneva, Switzerland, WMO.

WRI (World Resources Institute), UNDP (United Nations Development Programme), UNEP (United Nations Environment Programme) and World Bank. 2000. *World Resources 2000–2001: People and ecosystems: The fraying web of life*. Washington DC, WRI.

WWF (World Wide Fund for Nature). 2003. *Managing Rivers Wisely: Kafue Flats Case study, Mozambique*. www.panda.org/downloads/freshwater/mrwkafueflatscasestudy.pdf

WWF and WRI (World Resources Institute). 2004. *Rivers at Risk: Dams and the Future of Freshwater Ecosystems*. www.panda.org/downloads/freshwater/riversatriskfullreport.pdf

WWF/IUCN (Global Conservation Organization/World Conservation Union). 2001. *The Status of Natural Resources on the High Seas*. Gland, Switzerland

Zhulidov, A. V., Robarts, R. D., Headley, J. V., Liber, K., Zhulidov, D. A., Zhulidova, O. V. and Pavlov, D. F. 2002. Levels of DDT and hexachlorocyclohexane in burbot (*Lota lota*) from Russian Arctic rivers. *The Science of the Total Environment*, Vol. 292, pp. 231–46.

Zöckler, C. 2002. A comparison between tundra and wet grassland breeding waders with special reference to the ruff (*Philomachus pugnax*). *Schriftenreihe Landschaftspflege und Naturschutz*, Vol. 74.

FEWS (Famine Early Warning Systems Network). 2003. www.fews.net

Ramsar 2005. www.ramsar.org

Regional Ecosystem Office. 2005. Definitions N-Z. www.reo.gov/general/definitions_n-z.htm#R

UNEP-GEMS Water (Global Environment Monitoring System). 2004. www.gemswater.org

Wetlands International. 2005. Annual History of Ramsar Site Designations.
www.wetlands.org/RDB/global/Designations.html and www.wetlands.org/RDB/global/AreaTrend.html

World Lakes Organisation: www.worldlakes.org/

SECTION 3

Challenges for Well-being and Development

The provision of adequate drinking water is just one aspect of the role played by water in meeting basic needs and contributing to development. Having enough water to cover domestic hygiene needs promotes better health and well-being. Sanitation facilities help to ensure the safe disposal of human waste and reduce disease and death. Adequate water supplies improve the prospects of new livelihood activities, including agriculture, that are otherwise denied and which are often a key step out of poverty. Industry at all scales needs reliable water resources to prosper and grow. Water also plays a key role in energy generation and transportation.

We must examine the current conditions of and the different demands being placed on water for food, human health, industry and energy, as increased competition will demand integrated responses in order to ensure that there is enough water of adequate quality to meet each of these needs in a sustainable manner.

Global Map 5: *Domestic and Industrial Water Use*
Global Map 6: *Sediment Trapping by Large Dams and Reservoirs*

Chapter 6 – **Protecting and Promoting Human Health**
(WHO & UNICEF)

This chapter reviews the main components of the water cycle and provides an overview of the geographical distribution of the world's total water resources, their variability, the impacts of climate change and the challenges associated with assessing the resource.

Chapter 7 – **Water for Food, Agriculture and Rural Livelihoods**
(FAO & IFAD)

The demand for food is not negotiable. As the largest consumer of freshwater, the agriculture sector faces a critical challenge: producing more food of better quality while using less water per unit of output, and reducing its negative impacts on the complex aquatic ecosystems on which our survival depends. Better water management leads to more stable production and increased productivity, which in turn enhance the livelihoods and reduce the vulnerability of rural populations. This chapter examines the challenges of feeding a growing population and balancing its water needs with other uses, while contributing to sustainable development in rural areas.

Chapter 8 – **Water and Industry**
(UNIDO)

Despite industry's need for clean water, industrial pollution is damaging and destroying freshwater ecosystems in many areas, compromising water security for both individual consumers and industries. This chapter focuses on industry's impact on the water environment in routine water withdrawal and wastewater discharge, analysing a broad range of regulatory instruments and voluntary initiatives that could improve water productivity, industrial profitability and environmental protection.

Chapter 9 – **Water and Energy**
(UNIDO)

To be sustainable, economic development needs an adequate and steady supply of energy. Today's changing contexts require the consideration of a range of strategies to incorporate hydropower generation and other renewable forms of energy production to improve energy security while minimizing climate-changing emissions. This chapter stresses the need for the cooperative management of the energy and water sectors to ensure sustainable and sufficient supply of both energy and water.

By means of water we give life to everything

The Koran, Book of The Prophets 21:30

CHAPTER 6

Protecting and Promoting Human Health

By

WHO
(World Health Organization)

UNICEF
(United Nations Children's Fund)

In many parts of Africa the population faces intense year-round malaria transmission, resulting in a high disease burden, especially among children...

near dam sites, and provided evidence of the impact of water resources development on these diseases in different WHO sub-regions (Erlanger et al, 2005; Keiser et al., 2005a,b; Steinman et al., in press). The low level of association between water resources development and malaria and schistosomiasis in sub-Saharan Africa, where the estimated burden of these two diseases is highest, reflects the limited level of development of this continent's water resources potential rather than a lack of association (see **Chapter 14**). The at-risk population for Japanese encephalitis in rice irrigation schemes is highest in South Asia. While only 5.9 percent of the global population at risk of schistosomiasis lives in the western Pacific region (mainly China and the Philippines), relatively substantial parts of the population at risk living in irrigated areas or near dams (14.4 percent and 23.8 percent, respectively) are found in that region (see **Table 6.6**).

Malaria

Malaria remains one of the most important public health problems at a global level, causing illness in more than 300 million people each year. Its share of the global burden of disease has increased over the past few years and now stands at 46.5 million DALYs, 3.1 percent of the world's total. This is an increase of 23 percent, compared with the year 1990. Mortality increased by 27 percent from 926,000 in 1990 to 1,272,000 in 2002. The majority of the burden of malaria is concentrated in sub-Saharan Africa. In many parts of Africa the population

faces intense year-round malaria transmission, resulting in a high disease burden, especially among children below 5 years of age and pregnant women. In all malaria-endemic countries in Africa, on average 30 percent of all out-patient clinic visits are for malaria (WHO/UNICEF, 2003). In these same countries, between 20 percent and 50 percent of all hospital admissions are malaria-related. International efforts to reduce the malaria burden are coordinated by the WHO-led Roll Back Malaria (RBM) initiative, which was launched in 1998. The main strategy is to promote prompt diagnosis and treatment, and the use of insecticide-treated nets (ITNs).

Malaria control is hampered by a number of constraints. Vector mosquitoes are becoming increasingly resistant to insecticides and malaria parasites to inexpensive drugs. Climate and environmental change, population movements and behavioural change have helped malaria gain new grounds in many parts of the developing world. The difficulties in achieving a high coverage of ITNs among the vulnerable groups are a major issue, especially in Africa. In addition, operational constraints limit effective re-impregnation of ITNs. Most importantly, the countries facing severe malaria problems have an underdeveloped health care sector that is limited in its potential to implement the established strategies, particularly those related to ensuring early diagnosis and treatment, disease monitoring and community involvement in control activities.

Table 6.6: Global estimates of people at risk of four vector-borne diseases

Estimated numbers of	Malaria (million)	Lymphatic filariasis (million)	Japanese encephalitis (million)	Schistosomiasis (million)
People at risk globally	>2,000	>2,000	1,900	779
People at risk near irrigation schemes, globally	851.3	213	180–220	63
People at risk near dams, globally	18.3	n.a.	n.a.	42
People at risk in urban settings (no access to improved sanitation		395	n.a.	
People at risk near dams and irrigation schemes, sub-Saharan Africa	9.4	n.a.	n.a.	39
People at risk near dams and irrigation schemes, excluding sub-Saharan Africa	860.3	n.a.	n.a.	66
People at risk near dams and irrigation schemes, Western Pacific	n.a.*	n.a.	n.a.	40
People at risk near irrigation schemes, South East Asia and Western Pacific	n.a.*	n.a.	132 (in irrigated areas) 167 (in rice irrigated areas) } SE Asia 921 (in irrigated areas) 36 (in rice irrigated areas) } W. Pacific	

*Not segregated to this level.

Sources: Erlanger et al., 2005; Keiser et al., 2005a,b; Steinman et al., in press; www.who.int/water_sanitation_health/resources/envmanagement/en/index.html

Water management for malaria control

Water resources development projects, especially irrigation systems, can provide the ecological conditions suited to the propagation of malaria vectors. The relationship between malaria and water resources development is, however, highly situation-specific, depending on the ecology, biology and efficiency of local vectors, people's behaviour and climate. The opportunities for malaria vector breeding are often associated with faulty irrigation design, maintenance or water management practices. The case of irrigation-related malaria in the Thar Desert is described in **Box 6.1**.

In Africa, but also in parts of Asia, several empirical studies have shown the counter-intuitive result of no intensification of malaria transmission in association with irrigation development and increased mosquito vector densities; socio-economic, behavioural and vector ecological factors may all play a role in this phenomenon, dubbed the 'paddy paradox' (Ijumba and Lindsay, 2001; Klinkenberg et al., 2004). Studies in West Africa on rice irrigation and farmers' health showed that irrigation altered the transmission pattern but did not increase the burden of malaria (Sissoko et al., 2004). It was also documented that irrigated rice cultivation attracted young families, improved women's income and positively affected treatment-seeking behaviour by shortening the delay between disease and initiation of treatment.[9]

Globally, it is estimated that only 18.9 million people (most of whom are in India) live close enough to large dams to be at risk of malaria transmitted by mosquitoes associated with man-made reservoirs (Keiser et al., 2005a). The population living close to irrigation sites in malaria endemic areas is much larger and has been estimated at 851.5 million (see **Chapters 7 and 8**). However, in Africa, where the main burden of malaria rests, only 9.4 million people live near large dams and irrigation schemes. Hardly any information is available on the impact of small dams, of which there are many hundreds of thousands in malaria endemic areas in Africa and elsewhere. Cumulatively, these could well be more important for malaria transmission than large dams and irrigation schemes. The potential for the further expansion of small dams is considerable, particularly in sub-Saharan Africa. There is therefore a pressing need for strategic health impact assessment as part of the planning of small dams that should encompass a broad approach towards health, including issues of equity and well-being (Keiser et al., 2005a).

The role of the aquatic environment as an essential condition for malaria transmission was recognized long ago. Environmental management methods were used for malaria control, especially in Asia, Central America and the Caribbean, Europe and the US (Konradsen et al., 2004; Keiser and Utzinger, 2005). A lack of scientific evidence of effectiveness, uncertainty about the present-day feasibility of implementation and remaining vertical vector-control structures prevent environmental management methods from playing a more important role in present-day malaria control. The joint World Health Organization (WHO), Food and Agriculture Organization (FAO), United Nations Environment Programme (UNEP) Panel of Experts on Environmental Management for Vector Control (PEEM) has played a central role in research and capacity-building in this field since the early 1980s. Recently, international research initiatives have focused on possibilities for reducing malaria as part of an ecosystem approach to human health, by looking at the relationship between all components of an ecosystem in order to define and assess priority problems that affect the health and livelihood of people and environmental sustainability.[10]

The Consultative Group on International Agricultural Research's (CGIAR) Systemwide Initiative on Malaria and Agriculture (SIMA) looks at the interaction of people with land, water and crops as they farm existing agricultural areas or develop new areas for farming. This is expected to lead to the identification of specific environmental management measures for the reduction of the disease transmission potential. In the absence of an effective vaccine, treatment of patients and promotion of insecticide-treated nets will remain the main evidence-based strategies for malaria control. But even in the African context, vector control (largely by indoor house-spraying with residual insecticides) and proper management of the environment is increasingly recognized as an indispensable part of malaria control (see the recent work done in Sri Lanka discussed in **Box 6.3**). In low transmission areas such as in many parts of Asia and in the latitudinal and altitudinal fringes of malaria distribution in Africa, environmental management is re-emerging as an important component of an integrated approach to malaria control. In such areas, it is also important that health impact assessments be part of the planning process of hydraulic infrastructure projects, in order to identify, qualify and possibly quantify adverse health effects at the earliest possible stage and suggest preventive solutions (Lindsay et al., 2004). In rural areas of Africa where mosquito breeding places are diffuse and

Mosquitoes are becoming increasingly resistant to insecticides and malaria parasites to inexpensive drugs

9. See www.warda.cgiar.org/ research/health for more information

10. For more information, go to www.idrc.ca/ecohealth

Map 6.1: Coverage with improved drinking water sources, 2002

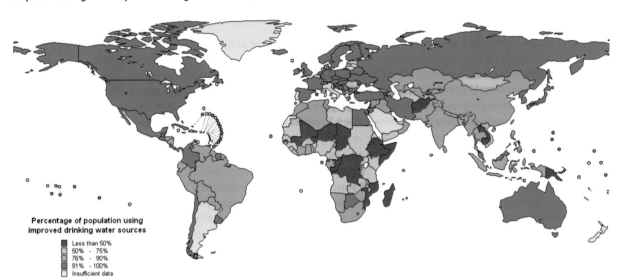

Percentage of population using improved drinking water sources
- Less than 50%
- 50% - 75%
- 76% - 90%
- 91% - 100%
- Insufficient data

Source: WHO/UNICEF, 2004. The boundaries shown on this map do not imply the expression of any opinion whatsoever on the part of the World Health Organization concerning the legal status of any country, territory, city or area or of its·authorities, or concerning the delimitation of its frontiers or boundaries. Dotted lines on maps represent approximate border lines for which there may not yet be full agreement.

A significant part of child mortality rates can be attributed to water-associated diseases

■ *MDG Target 2: Halve, between 1990 and 2015, the proportion of people who suffer from hunger*

One of the two indicators for monitoring progress towards achieving this target is the prevalence of underweight children under 5 years of age.

It is unlikely that the MDG target of reducing 1990-level prevalence of underweight children by 50 percent in the year 2015 can be met, mainly due to the deteriorating situation in Africa (de Onis et al., 2004). Worldwide, the percentage of underweight children has been projected to decline from 26.5 percent in 1990 to 17.6 percent in 2015, a decrease of 34 percent. However, in Africa, the rate was expected to increase from 24 percent to 26.8 percent. In developing countries, stunting has fallen progressively from 47 percent in 1980 to 33 percent in 2000, but with very little, if any, progress in large parts of Africa (de Onis et al., 2000). Estimated trends indicate that overall stunting rates in developing countries will continue to decrease to 16.3 percent in 2020 (de Onis and Blössner, 2003). The great majority of stunted children live in South Asia and sub-Saharan Africa, where only minor improvements are expected.

■ *MDG Target 5: Reduce by two-thirds, between 1990 and 2015, the under-5 mortality rate*

Progress in reducing child mortality is low. No country in sub-Saharan Africa is making enough progress to reach this target. The developing world only achieved a 2.5 percent average annual decrease during the 1990s, well short of the target of 4.2 percent (UNDP, 2003). A significant part of this mortality rate can be attributed to water-associated diseases.

■ *MDG Target 8: Have halted by 2015 and begun to reverse the incidence of malaria and other major diseases*

Throughout sub-Saharan Africa, the decrease in under-5 mortality from all combined causes, apparent during the 1970s and 1980s, levelled off in the 1990s, perhaps partially as a result of increased malaria mortality (WHO/UNICEF, 2003).

Map 6.2: Coverage with improved sanitation, 2002

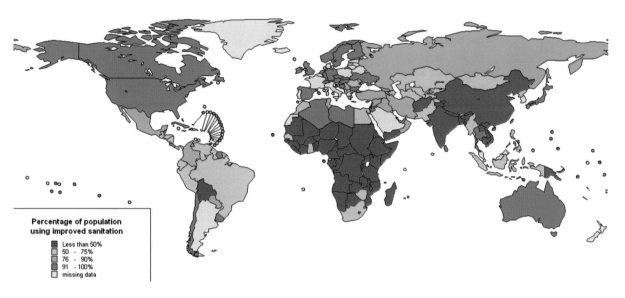

Percentage of population using improved sanitation

Less than 50%
50 - 75%
76 - 90%
91 - 100%
missing data

Source: WHO/UNICEF, 2004. The boundaries shown on this map do not imply the expression of any opinion whatsoever on the part of the World Health Organization concerning the legal status of any country, territory, city or area or of its authorities, or concerning the delimitation of its frontiers or boundaries. Dotted lines on maps represent approximate border lines for which there may not yet be full agreement.

Section 3: CHALLENGES FOR WELL-BEING & DEVELOPMENT

Part 4. Indicators

Good indicators must fulfil a number of criteria. They must have a scientific evidence base, be policy-relevant, make it possible to monitor progress towards internationally agreed targets (such as the targets of the MDGs), and reliable data necessary to compute the indicator values should be available in the public domain. Several indicators relevant to water and health are well-defined, well-established and backed by databases with global coverage that are updated at least on an annual basis. Examples include access to safe drinking water and adequate sanitation, under the WHO/UNICEF Joint Monitoring Programme (JMP); global burden of specific diseases, expressed in deaths and DALYs (WHO's *World Health Reports*); child mortality (UNICEF); and nutritional status (WHO Global Database on Child Growth and Malnutrition).

4a. Burden of water-related diseases

Databases on the number of deaths and DALYs by cause (disease), age, gender and region are maintained by WHO.[14] The major water-related diseases and hazards whose mortality rate and burden can be monitored in this way include diarrhoea, malaria, schistosomiasis, lymphatic filariasis, onchocerciasis, dengue, Japanese encephalitis, trachoma, intestinal helminth infections (separate for *Ascaris*, *Trichuris* and hookworm), and drowning. Some water-related diseases of interest are separately accounted for or not included, notably cholera, typhoid fever and Guinea worm disease. For these diseases, and for selected other diseases like diarrhoea and malaria as well, it is still useful to report the direct measures of disease frequency (incidence or prevalence) when data are available. Changing epidemiological patterns, with important implications for planning appropriate cost-effective interventions, make it preferable to segregate reported diarrhoea figures for watery diarrhoea, persistent diarrhoea and dysentery.

In the context of ongoing mass treatment campaigns, increasing numbers of baseline prevalence data will be generated for intestinal helminth infections. Such mass treatment campaigns will result in immediate prevalence

reductions. Over longer periods of time, the prevalence of intestinal helminth infections can be an important indicator for monitoring the impact of improvements in sanitation, so long as it is possible to control for other confounding factors, especially treatment. Spatial differences in prevalences following extended periods of mass treatment will indicate particular environmental risk factors linked to sanitation conditions and specific behaviours.

4b. Access to improved drinking water and sanitation: Standards and definitions

The question of what exactly constitutes access to safe drinking water and basic sanitation has been a topic of debate in recent years. Since the publication of the 2000 coverage estimates for access to improved facilities, produced by WHO, UNICEF and their Joint Monitoring Programme (WHO/UNICEF, 2000), in which definitions based on an expert consensus are presented, several publications have attempted to provide alternative definitions (see UN Millennium Project, 2004b).

JMP, responsible for monitoring progress towards the MDG targets, has used proxy indicators to estimate the number of people with and without access to safe

Table 6.7: Classification of improved and unimproved drinking water sources

Improved sources of drinking water	Unimproved sources of drinking water
Piped water (into dwelling, yard or plot)	Unprotected dug well
Public tap/standpipe	Unprotected spring
Tubwell/borehole	Vendor-provided water
Protected dug well	Tanker truck water
Protected spring	Surface water (river, stream, dam, lake, pond, canal, irrigation channel)
Rainwater collection	
Bottled water*	

*Bottled water is considered an 'improved' source of drinking water only where there is a secondary source that is 'improved'.

Source: WHO/UNICEF, 2005; www.wssinfo.org

14. See www.who.int/evidence/bod for more information.

Table 6.8: Classification of improved and unimproved sanitation facilities

Improved sanitation facilities	Unimproved sanitation facilities
Flush/pour flush to: piped sewer system septic tank pit (latrine)	Public or shared latrine
Ventilated Improved pit latrine	Pit latrine without slab or open pit
Pit latrine with slab	Hanging toilet/hanging latrine
Composting toilet	Bucket latrine
	No facilities (so people use any area, for example, a field)

Source: WHO/UNICEF, 2005; www.wssinfo.org

drinking water and basic sanitation. These are the official indicators for monitoring the MDG targets; these proxy indicators for access are defined as the type of facility that people use to obtain their drinking water and meet their sanitation needs. JMP categorized these facilities as 'improved' or 'unimproved' (**Tables 6.7** and **6.8**). People relying on an improved source as their main source of drinking water are counted as having access to safe drinking water, while those using an improved sanitation facility are counted as having access to sanitation.

Specifically, the JMP definition for monitoring the proportion of the population with access to an improved drinking water source is as follows:

> An improved drinking water source is more likely to provide safe drinking water than a not-improved drinking water source, by nature of its construction, which protects the water source from external contamination particularly with faecal matter.

The JMP definition for monitoring the proportion of the population with access to basic sanitation is expressed in terms of the proportion of a population that uses an improved sanitation facility, defined as a facility that hygienically separates excreta from human contact.

Rather than providing an all-inclusive definition of what constitutes access to safe drinking water and basic sanitation, the categorization into improved and unimproved facilities was a necessary step to make the available data comparable between countries and within countries over time. This allows JMP to monitor progress, using the best available nationally representative population-based data obtained from household surveys (see **Box 6.7**). **Chapter 3** gives more details on the accuracy of local surveys compared to national censuses in urban areas.

JMP estimates do not always reflect whether or not an improved source provides drinking water of an acceptable quality; nor do they take into account accessibility of the drinking water source (in terms of the distance or time) or the affordability of drinking water. Issues of intermittence, reliability or seasonality are not reflected either. For access to basic sanitation, JMP monitors the number of people using different types of sanitation facilities, not taking into account whether or not they provide privacy and dignity or whether or not they are used by all household members at all times. Nor does the outcome of the monitoring process reflect the actual level of hygiene or cleanliness of the facility. This type of information is generally not collected at national level.

Nonetheless, using the categorization 'improved/unimproved', JMP has a yardstick for measuring progress and change over time. It allows a reasonably accurate estimate of the number of people without access to any type of improved facility: the have-nots on which the MDGs focus.

However, access to safe drinking water and sanitation needs to be better defined. Howard and Bartram (2003) propose four access categories (see **Table 6.9**), based on the relationship between accessibility expressed in time or distance and the likely quantities of water collected or used. The four categories are: no access, basic access, intermediate access and optimal access. Global access, as monitored by JMP, corresponds to the level of basic access.

The definitions applied by WHO and UNICEF constitute a pragmatic approach to a complex global monitoring need and ensure consistency, replicability and a focus on those without access.

Over the years, a number of comprehensive definitions of access have been formulated. Such definitions and the accompanying standards may serve in the planning or design of new drinking water and sanitation services. The related indicators are specific, objective and measurable on an individual, setting-specific basis. However, when

Over longer periods of time, the prevalence of intestinal helminth infections can be an important indicator for monitoring the impact of improvements in sanitation...

Women and children collecting water for domestic use from a public water fountain, India

BOX 6.7: USER-BASED VERSUS PROVIDER-BASED DATA

Since 2000, JMP coverage estimates have been based on user data derived from nationally representative household surveys and national censuses. This marks an important shift away from the approach of using data originating from governments in the 1990s, which became possible after the introduction of the five-yearly Multiple Cluster Indicator Surveys (MICS) by UNICEF in sixty-four countries in 1995. Together with results of the Demographic and Health Surveys (DHS), or data from national censuses and other sources, including WHO's Water, Sanitation and Health Programme, this provides a large enough knowledge base to calculate coverage estimates supported by evidence-based datasets.

Why are data derived from household surveys better than those provided by governments or water utilities? The latter suffer from variations in the interpretation of what constitutes access. This complicates comparability between countries and even within a country over time. Often only those facilities that are constructed under government programmes or by water utility companies are counted. Facilities constructed by households, NGOs or the private sector may be partially or totally excluded. Water providers are inclined to report progressively on the number of facilities constructed and do not take into account facilities that are not used or that have fallen into disrepair. Household surveys, on the contrary, record, at a given point in time, the facilities people actually use – broken facilities are not counted.

Informal settlements and slums, even those that are home to hundreds of thousands of people, frequently do not appear in official government statistics because of questions of tenure or land ownership. In general, access to such areas tends to be poor and when not counted, a significant over-reporting of coverage will result. Household surveys usually do survey peri-urban areas when they fall into one of the selected sampling clusters, thus providing a better picture of the actual situation (see also **Chapter 3**). Household surveys including national censuses together provide the most reliable, nationally representative, comparable data, and they are available for almost every country in the world.

Source: www.wssinfo.org

---

used as a benchmark to assess globally whether or not existing services meet the required standards, the feasibility of measuring such indicators declines sharply and becomes a bottleneck for the frequent monitoring of progress and trends.

An example is provided by the lack of agreement on what exactly constitutes domestic and personal hygiene. The debate is centred around activities like bathing and clothes washing. Such activities usually require amounts of water equal to or larger than the amount used for all other basic personal and domestic water needs combined. In rural areas, bathing and clothes washing often takes place at the source or water point or in rivers or streams. In urban slum areas or during emergency situations, this might not be possible or desirable due to limited water availability, privacy concerns or public health concerns of contaminating the water source. Howard and Bartram (2003) argue that an improved source should provide adequate quantities for bathing and clothes washing as well, but recognize that the quantity per person required corresponds to the level of intermediate access and not to the level of basic access. It should be recalled that basic access is the current global standard for access. Drinking water for domestic and personal hygiene therefore does not necessarily include the use for extensive bathing and clothes washing.

4c. Water quality

The three principal international guidelines on water quality of relevance to human health are as follows:[15]

- *Guidelines for Drinking-Water Quality*

- *Guidelines for the Safe Use of Wastewater, Excreta and Greywater*[16]

- *Guidelines for Safe Recreational Water Environments.*

These guidelines are addressed primarily to water and health regulators, policy-makers and their advisors, to assist in the development of national standards. For a long time, in the absence of good epidemiological studies, guidelines and standards for water-related hazards were based on the technical feasibility of providing treatment and took a 'no or very low' risk approach. However, setting targets that are too high can be counter-productive: they may be ignored if they are not attainable. National standards should therefore reflect national conditions, priorities and capacities to improve water supplies. All the recently developed guidelines are based on risk-assessment methods. This considers the risk for disease, not just the presence or absence of pathogens or chemicals in the water.

15. All of these guidelines are available online at www.who.int/water_ sanitation_health/norms/

16. In four volumes: (1) Policy and regulatory aspects; (2) Wastewater use in agriculture; (3) Wastewater and excreta use in aquaculture; (4) Excreta and greywater use in agriculture. All of these are available at www.who.int/ water_sanitation_health/ norms/

Table 6.9: Requirements for water service levels and health implications

Service level	Access measure (distance or time)	Needs met	Level of health concern
No access – quantity collected often below 5 litres (L) per capita per day	More than 1,000 metres (m) or 30 minutes total collection time	Consumption cannot be assured Hygiene not possible (unless practised at the source)	Very high
Basic access – average quantity unlikely to exceed 20 L per capita per day	Between 100 and 1,000 m or 5 to 30 minutes total collection time	Consumption should be assured Handwashing and basic food hygiene possible; laundry and bathing difficult to assure unless carried out at source	High
Intermediate access – average quantity about 50 L per capita per day	Water delivered through one tap on plot or within 100 m or 5 minutes total collection time	Consumption assured All basic personal and food hygiene assured; laundry and bathing should also be assured	Low
Optimal access – average quantity 100 L per capita per day	Water supplied through multiple taps continuously	Consumption: all needs met Hygiene: all needs should be met	Very low

Source: Howard and Bartram, 2003.

...there is increasing recognition that a few key chemicals, notably fluoride and arsenic, cause large-scale health effects

Drinking water quality

An important recent event was the publication of the third edition of the *Guidelines for Drinking Water Quality* (WHO, 2004b). These guidelines are widely accepted in industrialized and developing countries. Recent developments in microbial risk assessment and its linkages to risk management are taken into account. Increased attention is paid to effective preventative management through a 'framework for drinking water safety', including 'water safety plans' (see **Box 6.8**). The guidelines pay attention to the adequacy of supply, which is not only determined by water quality but also by water quantity, accessibility, affordability and continuity. The importance of water quality at the point of use (within the house) is emphasized, while previously, quality guidelines tended to refer only to the source of the drinking water.

There is agreement that the best available indicator of faecal pollution of individual drinking water sources is *Escherichia coli* (or thermo-tolerant coliform bacteria). The presence of *E. coli* provides conclusive evidence of recent faecal pollution, but its absence does not automatically prove that the water is safe. There is certainly a need for additional indicators, especially for protozoa such as *Cryptosporidium parvum*. To date, no water quality standards regarding *Cryptosporidium* oocysts have been established, and the minimum concentration of oocysts in drinking water leading to

clinical illness in healthy individuals has not been conclusively defined.

Drinking water quality guidelines have always included permissible levels of chemical substances. Chemicals in drinking water can be naturally occurring or originate from pollution by agricultural activities (fertilizer, pesticides), human settlements and industrial activities. While the revised WHO guidelines state that microbial hazards continue to be a priority concern in both developed and developing countries, there is increasing recognition that a few key chemicals, notably fluoride and arsenic, cause large-scale health effects. For a risk analysis, information from the catchment on naturally occurring chemicals is essential. If chemicals such as fluoride or arsenic are present in unusually high concentrations in rocks, soil or groundwater, there is an elevated risk for public health. In many countries, the development of appropriate risk management strategies is hampered by a lack of information on the presence and concentrations of chemicals in drinking water and the lack of information on disease cases. In the case of chemical hazards with high measurable disease burden, the target would be to reduce the occurrence of disease cases. If the disease burden is low, it cannot be directly measured by public health surveillance systems, and quantitative risk assessment methods can be applied (see also **Chapter 10**).

BOX 6.8: WATER SAFETY PLANS (WSPs)

To ensure that drinking water is safe, a comprehensive strategy that looks at risks and risk management at all stages in water supply (WHO, 2004b), from catchment to consumer, is needed. In the WHO *Guidelines for Drinking-Water Quality*, such approaches are called water safety plans (WSPs). WSPs have built-in quality control at each step of the process, from source to tap, and represent a paradigm shift in

drinking water management, which previously tended to focus on the detection of contamination that had already taken place. WSP approaches exist for large (piped) supplies and smaller community or household supplies in developed and developing countries. The objectives of WSPs are the minimization of contamination of source waters, the reduction or removal of contamination through treatment

processes and the prevention of contamination during storage, distribution and handling of drinking water. This is achieved by an assessment of the entire drinking-water supply chain, effective operational monitoring, and management plans.

Source: WHO, 2005; Davison et al., 2005.

Wastewater use in agriculture and aquaculture

With the increasing scarcity of freshwater resources available to agriculture, the use of urban wastewater in agriculture will increase, especially in arid and semi-arid regions. Wastewater is often the only reliable source of water for farmers in peri-urban areas, and it is widely used in urban and peri-urban areas, in both treated and untreated forms. A nationwide survey in Pakistan showed that an estimated 25 percent of all vegetables grown in the country are irrigated with untreated urban wastewater and that these vegetables, cultivated close to the urban markets, were considerably cheaper than the vegetables imported from different regions of Pakistan (Ensink et al., 2004). Likewise, 60 percent of the vegetables consumed in Dakar, Senegal are grown with a mixture of groundwater and untreated wastewater within the city limits (Faruqui et al., 2004). In this context, the use of wastewater for peri-urban agriculture provides an opportunity and a resource for livelihood generation.

The major challenge is to optimize the benefits of wastewater as a resource (both the water and the nutrients it contains) and to minimize the negative impacts on human health. There is sufficient epidemiological evidence that infection with intestinal helminths poses the major human health risk associated with the agricultural use of untreated urban wastewater. In those countries where sewage and excreta are used to feed fish, there are important risks for infection with flukes. Foodborne trematode (fluke) infections are a serious and growing public health problem, with an estimated 40 million people affected worldwide. Transmission to humans occurs mostly via consumption of raw freshwater fish and aquatic plants. A recent analysis indicates that residents in endemic areas living

close to freshwater bodies more than double their risk of infection, and it is speculated that the exponential growth of aquaculture is the major contributing factor to this emerging disease trend (Keiser and Utzinger, 2005).

Mitigating health risks while maximizing benefits requires holistic approaches that involve all stakeholders in a process to enhance knowledge sharing, promote realistic measures for hygiene and sanitation improvement, generate income, produce food for better livelihoods and sustain the strengthening of water and sanitation services at household and community levels.

For the protection of public health in this context, WHO has developed updated *Guidelines for the Safe Use of Wastewater, Excreta and Greywater* (WHO, 2006a–d). They define an acceptable and realistic level of public health protection, which can be achieved through a combination of setting microbial water quality targets and implementing health protection measures, such as crop restriction, application techniques and irrigation timing. This approach is flexible and is applicable to both industrialized and less-developed countries. Countries can choose to meet the health target level by wastewater treatment alone, or through a combination of partial wastewater treatment and additional health protection measures.

In adopting wastewater use guidelines for national standards, policy-makers should consider what is feasible and appropriate in the context of their national situation. They should use a risk-benefit approach that carefully weighs the benefits to household food security, nutrition and local economic development against possible negative health impacts. The revised guidelines call for a progressive implementation of measures and incremental improvements in the public health situation.

4d. Child mortality

Children under the age of 5 are the most affected by poor water supply and sanitation. Diarrhoea is one of the directly preventable causes of under-5 mortality. Child mortality is the result of a complex web of determinants at many levels. The fundamental determinant is poverty, and an underlying determinant is under-nutrition. The under-5 mortality rate has become a key indicator of health and social development. It can be seen as a cross-cutting indicator for several of the challenge areas and for achieving the MDG targets.

There is sufficient evidence that improvements in water supply, sanitation and hygiene result in fewer cases of diarrhoea and lower overall child mortality. To obtain the maximum possible reduction in child mortality, these improvements would have to be combined, however, with other preventive interventions (breastfeeding, vitamin A supplementation) and treatment interventions (oral rehydration therapy and zinc) (Jones et al., 2003). This combination of interventions could save more than 1.8 million children under the age of 5 each year, which is 88 percent of the annual under-5 mortality due to diarrhoea.[17]

The infant mortality rate is a less suitable indicator than the under-five mortality rate in the context of water-related diseases, since only a small proportion of deaths in the neonatal period (first twenty-eight days of life) can be attributed to water-related diseases (Black et al., 2003). In the first six months of life, children are, to some extent, protected against diarrhoea (if they are being breastfed) and malaria. It is only towards the end of the first year of life that infectious diseases due to poor water, sanitation and hygiene take their huge toll on children's health.

4e. Nutritional status

Nutritional status is probably the single most informative indicator of the overall health of a population (see also **Chapter 7**). For evaluating the impact of water supply and sanitation interventions, nutritional status is as important and appropriate a measure as the incidence of diarrhoeal disease. Anthropometric measurements are well defined, and are easily and inexpensively performed. Data on childhood under-nutrition are available from the WHO Global Database on Child Growth and Malnutrition,[18] which is based on nationally representative anthropometric surveys. It is a good example of international collaboration in standardizing indicators and data collection systems (de Onis and Blössner, 2003).

One of the indicators for monitoring progress towards the MDG targets is the prevalence of underweight children under 5 years of age. Underweight (low weight-for-age) reflects the effects of acute as well as chronic under-nutrition. Weight-for-age is a composite indicator of height-for-age and weight-for-height, which makes its interpretation difficult. Stunting (low height-for-age) reflects chronic under-nutrition and is an indicator of the cumulative effects of standard of living, women's educational level, access to food, access to water supply and sanitation, and burden of infectious diseases. Stunting is a good indicator to monitor the long-term impact of improvements in water supply, sanitation and hygiene, provided it is possible to correct for confounding variables.

17. Child mortality data are available online from UNICEF at www.childinfo.org/cmr/revis/db2.htm

18. Available online at www.who.int/nutgrowthdb/

Part 5. Comparative Risk Assessment

Most water-related diseases have multiple risk factors. This raises a number of questions: What part of the burden of disease is attributable to inadequate water supply and sanitation? What would be the health gains of improvements in water supply and sanitation? Similar questions may be posed for water management in agriculture: What burden of disease can be attributed to poor water management, and what are the health benefits of improved water management?

To answer these questions, epidemiological measurements are needed that quantify the public health relevance of important risk factors. The population-attributable risk provides a measure of the amount of disease in the whole population, which is attributable to a certain level of exposure (risk to health), assuming that the association between exposure and the disease is one of cause-and-effect. The known attributable risks for a disease often add up to more than 100 percent, because some risk factors act through other more proximal factors, such as under-nutrition. The potential impact fraction expresses the proportion of disease that could be eliminated by reducing exposure. Risk

...estimated benefits of US $3 to 34 per US $1 invested if the water and sanitation MDG targets were achieved...

was found to be an important component in the overall benefits from water and sanitation improvements. When valued in monetary terms, using the minimum wage as a proxy for annual time savings, such savings outweigh the annual costs of the interventions.

The scenario scoring highest in actually reducing the burden of water-related disease to nearly zero is that where universal access to piped water and sewerage connections is provided, with an estimated cost of US $850 to 7,800 per DALY averted (Evans et al., 2004; Rijsberman, 2004). This is above income levels in developing countries. In the scenario that provides for low-cost technologies (standpipes and latrines, as opposed to piped water and sewerage connections to individual homes), the cost would improve to US $280 to 2,600 per DALY averted, if disinfection at the point of use is added.

A further analysis considering disease burden averted, costs to the health services and to individual households reduced, and opportunity costs (attending ill family members, fetching water) avoided arrived at estimated benefits of US $3 to 34 per US $1 invested if the water and sanitation MDG targets were achieved, with, on the whole, benefits from sanitation investments being greater than those from water interventions. In aggregate, the total annual economic benefits of meeting the MDG targets on water supply and sanitation accrue to US $84 billion (Hutton and Haller, 2004). While global estimates for the additional annual investment to meet the MDG water and sanitation targets all arrive at about US $11 billion, meeting the targets translates into 322 million

working days per year gained at a value of US $750 million (SIWI/WHO, 2005).

Based on a study in Burkina Faso, the cost of implementing a large-scale hygiene promotion programme was estimated at US $26.9 per case of diarrhoea averted (Borghi et al., 2002). Cost-effectiveness of a latrine revision programme in Kabul, Afghanistan ranged from US $1,800 to 4,100 per death due to diarrhoea averted, depending on age and payer perspective (Meddings et al., 2004). Fattal et al. (2004) estimated the cost of treating raw sewage used for direct irrigation to meet the WHO 1989 norms for safe irrigation of vegetables eaten raw with untreated wastewater at about US $125 per case of disease prevented.

6b. Water scarcity: Bridging the gaps between the different sectors

While the looming freshwater crisis is getting a lot of attention from water resources policy- and decision-makers, the provision of domestic water to rural populations is often not perceived as a problem in this context. Policy documents on integrated water resources management (IWRM), whether from governments or donor organizations, give first priority to water supply for agricultural production purposes in water allocation decisions; the domestic uses are only a small fraction of the total amount of freshwater utilized in a country. For example, the agriculture sector of the South Asian region receives about 96 percent of the total diversions. Even in sub-Saharan Africa, with a much less developed irrigation infrastructure than Asia, 84 percent of total water diversions is used in agriculture.

BOX 6.10: DOMESTIC USE OF IRRIGATION WATER

Millions of people around the world rely on surface irrigation water for most of their domestic needs. This is especially true of irrigation communities living in areas with low rainfall, under-developed drinking water supply systems, and in regions with low groundwater tables or unusable groundwater, due to high concentrations of salt or hazardous chemicals. In such circumstances, the way in which irrigation water is managed has a tremendous bearing on the health of the populations living in these areas. Unfortunately, irrigation water management is based entirely on crop

requirements and not on domestic water needs. Therefore, when decisions for water allocation are made, domestic uses are rarely taken into account. Also, with the looming freshwater crises, there is increasing pressure on the irrigation sector to make water use in agriculture more efficient. In this process, the non-agricultural uses of irrigation water need to be considered.

Studies in Punjab, Pakistan have documented the links between availability of irrigation water for domestic use and its impact on diarrhoea and the

nutritional status of children. It was concluded that irrigation water management has a clear impact on human health and that bridging the gap between the irrigation and domestic water supply sectors could provide great health benefits by taking into account the domestic water availability when managing irrigation water. In the same study, it was found that using irrigation seepage water as a safe source for domestic supplies was a possible option.

Source: Van der Hoek et al., 2001b; 2002a, b.

The difference between credible high and low estimates of the water globally required for agriculture in 2025 is in the order of 600 cubic kilometres (km^3) – more than is estimated to be required for all domestic uses. This has created a widely prevalent notion that a small diversion from the irrigation sector could fulfil the demands of a growing population for domestic water supply. In reality, this reallocation of water between sectors can be very difficult, and truly integrated water management is constrained by the traditional sectoral thinking and priorities set by professionals in the various disciplines and the existing power structure. The main concern of public health officials and researchers is the increasing deterioration of water quality due to industrial and urban waste, agricultural runoff and insufficient investments in the domestic water supply infrastructure.

This global concern for water quality is, to a large extent, a reflection of the very high quality standards traditionally imposed on drinking water by institutions and professionals in industrialized countries. On the other hand, the managers of water for agricultural production see their responsibilities largely confined to the provision of water in time and space in accordance with the cropping cycle requirements. Few irrigation managers would see it as part of their mandate to supply water for domestic use. To water planners, domestic uses in rural areas concern only a small fraction of the total amount of freshwater utilized and are therefore easily overlooked. This may lead to the situation that high investments have been made to mobilize freshwater into an area, without considering other uses than irrigation.

6c. Multiple uses of water

In many areas, the most readily available surface water is from irrigation canals and reservoirs. It has not been sufficiently recognized that apart from irrigating crops, irrigation water is used for many other purposes, including drinking, cooking, livestock rearing, aquaculture and wildlife. Washing clothes and bathing are probably the most frequently observed domestic uses of irrigation systems throughout the world. When there is a poor supply of domestic water from underground sources, but abundant supply for agricultural production, irrigation water from canals and reservoirs can be the only source of water for domestic use. In a few cases, such uses have been considered in the design of irrigation systems, but as a general rule, designers and engineers have tended to focus exclusively on water use in crop production. On the other hand, providers of domestic water rarely

consider the usage of irrigation water as an option, because the conventional strategy has been to utilize groundwater, not surface water for domestic purposes.

As a result, the non-agricultural household uses of irrigation water have neither been systematically documented, nor have the possibilities they offer been seriously explored. A large gap therefore remains between what happens in irrigation schemes (what people do) and what is taken into account in water resources planning and policies. With increasing focus on improved water use efficiency within irrigation systems, there is a risk that recognized uses of water (crop irrigation) will be prioritized to the detriment of other valuable but non-recognized uses, such as domestic needs (see **Box 6.6** for an example in Sri Lanka). There is a critical need, therefore, to understand the health dimensions of the multiple uses of irrigation water, the determinants of its use, the realistic alternatives, and the consequences of these uses in order to promote informed water policy formulation (see **Box 6.10**).

6d. Falling groundwater levels

The over exploitation of groundwater for agricultural and industrial purposes renders the availability of shallow groundwater for drinking and domestic purposes increasingly problematic. In some of the major breadbaskets of Asia, such as the Punjab in India and the North China Plain, water tables are falling 2 to 3 metres a year. The wealthier farmers can continue to drill deeper tubewells with larger, more expensive pumps, but poor farmers are unable to do so. The problem of falling groundwater levels is now seen by all stakeholders as a threat to food security. What has received less attention is that it also causes the shallow drinking water wells of poor communities to run dry. Deepening these wells is very costly and beyond the resources of the poor. In coastal areas such as the State of Gujarat, India, over-pumping causes salt water to invade freshwater aquifers, making them unsuitable for drinking. Over-pumping has also been linked to the contamination of drinking water with arsenic. Clearly, pumping groundwater has become a key policy issue that can only be dealt with in the context of IWRM.

6e. Poverty Reduction Strategy Papers

One of the main instruments for national governments in their attempts to reduce poverty are the Poverty Reduction Strategy Papers (PRSPs), which give clarity and direction to all the development work in a country. These

The main concern of public health officials and researchers is the increasing deterioration of water quality due to industrial and urban waste...

BOX 6.11: SUCCESSFUL WATER SUPPLY IN PHNOM PENH, CAMBODIA

Cambodia is one of the poorest countries in South-East Asia. It is still recovering from decades of conflict, and all sectors, including the health sector, require reconstruction. The life of most people in Cambodia is still defined by poverty and a very high burden of disease with a government health care system that is ill-equipped to deal with a range of health problems. Access to improved drinking water sources (estimated at 34 percent in 2002) is extremely low, even by developing country standards (WHO/UNICEF, 2004). In the capital, Phnom Penh, the water supply and drainage systems have deteriorated over the years due to war, poor management and lack of maintenance. This problem has been worsened by the rapid growth of the urban population. However, successful rehabilitation projects have taken place with foreign aid and technical assistance. Since 1993, the Phnom Penh Water Supply Authority (PPWSA) has increased its distribution network from serving 40 percent of the Phnom Penh population to over 80 percent. Non-revenue water – the result of leaks, mismeasurement, illegal connections and illegal sales – has been reduced to 22 percent (from 72 percent) and collections are at almost 99 percent with full cost recovery achieved. By mid-2004, it is predicted that the water supply capacity in the city will have increased to 235,000 cubic metres per day. This is now considered a success story for which the PPWSA was awarded the Water Prize of the Asian Development Bank.

Charging for water and the relative roles of public versus private management are controversial issues (see **Chapters 2 and 12**). Phnom Penh provides a rare example of an efficient water-delivery system in a large city run by a public body.

Source: www.adb.org/Documents/News/2004/nr2004012.asp.

are country-owned development strategies demanded by the World Bank and the International Monetary Fund of countries that want to be eligible for loans. Reducing an excessively-high disease burden will have a positive economic impact, and strategies on communicable disease control and child health can be seen as evidence of a pro-poor approach. A review of twenty-one PRSPs found that all of them included strategies on communicable disease control, child health and water and sanitation improvement (WHO, 2004c). However, the emphasis was overwhelmingly on government delivery of health services to reach health goals without examination of the role of non-government providers and other sectors. Furthermore, quantifiable targets were mostly not mentioned, making it difficult to link PRSP indicators with the MDGs. One of the overarching criticisms of the PRSPs from NGO sources has been that participation – the widely proclaimed centrepiece of national ownership of the PRSPs – is poorly implemented (UN Millennium Project, 2004a).

Part 7. Water for Life: Making it Happen

With respect to human health, this second edition of the World Water Development Report consolidates our new and updated insights into the diverse nature and broad scope of conditions where the development, management and use of water resources are associated with community health status. The concept of burden of disease, expressed in Disability-Adjusted Life Years lost, has strengthened its position as a universal indicator of that status with valid applications in economic evaluation as well as development planning. New tools have also become available to better estimate the costs and benefits of different options, particularly for improving access to drinking water and sanitation.

Water taps provided by relief organizations at the Virginia Newport high school in Monrovia, Liberia, where some of the 25,000 internally-displaced people had taken refuge

The basic driving forces of the water–health nexus have not changed in nature and include population expansion, rapid urbanization, globalization and increasing scarcity of good-quality freshwater resources. At the global policy level, the MDGs are exerting an increasingly marked pressure on both thinking about and acting on water-health issues; newly emerging economic realities (particularly the rapid developments in China and India) further modulate these pressures.

Positive and negative trends can be distinguished. The positive trends include:

- Global progress towards achieving the MDG target on drinking water.

- A significant reduction in mortality due to childhood diarrhoea.

- The availability of good indicators for monitoring progress towards achieving health-related MDG targets at the global and regional level.

- A significant evolution in approaches to managing the quality of drinking water, recreational waters and wastewater, from a technical no-risk concept to a comprehensive system of risk assessment and management.

- Greater recognition of health impact assessment as the critical starting point for a functional incorporation of human health considerations, especially into integrated water resources development and management.

Together, these trends will influence and improve the governance of water and health issues in the coming years. Authorities now can apply adaptive management and ensure optimal solutions in local settings. Decision-making will have a stronger evidence base, even though

the indicators used need further development and refinement. An example of this is provided by the new vision on the safe use of wastewater, excreta and greywater in agriculture and aquaculture that assesses and manages health risks and that balances health costs and benefits rather than applying rigid water quality standards. In many parts of the world rigid standard setting has proved to be neither feasible nor enforceable, whereas through water safety plans, through safe household water management and storage or through safe use of wastewater, governments can achieve solid and sustainable progress.

On the downside, the following constraints and bottlenecks can be observed:

- Lack of progress towards achieving the MDG sanitation target left 2.6 billion people without access to improved sanitation at the end of 2002.

- The significant increase in the absolute number of people without access to an improved drinking water source and improved sanitation, in both urban and rural areas, since 1990 as exclusively experienced in sub-Saharan Africa.

- The problematic health situation (with no signs of improvement) in sub-Saharan Africa, as reflected in practically all indicators, and in particular by the increasing malaria burden.

- Lack of progress in the implementation of the IWRM concept specifically, and in the realization of intersectoral action for health in general.

- An inadequate evidence base needed to advocate for increased investment in urban sewage treatment, resulting from a lack of indicators and mechanisms for monitoring the sewerage discharge and the added burden of disease for people downstream.

International Development Research Centre (IDRC Canada) Ecohealth Programme: www.idrc.ca/ecohealth

International Water and Sanitation Centre, the Netherlands: www.irc.nl

International Water Association: www.iwahq.org.uk

International Commission for Irrigation and Drainage: www.icid.org

WHO Collaborating Centres in Water, Sanitation and Health:
  Water Quality and Health Bureau, Health Canada: www.hc-sc.gc.ca/waterquality
  Office national de l'Eau potable (ONEP), Morocco: www.onep.org.ma
  Institute of Environmental Engineering and Research: www.uet.edu.pk/Departments/Environmental/environmental_main.htm
  DBL Institute for Health Research and Development, Denmark: www.dblnet.dk
  DHL Water and Environment Denmark: www.dhi.dk
  Institute for Water, Soil and Air Hygiene, Federal Environment Agency, Germany: www.umweltbundesamt.de
  Institute for Hygiene and Public Health, Bonn, Germany: www.meb.uni-bonn.de/hygiene
  Institute for Water Pollution Control (VITUKI), Hungary: www.vituki.hu
  University of Surrey, School of Engineering: www.surrey.ac.uk/eng
  National Centre for Environmental Toxicology: www.wrcplc.co.uk/asp/business_areas.asp#ncet
  British Geological Survey, Groundwater Systems and Water Quality Programme: www.bgs.ac.uk
  International Water Management Institute, Sri Lanka: www.iwmi.cgiar.org
  Faculty of Tropical Medicine, Mahidol University, Bangkok, Thailand: www.tm.mahidol.ac.th
  Asian Institute of Technology, Urban Environmental Management Programme: www.ait.ac.th
  Queensland Institute for Medical Research, Mosquito Control Laboratory, Australia:
  www.qimr.edu.au/research/labs/briank/index.html
  National Institute of Public Health, Department of Water Supply Engineering, Japan: www.niph.go.jp
  Centre regional pour l'Eau potable et l'Assainissement à faible Coût, Burkina Faso: www.reseaucrepa.org

Future Harvest centres associated with the CGIAR doing research on water management/health
  International Food Policy Research Centre: www.ifpri.org/events/seminars/2005/20050623AgHealth.htm
  Africa Rice Centre (formerly: West African Rice Development Association): www.warda.cgiar.org/research/health
  International Water Management Institute (IWMI): www.iwmi.org

Starvation is the characteristic of some people not having enough food to eat. It is not the characteristic of there being not enough food to eat.

Amartya Sen

CHAPTER 7

Water for Food, Agriculture and Rural Livelihoods

By
FAO
(Food and Agriculture Organization of the United Nations)
IFAD
(International Fund for Agricultural Development)

Rice terraces, China

Key messages:

Above: Farmer ploughing a rice field, Indonesia

Below: Wollo women diverting a stream to irrigate land, Ethiopia

Bottom: Rendille livestock enclosures, Kenya.

Bottom right: Fruit and vegetable market, Jordan

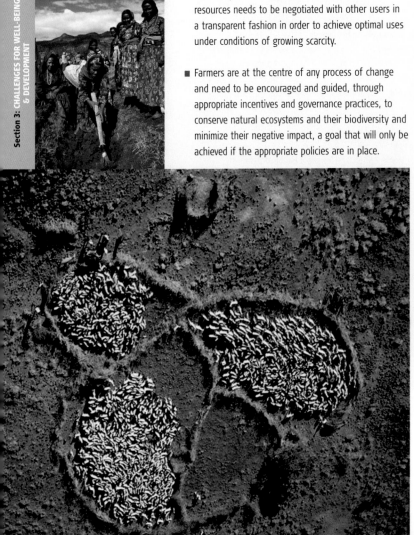

In the context of demographic growth, increased competition for water and improved attention to environmental issues too often left out by agricultural policies, water for food remains a core issue – that can no longer be tackled through a narrow sectoral approach. New forms of water management in agriculture, including irrigation, are to be explored and implemented, in order to focus on livelihoods rather than just on productivity.

■ To satisfy the growing demand for food between 2000 and 2030, production of food crops in developing countries is projected to increase by 67 percent. At the same time, a continuing rise in productivity should make it possible to restrain the increase in water use for agriculture to about 14 percent.

■ As competition for water increases among different sectors, irrigated agriculture needs to be carefully examined to discern where society can benefit most effectively from its application. Access to natural resources needs to be negotiated with other users in a transparent fashion in order to achieve optimal uses under conditions of growing scarcity.

■ Farmers are at the centre of any process of change and need to be encouraged and guided, through appropriate incentives and governance practices, to conserve natural ecosystems and their biodiversity and minimize their negative impact, a goal that will only be achieved if the appropriate policies are in place.

■ Irrigation institutions must respond to the needs of farmers, ensuring more reliable delivery of water, increasing transparency in its management and balancing efficiency and equity in access to water. This will not only require changes in attitudes, but also well targeted investments in infrastructure modernization, institutional restructuring and upgrading of the technical capacities of farmers and water managers.

■ The agriculture sector faces a complex challenge: producing more food of better quality while using less water per unit of output; providing rural people with resources and opportunities to live a healthy and productive life; applying clean technologies that ensure environmental sustainability; and contributing in a productive way to the local and national economy.

■ Action is needed now to adapt agricultural and rural development policies, accelerate changes in irrigation governance and, through adequate water laws and institutions, support the integration of the social, economic and environmental needs of rural populations.

Part 1. Water's Role in Agriculture

During the second half of the twentieth century, the global food system responded to a twofold increase in the world's population by more than doubling food production, and this in an environment of decreasing prices for agricultural products. During the same period, the group of developing countries increased per capita food consumption by 30 percent and nutritional situations improved accordingly. In addition, agriculture continued producing non-food crops, including cotton, rubber, beverage crops and industrial oils. However, while feeding the world and producing a diverse range of commodities, agriculture also confirmed its position as the biggest user of water on the globe. Irrigation now claims close to 70 percent of all freshwater appropriated for human use.

In the absence of competition for raw water, and with little initial concern for environmental implications, agriculture has been able to capture large quantities of freshwater and ensure its claim to freshwater use. In the near future, the need to produce and process more food for the world's growing population will translate into an increased demand for irrigation. However, agriculture is now increasingly obliged to accommodate its claims on water within a complex framework in which social, economic and environmental objectives have to be negotiated with other sectors. The basis for well-informed negotiation hinges upon the degree of effective governance that can be found within the respective social, economic and environmental sectors.

Food production, whether on a large commercial farm, a homestead garden plot or a fish pond, is a local activity. However, the decisions underlying the way in which food is produced are increasingly beyond the reach and influence of local communities and of local agricultural organizations. Prices and specifications for agricultural export products are decided at far away market places. National governments in many developing countries have discriminated against the rural sector in order to favour urban constituencies, and rich countries have subsidized their agricultural exports, with dire consequences for undercapitalized rural producers operating in an environment of poor or non-existing physical, financial, educational and health infrastructure. At present, about 13 percent of the world's population does not have access to enough food to live a healthy and productive life, yet the ability, technology and resources needed to produce enough food for every man, woman and child in the world do currently exist. Lack of health, financial or natural resources such as land and water, and lack of skills to link productive activities with remote markets and ensure employment, are all intimately related to poverty.

Table 7.1 presents the various levels of governance linked to agricultural water management. Water governance issues emerge around water allocation and distribution, but governance aspects other than those concerning water are equally important. Secure tenure of sufficient land is fundamental to water governance, as is the availability of supporting infrastructure related to distribution and marketing. Market access is critical to income generation. Clearly, the management of rural water, including irrigation facilities, calls for some form of local governance. Recent trends towards increased responsibility of water users present new challenges for such arrangements. Again, beyond water management, the whole system of food governance arises when the implementation of national food policies (through subsidies, taxes, tariffs and even food aid in some instances) distorts markets and marginalizes the rural poor.

With current trends towards international trade liberalization, the complexity of these governance problems and their interconnection is growing. Water governance and related food system issues have to be examined from local, national and global perspectives. This chapter reviews the main links between water, food production, markets and rural livelihoods, as well as their implications in terms of governance at all levels.

1a. The water variable in agriculture
Feeding the world's population: from need to surplus
For adequate nutrition, a person's daily diet should be complete (in energy terms) and balanced (in nutritional terms). The indicator used as a proxy to assess the nutritional situation of a population is the average dietary energy intake in the form of kilocalories per person per day (kcal/person/d). The dietary energy supply (DES) value of 2,800 kcal/person/d is taken as a threshold to

...agriculture is now increasingly obliged to accommodate its claims on water within a complex framework in which social, economic and environmental objectives have to be negotiated with other sectors

Figure 7.5: Evolution of cropland, 1961–2000

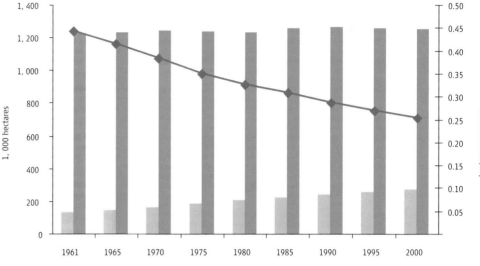

Note: In forty years, cropland has increased only slightly while population was more than doubling, leading to a sharp reduction in the amount of land needed to produce food for one person. These rapid increases in productivity were obtained through intensification of agricultural production, in which irrigation has played an important role.

Source: FAOSTAT, 2005.

A farmer and his cattle return home across rice terraces, Indonesia

1.4 percent. This growth would occur mostly in developing countries, where about 80 percent of the projected growth in crop production will come from intensification in the form of yield increases (67 percent) and increased cropping intensity (12 percent). The remaining 20 percent will come from cropland expansion in some countries of sub-Saharan Africa, Latin America and East Asia that still have land potential (FAO, 2003a).

In 2030, irrigated agriculture in ninety-three developing countries would account for over 70 percent of the projected increase in cereal production. In these countries, the area equipped for irrigation is expected to expand by 20 percent (40 million ha) between 1998 and 2030. This projected increase in irrigated land is less than half of the increase of the preceding period (100 million ha). Thanks to increased cropping intensity, the area of harvested crops in irrigation is expected to increase by 34 percent by 2030. In the same period, the amount of freshwater that will be appropriated for irrigation is expected to grow by about 14 percent to 2,420 km^3 in 2030. Compared to the projected 34 percent increase in harvested irrigated area and the 55 percent increase in food production, the 14 percent increase in water withdrawal for irrigation is modest. Irrigation in the ninety-three developing countries, aggregated as a group, still claims a relatively small part of their total water resources. At the local level, however, where there

are already water shortages, such as in the Near East and North Africa, growing competition between agriculture, cities and industries will exacerbate water scarcity, and it is likely that the share of freshwater available for agriculture will decrease (Faurès et al., 2003). In countries and regions facing serious water scarcity problems, the gap between demand and production will grow, forcing them to rely increasingly on importing food to satisfy domestic needs. Already today, several countries like Egypt or Jordan have a structural food deficit and cannot produce the food they need to satisfy domestic demand.

1b. Drivers of change in agricultural production
Changing patterns of demography, food production, food demand and diets
Global demographic projections point to declining rates in population growth. Deceleration of demographic growth and gradual saturation in per capita food consumption will contribute to a slowing growth of food demand. Nevertheless, the expected absolute annual increments in population growth continue to be large, of the order of 76 million people per year at present and 53 million people per year towards 2030. Almost all of this population growth will take place in developing countries, with large regional differences. These countries have to find an adequate mix of policies stimulating local food

Map 7.1: Distribution of areas under irrigation in the world, 2000

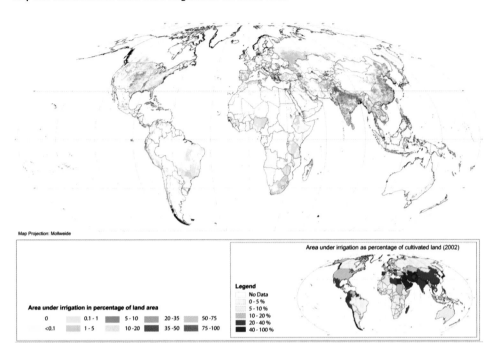

Map Projection: Mollweide

Area under irrigation in percentage of land area

| 0 | | 0.1 - 1 | | 5 - 10 | | 20 - 35 | | 50 - 75 |
| <0.1 | | 1 - 5 | | 10 - 20 | | 35 - 50 | | 75 - 100 |

Area under irrigation as percentage of cultivated land (2002)

Legend
No Data
0 - 5 %
5 - 10 %
10 - 20 %
20 - 40 %
40 - 100 %

Note: Irrigation is concentrated in arid and semi-arid areas, where it represents a significant share of cropland, and in the humid tropics of Southeast Asia, where it made it possible to move from one to two or even three harvests of rice per year.

Source: Siebert et al., 2005; FAO/AQUASTAT, 2005.

production, income generation for the poorer, mostly rural, segments of the population and generation of foreign exchange to import the complement of food needed to satisfy domestic food requirements.

Agricultural commodity supply and demand are also changing (Schmidhuber, 2003). In addition to the required quantity, many factors in changing food demand and production patterns, sometimes cancelling out one another, influence agricultural production and the way inputs are managed. The distribution of bulk grain has become more reliable and 'just-in-time', allowing world reserves to be progressively reduced over the past decades from about four months to less than three months of global demand (FAO, 2005). Food commodities are produced, conditioned, refrigerated and transported over increasing distances at the cost of energy and environmental degradation.

Meat demand has been shifting towards poultry, and the world is now consuming more poultry meat than bovine meat. Given that poultry has a much better conversion rate of cereals into meat (two to one) than cattle

(between five and seven to one), this shift releases some of the pressure projected on the cereal sector and water demand for the irrigated cereal production.

As diets diversify and become healthier and better balanced, the demand for fresh vegetables and fruits increases. These goods are produced under intensive farming methods, including the use of greenhouses and irrigation for timely year-round production following exacting specifications. The controlled agro-ecological environment under which vegetables and fruits are produced also allows for accurate water control with minimum wastage. However, this form of agriculture is only possible under full control of water, which should be available on demand and in good quality. Many irrigation systems are not equipped with the necessary storage, conveyance and control systems and do not have the capacity to deliver water under these stringent conditions.

In countries and regions facing serious water scarcity problems, the gap between demand and production of food will grow, forcing them to rely increasingly on importing food to satisfy domestic needs

Table 7.2 Virtual water content of selected products

Product	Litres of water per kilo of crop
Wheat	1, 150
Rice	2, 656
Maize	450
Potatoes	160
Soybeans	2, 300
Beef	15, 977
Pork	5, 906
Poultry	2, 828
Eggs	4, 657
Milk	865
Cheese	5, 288

Note: Virtual water is the total amount of water used in the production and processing of a given product.

Source: Adapted from Hoekstra, 2003.

During the twentieth century, the world population increased threefold, while water used in agriculture through irrigation increased sixfold and some major rivers approached an advanced level of water depletion

crops and thus releasing water for more financially productive uses. Such policies usually imply long-term trade agreements between importing and exporting countries and therefore tend to facilitate increased stability in international relations.

2b. Improving irrigation

During the twentieth century, the world population increased threefold, while water used in agriculture through irrigation increased sixfold and some major rivers approached an advanced level of water depletion. The 'green revolution' was based on a technology package comprising components of improved high-yielding varieties of cereals, irrigation, improved soil moisture utilization and the application of plant nutrients, pest control, and associated management skills. The use of these technology packages on good land in suitable socio-economic environments resulted in increased crop yields and increased incomes for millions of farmers, particularly in Asia. Statistics indicate that yields of rice, wheat and maize approximately doubled between the 1960s and the 1990s. The green revolution has been a major achievement, and its effects are continuing, but the need for systematic use of irrigation, mineral fertilizers and agrochemical-based pest and weed control created environmental and health problems.

Achievements and failures of irrigation

The aim of large-scale irrigation projects was to drive regional and national development through the participation of significant segments of populations in direct and indirect project benefits. This socio-economic objective justified the implementation, at substantial public cost, of hydraulic infrastructure, including dams

and canals, financed mostly by national governments, with support from international lending institutions. However, irrigation project performance problems started to emerge as early as the mid-1960s: not all the irrigation areas created were actually irrigated; crop yields were below projections; maintenance was substandard, and rehabilitation too frequently required; in some areas, soils started to become salinized; the return on investments was lower than expected; and the benefits to poor people were fewer than foreseen when calling for public funding (Mollinga and Bolding, 2004).

Understanding of the causes of poor performances in irrigation has improved. Design faults, including missing or inadequate drainage infrastructure, were often observed and sometimes traced to the application of inappropriate design standards (i.e. calling on materials, equipment and skills that were not locally available). Today's economic context calls for changes in agricultural policies and practices that these schemes cannot easily accommodate. In the Indus River Basin, for example, large irrigation schemes were initially designed and built to spread and share water thinly and equitably in order to reach as many farmers as possible, with deliveries covering only part of water needs when the entire area is considered. These systems cannot accommodate current demands for crop diversification and intensification. Other dysfunctions can be traced to disregard for relevant socio-economic conditions, lack of consultations with stakeholders and target groups, and generally poor governance both at the level of the countries implementing the irrigating works and of the financing institutions and donors. In many cases, women were excluded from the benefits of irrigation, because, according to social traditions, they could not have access to land rights and/or would not be allocated water rights (see **Box 7.3**). Among typical governance problems in the irrigation sector are the capture of benefits, including the control of water by the most influential farmers at the expense of poorer smallholders, and control of irrigation systems by rent-seekers, usually well-connected with local decision-makers.

Institutional reforms in irrigation management

By the 1990s, the major agencies funding development were making their loans conditional on the adoption of reform packages that required a balanced fiscal budget, a reduced role for the state and a larger role for the private sector. These packages emphasized economic water pricing, financial autonomy for irrigation agencies and the devolution of management responsibilities to lower levels.

BOX 7.3: THE ROLE OF WOMEN IN IRRIGATED FARMING IN SUB-SAHARAN AFRICA

In most countries, access to irrigation water is mediated by race, social status and gender. In sub-Saharan Africa, a complex set of rights and obligations reflecting social and religious norms prevails within rural communities and dictates the division of labour between men and women farmers. Irrigation projects have often been implemented without considering existing social and cultural practices like the gendered division of labour and responsibilities.

In Burkina Faso, a case study showed that overall productivity increased when women and men were allocated small separate plots rather than larger household plots. Women proved to be good irrigation managers and preferred to work on their own plots. As they became economically less dependent upon their husbands, they were able to help support their relatives and increase their own opportunities for individual accumulation of wealth in the form of

livestock. The effects of having an individual plot also significantly improved the bargaining position of women within households.

Sources: FAO, 2002a; Rathgeber, 2003.

Among these reforms, irrigation management transfer (IMT) appears to be the most systematic and far-reaching effort so far. The philosophy behind IMT lies in the perception that increased ownership, representation and active participation of farmers in the operation and maintenance of irrigation systems would be more effective than publicly run systems and would create an incentive for farmers to be more responsible towards their common obligations. IMT is based on the principle of subsidiarity, which holds that no responsibility should be located at a higher level than necessary.

Several approaches were developed to reform irrigation institutions, often in combination with each other. Decentralization, devolution, privatization and the development of public–private partnerships for irrigation management are all possible elements of institutional reform packages being implemented at various levels in over fifty countries, including Australia, India, Mexico, the Philippines and Turkey. All of them imply substantial changes in the way water governance is being practised. **Figure 7.8** schematically presents the implications of these institutional packages in terms of ownership and management of water for a range of typical situations.

Cattle drinking from the riverbank, Ethiopia

Figure 7.8: Examples of institutional reforms and implications in terms of ownership and management

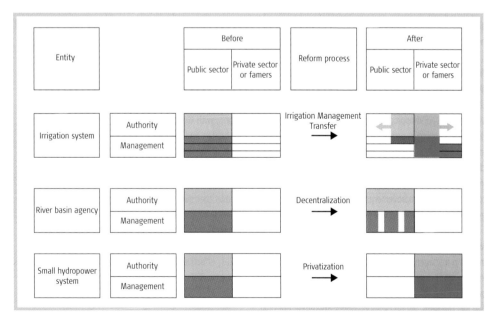

Note: Institutional reforms in irrigation management can take many forms. In most cases, they imply changes in the ownership, responsibility and authority over different parts of the irrigation system, land, water and infrastructures. The figure shows a sample of possible changes, and the new roles of governments, farmers and the private sector (including farmers' associations).

Source: Adapted from FAO, forthcoming.

and farmers progressively shift self-sufficient activities into more business-oriented activities, irrigation is increasingly used for precision agriculture. Precision agriculture is an agricultural concept relying on the existence of in-field variability. It seeks to tailor agricultural practices to suit local conditions. Precision agriculture is well adapted to markets that demand delivery on a precise schedule of products subject to stringent specifications. Precision agriculture calls for optimal control of water deliveries and is an ideal condition for the application of pressurized irrigation technologies (sprinkler and localized irrigation). Localized irrigation finds its most rewarding applications in horticulture and fruit tree production. Combined with automatic fertilizer application, or 'fertigation', it usually guarantees high returns on investments, reliability in the control of soil moisture, and reduced labour costs. When it is well managed, it can ensure an irrigation efficiency of close to 100 percent, thus contributing to minimizing water loss. Precision agriculture has a bright future in serving an increasing number of consumers in urban areas, but its application to low-cost staple food and commodities, representing the largest share of irrigation, is unlikely to materialize.

Part 3. Towards More Sustainable Agriculture

Agriculture has significant impacts on environment and people's health and too often, pursuing a narrow development goal of increased productivity has lead to the breakdown of the resilience of natural ecosystems. The negative impacts of water management in agriculture are related to land and water uses, in particular through encroachment on natural ecosystems, water extraction, erosion, or loss of soil biodiversity. The drainage and return of flows from irrigation often result in unwanted impacts, including loss of water quality. Inappropriate agricultural practices like excessive application of pesticides and fertilizers have direct impacts on water quality and affect people's health; waterlogging and salinization is also the result of inadequate planning and management of irrigation and drainage in agriculture. Finding alternative ways to alleviate these impacts is therefore essential to maintain the integrity and productivity of the ecosystems on which it depends and to create the conditions for agriculture to contribute, in a sustainable way, to food security, poverty alleviation and economic growth.

3a. Water storage and the evolution of groundwater-based economies

Irrigation backed by water storage has been conceived to provide a high degree of water security to reduce agricultural risk and encourage farmers to invest. Water stored in reservoirs is a secure asset on which farmers can rely. Surface water storage in reservoirs, however, contends with several problems, including the cost and liability of the impounding structure; the loss of water through evaporation; reservoir and canal sedimentation; river fragmentation and changes in river regimes; and the destruction of local livelihoods and resources. In the past, these costs (externalities) tended to be systematically underestimated while the potential benefits of dams were overestimated. The World Commission on Dams (WCD, 2000) represented significant progress in stating that all costs (social, economic and environmental) must be assessed against potential benefits derived from the construction of reservoirs.

Groundwater, where it is available, is a highly reliable source of water and provides an attractive alternative to surface storage. In the last few decades, groundwater has played a central role in enabling the transformation of rural communities from low productivity subsistence agriculture to more intensive forms of production. In contrast to surface water systems based on reservoirs and canals, users pump the aquifer as and when needed, and because groundwater extraction occurs through a pressurized system instead of open channels, precision application, which can greatly increase yields, is also possible. Except in places where energy is subsidized, groundwater productivity tends to be good, as pumping costs provide an incentive to saving water. For farming populations, groundwater access enables increases in production while reducing agricultural risk, enabling them to invest in more intensive forms of production and improve their livelihoods. Consequently, groundwater has played a particularly large role in yield and production increase. Evidence also suggests that groundwater access often plays a role in reducing rural poverty (Moench, 2001). Groundwater-based rural development has been central to major productivity gains in agriculture and the improvement of rural livelihood. But groundwater-based rural economies also show signs of vulnerability as aquifers are depleted (see also **Chapter 4**).

Managing groundwater

Private irrigation often uses groundwater, and its individualistic nature makes groundwater extraction difficult to control, leading to risks of anarchic exploitation and unequal water access. As water levels drop, competition among users increases, progressively excluding poorer farmers who cannot afford the cost of competitive well deepening, whereas those farmers who develop groundwater early, and those who already possess diverse forms of social or other capital, often consolidate their economic advantage. Managing a groundwater body consists mainly in ensuring that the extraction of water by a large number of individual users is performed in a controlled manner. This is technically feasible, but in reality meets major legal, institutional and social obstacles. Conventional bureaucratic controls based on well-licensing procedures, water pumping quotas and policing entail large transaction costs and have generally proven ineffective. It is a cause for concern that many aquifers continue to be drawn from until declining discharges, growing salinity and increasing pumping costs announce groundwater depletion (Burke and Moench, 2000).

Few examples exist of successful groundwater management. In Guanajuato State, Mexico, an experiment involving users at the local level has led to the creation of Aquifer Management Councils that have resulted in reduced transaction costs and progressive changes in users' behaviour. The sustainability and replicability of such a model remains to be ascertained (see also **Chapter 14**).

3b. Environment and water quality

Water abstractions for agriculture and other purposes modify the water balance and reduce the quantity of water that flows its natural course. The impact on the aquatic environment ranges from negligible to deleterious and deadly in extreme cases. The return of contaminated water into natural water bodies, when exceeding the natural recovery capacity of these systems, further reduces the amount of freshwater of adequate quality available for various uses and for sustaining the aquatic environment. Agriculture is a major cause of river depletion in the regions of the world sustained by irrigation and is the main source of nitrate pollution of groundwater and surface water, as well as a principal source of ammonia pollution. It is also a major contributor to the phosphate pollution of lakes and waterways and to the release of methane and nitrous

oxide into the atmosphere. The improper use of pesticides has detrimental impacts on the environment, resources and human health. (see **Chapters 5** and **6**).

While there is no question that agriculture must reduce the impact of its negative externalities, there is also wide recognition that agriculture must not necessarily be considered in opposition to natural ecosystems: positive externalities generated by agriculture go beyond the strict economic systems of crop production. In the same way that humans have for millennia drawn their food from the environment, agricultural systems that have proved sustainable in the long term can go far in the preservation of ecosystems and their biodiversity, while enhancing rural livelihoods. The twentieth century has been a time of productivity, based on the application of agronomic practices that favour a limited number of strategic crops. In this aspect, much indigenous knowledge has been neglected and partly lost in the drive to always apply agricultural systems that are high in energy inputs and low in species and cultivar diversity. As conditions now exist to release the pressure on natural resources, the trend, in numerous developed countries, is to transform agriculture into a landscape management practice, offering new avenues for better integration of agriculture with its environment (see also **Chapter 13**).

In addition to producing food and other goods for farm families and markets, sustainable agriculture also contributes to a range of public goods, such as clean water, wildlife, management of living aquatic resources, carbon sequestration in soils, flood protection and landscape quality. Certain non-food functions of sustainable agriculture cannot be produced by other sectors, including on-farm biodiversity, groundwater recharge, or social cohesion. Thus, what many see as an almost unbearable challenge for the agriculture sector – internalizing externalities – might in fact also be seen as a major opportunity to promote sustainable development in rural areas (FAO and MAFF, 2003).

Salinity, a hazard of irrigation in arid zones

Irrigation development has caused numerous cases of soil and water salinization, which is mostly restricted to arid and semi-arid areas, where about 40 percent of the world's irrigated land is located and where the rate of evapotranspiration is high. By withdrawing water from rivers for application on land, irrigation tends to accelerate the rate of accumulation of salts on land through evaporation and increase its concentration in rivers. Salinization is also likely to become a problem on poorly

Fields near Quito, Ecuador. The plateaus of Quito benefit from the humid, gentle climate of the Sierra, which favours the cultivation of cereals and potatoes

Heavy monsoon rains submerge villages, roads and fields in India

Salinization seriously affects 20 to 30 percent of the area under irrigation in arid and semi-arid zones

drained soil, when the groundwater level is close to the surface. In such cases, water tends to rise from the water table to the surface by capillary action and then evaporate from the soil surface, leaving salts accumulating at the surface. In more humid regions, rainfall usually provides enough leaching to prevent harmful salt accumulation.

No exact assessments are available on the extent and severity of salinization, but Smedema and Shiati (2002) suggest that it seriously affects 20 to 30 million ha worldwide, that is, about 25 percent of the area under irrigation in arid and semi-arid zones and about 10 percent of all areas under irrigation. Most of this is a legacy of large-scale water works developed from the 1950s. The spread of salinization in these 'old' irrigation areas is now drastically reduced. Current global estimates of the rate of extension of salinization are in the order of 0.25 to 0.50 million ha per year.

To a large degree, irrigation-induced land and river salinization is inherent to the practice of irrigation in arid and semi-arid areas. The adverse impacts of salinization can, to some extent, be prevented and mitigated, but large-scale development in arid regions will always represent a salinity hazard that goes beyond the single irrigation scheme and amplifies as one travels downstream. Of particular concern are the major rivers that have their sources in the Himalayas and flow into desert areas in Pakistan and Central Asia. Preventive action includes planning irrigation development better, avoiding highly saline areas and establishing drainage infrastructure. Among the measures that can be applied are the application of river basin-level salt balance models to predict and monitor the incidence of salinization and the interception and disposal of highly saline runoffs. Salt control programmes have contributed to arresting river salinization. However, significant lowering of salt concentrations in rivers would generally require radical measures such as a substantial reduction in land under irrigation.

Recycling: Achieving an adequate urban–rural balance of wastewater use

Cities produce large quantities of solid and liquid waste that are disposed of and more or less treated back into the environment. If this process is not adequately considered in all its steps and consequences – and in developing countries it generally is not – the impact can be devastating to the environment and to people living close to disposal sites, causing the disruption of ecosystems and putting people at risk of poisoning (see **Chapter 3**). Liquid waste (the contents of sewers) is discharged into rivers and coastal zones, where it may overtax the recovery capacity of natural water bodies, leading to the establishment of new, less desirable ecological systems (i.e. anaerobic systems).

Agriculture around cities is generally dynamic and well connected to markets, making profitable use of water. Wastewater provides users with a stable source of water with a high nutrient content. However, the use of untreated wastewater in agriculture poses risks to human health. Governments have usually responded to such risks by implementing strict regulations limiting or preventing the use of wastewater and advocating treatment before use. Full treatment, however, can be expensive, and achieving an adequate urban–rural balance and distribution of charges and benefits continues to elude governance. While the uncontrolled use of wastewater cannot be encouraged, unconditional restriction is not a practical option, as wastewater is too valuable a resource for farmers who have no other alternatives.

A more pragmatic approach to wastewater use in agriculture is now emerging. It includes enhanced monitoring, health protection and education, and alternative agricultural practices. This approach is being adopted in the revision of the WHO guidelines for wastewater use in agriculture (see **Box 7.5**).

BOX 7.5: REVISED WORLD HEALTH ORGANIZATION (WHO) GUIDELINES FOR THE SAFE USE OF WASTEWATER IN AGRICULTURE

WHO first published its 'Guidelines for the safe use of wastewater and excreta in agriculture and aquaculture' in 1989. A revision of these guidelines is currently under preparation. The revised WHO guidelines will incorporate a risk-benefit approach, in which the assessment of tolerable risks takes place before the setting of

health targets. This framework allows more flexibility to countries in adapting what would be available and achievable in the context of local social, economic and environmental factors. In addition, the interaction between wastewater use and poverty in the political context and international development targets is mentioned

with expanded sections on risk analysis and management, revised microbial guideline values and further elaboration of chemical contaminants, including pharmaceuticals and endocrine disrupting substances, health-impact assessment, and wastewater use planning strategies at sub-national levels.

BOX 7.6: **TONLE SAP: THE BENEFITS OF SEASONAL FLOODING FOR LIVELIHOODS, NUTRITION AND BIODIVERSITY**

Tonle Sap, in central Cambodia, is the largest freshwater lake in Southeast Asia. The annually flooded area includes a ring of freshwater mangrove forest, shrubs, grassland and rice fields. The Tonle Sap is also a rich fishing ground, with an estimated catch of 250,000 metric tonnes (t) per year on average.

Traditionally, the people living around the lake in areas subject to flooding have cultivated rice varieties that could cope with the high water level by elongating their stems up to five metres, with a maximum growth of 10 cm per day. Where the flooding is not as deep, normal wet rice varieties are transplanted into the fields once the flood has reached them. In some areas, rice is planted in the fields as floodwaters recede.

Licensed fishing lots occupy the most productive areas in terms of fish catch. There is a tendency to underestimate the importance of rice field fisheries in the Tonle Sap, because they tend to yield only small amounts of fish at a time, but this provision of fish is available for many people on a regular basis (it is estimated that fish consumption around the lake averages about 60 to 70 kg per person per year).

The Tonle Sap is also an important source of biodiversity. A survey carried out in 2001 identified seventy different species of fish and other organisms captured in rice field ecosystems for consumption as food and for other purposes. They include several species of fish, snake, turtle, crab, shrimp and amphibians,

all of them tradable on local markets. In the vegetal world, besides rice, thirteen plant species were recorded, of which six were marketed.

In conclusion, the Tonle Sap ecosystem is of major importance to the local population, not only for the supply of rice, but also for animal protein and vegetables. Development that focuses only on increasing yields of rice through intensification and the use of agrochemicals may provide more rice to eat, but may also eliminate many aquatic animals and vegetables harvested from and around the rice fields.

Source: Adapted from Balzer et al., 2002.

Wetlands: Fragile ecosystems, sources of livelihood

Wetlands are fragile ecosystems and an important source of biodiversity, with complex hydrological and livelihood support functions, including regulation, silt retention, grazing land, hunting, fishing and wood production. In the past, the attractive characteristics of wetlands for agricultural production (particularly their fertility and soil moisture) have led planners to undervalue their environmental and socio-economic functions and promote their conversion into agricultural production. Conversion of wetlands into farmland, largely a matter of the past in developed countries, is still actively underway in regions with high demographic growth that suffer from food insecurity, as in sub-Saharan Africa. Not all wetlands can be preserved, and research is needed to identify critical wetlands of particular importance for biodiversity, so that a critical core of wetlands can be preserved. The Ramsar Convention, which initially focused on wetland conservation to ensure the survival of migrating bird species, now works with its partners to promote a wise use of wetlands in general, emphasizing the needs of local populations and the complex livelihood support functions of the wetlands. Resolution VIII.34 of the 8th Conference of the Contracting Parties (2002) focuses on the necessary interactions between agriculture, wetlands and water resources management (see **Box 7.6**).

3c. Water to combat hunger and poverty in rural areas

The projections of total food demand suggest that per capita food consumption will continue to grow significantly, and the world average will approach 3,000 kcal in 2015, compared to 2,800 kcal around 2000. The world will be producing enough food for everyone, but its distribution will continue to be unequal. In absolute figures, the number of undernourished people in the world has been stagnating since the early 1990s, and was estimated at 850 million in 2000–02, of which 815 million were in developing countries (see **Map 7.2**, **Figures 7.10** and **7.11**). Projections show a decline to 610 million in 2015, which is progress, but still distant from the 1996 World Food Summit target of 400 million in 2015 (FAO, 1997). Although the Millennium Development Goal of reducing by half the proportion of people living in extreme poverty and hunger by the year 2015 is well within grasp, at present, 15,000 children under the age of five die every day as a consequence of chronic hunger and malnutrition (see **Chapters 1** and **6**).

Chronic hunger is a reflection of extreme poverty, as those affected by hunger do not have the resources needed to produce or buy food. Hunger is not only a result of poverty but also contributes to poverty by lowering labour productivity, reducing resistance to disease and depressing educational achievements.

Irrigation in the Eastern Cape, South Africa

Access is a pivotal concept in the development of livelihoods, and is allied with the notion of entitlement. Poverty results from the failure to express such entitlements...

Decades of international concern about an ethically unacceptable global level of extreme poverty and hunger, and national and international policies and governance formulated in this spirit, have been insufficient to transform the livelihoods of the poor for the better. Forty years ago, there was hope that the green revolution, with its new high-yielding varieties of rice, wheat and maize, would bring world hunger to an end by increasing food supply. The green revolution boosted food production and, in relative terms, the global situation has improved. Nevertheless, universal food security has not been achieved, and the absolute number of chronically hungry people remains high. So what options are now available to eradicate hunger and poverty, and what role does water play in this endeavour?

Water in livelihood as a pathway out of poverty
The livelihoods approach to understanding and tackling poverty, its causes and consequences, is gaining momentum across the developing world and among the development partners. For water and food, it means a fundamental shift beyond considering water as a resource for increasing food production to focusing on people and the role that water plays in their livelihood strategies. This puts people at the centre of development and means that issues such as drought and secured access to water become problem-led

rather than discipline-led, leading to a focus on institutional and political barriers to water access and on physical infrastructure needed for its management.

At the heart of the livelihoods approach are the 'capital' assets of households, a particularly relevant approach in rural areas. These include not only natural assets, such as land and water, but also social, human, physical and financial assets, presenting a comprehensive view of the basis of livelihood, as opposed to the more classical approach that tends to address single issues separately (see **Table 7.3**). Within a sustainable livelihoods approach, water is treated as an economic good and as an asset that can be invested to generate benefits and income. To consider only the role of water in agricultural production is not sufficient; in a livelihoods approach, it is necessary to understand the impacts of improved water supplies on the socio-economic livelihood circumstances of households. The challenge for the future is to introduce this systemic approach in places where the majority of organizations and the professionals working in them are still driven by a sectoral approach (see **Chapter 12**).

Irrigation is a direct source of livelihood for hundreds of millions of the rural poor in developing countries because of the food, income options and indirect benefits it

Table 7.3: Shifting towards a livelihood-based approach in rural areas

Capital	Issue	Production-based approach	Livelihood-based approach
Physical capital	Infrastructure for rainfed and irrigation systems	Rainfed and irrigation farming systems improved to increase agricultural production.	Improves decision-making ability through better rainfed and irrigation farming systems. Removes risk and uncertainty including maintenance and management of natural capital stocks.
Social capital	Community approach needed to raising or managing other forms of capital, of crucial importance in irrigation management, water user associations (WUA), networks	Communities mobilized to establish water user associations (WUA) to improve agricultural water management.	Identifies poorest households and strengthens participation in, and influence on, community management systems; creates safety-nets within communities to ensure the poor have access to water; improves rights to land and water and establishes right to access by poor households within communities.
Natural capital	Land and water availability	Develops new and enhances existing water resources using physical and social assets.	Enhanced through training in catchment protection and maintaining natural environment.
Financial capital	Cash, credit, savings, animals	Develops individual or community-based tariffs and charges mechanisms for water use.	Secured through access to small-scale credit.
Human capital	Labour, knowledge (through education, experience)	Trains people in agricultural water management and promotes gender equity.	Knowledge of demand, responsive approaches, community self-assessment of needs, participatory monitoring, gender mainstreaming.

Source: Adapted from Nicol, 2000.

BOX 7.7: POSITIVE IMPACTS OF IRRIGATION ON RURAL COMMUNITIES

- Employment and income for landowners and the landless who benefit from new employment opportunities.

- Increased production options throughout the year, used for both home consumption and sale.

- Health improvements through access to safe domestic water supply and sanitation.

- Attraction of immigration and improved provision of services, such as education.

- Widening of social networks through participation in water committees.

- Boost to local economy and family welfare.

Source: Adapted from Vincent, 2001; Meinzen-Dick and Bakker, 1999; Zwarteveen 1996.

---

generates (Vincent, 2001). The anti-poverty effects of irrigation can be assessed on two levels: (1) production, related to the national or regional economy, and (2) livelihoods, related to the household and its well-being. The former has been the method traditionally used to assess irrigation impacts; conversely, a livelihoods approach to irrigation places adequate and secure livelihood aims before increased production. Negative impacts of irrigation systems and provision on livelihoods, such as water-borne infections, waterlogging and salinity, increases in land prices and in women's unpaid workload, displacement and disparity of benefits between inequity in irrigation water distribution, are outweighed in most cases by benefits (see **Box 7.7**).

The balanced achievement of these livelihoods benefits, without a disproportionate gap between those who lose and those who gain in irrigation processes, can only be reached if access to water or to the benefits it generates to third parties is secured by the poor and landless. Access is a pivotal concept in the development of livelihoods, and is allied with the notion of entitlement. Poverty results from the failure to express such entitlements, not from the lack of individual rights to the commodities at stake.

Despite difficulties in participatory irrigation management processes, a beneficial by-product has been the strengthening of social capital, increasingly accounted for in livelihood improvements (see **Box 7.8**). Increasing the positive impacts of water in supporting and enhancing the livelihood of the poor has three implications:

- recognizing the role and importance of water in non-agricultural uses in single purpose management systems and identifying complementarities among uses (Meinzen-Dick, 1997)

- supporting people's capacity to manage their water in a fair and sustainable manner (Vincent, 2001)

- engaging a policy move from production and health to sustainable livelihoods in water assessments (Nicol, 2000), that is, moving from supply-led to demand-responsive policies that take requirements and claims of user groups into account and make more efficient and equitable use of existing supplies (Winpenny, 1997).

BOX 7.8: LOCAL GOVERNANCE TO SECURE ACCESS TO LAND AND WATER IN THE LOWER GASH WATERSHED, SUDAN

In Sudan, the livelihood of more than 67,000 poor farming families is to be improved on a large irrigation scheme in the Gash watershed in the arid eastern part of the country. Set up in the 1920s in order to settle nomadic people, the project fell into decline in the 1970s. The management was fragmented and nepotistic, and farmers complained about its ineffectiveness in meeting their needs for social and economic development. Soon, production shifted to low-return subsistence crops, farmers stopped paying irrigation fees and the system fell into disrepair.

Traditional approaches to rehabilitating such projects usually focus on infrastructure repairs, with little room for adaptation. In the Gash Sustainable Livelihood Regeneration Project (GSLRP) (2004–12), the improvement of farmers' livelihood was selected as the first objective. Capacity development and institutional reforms have been designed to ensure that all stakeholders are involved in the decision-making process. This is seen as critical to the success of the project. New organizations are being set up to ensure that citizens gain more secure rights to

land and water by building on existing local community organizations. Efforts are underway to counter the strong tradition of supply-driven irrigation management, where farmers are tenants, and empower farmers to take on more management responsibility. This puts household livelihood, rather than infrastructure development, firmly at the core of future investments.

Source: IFAD, 2003.

In many parts of the world, poor farmers rank soil erosion and lack of soil fertility among the main constraints to improving crop yields – both of which are linked to water management. Technical solutions have long been available, yet the problems and the solutions do not appear to be connected and so the rate of adoption of good practices remains poor. The links between research, extension and poor farmers need to be strengthened in new and innovative ways that encourage two-way communication with farmers (IFAD, 2001).

Water mobilization targeted towards benefiting the poor can effectively contribute to reducing extreme poverty and hunger. Safe water supply improves personal health, the primary physical capital, thus facilitating the undertaking of gainful activities. Water availability sustains the natural ecosystems on which the livelihoods of the rural poor largely depend. Irrigation can reduce the risk of droughts and increase cropping intensities by 'extending' the wet season in the humid and tropical zones. Introducing irrigation technology can reduce household risks by raising incomes. Groundwater access often plays a particularly important role in reducing rural poverty. However, while irrigation is one of the success stories of the twentieth century, providing significant increases in food production, its poverty-reduction impact is not a foregone conclusion. Inequality in access to land and water resources, such as in southern Africa and Latin America, tends to exacerbate social inequities. If not properly managed, resources tend to end up in the hands of large influential farmers, thereby leaving almost none for small poor farmers to control (Lipton et al., 2003). Access to financial capital is also important; most often poor farmers have neither the money to invest in irrigation nor the collateral, such as land tenure rights, to obtain credit.

In the future, a purely sectoral approach to water management will no longer be possible...

Part 4. Governance Matters at All Levels in Agriculture

Agriculture requires that large quantities of water be taken up by crops from the soil in the root zone. The production of meat requires substantially more water, and fish production needs large quantities of clean water in ponds, rivers and estuaries. Globally, irrigated agriculture claims close to 70 percent of all freshwater withdrawn from its natural course, but this represents only about 10 percent of water used by agriculture – rainfall that replenishes soil moisture provides the larger part. However, irrigation has a strategic role in agriculture. Depending on various circumstances, irrigation helps to produce two to three times as much per hectare than non-irrigated agriculture. It is of crucial importance in boosting agricultural productivity and limiting horizontal expansion of cropland.

However, agriculture is now coming under much more scrutiny as competition for water between sectors increases. Degraded land and water systems, competition from other economic sectors and the need to conserve the integrity of aquatic ecosystems are progressively limiting water availability to agriculture and imposing cleaner production methods. In the future, a purely sectoral approach to water management will no longer be possible, and substantial adaptations of agricultural policies will be necessary to align production with overall river basins and aquifer management objectives.

As competition increases, irrigated agriculture will need to be systematically examined to discern where society can most effectively benefit from its application. Access to natural resources needs to be negotiated with other users in a transparent fashion in order to achieve optimal allocation and uses under conditions of growing demand for water.

The modernization of irrigated agriculture, through technological upgrading and institutional reform, will be essential in ensuring much-needed gains in water productivity. Irrigation institutions will have to respond to the needs of farmers, ensuring flexible and reliable delivery of water, increasing transparency in its management and balancing efficiency and equity in access to water. This will not only require changes in attitudes, but also well-targeted investments in infrastructure modernization, institutional restructuring and upgrading of the technical capacities of farmers and water managers.

Agriculture is under pressure to reduce its negative impact on the environment and other sectors, particularly when associated with the use of fertilizers and pesticides, as well as wasteful water use. However, there is currently a much wider recognition that better agricultural water management can also have a profoundly positive impact, reaching far beyond the strict economic system of crop production. Farmers are at the centre of any ecological process of change. They need to be encouraged and enabled, through appropriate incentives and governance practices, to conserve natural ecosystems and their biodiversity and minimize the negative impacts of agricultural production, a goal that will only be achieved if the appropriate policies are in place.

Farmers around the world are deeply affected by economic factors out of their control. Historically, governments in developing countries have tended to neglect agricultural development in favour of industrialization and national and urban activities. However, it is now more generally acknowledged that agriculture is the main engine of growth in many developing economies. Thirty countries, most of them in Africa, are highly dependent on agriculture, and progress in improving their food security situation depends on, more than any other factor, the development of local food production. In most cases, there is a need for substantial increase in investment in rural areas, where water management plays a central role in raising the productivity of agriculture and related rural activities.

At the same time, targeted policies are needed to address the causes of chronic hunger and poverty. To be effective, such policies need to focus on people and develop the assets they control. Titles to land and secure and equitable access to water and basic rural services (education, finance, etc.) are also needed if rural populations are to emerge from marginalization and integrate their farming activity in their region's economy.

The agriculture sector faces complex challenges: producing more food of better quality, while using less water per unit of output; providing rural people with resources and opportunities to live healthy and productive lives; applying clean technologies that ensure environmental sustainability; and contributing in a productive way to the local and national economy. Continuing 'business as usual' is unlikely to deliver the Millennium Development Goals on the path towards freeing humanity of extreme poverty and hunger and ensuring environmental sustainability. Action is needed now to adapt agricultural and rural development policies, accelerate changes in irrigation governance and, through adequate water laws and institutions, support the integration of the social, economic and environmental needs of rural populations.

Ultimately, the reduction of rural hunger and poverty depends on the decisions and actions of the farming community in developing countries – 500 million farm households. Their potential contribution will not be fully realized in the absence of a socio-economic environment that encourages, supports and protects their aspirations, ideas and initiatives.

A class of children from Shanghai, China, drew their vision of their environment for the 'Scroll around the world' project

Workers harvest carp raised in a stock pond, India

References and Websites

Allan, J. A. 2003. Virtual water – the water, food and trade nexus: useful concept or misleading metaphor? *Water International*, Vol. 28, pp. 4–11.

Balzer, T., Balzer, P. and Pon, S. 2002. Kampong Thom Province, Kingdom of Cambodia. M. Halwart, D. Bartley, and H. Guttman (eds), *Traditional Use and Availability of Aquatic Biodiversity in Rice-based Ecosystems*. CD-ROM, Rome, FAO.

Barker, R. and Molle, F. 2004. Evolution of Irrigation in South and Southeast Asia. *Comprehensive Assessment Research Report 5*. Colombo, Sri Lanka, International Water Management Institute.

Bennett, J. 2003. Opportunities for increasing water productivity of CGIAR crops through plant breeding and molecular biology. J. W. Kijne, R. Barker and D. Molden (eds), *Water Productivity in Agriculture: Limits and Opportunities for Improvement*. Wallingford, UK, CABI Publishing and IWMI.

Burke, J. and Moench, M. H. 2000. *Groundwater and Society: Resources, Tensions and Opportunities*. New York, UN DESA and ISET.

Commission for Africa. 2005. *Our Common Interest*. Report of the Commission for Africa. www.commissionforafrica.org

Dixon, J., Gulliver, A. and Gibbon, D. 2001. *Farming Systems and Poverty: Improving Farmers' Livelihoods in a Changing World*. Rome/Washington DC, FAO/World Bank.

Facon, T. 2005. Asian irrigation in transition – service orientation, institutional aspects and design/operation/infrastructure issues. G. Shivakoti, D. Vermillion, W. F. Lam, E. Ostrom, U. Pradhan and R. Yoder (eds), *Asian Irrigation in Transition: Responding to Challenges*. London, Sage Publications Ltd.

FAO (Food and Agriculture Organization of the United Nations). Forthcoming. *Irrigation Management Transfer: Worldwide Efforts and Results*. Rome, FAO.

——. 2005. *FAO Food Outlook*. Quarterly Report No. 1, April 2005, Global information and early warning system on food and agriculture (GIEWS). Rome, FAO.

——. 2004a. *The State of Food Insecurity in the World 2004*. Rome, FAO.

——. 2004b. *The State of Food and Agriculture 2003–2004: Agricultural Biotechnology: Meeting the Needs of the Poor?* Rome, FAO.

——. 2003a. *World Agriculture Towards 2015/2030: An FAO perspective*. Rome/London, FAO/Earthscan Publishers.

——. 2003b. International scientific symposium on measurement and assessment of food deprivation and undernutrition. Summary of Proceedings. 26–28 June 2002. Rome, FAO.

——. 2003c. *Report of the FAO Expert Consultation on Environmental Effects of Genetically Modified Crops*. 16–18 June 2003, Rome, FAO.—— 2003d. *Review of the State of World Fishery Resources: Inland Fisheries*. FAO Fisheries Circular, No. 942, Rev. 1, Rome, FAO.

——. 2002a. *The State of Food and Agriculture 2002*. Rome, FAO.

——. 2002b. *Crops and Drops: Making the Best Use of Water for Agriculture*. FAO, Rome.

——. 1999. Global issues and directions in inland fisheries. *Review of the State of World Fishery Resources: Inland Fisheries*. FAO Fisheries Circular. No. 942, Rev. 1. Rome, FAO.

——. 1998. Integrating fisheries and agriculture to enhance fish production and food security. *The State of Food and Agriculture, 1998*, No. 31, pp. 85–99. Rome, FAO Agriculture Series.

——. 1997. Report of the World Food Summit, 13–17 November 1996, Part 1. Rome, FAO.

FAO and MAFF (Ministry of Agriculture, Forestry and Fisheries of Japan). 2003. Issue paper for the Ministerial meeting on Water for food and agriculture. Rome, FAO and MAFF.

FAO and WDD (World Development Department of Cyprus). 2002. Reassessment of the water resources and demand of the island of Cyprus. Synthesis report. Rome/Nicosia, FAO/WDD.

FAO-IPTRID (International Programme for Technology and research in Irrigation and Drainage). 2003. The irrigation challenge: Increasing irrigation contribution to food security through higher water productivity from canal irrigation systems. Issue Paper 4. Rome, FAO and IPTRID.

Faurès, J. M., Hoogeveen, J. and Bruinsma, J. 2003. *The FAO Irrigated Area Forecast for 2030*. Rome, FAO www.fao.org/ag/agl/aglw/aquastat/reports/index.htm

Hoekstra, A. Y. (ed). 2003. Virtual water trade, proceedings of the international expert meeting on virtual water trade, *Value of Water Research Report* No. 12. Delft, the Netherlands, IHE.

IFAD (International Fund for Agricultural Development). 2003. Republic of the Sudan, Gash sustainable livelihoods regeneration project, project document. Rome, IFAD.

——. 2001. *Rural Poverty Report 2001: The Challenge of Ending Rural Poverty*. Oxford, IFAD.

IPCC (International Panel on Climate Change). 2001. *Third Assessment Report – Climate Change 2001: Synthesis Report*. Geneva, IPCC.

IWMI (International Water Management Institute). 2003. *Confronting the Reality of Wastewater Use in Agriculture*. Water Policy Briefing No. 9. Colombo, Sri Lanka, IWMI.

Johnson III, S., Svendsen, M. and Gonzalez, F. 2002. Options for institutional reform in the irrigation sector. International Seminar on Participatory Irrigation Management, Beijing.

Kijne, J. W., Barker, R. and Molden, D. (eds). 2003. *Water Productivity in Agriculture: Limits and Opportunities for Improvement*. Wallingford, UK, CABI Publishing.

Lipton, M., Litchfield, J. and Faurès, J. M. 2003. The effects of irrigation on poverty: a framework for analysis. *Water Policy*, Vol. 5, No. 5/6, pp. 413–27.

Mason, J. B. 2002. Measuring hunger and malnutrition. Measurement and assessment of food deprivation and undernutrition. Proceedings of an international scientific symposium convened by FAO, 26–28 June, Rome.

Meinzen-Dick, R. 1997. Valuing the multiple uses of irrigation water. M. Kay, T. Frank and L. Smith (eds), *Water: Economics, Management and Demand*. London, E. & F. N. Spon.

Meinzen-Dick, R. and Bakker, M. 1999. Irrigation systems as multiple-use commons: Water use in Kirindi Oya, Sri Lanka. *Agriculture and Human Values*, No. 16, pp. 281–93.

Moench, M. 2001. Groundwater: Potential and Constraints. *2020 Vision Focus (Overcoming Water Scarcity and Quality Constraints)*, No. 9. Washington, DC, IFPRI.

Molden, D., Murray-Rust, H., Sakthivadivel R. and Makin, I. 2003. A water productivity framework for understanding and action. J. W. Kijne, R. Barker, and D. Molden (eds), *Water Productivity in Agriculture: Limits and Opportunities for Improvement*. Wallingford, UK, CABI Publishing and IWMI.

Mollinga, P. P. and Bolding, A. 2004. *The Politics of Irrigation Reform: Contested Policy Formulation and Implementation and Implementation in Asia, Africa and Latin America*. Aldershot, UK, Ashgate Publishing.

Nicol, A. 2000. Adopting a sustainable livelihoods approach to water projects: Implications for policy and practice. Working Paper 133, London, Overseas Development Institute.

Rathgeber, E. 2003. *Dry taps... Gender and Poverty in Water Resources Management*. Rome, FAO.

Renault, D. 2003. Value of virtual water in food: principles and virtues. A.Y. Hoekstra (ed.), *Virtual Water Trade, Proceedings of the International Expert Meeting on Virtual Water Trade*. Delft, the Netherlands, UNESCO-IHE.

Ringersma, J., Batjes, N. and Dent, D. 2003. *Green Water: Definitions and Data for Assessment*. Wageningen, the Netherlands, ISRIC.

Rockström, J. 1999. On-farm green water estimates as a tool for increased food production in water scarce regions. *Phys. Chem. Earth B*, Vol. 24, No. 4, pp. 375–83.

Rockström, J., Barron, J. and Fox, P. 2003. Water productivity in rain-fed agriculture: Challenges and opportunities for smallholder farmers in drought-prone tropical agro-ecosystems. J. W. Kijne, R. Barker and D. Molden (eds), *Water Productivity in Agriculture: Limits and Opportunities for Improvement*. Wallingford, UK, CABI Publishing.

Schmidhuber, J., 2003. The outlook for long-term changes in food consumption patterns: Concerns and policy options. Paper prepared for the FAO Scientific Workshop on Globalization of the Food System: Impacts on Food Security and Nutrition, 8–10 October 2003, Rome, FAO.

Seckler, D., Molden, D. and Sakthivadivel, R. 2003. The concept of efficiency in water-resources management and policy. J. W. Kijne, R. Barker and D. Molden (eds), *Water Productivity in Agriculture: Limits and Opportunities for Improvement.* Wallingford, UK, CABI Publishing.

Shiklomanov, I. 2000. Appraisal and assessment of world water resources. *Water, International*, Vol. 25, No. 1, pp. 11–32, March 2000. IWRA.

Siebert, S., Döll, P., Feick, S. and Hoogeveen, J. 2005. *Global Map of Irrigated Areas.* Version 3.0, interactive map. Frankfurt/Rome, Johann Wolfgang Goethe University and FAO.

Smedema, L. K. and Shiati, K. 2002. Irrigation and salinity: A perspective review of the salinity hazards of irrigation development in the arid zone. *Irrigation and Drainage Systems*, Vol. 16, No. 2, pp. 161–74.

UN (United Nations). 2004. *World Population Monitoring 2003: Population, Education and Development.* Department of Economic and Social Affairs, Population Division. New York, United Nations.

UN (United Nations) Millennium Project Task Force on Hunger. 2004. Halving hunger by 2015: A framework for action. Interim report. Millennium project. New York, United Nations.

Vincent, L. 2001. Water and rural livelihoods. R. Meinzen-Dick and M. W. Rosegrant (eds), *2020 Vision Focus 9 (Overcoming Water Scarcity and Quality Constraints).* Brief 5. Washington, DC, International Food Policy Research Institute.

Wani, S. P., Pathak, P., Sreedevi, T. K., Singh, H. P. and Singh, P. 2003. Efficient management of rainwater for increased crop productivity and groundwater recharge in Asia. J. W. Kijne, R. Barker and D. Molden (eds), *Water*

Productivity in Agriculture: Limits and Opportunities for Improvement. Wallingford, UK, CABI Publishing.

Winpenny, J. T. 1997. Demand management for efficient and equitable use. M. Kay, T. Frank and L. Smith (eds), *Water: Economics, Management and Demand.* London, E. & F.N. Spon.

WCD (World Commission on Dams). 2000. *Dams and Development, A New Framework for Decision-making: The Report of the World Commission on Dams.* London and Sterling, VA, Earthscan Publications Ltd.

Zwarteveen, M. Z. 1996. *A Plot of One's Own: Gender Relations and Irrigated Land Allocation Policies in Burkina Faso.* Washington, DC, The Consultative Group on International Agricultural Research (CGIAR).

CGIAR (Consultative Group on International Agriculture Research) – Challenge Program on Water and Food:
www.waterforfood.org/
One of the greatest challenges of our time is to provide food and environmental security. The CGIAR Challenge Program on Water and Food approaches this challenge from a research perspective.

Comprehensive Assessment of Water Management in Agriculture (CA): www.iwmi.cgiar.org/Assessment/Index.asp
A multi-partner assessment process hosted by International Water Management Institute (IWMI). The CA Synthesis Report will be released in August 2006. It will examine trends, conditions, challenges and responses in water management for agriculture in order to identify the most appropriate investments for enhancing food and environmental security over the next fifty years.

FAO-AQUASTAT: www.fao.org/ag/aquastat/
Global information system of water and agriculture. Provides users with comprehensive information on the state of agricultural water management across the world, with emphasis on developing countries and countries in transition (statistics, country profiles, maps and GIS).

FAO-FAOSTAT: faostat.external.fao.org/
Online multilingual database containing over 3 million time-series records covering international statistics in the areas of food production, prices, trade, land use, irrigation, forests, fisheries, etc.

FAO – Global Perspective Studies: www.fao.org/es/ESD/gstudies.htm
Includes the report, *World Agriculture: Towards 2015/2030*, which is FAO's latest assessment of the long-term outlook for the world's food supplies, nutrition and agriculture.

FAO – The State of World Fisheries and Aquaculture (SOFIA): www.fao.org/sof/sofia/index_en.htm
Published every two years with the purpose of providing policy-makers, civil society and those who derive their livelihood from the sector with a comprehensive, objective and global view of capture fisheries and aquaculture, including associated policy issues.

FAO – The State of Food Insecurity (SOFI): www.fao.org/sof/sofi/index_en.htm
Reports annually on global and national efforts to reduce by half the number of undernourished people in the world by the year 2015.

ICID (International Commission on Irrigation and Drainage): www.icid.org/
ICID is a non-profit organization dedicated to enhancing the worldwide supply of food and fibre by improving the productivity of irrigated and drained lands through the appropriate management of water and environment and the application of irrigation, drainage and flood management techniques.

IFAD (International Fund for Agricultural Development) – Rural Poverty: www.ifad.org/poverty/
In its *Rural Poverty Report 2001, The Challenge of Ending Rural Poverty*, the International Fund for Agricultural Development argues that, to be successful, poverty-reduction policies must focus on rural areas.

We are no longer able to think of ourselves as a species tossed about by larger forces – now we _are_ those larger forces.

Bill McKibben, *The End of Nature*

CHAPTER 8

Water and Industry

By

UNIDO
(United Nations Industrial Development Organization)

Aerial view of the disposal of mine wastes into a water body, Ishpeming, Michigan, US

Key messages:

For the majority of the world's population, a thriving economy and improvement in the quality of life are closely linked to better access to consumer goods. Growing local industries create much-needed jobs, so people have more disposable income to spend on manufactured products. This often comes at the cost of increasing volumes of dumped solid waste, deteriorating water quality, and increased air pollution, when industry discharges untreated wastes onto land and into water and air. However, the linkage between industry and pollution is not inevitable. The purpose of this chapter is to show that manufacturing activities can be both clean and profitable. Indeed, industry can lead the way in pricing water at its true value and conserving high-quality water resources. Governance has an important role to play in creating the conditions that promote healthy and sustainable industrial growth.

- Industry is a significant engine of growth providing 48 percent of gross domestic product (GDP) in East Asia/Pacific, 26 percent of GDP in lower-income countries and 29 percent of GDP in higher-income countries, although this last figure is declining.

- Much industrial activity in middle- and lower-income countries is accompanied by unnecessarily high levels of water consumption and water pollution.

- Worldwide, the total rate of water withdrawals by industry is slowing, whereas the rate of water consumed is steadily increasing.

- It is possible to decouple industrial development from environmental degradation, to radically reduce natural resource and energy consumption and, at the same time, to have clean and profitable industries.

- A very wide range of regulatory instruments, voluntary initiatives, training and advice is available to help industrial managers improve water-use productivity and to reduce polluting emissions to very low levels. At the same time, these tools can aid production efficiency, reduce raw material consumption, facilitate recovery of valuable materials and permit a big expansion of re-use/recycling.

Top to bottom:
Industrial site in
Grangemouth, Scotland

Dockside construction site
in the US

Water treated on site at a
rubber factory, Malaysia

Section 3: CHALLENGES FOR WELL-BEING & DEVELOPMENT

Part 1. Industry in an Economic Context

Industry is the engine of growth and socio-economic development in many developing countries. In the fast-growing East Asia and Pacific region, industry now provides 48 percent of the total gross domestic product (GDP), and this proportion is still increasing. In heavily indebted poor countries, the proportion of GDP provided by industry grew quickly from 22 percent to 26 percent between 1998 and 2002. In rich countries, by contrast, the proportion of GDP coming from the production of manufactured goods is slowly declining, currently providing some 29 percent of GDP, with services making up the bulk of the economy. Overall however, industrial production continues to grow worldwide, as economies grow (World Bank, 2003).

The total water withdrawal from surface water and groundwater by industry is usually much greater than the amount of water that is actually consumed

1a. Water use by industry

Water is used by industry in a myriad of ways: for cleaning, heating and cooling; for generating steam; for transporting dissolved substances or particulates; as a raw material; as a solvent; and as a constituent part of the product itself (e.g. in the beverage industry). The water that evaporates in the process must also be considered in accurate assessments as well as the water that remains in the product, by-products, and the solid wastes generated along the way. The balance is discharged after use as wastewater or effluent. The total water *withdrawal* from surface water and groundwater by industry is usually much greater than the amount of water that is actually consumed, as illustrated by the graphs in **Figures 8.1** and **8.2**. Industrial water use tends to be measured in terms of water withdrawal, not water consumption.

Following major growth between 1960 and 1980, water withdrawal for use by industry worldwide has pretty much stabilized. Industrial water withdrawal in Europe has actually been dropping since 1980, although industrial output continues to expand. In Asia, the growth in industrial water withdrawal was rapid up to 1990, and has since been growing much more slowly, despite the region's high growth in manufacturing output. As shown by these figures, the intensity of water use in industry is increasing in these regions, as is the value added by industry per unit of water used (see **Table 8.4** at end of chapter).

Once more information becomes available on environmental water flow requirements in many rivers and rainfed agriculture, a fuller picture may be presented of the allocation of water among all its various uses. It will also be necessary to analyse actual water use in terms of consumption by the various sectors (see **Figure 8.3**). The return flows from the different sectors to surface water and groundwater must be accurately depicted, with the inclusion of water reuse cycles (and water reclamation, see discussion below). Only then can a realistic water balance be prepared for a given river basin or country.

1b. Negative industrial impacts on the water environment

Frequently of greater concern than the actual volume of water used by industry is the negative impact of industry on the water environment. Water quality is deteriorating in many rivers worldwide, and the marine environment is also being affected by industrial pollution. How does this take place? Much of the water used by industry is usually disposed of 'to drain'. This can mean one of the following things:

■ direct disposal into a stream, canal or river, or to sea

■ disposal to sewer (which may be discharged, untreated, further downstream, or may be routed to the nearest municipal sewage treatment plant)

■ treatment by an on-site wastewater treatment plant, before being discharged to a watercourse or sewer treatment in a series of open ponds.

There are many instances of water reclamation (treating or processing wastewater to make it reusable), where industrial effluent is not returned immediately to the natural water cycle after use. It can be recycled or reused directly on-site, either before or after treatment. The water may also be treated and then reused by other industries nearby or agricultural or municipal users, as well as for cropland irrigation or local parks and gardens. All these possibilities for water reclamation and reuse are dependent on the quality of the discharge and are discussed in more detail in Part 3. Reclaimed water that has been treated can also help to conserve the water environment by being injected to replenish underground aquifers or prevent salt-water intrusion or by being discharged into a drought-stricken wetland.

Of major concern are the situations in which the industrial discharge is returned directly into the water cycle without adequate treatment. If the water is contaminated with

Figure 8.1: Trends in industrial water use by region, 1950–2000

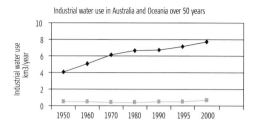

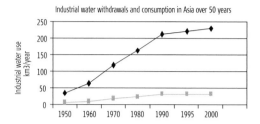

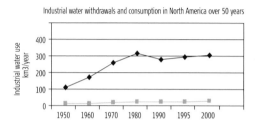

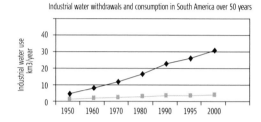

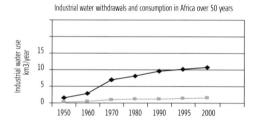

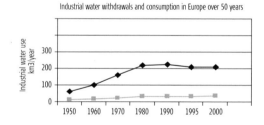

Note: Vertical scale varies among the graphs. Industrial water withdrawals in Africa and South America are still rising, albeit off a very low base. In Asia, North America and Europe, industrial water use accounts for the bulk of the global figure for industrial water withdrawals. Note that industrial water consumption is everywhere much lower than the volume of water withdrawn.

Source: Shiklomanov, 2000.

Figure 8.2: Total world industrial water use, 1950–2000

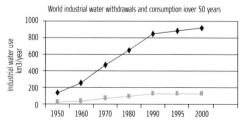

Source: Shiklomanov, 2000.

Figure 8.3: Water use by industry vs. domestic use and agriculture

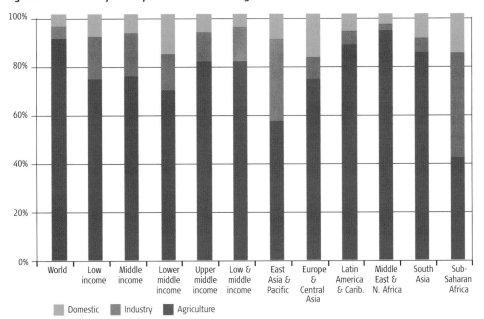

Legend:
- ■ Domestic
- ■ Industry
- ■ Agriculture

(Categories along x-axis: World, Low income, Middle income, Lower middle income, Upper middle income, Low & middle income, East Asia & Pacific, Europe & Central Asia, Latin America & Carib., Middle East & N. Africa, South Asia, Sub-Saharan Africa)

Note: There is increasing competition for water among the various water use sectors in many river basins. If we compare water use (i.e. water withdrawal) by industry to water use by other sectors, namely agriculture and domestic use, it is clear that globally, industry uses only a fraction of the amount of water used by agriculture. However, in East Asia and the Pacific, industrial water use has grown to a significant proportion of total use, in line with its significance to the economies of those countries. In sub-Saharan Africa, although overall water use is low, the water used by industry is a larger proportion of the total, because more agriculture is rainfed, rather than irrigated. These data exclude rainfed agriculture from the calculations of water use, and do not include environmental flow requirements as a water use category. In many catchment areas and river basins, environmental needs have not yet been calculated (see **Chapter 5**).

Source: World Bank, 2002.

Above: An Ijaw child shows off the oil that has damaged the communal forest around her village in the Delta region of Nigeria. The fish catch has dropped dramatically as a result of oil spillage from a nearby extraction pipe

Below: Wastewater from bleaching cotton in a mill, Ndola, Zambia

heavy metals, chemicals or particulates, or loaded with organic matter, this obviously affects the quality of the receiving water body or aquifer. The sediments downstream from the industrial discharge can also be contaminated. Water that has a high organic content (called the biochemical oxygen demand, or BOD) often appears cloudy or foamy, and is characterized by the rapid growth of algae, bacteria and slime (see **Figures 8.4** and **8.5** and **Chapter 5**). The growth of these organisms depletes the level of oxygen in the water. It is more difficult for fish, insects, amphibians and many species of aquatic plants to live and breed in such oxygen-depleted water. If the water discharged is still hot, this 'thermal pollution' may also affect the aquatic ecosystems downstream, which have to adjust to a temperature that is higher than normal (see also **Chapter 9**).

A much larger volume of water may actually be affected than the volume of the industrial discharge itself. Industries and water quality regulators in some places still rely on the so-called 'dilution effect' to disperse contaminants within the water environment to the point where they fall below harmful levels. In areas where industries are growing fast and more industrial plants are coming on-stream with many newly created discharge points, this approach can quickly result in polluted rivers and reservoirs. The toxicity levels and lack of oxygen in the water can damage or completely destroy the aquatic ecosystems downstream as well as lakes and dams, ultimately affecting riverine estuaries and marine coastal environments. In international river basins, routine pollution and polluting incidents such as industrial accidents and spillages may have transboundary effects. Significant pollution sources in river basins, such as large industrial plants, may be termed 'hot spots' and prioritized for clean-up within a river basin management plan (see **Box 8.1**).

It is important to consider not only the level or concentration of individual substances, but also their combined effect. It is very expensive to monitor water quality for the presence of numerous chemicals, each of which must be tested for separately. By monitoring the populations of certain organisms, called indicator organisms (such as frogs, molluscs or certain insect species), it is possible to create a picture of how the water body is being affected over time. These eco-toxicological methods provide a more cost-effective way of assessing the impact of industrial discharges and are discussed in more detail in **Chapter 5** on ecosystems.

Direct human health impacts can result if the industrial discharge is located upstream of:

- a recreational bathing and swimming area or commercial, recreational or subsistence fishing grounds

- a point where farmers withdraw water in order to irrigate their crops

- a point where a municipality withdraws water for domestic use

- a point where people without a formal water supply withdraw water for drinking.

Many municipalities now find that the quality of the drinking water which they supply is compromised by industrial pollution. This raises water treatment costs for the water supply utility. Where the problem is variable freshwater quality, caused by irregular effluent discharges, the water treatment plant may not be able to cope adequately with the contaminants. In such cases the health of local people may be affected in the longer term, depending on the concentration and type of substances involved.

Two additional ways in which industries may more indirectly affect the water environment are through the following:

BOX 8.1: IDENTIFICATION, ASSESSMENT AND PRIORITIZATION OF POLLUTION 'HOT SPOTS'

The methodology for evaluating hot spots was developed within the framework of the Global Environment Facility (GEF) regional project preparing a Strategic Action Plan for the transboundary Dnieper River Basin, including areas of the three countries involved, namely Russia, Ukraine and Belarus. The objectives of the Strategic Action Plan are to facilitate the reduction of pollution in the river basin, and ultimately to contribute to the protection of the Black Sea.

As in many river basins in populated areas, there are thousands of pollution sources in the Dnieper River Basin. The Hot Spot methodology identifies, assesses and prioritizes the most significant sources of pollution, based on their impacts and characteristics. These include point sources, such as industrial and municipal effluents, and non-point sources, such as agricultural and urban runoff. Each contributes to human health risk and environmental degradation, including significant impacts to environmentally sensitive areas where biodiversity is threatened.

A multi-stage screening system, developed by the United Nations Industrial Development Organization (UNIDO), is used to identify priority hot spots. They are evaluated according to pollution control issues, water quality issues and biodiversity issues, as well as economic and employment criteria. Point sources of pollution are scored on a number of criteria under each of these general headings, which are then weighted according to their significance, before a total score is assigned. Non-point sources and areas that are difficult to characterize quantitatively (e.g. abandoned military facilities, or large tailings ponds) may still rank as hot spots but are described qualitatively, based upon the professional judgement of national experts. Finally, for a small group of priority hot spots, mitigation measures are proposed together with an estimation of implementation costs and a cost-benefit analysis.

An example of water quality issues scored includes the following criteria:

- location of nearest municipal drinking water withdrawal downstream
- influence of river quality on the nearest municipal drinking water withdrawal point
- population being supplied by river water within 25 kilometres downstream of the hot spot
- recreational bathing areas located near the hot spot
- other aquatic recreational activities near the hot spot
- any illnesses attributed to the recreational areas
- hot spot directly identified as the source of illnesses
- proximity of recreational fishing areas and sustainability
- proximity of commercial fishing areas and sustainability
- agricultural water utilization in proximity to the hot spot
- sediment quality
- proximity to national boundaries.

Source: UNIDO, 2003.

■ The leaching of chemicals from solid wastes: The solid wastes generated by industrial activity may contain a quantity of contaminated water or other liquids, which gradually seep out once the waste is disposed of. In the rain (or in groundwater, if the waste is buried in a landfill), further chemicals may be leached or mobilized from the solid waste over time. This leachate eventually reaches a stream or an aquifer. Industrial dumpsites and municipal landfill sites, if not adequately constructed, are frequently found to generate such 'leachate plumes' that can be significant pollution hot spots.

■ The atmospheric deposition of chemicals distributed through air and rain pollution: Some industries emit significant quantities of sulphur and nitrogen compounds (SOx and NOx) into the atmosphere. These may dissolve into raindrops, and fall as acid rain. Many streams, rivers and lakes in Europe are more acid than they would naturally be, due to this process. Other compounds such as dioxins and furans may also be released into the atmosphere from furnaces, and thereby enter the water cycle.

More detailed information on industrial pollution in Europe is available since the introduction of the European Pollutant Emissions Register. All factories in the European Union over a certain size are required to report their emissions. **Figure 8.5** shows figures on total organic carbon releases to water (a more accurate measure than the BOD data available). **Table 8.1** shows the amount of benzene, toluene, ethylbenzenes and xylenes being released annually to the water environment, both directly and indirectly. These toxic hydrocarbons are emitted by a range of industries, from oil refineries to pharmaceutical plants.

1c. Natech disasters

Natech disasters are a new disaster category, identified by the UN International Strategy on Disaster Reduction (UN-ISDR) as a technological disaster triggered by a natural hazard (see **Box 8.2**). In Europe, for instance, there are many vulnerable installations close to rivers or in earthquake-prone regions, which are vulnerable to flooding or strong tremors (see **Chapter 10**).

For example, the magnitude of an earthquake in Turkey that measured 7.0 on the Richter Scale in August 1999 triggered unprecedented multiple and simultaneous hazardous materials releases, wreaking havoc on relief operations assisting earthquake victims. In one incident, the leakage of 6.5 million kilograms (kg) of toxic acrylonitrile (ACN) contaminated air, soil and water,

Figure 8.4: Industry shares of biological oxygen demand (BOD), by industrial sector and in selected countries

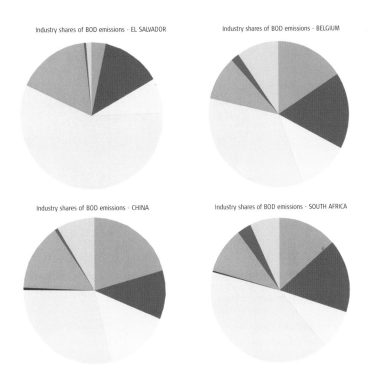

Industry shares of BOD emissions - EL SALVADOR

Industry shares of BOD emissions - BELGIUM

Industry shares of BOD emissions - CHINA

Industry shares of BOD emissions - SOUTH AFRICA

■ Primary metals
■ Paper and pulp
■ Chemicals
  Food and beverages
■ Stone, ceramics and glass
■ Textiles
■ Wood
  Other

Note: This figure shows the industry shares of organic pollution emissions (using BOD as an indicator), by industrial sector in selected countries. The data on BOD is the only pollution data available, and it is not very accurate as it is calculated indirectly from employment data in the various industrial sectors.

In less developed economies, such as in El Salvador, the food and beverage industry generates the majority of the organically loaded effluent. In developed countries such as Belgium, where the economy is more diversified, effluent from the food and beverage industry is still significant, but there is a wider spread of other contributing sectors. In China, the primary metals sector, chemicals and textiles contribute the lion's share. In all countries, the pulp and paper sector can be a significant polluter of the aquatic environment, if untreated effluent is released.

Source: World Bank, 2002.

threatening residential areas. Automatic foam sprayers were available at the industrial facility at the time of the earthquake, which would normally have contained the ACN release, but these were rendered useless due to a lack of water and power. These technological disasters posed additional health and psychological problems to an already devastated population. Hence current industrial risk management regulations should be carefully revised to ensure that this kind of 'natech' risk is being addressed.

Figure 8.5: Release of total organic carbon (TOC) directly or indirectly to water in thirteen EU Member States, 2003

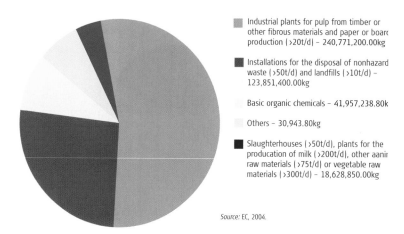

Industrial plants for pulp from timber or other fibrous materials and paper or board production (>20t/d) – 240,771,200.00kg

Installations for the disposal of nonhazard waste (>50t/d) and landfills (>10t/d) – 123,851,400.00kg

Basic organic chemicals – 41,957,238.80k

Others – 30,943.80kg

Slaughterhouses (>50t/d), plants for the producation of milk (>200t/d), other aanir raw materials (>75t/d) or vegetable raw materials (>300t/d) – 18,628,850.00kg

Source: EC, 2004.

Table 8.1: Release of benzene, toluene, ethylbenzene and xylenes directly or indirectly to water in eight EU Member States, 2003

Activity releasing benzene, toluene, ethylbenzene and xylenes	Directly to water (kg/year)	Indirectly to water (kg/year)
Combustion installations (> 50 MW)	967	2,830
Mineral oil and gas refineries	67,486	880
Coke ovens	390	–
Coal gasification and liquefaction plants	1,020	–
Metal industry and metal ore roasting or sintering installations	16,080	8,080
Basic organic chemicals	40,328	127,158
Basic inorganic chemicals or fertilisers	57,996	–
Biocides and explosives	6,170	365
Pharmaceutical products	1,282	7,550
Installations for the disposal or recovery of hazardous waste (>10 tons/day)	2,300	2,136
Plants for the pre-treatment of fibres or textiles (>10 tons/day)	–	707
Installations for surface treatment or products using organic solvents (>200 tons/year)	–	3,773
Total	**194,019**	**153,479**

Source: EC, 2004.

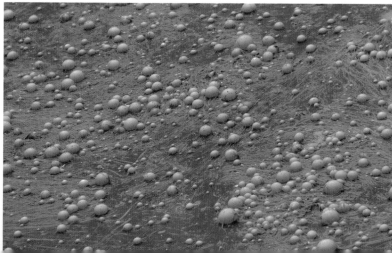

BOX 8.2: INDUSTRIAL DISASTERS AROUND THE WORLD

The Tisza tailings dam disaster

On 30 January 2000, a breach in a tailings dam released some 100,000 cubic metres (m^3) of cyanide-rich tailings waste into the river system near Baia Mare in northwest Romania (see also **Chapter 14**). This spill released an estimated 50 to 100 tonnes (t) of cyanide, as well as heavy metals, into the Somes, Tisza and finally the Danube Rivers before reaching the Black Sea. Ice on the rivers and low water levels in Hungary delayed the dilution of the cyanide, increasing the risk to municipal water supplies. High concentrations of copper, zinc and lead, leached by the cyanide, compounded the problem. Impacts included:

■ contamination and interruption of the drinking water in twenty-four locations, affecting 2.5 million people
■ massive fish kill and destruction of aquatic species in the river systems
■ severe negative impact on socio-economic conditions of the local population
■ long-term reduction of revenue from tourism and canoeing
■ drop in real estate prices.

The Red Rhine Incident

In 1986 a fire destroyed a chemical store in Basel, Switzerland, near the borders of France and Germany. Chemicals reached the water in the Rhine River through the plant's sewage system when huge amounts of water (10,000-15,000 m^3) were used to fight the fire. The store contained large quantities of thirty-two different chemicals, including insecticides and raw ingredients, and the water implications were identified through the presence of red dye in one of the substances, which turned the river red. The main wave of chemicals destroyed eels, fish and insects, as well as habitats for small animals on the riverbanks. The total eel population was destroyed for 500 kilometres (km) downstream, from Basel in Switzerland down to Loreley in Germany. It took three months after the incident for the contaminant concentrations to drop to normal values. As a result of new regulations and precautions put in place following this incident, the permanent chemical load in the Rhine has been reduced, and information systems on potential incidents improved.

Arsenic contamination from mines in Thailand

Past mining activities caused heavy arsenic contamination of groundwater and topsoil over a 40 km^3 area in Nakhon Si Thammarat province, Thailand (see **Chapter 14**). The contamination was revealed in a study commissioned by the Japan International Cooperation Agency (JICA) in 2000. One conclusion of the study was that the contamination would last for the next thirty to fifty years. Testing of 1,000 samples showed arsenic contamination in some groundwater wells to be 50 to 100 times higher than the World Health Organization's guideline value for drinking water (0.01 milligrams per litre). Most people in the affected district stopped drinking well water in 1993, after the local health effects were found, and are now paying a very high cost for tap water.

Martin County, Kentucky, United States

On 11 October 2000, a coal tailings dam failed after the collapse of an underground mine beneath the slurry impoundment, and 950,000 m^3 of coal waste slurry was released into local streams. About 120 km of rivers and streams turned an iridescent black, causing a fish kill along the Tug Fork of the Big Sandy River and some of its tributaries. Towns along the Tug were forced to turn off their drinking water intakes.

Nandan County, Guangxi Province, China

Also in October 2000, after a tailings dam failure, at least 15 people were reported killed and 100 missing. More than 100 houses were destroyed by the tailing wave downstream.

Sebastião das Águas Claras, Nova Lima District, Minas Gerais, Brazil

On 22 June 2001, the failure of an iron mine waste dam caused a tailings wave to travel at least 6 km. Five mine workers died in the incident.

San Marcelino, Zambales, Philippines

In August 2002, at the Dizon Copper Silver Mines, after heavy rain, the overflow and spillway failure of two abandoned tailings dams caused some tailings to spill into Mapanuepe Lake and eventually into the St. Tomas River. By 11 September, several low-lying villages had been flooded with mine waste: 250 families were evacuated; no injuries were reported.

Source: WHO, 2004.

Part 2. Governance Issues and Sustainable Development in Industry Regulation

Environmental governance is central to ensuring that growing industries undertake an acceptable and affordable level of pollution control and environmental management. This section discusses a number of international conventions and multilateral environmental agreements (MEAs) that exist in order to regulate industries, and in particular those dealing with hazardous and toxic chemicals (see Table 8.2**). It is also important to note that voluntary systems go a long way towards demonstrating that industries can be both clean and profitable. Various voluntary approaches have been developed over time and are discussed later in this chapter.**

The 'polluter pays principle', or the 3Ps, was first widely discussed at the 1992 United Nations Conference on Environment and Development held in Rio de Janeiro, Brazil (Rio Principle 16). The principle was endorsed by the attending country representatives, and was also adopted by the Conference of the Parties of the Basel Convention among others (see section 2a below). Under the Basel Convention, the 3Ps states that the potential polluter must act to prevent pollution, and that those who cause pollution must pay for remedying the consequences of that pollution. With the development of the concept of Cleaner Production (see section 3b below), the 3Ps now stand for Pollution Prevention Pays: in other words, good environmental management need not be simply an extra cost for a company to bear, but can actually improve production processes, save money and resources, and make the company more efficient, more profitable and more competitive in the global marketplace.

The World Summit on Sustainable Development (WSSD), held in Johannesburg, South Africa, in August 2002 proposed a Plan of Implementation, which makes a strong link between the related goals of industrial development, poverty eradication and sustainable natural resource management[1] (see **Box 8.3**). The Johannesburg targets proposed for industry to build on what was defined in Goal 7 of the Millennium Development Goals (MDGs) in 2000 by doing the following:

■ ensuring environmental sustainability

■ integrating the principles of sustainable development into country policies and programmes

■ reversing the loss of environmental resources.

For countries adopting poverty-reduction policies, industrial growth is desirable in order to diversify their economy, create jobs and add value to primary products and raw materials being produced. However, it is very important that the necessary legal and institutional arrangements be in place to enable this growth to take place sustainably. Since water pollution can have significant transboundary effects, good environmental governance at the national level includes committing to international agreements and conventions on transboundary cooperation on shared waters (see **Chapter 11**).

2a. Best environmental practices and international standards for industry

Voluntary measures and self-regulation are the means whereby industries can demonstrate their commitment to improving the environment and monitoring their own performance. The extent of self-regulation tends to vary with the size of the enterprise, and the industrial sector in question. Consumers and media pressure can often influence the level of eco-awareness of companies in a particular sector. Women working through consumer organizations and environmental pressure groups have been particularly successful in bringing about good environmental practices in the companies making household products such as detergents. Eco-labelling is a growing practice whereby consumers can choose to buy certain products labelled to indicate that they are produced in a cleaner and more environmentally responsible way.

The international competitiveness of a company and its products in the global market is therefore often enhanced by its commitment to best environmental practices (BEP).[2] A company can show its high quality of self-regulation by seeking certification through ISO 14001, which is the current international environmental standard administered

---

1. See www.un.org/esa/sustdev/documents/WSSD_POI_PD/English/POIToc.htm

2. Best Environmental Practices (BEP) are guidelines that exist for all sectors of human society striving to co-exist with the natural environment, such as housing, infrastructure, industry and tourism. BEPs for industry include carrying out environmental impact assessments for new projects, environmental audits for existing projects and using best available technology.

by the International Organization for Standardization. By the end of 2002, nearly 50,000 companies in 118 countries had received this certification (see **Table 8.2**).

Some of the approaches to BEP, discussed below, have been made mandatory in national environmental law in some countries, but not in others. BEP can begin at the planning and design stage of a new industrial installation, with an environmental impact assessment (EIA), and be continued by putting in place an environmental management system (EMS) for the plant. Periodic or occasional environmental audits can be carried out during the plant's lifetime in order to assess the effectiveness of the environmental management system, and the plant's compliance with environmental regulations. The use of Best Available Technology (BAT) usually goes hand-in-hand with BEP (see **Box 8.4**).

Environmental Impact Assessment (EIA)

The EIA process is now required by law for new projects and significant extensions of existing projects in many countries. It covers a broad range of activities ranging from industrial to infrastructure projects. The process introduces procedural elements, such as the provision of an environmental impact statement and consultation with the public and environmental authorities, within the framework of development consent procedures for the activities covered.

...good environmental management need not be simply an extra cost for a company to bear...

BOX 8.3: INTERNATIONAL AGREEMENTS AND MULTILATERAL ENVIRONMENTAL AGREEMENTS (MEAs)

The Basel Convention on the Control of Transboundary Movements of Hazardous Wastes and their Disposal	**Entered into force in May 1992.** As of 28 May 2004, 159 states and the European Union were Parties to the Convention, which is an effective mechanism for addressing waste generation, movement, management and disposal. It plays a significant role in the safe management of chemicals. Recently, the Basel Convention joined with other existing international organizations in the creation of the Africa Stockpile Project, aimed at eliminating harmful stockpiles of pesticides on that continent. The Basel Convention is also working to create useful partnerships in areas as diverse as e-waste[1], biological and medical waste, and a global partnership aimed at addressing the stockpile of used oils in Africa.
The Rotterdam Convention on the Prior Informed Consent (PIC) Procedure for Certain Hazardous Chemicals and Pesticides in International Trade	**A voluntary procedure from 1980 onwards**, and is now mandatory in the 73 countries that are party to the Convention. This Convention entered into force in February 2004. A total of 27 hazardous chemicals are currently subject to the PIC Procedure. To put this into perspective, about 70,000 chemicals are currently on the market, with 1,500 new ones being added each year. This poses a significant challenge to governments, which must monitor and manage the use of these chemicals. The treaty helps countries to reduce the risks associated with the manufacture, trade and use of hazardous chemicals.
The Stockholm Convention on Persistent Organic Pollutants (POPs)	**A global treaty, which entered into force in May 2004** and is designed to protect human health and the environment from persistent organic pollutants (POPs). POPs are chemicals that remain intact in the environment for long periods, become widely distributed geographically, accumulate in the fatty tissue of living organisms, and are toxic to humans and wildlife. They have been shown to cause cancer and to damage the nervous, reproductive and immune systems, as well as causing birth defects. At present, twelve hazardous chemicals, including DDT, dioxins and furans, are listed as POPs. In implementing the Convention, governments take measures to eliminate or reduce the release of POPs into the environment.

BOX 8.3: CONTINUED

The European Union Water Framework Directive (WFD) on Integrated River Basin Management for Europe

Adopted in October 2000, it coordinates the objectives of European water policy in order to protect all waters, including surface water and groundwater, using a river basin management approach. The WFD coordinates with all previous EU directives relating to water, including the **Integrated Pollution Prevention and Control Directive** (IPPC) of 1996, which addresses industrial installations with a high pollution potential. Such installations may only be operated if the operator holds a permit containing requirements for the protection of air, water and soil, waste minimization, accident prevention and, if necessary, site clean-up. These requirements must be based on the principle of **Best Available Techniques** (BAT) (see following section). The European Pollutant and Emissions Register, which has been compiled under the IPPC Directive, contains information on the emissions to air and water of nearly 10,000 industrial installations across Europe.[2]

The UNECE Convention on the Protection and Use of Transboundary Waters and International Lakes (UNECE Water Convention)

Intended to strengthen national measures for the protection and ecologically sound management of transboundary surface water and groundwater. It obliges Parties to prevent, control and reduce water pollution from point and non-point sources. More than 150 major rivers and 30 large lakes in the UNECE region run along or straddle the border between two or more countries. **The Convention entered into force in October 1996** and has been ratified by 34 countries and by the European Community. It is open for accession by all UN Member States.

The 1992 UNECE Convention on the Transboundary Effects of Industrial Accidents

Entered into force in April 2000, and 32 countries and the European Community are currently Parties to the Convention. This Convention cooperates with the UNECE Water Convention on issues related to the prevention of chemical accidents and the limitation of their impact on transboundary waters. In 2003 this resulted in the signing of the joint Protocol on Civil Liability and Compensation for Damage caused by Industrial Accidents on Transboundary Waters. The following work is being undertaken under both Conventions:

- An inventory of existing safety guidelines and best practices for the prevention of accidental transboundary water pollution[3]
- Safety guidelines and best practices for tailing dams, pipelines, and navigation of ships on rivers
- Alarm and notification systems
- International response exercises[4]
- Transboundary contingency planning.

1. E-waste is electronic and electrical waste including domestic computers and appliances.
2. The upgraded register, the European Pollutant Release and Transfer Register, should go online in 2009 and will then replace the present one, the European Pollutant and Emissions Register, EPER. Just like EPER, it will provide clear information about the level of specific pollutants, the quality of our local environment, emissions from specific industrial facilities and activities, and by country. But while EPER reports on 50 substances emitted to air and water, the PRTR will report on more than 90 substances released to air, water and land. The present register covers 56 industrial activities; the new one will cover 65. It will also have information on what the industrial installations do with their waste and waste water. The reporting cycle will be annual instead of every three years. What is more, the PRTR will compile reporting of pollution from diffuse sources such as road traffic, aviation, shipping and agriculture.
3. For more information see www.unece.org/env/teia/water/inventory.htm
4. For more information see www.unece.org/env/teia/response.htm

Table 8.2: Trends in ISO 14001 certification regionally and globally, 1997–2002

National standards institutes from individual countries have created the ISO 14000, which provides voluntary environmental management systems standards. The table below shows the number of companies in each region that have received the International Organization for Standardization (ISO) 14001 certification by December of any given year. Companies adhering to the ISO 14001 implement environmental management systems, conduct environmental audits, and evaluate their environmental performance. Their products adhere to environmental labelling standards, and waste streams are managed through life cycle assessments. However, the ISO does not require companies to provide public reports on their environmental performance.

The number of companies with ISO 14001 certification globally increased more than tenfold between 1997 (two years after the introduction of the standard) and 2002. Europe and the Far East dominate the statistics, with 47 percent and 36 percent respectively of all companies certified worldwide. (ISO 14001 replaced ISO 14000 in 1995).

Regions	Number of companies with ISO 14001 certification					
	1997	1998	1999	2000	2001	2002
North America	117	434	975	1,676	2,700	4,053
Share in percent	2.64	5.50	6.91	7.32	7.35	8.20
No. of countries	3	3	3	3	3	3
Europe	2,626	4,254	7,365	11,021	18,243	23,316
Share in percent	59.24	53.94	52.21	48.13	49.62	47.14
No. of countries/economies	25	29	32	36	41	44
Central and South America	98	144	309	556	681	1,418
Share in percent	2.21	1.83	2.19	2.43	1.86	2.87
No. of countries/economies	5	12	14	18	22	21
Africa/West Asia	73	138	337	651	923	1,355
Share in percent	1.65	1.75	2.39	2.84	2.51	2.74
No. of countries/economies	10	15	21	25	29	31
Australia/New Zealand	163	385	770	1,112	1,422	1,563
Share in percent	3.68	4.88	5.46	4.86	3.87	3.16
No. of countries	2	2	2	2	2	2
Far East	1,356	2,532	4,350	7,881	12,796	17,757
Share in percent	30.59	32.10	30.84	34.42	34.81	35.90
No. of countries/economies	10	11	12	14	16	17
World total	4,433	7,887	14,106	22,897	36,765	49,462
Number of countries/economies	55	72	84	98	112	118

This rapid worldwide increase in the number of companies certified is accompanied by a dramatic rise in environmental awareness of managers and workers, because there is a substantial element of training and capacity-building involved in the certification process. This capacity-building and development of the environmental knowledge base necessarily goes hand-in-hand with the introduction of new management systems and performance yardsticks in these companies (see **Chapter 13**).

Source: www.iso.org/iso/en/prods-services/otherpubs/iso14000/index.html

Water can be saved either by cutting down on water input... or by water recycling and reuse...

Part 3. The Vision: Towards High Water Productivity and Zero Effluent Discharge

Both water quantity and quality need to be considered in the challenge of improving industrial water use. Where water *quantity* is concerned, it is useful to consider water productivity, in terms of the industrial value added per unit of water used (see Table 8.5 at end of chapter). The higher the water productivity, the greater the intrinsic value being placed on the water. In water-scarce regions, where there is competition for water among various users, water is likely to be allocated to the more highly productive uses. Industry achieves higher water productivity than agriculture, but as it is difficult to compare the water productivity of domestic use or environmental flow requirements, because the adequate data and economic instruments are not available to make such comparisons. Within industry, as in other sectors, it is important to strive towards greater water productivity.

Where water *quality* is concerned, zero effluent discharge is the ultimate goal, in order to avoid any releases of contaminants to the water environment. Zero effluent discharge entails water recycling, which also contributes to raising water productivity. If zero effluent discharge is not economically and technically feasible, there are some valuable intermediate strategies, which can be pursued to reduce pollution and to ensure that waste substances are recovered and water reused.

3a. Strategies for saving water and increasing industrial water productivity

Water auditing
Conducting a water audit of an industrial plant or manufacturing facility clearly shows where the water supplied to the plant is being used, how much is used in each process, and where it ultimately ends up. Rainwater that falls on the site, as well as the natural evaporation that occurs, should also be included in the audit. Once a water audit has been done, it is possible to draw a flow chart and show the water balance across the plant, or over individual units of the process. This is the first step in finding innovative ways to save water on an industrial site.

Water can be saved either by cutting down on water input, where it is being unnecessarily wasted, or by identifying water recycling and reuse opportunities, discussed in more detail below. On-site rainwater harvesting may also be considered, since this is preferable to allowing rainwater (which may have become contaminated) to simply run off into the stormwater system. Case studies from the same industrial sector can provide some ideas and general lessons on saving water, but each site needs to be audited and analysed individually.

Matching water quality to use requirements
In many instances, the water used in industry is of an unnecessarily high quality for the use to which it is put. The analogy in domestic water use is, for instance, using water of drinking quality in order to flush toilets or water the garden. Similarly, in industrial processes there are many applications where lower water quality could be used. This offers recycling opportunities. Often 50 percent or more of an industrial plant's water intake may be used for the purpose of process cooling, a need that can often be met with lower quality water. On the other hand, some industries (such as the pharmaceutical industry) require water of exceptionally high quality. In such processes, additional water treatment is carried out on the water received from the local water utility, or withdrawn from groundwater or surface waters, in order to further improve the water quality before it is used.

There are cases in industry where water is used inappropriately, where a completely different approach could be taken to save water in water-scarce areas. An example of this would be switching to using pneumatic or mechanical systems for transportation, instead of using water to move the products, as is often done in the poultry and other food industries.

Water recycling and on-site reuse
Water recycling is the primary means of saving water in an industrial application: taking wastewater that would otherwise be discharged and using it in a lower quality application (often after treatment). Each cubic metre (m^3) of water that is recycled on-site represents one cubic metre that will not have to be withdrawn from a surface water source or from groundwater. Water can even be used many times over. In such cases, where, for instance, a

*The most
common uses
of reclaimed
water are
industrial cooling
and power
generation,
followed by
boiler feed and
quenching*

given cubic metre of water is used ten times in the process (a 'recycle ratio' of ten to one), this represents 9 m³ that are not withdrawn from a freshwater source. Increased water savings can be made by raising the recycle ratio. The industrial water productivity of the product is thereby also greatly increased, as far less freshwater is used to produce the same quantity of product.

The way in which water recycling is done on-site must be governed by the principle of matching water quality to use requirements, as mentioned above. This is dependent on the nature of the manufacturing process, as well as on the degree of wastewater treatment carried out on the site. Processes such as heating, cooling and quenching are the most common applications for lower quality water. It can also be used as washdown water, and for site irrigation.

A second consideration in recycling industrial water is the cost of treating the wastewater to the required level, including the cost of new or additional pipes and pumps, as compared to the cost of 'raw' water supplies (freshwater). Where the quality of freshwater is declining locally, or where freshwater supplies are becoming unreliable due to water scarcity in the region (droughts or falling groundwater levels), on-site industrial water recycling becomes an increasingly attractive option. On-site

water recycling can be regarded as a component of industrial risk management, since it contributes to reducing the risk related to the unreliability of freshwater supplies.

For example, the micro-chip manufacturer, Intel, established the Corporate Industrial Water Management Group to improve water use efficiency at its major manufacturing sites, which use large amounts of highly treated water for chip cleaning. The group includes representatives from fabrication sites, corporate technology development experts, and regulatory compliance staff. Intel's initial goal was to offset by 2003 at least 25 percent of its total incoming freshwater supply needs by using recycled water and installing more efficient systems. In 2002, the company exceeded this goal by achieving 35 percent water savings through recycling water and efficiency gains.

Using reclaimed water
A more indirect means of recycling water occurs when an industrial enterprise reuses the wastewater produced by another industrial plant close by (with a treatment step in between, if necessary). Again, the principle of matching water quality to use requirements must be followed. The availability of wastewater, when needed, and its variability in terms of quality also need to be considered. For instance, an industrial plant could use wastewater from a

BOX 8.5: DEFINITIONS OF WATER RECLAMATION, REUSE AND RECYCLING

'Water reclamation', 'reuse' and 'recycling' should not be used interchangeably. In the wastewater treatment industry, the following definitions are used:

Water recycling normally involves only one use or user, and the effluent from the user is captured and redirected back into that use scheme. Water recycling is predominantly practised by industry.

Wastewater reclamation is the treatment or processing of wastewater (industrial or municipal) in order to make it reusable.

Reclaimed water is treated effluent suitable for an intended water reuse application.

Water reuse is the use of treated wastewater for beneficial purposes such as agricultural irrigation and industrial cooling. Water reuse can be done directly or indirectly.

Direct water reuse requires the existence of pipes or other conveyance facilities for delivering reclaimed water.

Indirect water reuse is the discharge of an effluent to receiving waters (a river, lake or wetland) for assimilation and further withdrawals downstream. This is recognized to be important and can be planned for, but does not constitute direct water reuse.

Water recycling and reuse has far-reaching benefits in industries beyond the mere requirement of complying with the effluent discharge permits:

1. Reduction in freshwater withdrawal and consumption
2. Minimization of wastewater discharge by reclaiming wastewater, thereby reducing clean-up costs and discharge liabilities
3. Recovery of valuable by-products
4. Improvement of the profit margin by cost reduction
5. Enhancement of corporate image, public acceptance and environmental responsibility.

Source: Asano and Visvanathan, 2001.

Above: This golf course in Arizona, US, is watered with recycled water from the city of Page

nearby municipal sewage treatment plant. The result is usually called reclaimed water and is sold to industry by municipalities in many countries, including Australia, South Africa and the US. The most common uses of reclaimed water are industrial cooling and power generation, followed by boiler feed and quenching. In such arrangements, the use of reclaimed water by industry eases the pressure on scarce water resources in the region.

In the metropolitan region of Durban, South Africa, an innovative public-private partnership has been supplying reclaimed water to industries since 1999 (see **Chapter 14**). The Southern Sewage Works of the Durban Metro Water Services treats over 100,000 m³/day of domestic and industrial effluent (through primary treatment only), prior to discharging it to sea through a long sea outfall. Projections showed that the capacity of the sea outfall would soon be reached, due to the growing population and industrial water discharges in the area. A secondary treatment plant with a capacity of 48,000 m³/day was built, which was allowed to discharge water into a canal that flows over the beach into the sea. A nearby paper mill then contracted to take 9,000 m³/day of the treated water. A local survey was undertaken, which found that further (tertiary) treatment would be required to sell reclaimed water to other industries in the area, which needed higher quality water than the paper mill. Since it was not economically feasible for the municipal water utility to construct and operate such a high-tech plant, the tertiary treatment works (which currently treats and sells up to 30,000 m³/day of reclaimed water to local industries) was built through a public-private partnership.

Agricultural irrigation and urban irrigation (of parks, sports fields and golf courses) are also major applications for reclaimed water, which is important since irrigation is usually the largest water user in any region (see **Chapter 7**). Israel currently reuses some 84 percent of its treated sewage effluent in agricultural irrigation. The World Health Organization has laid down guidelines for the use of reclaimed water in irrigation, as there may be health implications when reclaimed water is sprayed in the open (WHO, 2005). Reclaimed water can also be used to recharge aquifers, for instance to avoid saline water intrusion into the aquifer, or simply to augment the groundwater supply. In the Adelaide region of Australia, half of the city's water demand is met through reclaiming water by aquifer storage and recovery.

In construction applications, reclaimed water can be used for dust control, soil settling and compaction, aggregate washing and concrete production. Domestic applications for reclaimed water include fire fighting, car washing, toilet flushing and garden watering. Supplying reclaimed water in urban areas requires two sets of piping: one for potable water (drinking water) and the other for reclaimed water – termed 'dual reticulation'. The installation of dual reticulation is usually done in new housing developments, as laying it retrospectively may be prohibitively expensive. The Tokyo Metropolitan Government in Japan has long encouraged the fitting of new office blocks and apartments in Tokyo with dual reticulation (see also **Chapter 14**). There are even a few cities in arid regions, such as in Windhoek, Namibia, where reclaimed water is treated to a very high standard and then reused directly to augment the potable water supply.

Table 8.3: Wastewater treatment requirements as a function of end-use for industrial water supply

Industrial water use	Nitrogen and Phosphorus removal	Chemical precipitation	Filtration
Cooling tower makeup	Normally	Yes	Yes
Once through cooling			
– Turbine exhaust condensing	Sometimes	Seldom	Sometimes
– Direct contact cooling	Seldom	No	Sometimes
– Equipment and bearing cooling	Yes	Yes	Yes
Process water	Yes	Yes	Yes
Boiler feed water	Requires more extensive treatment; use of reclaimed wastewater generally not recommended		
Washdown water	Sometimes	Seldom	Yes
Site irrigation	No	No	Normally

Source: Asano and Visvanathan, 2001.

Both freshwater and reclaimed water can contain constituents that can cause problems, but their concentrations in reclaimed water are generally higher.

■ **Scaling:** This refers to the formation of hard deposits on surfaces, which reduce the efficiency of heat transfer processes. Due to repetitive recycling of feed water in the cooling water, water lost by evaporation leads to increases in the concentration of mineral impurities such as calcium, magnesium, sodium, chloride and silica, which eventually lead to scale formation. Scale forming constituents can be eliminated using appropriate chemical precipitation techniques.

■ **Corrosion:** Ammonia, which may be present in significant concentration in reclaimed municipal wastewater, is one of the prime causes of corrosion in many industrial water reuse installations. Dissolved oxygen and certain metals (manganese, iron, and aluminium) may also promote corrosion because of their relatively high oxidation potential. The corrosion can be controlled by adding chemical corrosion inhibitors.

■ **Biological growth:** Slime and algal growth are common problems in reclaimed water due to a high nutrient content, which promotes biological growth. This growth can be controlled or eliminated by addition of biocides during the internal treatment process.

■ **Foaming:** Associated with the presence of biodegradable detergents, foaming problems can be avoided by using anti-foaming chemicals.

■ **Pathogenic organisms:** When reclaimed water is used in industry, the assurance of adequate disinfection is a primary concern for protecting the health of workers and plant operators. The most stringent requirement, similar to unrestricted reclaimed water use in food crop irrigation, would be appropriate if there exists a potential for human exposure to spray.

Minimizing virtual water in manufactured products
The concept of the virtual water trade has been mentioned in **Chapters 7, 11** and **12**, in relation to trade in crops and food products. The same concept applies in relation to manufactured products, where the virtual water of a particular finished product represents the volume of water that was used to produce it. This can be calculated

in two ways: either as m^3/t of product, or as m^3/dollar of added value. By looking at the imports and exports of each type of product, it is possible to calculate the virtual water flows into and out of the region. One can also calculate the industrial water productivity of various products and sectors, in terms of the industrial value added per unit of water used (see **Table 8.4** at end of chapter). In water-scarce regions, it makes sense to focus on the manufacture of products that use little water, and to therefore only export products with a high water productivity. This minimizes the amount of virtual water that is exported. Conversely, water-intensive products and products with low water productivity, such as aluminium and beer, should be imported into water-scarce regions, as this represents a way of indirectly importing water.

Better policy instruments and economic incentives
Industrial water management strategies that intend to minimize water consumption and wastewater generation, and thereby improve water productivity, can be either internal or external to the enterprise itself. Internal strategies are those measures that are required to be taken at a factory level in order for water consumption and wastewater generation to be controlled, such as water recycling. These measures can be taken more or less independently of external strategies.

External strategies, on the other hand, are measures that are required at the industry level in the context of local, regional or national industrial water management. Generally, the factory management does not control these strategies, although in certain cases some measures are required at the factory level in response. The nature and number of a particular type of industry present in a locality or a region can significantly influence these strategies. Some of these strategies are summarized as follows:

■ national water recycling and reuse policies

■ grouping of industries in a particular site (industrial parks) coupled with combined treatment methods and reuse policies

■ rationing the water use within industry, so that each process uses a defined quantity of water

■ applying economic instruments such as penalties, water charges, subventions, credits and grants.

...the virtual water of a particular finished product represents the volume of water that was used to produce it

BOX 8.7: CLEANER BEER PRODUCTION IN CUBA

Tinima Brewery is the second largest brewery in Cuba, producing 47,600 cubic metres (m³) of beer per year. In 2002, the National Cleaner Production Network responded to a request from the brewery's management for a cleaner production assessment (CPA) of the brewery.

Beer is produced by mixing, milling and boiling three main components: barley malt, sugar and water. This process produces a sugary liquid called wort, which is cooled, fermented and filtered in order to obtain the final product. A new technology was proposed to Tinima Brewery, in which the concentrated sugar syrup and water short-circuit the hot section and are added directly to the fermentation tank. This

means that the main volume of liquid does not pass through the hot section. The investment required was low, as these changes needed only some new pipeline arrangements.

This new technology was implemented at Tinima Brewery in 2003. The beer produced was found to be just as acceptable to consumers, and the technology is now approved for all breweries in Cuba. The following savings were achieved by Tinima Brewery as a result of the cleaner production technology:

- 74 percent reduction in cooling water consumption
- 7 percent reduction in total water consumption

- 11 percent reduction in the volume of wastewater
- 4 percent savings on sugar consumption (used as an additive to the beer)
- 3 percent savings on caustic cleaning solution consumption
- 50 percent savings on thermal energy consumption in the heating and evaporating stages
- 30 percent savings on thermal energy consumption in the cooling stages
- 12 percent savings in total electricity consumption
- 21 percent reduction in greenhouse gas emissions.

Source: UNIDO, 2004.

BOX 8.8: THE TEST STRATEGY IN THE DANUBE BASIN

The implementation of the TEST programme in the Danube River Basin began in May 2001 and was completed in December 2003, successfully introducing the TEST approach in seventeen companies in five countries (Bulgaria, Croatia, Hungary, Romania and Slovakia). The companies were identified as hot spots of industrial pollution, from various industrial sectors, including chemicals, food, machinery production, textiles, pulp and paper. Tangible results were achieved in terms of increased productivity and improved environmental performance. These results are used to show other enterprises in the basin that it is possible to reduce environmental impacts to acceptable levels while becoming more competitive.

There were 224 Type A (no cost or low cost) measures identified, of which 128 were implemented by the 17 participating enterprises. These were mostly 'good housekeeping' measures involving the following:
- process improvement (with small technological changes using existing equipment)
- raising the skills of operational staff
- revising laboratory procedures

- improving scheduling management and maintenance
- improving raw materials storage
- adjusting water consumption by reducing wastage and leaks, and improving process control.

There were 260 Type B (involving a relatively small investment with a short payback period) measures identified, of which 109 were implemented by the end of the project. The total investment undertaken by the 17 enterprises to implement the Type B measures was US $1,686,704, while the estimated financial savings as a result of these measures are US $1,277,570 per year.

It is interesting to note that the Bulgarian, Romanian and Slovak companies had the highest number of Type A and B measures identified. This can be explained by the fact that these companies used relatively outdated technology, thus many more measures could be identified to optimize the existing process. The environmental benefits were significant in terms of reduced consumption of natural resources (including

freshwater and energy), reduced wastewater discharges and pollution loads into the Danube River and its tributaries, as well as reduction of waste generation and air emissions. The total reduction in wastewater discharge into the Danube River Basin, achieved by the end of 2003 as a result of implementing Type A and B measures, was 4,590,000 m³ per year. Pollution loads in the wastewater were reduced in most of the companies, including chemical oxygen demand (COD), biochemical oxygen demand (BOD), oily products, total suspended solids, heavy metals and toxic chemicals.

Finally, 141 Type C (requiring a significant financial investment) measures were identified, of which 38 were approved by top management of the various enterprises for implementation. The total investment required for the approved Type C measures is US $47,325,000 and they are scheduled for completion by 2007. The total additional reduction in wastewater discharges will be 7,863,000 m³ per year, with estimated annual savings by the companies of US $5,362,000.

Source: UNIDO, 2004.

Stream separation

The principle of stream separation is a useful tool when assessing wastewater flows for treating the final discharge and when identifying flows of process water that may be recycled and reused. Wastewater containing a variety of contaminants is much more difficult and expensive to treat effectively than wastewater containing only one contaminant. Also, mixing a concentrated stream of effluent with a more diluted stream may result in much larger volumes of wastewater entering an expensive treatment process. The diluted stream alone may be suitable for discharge directly into a sewer, to be dealt with by a municipal wastewater treatment plant or may be suitable for on-site recycling for direct reuse in another part of the process. Treating the concentrated stream alone may become easier, because it may contain fewer contaminants and is likely to be cheaper, because the volume is much smaller. Now that a wide range of treatment technologies is available, stream separation may provide better and more cost-effective solutions in comparison to producing a single mixed effluent. The larger the enterprise, the more cost-effective this approach becomes. However, even small and medium-sized enterprises may benefit from considering stream separation.

Raw material and energy recovery from waste

An important aspect of reducing pollution is to look carefully at the solid and liquid waste generated by a given production process in order to calculate the quantities of unconverted raw material remaining in the waste streams. This unconverted raw material can potentially be reused. The feasibility of the recovery process can be assessed by determining the following:

- the cost of the separation process, which can recover the raw materials from the remainder of the waste
- the quantities of recoverable material
- the cost of the raw material
- the cost of waste disposal.

If the cost of the separation process is too high, or if the quantities of recoverable material are too small, material recovery becomes unprofitable. Similarly, very cheap raw materials and a low cost of waste disposal mitigate against the feasibility of the process.

Energy recovery may be possible in the same way from wastewater carrying waste heat. Once discharged, the waste heat becomes thermal pollution in the receiving water body. However, the heat could potentially be recovered and reused in another part of the process, or indeed in another enterprise nearby, which requires lower grade heat. Indirect energy recovery can be done through a biological form of wastewater treatment, in which anaerobic bacteria break down organic matter in the wastewater and produce methane (biogas). The methane may then be used to fire a boiler or to generate electricity (see **Chapter 9**).

Reuse of waste

The recycling of glass, paper and various types of plastics are the best-known examples of waste reuse. However, there are many cases in industry where used solvents, oils, concentrated wastewater containing starch, or various solid wastes can be traded for their residual value and reused. One innovative industrial park in Cape Town, South Africa, has set up a voluntary Waste Register for the companies located within the park (see **Chapter 14**). Each company is required to log its waste production, the quantity and the type of waste, as well as the types of raw materials used as inputs and whether these may be reclaimed materials. The Waste Register may be searched on the industrial park's website, so that companies can identify sources that fit their requirements. This approach results in savings on raw materials and waste disposal costs for the companies involved.

Wastewater treatment technologies

These technologies are applicable both to recycling water and treating it prior to discharge back into the water environment. End-of-pipe treatment is often applied prior to discharging wastewater into the sewage system, as municipalities can charge industries for accepting their wastewater, with a rising tariff according to the concentration of the discharge. Some of the technologies mentioned below result in the recovery of energy or raw materials from the wastewater, such as anaerobic treatment, which produces biogas, and sulphate removal, which produces gypsum.

Today, there is a very wide range of treatment technologies available. Wastewater treatment technologies typically fall into two broad categories:

- physical/chemical treatment (e.g. settling, filtration, reverse osmosis, adsorption, flocculation, chlorination) and biological treatment (aerobic or anaerobic treatment which remove organic matter)

- other more specialized processes such as phosphate reduction and sulphate removal.

...there are many cases in industry where used solvents, oils, concentrated wastewater containing starch, or various solid wastes can be traded for their residual value and reused

Washing sugarbeets as they are unloaded at a sugar factory, Antois-Picardy River Basin, France

...industries often lead the way towards a more sustainable society by implementing water recycling and putting environmental management systems in place...

increasingly affected by water shortages and deteriorating water quality.

Industries therefore have a dramatic effect on the state of the world's freshwater resources, both by the quantity of water that they consume and their potential to pollute the water environment by their waste discharge. Yet industries often lead the way towards a more sustainable society by implementing water recycling and putting environmental management systems in place in their factories and offices. As discussed, there has been an exponential increase over the past decade in the numbers of industrial companies worldwide seeking certification with ISO 14001, the international environmental standard. This demonstrates many companies' commitment to being environmentally responsible as well as profitable, enhancing both their corporate image and their competitiveness.

As stated by the WSSD Plan of Implementation, poverty eradication and sustainable natural resource management are strongly linked. For countries adopting poverty-reduction policies, industrial growth is highly desirable in order to diversify the economy, create jobs, and add value to primary products and raw materials being produced. However, it is important that the necessary legal and institutional arrangements be in place to enable this growth to take place sustainably, keeping in mind that environmental commitment can be a highly efficient tool for enhancing profitability and competitiveness.

Table 8.4: Industrial water productivity by country, 2000/01

Country	Industrial value added (IVA): 2001* (billion constant 1995 US $) (1)	Industrial water use: 2000 (Km³/year) (2)	Population: 2000 (million) (3)	Industrial water productivity (IWP) (US $ IVA/m³) (4) = (1)÷(2)	IWP per capita (US $ IVA/m³/c) (5) = (4)÷(3)
Algeria	23.21	0.80	30.29	28.97	0.96
Angola	4.84	0.06	13.13	86.13	6.56
Argentina	69.13	2.76	37.03	25.07	0.68
Armenia	1.19	0.13	3.79	9.18	2.42
Australia	107.29	2.40	19.14	44.70	2.34
Austria	82.15	1.35	8.08	60.85	7.53
Azerbaijan	1.02	4.77	8.04	0.21	0.03
Bangladesh	13.10	0.52	137.44	25.25	0.18
Belarus	5.76	1.30	10.19	4.44	0.44
Benin	0.40	0.03	6.27	15.04	2.40
Bolivia	2.25	0.05	8.33	46.86	5.63
Botswana	3.41	0.03	1.54	127.97	83.05
Brazil	239.36	10.65	170.41	22.48	0.13
Bulgaria	3.48	8.21	7.95	0.42	0.05
Cambodia	0.79	0.02	13.10	35.14	2.68
Cameroon	2.67	0.08	14.88	33.69	2.26
Canada	205.98	31.57	30.76	6.52	0.21
Central African Republic	0.23	<0.01	3.72	56.08	15.09
Chad	0.30	<0.01	7.89	93.97	11.92
Chile	26.29	3.16	15.21	8.33	0.55
China	593.70	161.97	1,282.44	3.67	<0.01
Colombia	25.24	0.40	42.11	62.36	1.48
Congo, Dem. Republic	0.86	0.06	50.95	14.66	0.29
Costa Rica	4.16	0.46	4.02	9.11	2.26
Côte d'Ivoire	2.40	0.11	16.01	21.79	1.36
Czech Republic	20.97	1.47	10.27	14.31	1.39
Denmark	44.90	0.32	5.32	138.59	26.05
Ecuador	7.18	0.90	12.65	7.96	0.63
Egypt	24.03	9.57	67.88	2.51	0.04

Table 8.4: *continued*

Country	Industrial value added (IVA): 2001* (billion constant 1995 US $) (1)	Industrial water use: 2000 (Km³/year) (2)	Population: 2000 (million) (3)	Industrial water productivity (IWP) (US $ IVA/m³) (4) = (1)÷(2)	IWP per capita (US $ IVA/m³/c) (5) = (4)÷(3)
El Salvador	3.39	0.20	6.28	16.89	2.69
Estonia	1.72	0.06	1.39	26.80	19.24
Ethiopia	0.77	0.15	62.91	5.30	0.08
Finland	53.22	2.07	5.17	25.66	4.96
France	430.02	29.76	59.24	14.45	0.24
Gabon	2.85	0.01	1.23	198.17	161.12
Germany	748.18	31.93	82.02	23.43	0.29
Ghana	2.04	0.08	19.31	26.52	1.37
Greece	28.18	0.25	10.61	114.44	10.79
Guatemala	3.53	0.27	11.39	13.20	1.16
Guinea	1.59	0.03	8.15	45.85	5.62
Honduras	1.32	0.10	6.42	13.63	2.12
Hungary	17.26	4.48	9.97	3.85	0.39
India	120.24	35.21	1,008.94	3.42	<0.01
Indonesia	94.42	0.56	212.09	169.18	0.80
Iran, Islamic Republic	29.51	1.69	70.33	17.50	0.25
Italy	332.94	16.29	57.53	20.44	0.36
Jamaica	1.95	0.07	2.58	28.08	10.90
Japan	1,889.94	15.80	127.10	119.62	0.94
Jordan	1.80	0.04	4.91	40.27	8.20
Kazakhstan	8.39	5.78	16.17	1.45	0.09
Kenya	1.32	0.10	30.67	13.60	0.44
Korea, Republic	285.64	3.05	46.74	93.66	2.00
Kyrgyz Republic	0.36	0.31	4.92	1.17	0.24
Lao PDR	0.59	0.17	5.28	3.46	0.66
Latvia	1.88	0.10	2.42	19.60	8.10
Lebanon	2.52	0.01	3.50	333.78	95.47
Lesotho	0.43	0.02	2.04	19.31	9.49
Lithuania	2.48	0.04	3.70	60.34	16.33
Malawi	0.28	0.05	11.31	5.90	0.52
Malaysia	48.65	1.90	22.22	25.58	1.15
Mali	0.81	0.02	11.35	49.92	4.40
Mauritania	0.31	0.05	2.67	6.34	2.38
Mexico	99.69	4.29	98.87	23.25	0.24
Moldova	0.78	1.33	4.30	0.59	0.14
Mongolia	0.26	0.12	2.53	2.06	0.81
Morocco	13.36	0.20	29.88	66.51	2.23
Mozambique	1.50	0.01	18.29	102.65	5.61
Namibia	0.94	0.01	1.76	73.34	41.74
Netherlands	119.90	4.76	15.86	25.17	1.59
New Zealand	15.85	0.20	3.78	79.26	20.98
Nicaragua	0.48	0.03	5.07	14.34	2.83
Niger	0.39	0.01	10.83	31.69	2.93
Nigeria	14.31	0.81	113.86	17.65	0.16
Norway	49.05	1.46	4.47	33.56	7.51
Pakistan	15.71	3.47	141.26	4.53	0.03
Panama	1.49	0.04	2.86	34.47	12.07
Papua New Guinea	1.65	0.03	4.81	51.24	10.66

For countries adopting poverty-reduction policies, industrial growth is highly desirable in order to diversify the economy

Table 8.4: *continued*

Country	Industrial value added (IVA): 2001* (billion constant 1995 US $)	Industrial water use: 2000 (Km³/year)	Population: 2000 (million)	Industrial water productivity (IWP) (US $ IVA/m³)	IWP per capita (US $ IVA/m³/c)
	(1)	(2)	(3)	(4) = (1)÷(2)	(5) = (4)÷(3)
Paraguay	2.61	0.04	5.50	61.90	11.26
Peru	17.08	2.03	25.66	8.42	0.33
Philippines	28.07	2.69	75.65	10.42	0.14
Poland	50.65	12.75	38.61	3.97	0.10
Portugal	36.71	1.37	10.02	26.87	2.68
Romania	12.32	7.97	22.44	1.55	0.07
Russian Federation	139.79	48.66	145.49	2.87	0.02
Rwanda	0.37	0.01	7.61	35.11	4.61
Senegal	1.42	0.06	9.42	24.32	2.58
Sierra Leone	0.17	0.01	4.41	24.86	5.64
South Africa	51.35	1.61	43.31	31.99	0.74
Spain	208.17	6.60	39.91	31.54	0.79
Sri Lanka	4.11	0.31	18.92	13.33	0.70
Sweden	81.68	1.61	8.84	50.67	5.73
Syrian Arab Republic	3.18	0.36	16.19	8.74	0.54
Tajikistan	0.70	0.56	6.09	1.25	0.21
Tanzania	1.07	0.03	35.12	42.31	1.20
Thailand	69.52	2.14	62.81	32.46	0.52
Togo	0.33	0.01	4.53	25.22	5.57
Trinidad and Tobago	3.46	0.08	1.30	41.98	32.44
Tunisia	7.04	0.07	9.46	105.03	11.10
Turkey	50.00	4.11	66.67	12.18	0.18
Turkmenistan	3.46	0.19	4.74	18.34	3.87
Uganda	1.34	0.05	23.30	29.40	1.26
Ukraine	21.62	13.28	49.57	1.63	0.03
United Kingdom	340.03	7.19	59.63	47.28	0.79
United States	2,147.80	220.69	283.23	9.73	0.03
Uruguay	5.32	0.04	3.34	147.69	44.26
Uzbekistan	2.79	1.20	24.88	2.33	0.09
Venezuela, Bolivian Republic	31.69	0.59	24.17	53.82	2.23
Viet Nam	10.89	17.23	78.14	0.63	0.01
Yemen	1.86	0.04	18.35	43.74	2.38
Zambia	1.11	0.13	10.42	8.45	0.81
Zimbabwe	1.58	0.12	12.63	13.15	1.04

*For some countries only 2000 statistics are available.

Note: Values for IVA and population have been rounded to two decimal places. *Source:* World Bank, 2001; FAO, 2003.

References and Websites

Asano, T. and Visvanathan, C. 2001. Industries and water recycling and reuse. *Business and Industry – A Driving or Braking Force on the Road towards Water Security.* Founders Seminar, organized by Stockholm International Water Institute, Stockholm, Sweden, pp. 13–24.

EC (European Commission). 2004. *European Pollutant Emissions Register.* Luxemburg, Office for Official Publications of the European Communities.

ISO (International Organization for Standardization). 2004. The ISO Survey of ISO 9000 and ISO 14001 Certificates, Twelfth cycle: up to and including 31 December 2002, ISO, Geneva.

Kuylenstierna, J. and Najlis, P. 1998. The comprehensive assessment of the freshwater resources of the world - policy options for an integrated sustainable water future. *Water International,* Vol. 23, No.1, pp. 17–20.

Levine, A. D. and Asano, T. 2004. Recovering sustainable water from wastewater. *Environmental Science & Technology.* June, 2004, pp. 201-08.

McDonough, W. and Braungart, M. 2002. *Cradle to Cradle: Remaking the Way We Make Things.* New York, North Point Press.

Morrison, J. and Gleick, P. 2004. *Freshwater Resources: Managing the Risks Facing the Private Sector,* Pacific Institute, Oakland, California.

Shiklomanov, I.A. 1999. *World Water Resources and their Use.* Paris, UNESCO and the State Hydrological Institute, St Petersburg.

UN (United Nations). 2002. Johannesburg Plan of Implementation. New York, UN. www.un.org/esa/sustdev/documents/WSSD_POI_PD/English/POIToc.htm

UNECA (United Nations Economic Commission for Africa). 2002. The Way Forward. Addis Ababa, UNECA.

UNIDO (United Nations Industrial Development Organization). 2004. *Industry, Environment and the Diffusion of Environmentally Sound Technologies.* Annual Report, 2004. Vienna, UNIDO.

——. 2003. Identification, assessment and prioritisation of Pollution Hot Spots: UNIDO Methodology.

Unilever. 2003. *Unilever Environment Report.* Unilever, N.V. Netherlands, Unilever.

WHO (World Health Organization). 2006. Guidelines for the Safe Use of Wastewater, Excreta and Greywater. Geneva, WHO.

——. 2004. Guidelines for Drinking Water Quality. Geneva, WHO. www.who.int/water_sanitation_health/dwq/gdwq3/en/index.html

World Bank. 2003 *World Development Indicators.* New York, World Bank.

Basel Convention: www.basel.int/
Chronology of major tailings dams failures: www.wise-uranium.org/mdaf.html
The European Pollutant Emission Register: www.eper.cec.eu.int/eper/default.asp
The EU Water Framework Directive: europa.eu.int/comm/environment/water/water-framework/index_en.html
International Standards Organization: www.iso.org
Pacific Institute: www.pacinst.org
Rotterdam Convention: www.pic.int/
Stockholm Convention: www.pops.int/
UNECE Convention on the Protection and Use of Transboundary Watercourses and International Lakes (Water Convention): www.unece.org/env/water/
UNECE Convention on the Transboundary Effects of Industrial Accidents: www.unece.org/env/teia/welcome.htm
UNEP description of technological disasters: www.uneptie.org/pc/apell/disasters/lists/technological.html
UNEP Disaster database: www.uneptie.org/pc/apell/disasters/database/disastersdatabase.asp
UNEP Division of Technology, Industry and Economics: www.uneptie.org/
UNIDO: www.unido.org/
Unilever: www.unilever.com/environmentsociety/
World Resources Institute: www.wri.org/
World Water Resources and Their Use – a joint SHI/UNESCO product: webworld.unesco.org/water/ihp/db/shiklomanov/index.shtml

And what is a man without energy?
Nothing – nothing at all.

Mark Twain

CHAPTER 9

Water and Energy

By

UNIDO

(United Nations Industrial Development Organization)

Colorado River dam in Arizona, United States

Key messages:

Water and energy are two highly interconnected sectors: energy is needed throughout the water system, from supplying water to its various users, including urban people, to collecting and treating wastewater. On the other hand, water is essential to producing energy, from hydropower to water cooling in power stations.

In the context of a growing world population, leading to increasing demands and competition for water and energy, it is time to integrate the management of these resources. This chapter takes stock of the various possibilities to be explored in order to enhance water and energy efficiency and ensure sustainable development.

While much progress has yet to be made for ensuring universal access to water supply and sanitation, even more progress is needed to provide electricity for all. In order to achieve these challenging and urgent targets, water supply and energy production systems both need improvements that do not jeopardize the environment.

■ There are very strong links between water and electrical power usage which at present are not fully taken into account in policy-making, management and operation of both water and electricity generation systems. The consequence is that many opportunities for both energy and water savings are being lost.

■ Access to electricity for many poor people in lower-income countries continues to lag a long way behind access to an improved water supply. Access to electricity plays a big role in poverty alleviation, improved health and socio-economic development. Accelerating access to electricity for the poor, although not one of the Millennium Development Goals (MDGs), was one of the targets set at the World Summit on Sustainable Development (WSSD) in Johannesburg in 2002.

■ Concern about the impact on the environment of traditional methods of electrical power generation is driving the introduction of a variety of non-polluting, renewable energy sources. However, economies of scale on large thermal and hydropower plants, existing transmission/distribution grids plus government subsidies for these traditional systems, put the renewable approaches at a cost disadvantage. A wide range of renewable electricity production options is now available, together with a growing range of incentives and economic instruments to promote their use and also to promote increased efficiency of energy usage.

■ Hydropower is available at different scales from very large systems to small systems. It is very flexible, permits rapid start up and can augment both thermal power plant base loads at peak times and compensate for fluctuating renewable supplies, as well as providing stand-alone generating capacity for smaller and remote communities. There is some controversy over whether large hydropower schemes are renewable power sources, but run-of-river systems are and there are now many options to increase sustainability.

■ The supply of water and wastewater services of all kinds to urban areas generally involves high electrical energy consumption. However, by taking a total system approach to energy management in these systems, including energy audits, it is possible to achieve big energy savings. Desalination of saline and brackish water for urban water supply is growing as technology improvements bring significant decreases in costs.

■ Experience has shown that the simultaneous analysis of water and energy use at the policy level can enable significant increase in productivity in the use of both resources. Water conservation can lead to large energy savings, as can taking full account of energy efficiency approaches in water policy decisions.

This page from top: Kut Al Amara dam, Iraq; Glen Canyon Dam, Arizona; Villagers draw water from a pump powered by solar panels, Tata, Morocco; Water pipeline transporting water up to a valley accumulation station

Right: The Blue Lagoon is an artificial lake fed by the surplus water drawn from the geothermal power station at Svartsengi, Iceland. Captured at 2,000 m below ground, the water reaches the surface at a temperature of 70°C, at which point it is used to heat neighbouring cities

Water and electricity use are inextricably linked. Large quantities of water are used for cooling in many electricity generating methods, such as coal and nuclear power stations. Hydropower, while not a consumptive use of water, often requires the construction of reservoirs and other large engineering works, which modify the aquatic environment. Conversely, large amounts of electrical power are used to pump water from its sources to the places it is used, especially in irrigated agriculture and municipal water systems.

Further links between the water and energy sectors are created by the frequent inefficiency and wastage in the way both resources are used. There are serious inefficiencies in many parts of the world in electricity generation, transmission, distribution and usage. Likewise, there are inefficiencies and leaks in water distribution systems. It follows that substantial efficiency gains in water use will reduce electric power requirements, which in turn will lead to more savings of water otherwise used in power generation.

A great deal of the infrastructure for both power and water in middle- and lower-income countries is poorly maintained. There is also a serious lack of the infrastructure needed to extend necessary power and water services to the many people presently unserved. Access to electricity for the poor lags far behind access to drinking water supply in many countries. For example, in sub-Saharan Africa, only 25 percent of the population have access to electricity, while 83 percent of the urban population and 46 percent of the rural population have access to a water supply (see **Table 9.5** at the end of this chapter).

Thus there is great pressure on governments in developing countries to build power stations and to deliver more electricity for domestic use and industrial development. Yet increasing power generation through burning coal, oil and gas presents its own set of sustainability issues linked to the generation of carbon dioxide (CO_2) and the greenhouse effect. The majority of electricity worldwide is generated by fossil fuel power stations from which emissions exacerbate the problems of climate variability and changes, raising the intensity of natural disasters, which mainly impact the poor. Moving away from a carbon-rich power-generating environment to more sustainable generation methods and reducing the inefficiencies mentioned earlier will help to alleviate this problem.

In the rapidly growing urban environments in developing countries, energy costs draw budgetary resources from other municipal functions, such as education, public transportation and health care. Without the provision of reliable sustainable energy supplies, it is unlikely that the Millennium Development Goals (MDGs) of reducing hunger, providing safe drinking water, providing sanitation and improving health will be achieved.

Access to electricity for the poor lags far behind access to drinking water supply in many countries...in sub-Saharan Africa, only 25 percent of the population have access to electricity...

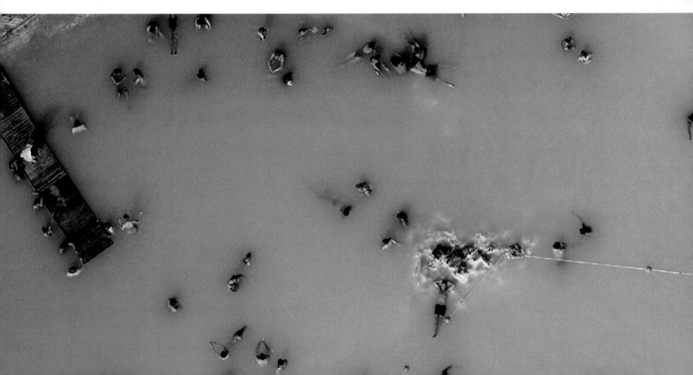

Part 1. Energy for Water Supply

In many countries, agricultural irrigation, groundwater pumping, interbasin transfers, and urban water supply and sanitation systems are major electricity users. Improving water use efficiency and introducing water conservation measures can therefore significantly reduce energy use. This section sets out to show how the two issues are interlinked, focusing upon urban water supply, and how the two systems should be co-managed, with future implications for both water and energy policies.

...the energy required by the end uses of water is far greater than in the other steps of the urban water cycle

1a. Energy use in water supply and sanitation services

Nearly all modern urban water and wastewater systems require energy in all phases of the treatment, delivery, collection, treatment and disposal cycle. Where historical systems once depended on surface water sources, gravity distribution systems and dilution for wastewater treatment, the water needs of growing urban areas need additional energy input to safeguard human health.

Extraction, conveyance and treatment

The first step of the urban water cycle is extraction, conveyance and treatment. The most widely used sources of potable water are surface sources and groundwater wells. The use of a particular source in a region depends on the availability and the cost of water extraction. Surface sources such as lakes, rivers and reservoirs typically require some treatment to achieve potable quality. The quality of the water body and the desired level and type of treatment are key variables in energy inputs required at this step. Groundwater sources have a more direct energy requirement, since energy is needed to pump the water up out of the ground, usually from bore. The amount of energy required by a pump and motor system to extract groundwater depends on the depth of the water table beneath the ground. It is important to note that water recycling and reuse, including a treatment step, is generally far less energy-intensive than developing any new physical source of water, other than local surface water.

Distribution

Distribution of potable water is often the most variable step in the urban water cycle. Ideally, the water source is at a higher elevation than the intended destination. In this case, gravity is used to distribute water and no energy input is required. In most cases, though, varied topography requires energy input through booster pumps to generate sufficient pressure in the system to distribute water to communities at higher elevations. Pumped storage,[1] which is further discussed later in this chapter, is often used at this stage to take advantage of off-peak

energy rates, converting pumping mechanical energy to potential energy by storing water at higher elevations. There are areas where conveying water can be highly energy intensive. Since water conservation saves all of the upstream energy inputs as well as the end-use energy inputs, water conservation in areas with energy intensive water supplies will save substantially more energy than water conservation in other areas.

Consumer end-use

Once water is delivered for consumer use, additional energy inputs come from heating and cooling water. Residential and commercial consumers heat water for bathing, radiant heating and dishwashing and cool water for air conditioning. Industrial consumers vary widely in their needs for heated and cooled water based on the industrial application and their process needs. However, the energy required by the end-uses of water is far greater than in the other steps of the urban water cycle. While there are efficiency improvements that can reduce the energy inputs required at each stage of the water use cycle, the greatest energy and water savings come from reducing water consumed by various end-uses (see **Box 9.1**). Water conservation at the end-use stage eliminates all of the upstream energy required to bring the water to the point of end-use, as well as all of the downstream energy that would otherwise be spent to collect, treat and dispose of this water.

Wastewater collection

Like distribution, wastewater collection is ideally done using gravity systems. When this is not possible, pumps are used to boost the wastewater to treatment facilities. In combined sanitary and storm-water sewers, precipitation affects the energy requirements of collection systems and heavy rains sometimes overwhelm the available infrastructure.

Wastewater treatment requires energy to remove contaminants and prepare the water for discharge or reuse. In aerobic wastewater treatment, the largest energy input is in the aeration system itself. Some types of wastewater

1. This involves pairs of reservoirs with a significant height difference. Water is pumped up when there is spare capacity in the network and then allowed to flow down again and generate power at times of peak demand.

treatment require very little energy (e.g. lagoons) but large amounts of land. In urban areas where land is scarce, more energy is required to treat large amounts of wastewater in a treatment plant requiring less land area. Opportunities exist to recover some of the energy embodied in the organic material present in wastewater, by recovering methane gas through anaerobic treatment and then using this fuel to power the treatment facility. Indeed, some wastewater treatment plants even provide electricity to the national grid.

1b. Approaches to energy and water efficiency

Because of the interconnectedness of water and energy, it is vital to manage them together rather than in isolation. The energy savings from water conservation and the water savings from energy efficiency are inextricably linked, and these linkages should be considered when determining the best course of action from an economic, social or environmental perspective. Energy efficiency in the water and wastewater industry saves money in operations and maintenance costs, reduces capital costs of new supply, improves solvency and operations capacity of water utilities, improves service coverage, reduces emissions and improves water quality, among a host of other related benefits.

In order to support larger efforts to reduce energy use in water and wastewater systems, larger-scale energy and water management should be entrusted to the local level for implementation. The term 'watergy' efficiency has been coined to describe the combined water and energy efficiencies which are available to municipalities and water users (see **Box 9.2**).

Involvement of the energy utility provides the needed support for implementing energy efficiency measures and ensuring that efforts to reduce energy and water waste are sustainable as a business practice. Energy efficiency in any water utility never has a beginning or an end. To sustain its energy savings, a water utility must continue to monitor its energy use and set goals for improvement.

Identifying water/energy efficiency opportunities

Energy and water audits are used to identify areas of concern in water and wastewater systems. The boundaries of the system to be audited are usually chosen based on budgetary considerations and areas that are presumed to yield the largest energy savings for the investment.

Major areas that are frequently identified as water/energy savings opportunities in water supply systems include the following:

▪ Repairing leaks from valves, distribution pipes, etc. Many urban water distribution systems in developed cities were installed more than fifty years ago, and leaks caused by corrosion of pipe material or other problems

Small-scale hydro-energy generation in Lao Cai, Viet Nam

BOX 9.1: WATER CONSERVATION VERSUS ENERGY CONSERVATION

Energy intensity measures the amount of energy used per unit of water. Some water sources are more energy intensive than others; for instance, desalination requires more energy than wastewater recycling. Water conservation technology may either increase or decrease energy intensity. Yet when water planners make decisions, they should look not just at energy intensity, but also at the total energy used from source to tap. In the case of water conservation, some programmes may consume a lot of energy at one stage in the energy/water use cycle, but still decrease the amount of energy used overall. The following three examples illustrate the interplay between energy intensity and total energy use:

▪ Water conservation may increase energy intensity and increase total energy use: A particular irrigation technology could reduce water use by 5 percent but require so much energy to operate that it increases the energy intensity by 10 percent. This would increase total energy use by 4.5 percent.

▪ Water conservation may increase energy intensity and decrease total energy use: The average high-efficiency dishwasher increases the energy intensity of dishwashing by 30 percent, but reduces water use by 34 percent. As a result of using less water (and therefore less energy to convey water from the source to the dishwater) the net total energy needed to wash dishes declines by 14 percent.

▪ Water conservation may decrease energy intensity and decrease total energy use: The average high-efficiency clothes washer reduces water use by 29 percent, compared to average low-efficiency machines, and simultaneously lowers energy intensity by 27 percent. Energy intensity declines, because mechanical aspects of the machines are also improved. By reducing total water use as well as energy intensity, total energy use is reduced by 48 percent.

Source: NRDC, 2004.

Reverse osmosis desalination unit in the Virgin Islands, United States

By 2003 there had been about 29 million domestic solar water heaters installed worldwide, of which 21 million were in developing countries

increased energy consumption. These must all be explored and adequately addressed before the development of desalination facilities begins. In most cases, water conservation and water recycling offer cheaper and better alternatives. The heavy energy cost of desalination also suggests the need to consider desalination plants as an emergency water supply, to be used during water demand peaks or droughts, rather than as a base supply.

1d. Solar energy for water supply

Small and inexpensive solar units are now available for many water-related applications, including pumping, water purification and solar water heating.

Solar pumping

Solar power can be used to help achieve the MDG of providing safe and accessible drinking water in countries that have plenty of sunlight. The great potential of solar pumping is to bring freshwater to villages that have no electricity and pump groundwater. There are many different types of solar pumps now available for various applications. At present, sales of solar pumps are largely to developed countries, because the prices of the systems are still rather high, but they are dropping rapidly as demand grows.

Solar water purifiers

The simplest and cheapest solar water disinfection system has been named SoDis (Solar Disinfection), and is designed for use at the household level. It improves the microbiological quality of drinking water by using solar ultraviolet-A (UV-A) radiation and heat to inactivate the pathogens that cause diarrhoea. The system uses commonly available plastic soft drink bottles. Contaminated water is filled into the transparent plastic bottles and exposed to full sunlight for six hours. The water must be relatively clear, and the bottles must be clean and unscratched. The required heating can be achieved by placing the bottles on a corrugated iron sheet or on a rooftop.

A more sophisticated solar water disinfection system called Naiade has been developed for use in developing countries. It produces safe drinking water from polluted water in a sustainable manner, without the use of chemicals, by means of UV irradiation. The unit weighs 44 kg and can produce on average up to 2,000 litres per day of high-quality drinking water. Water from a well or surface source is poured into the unit, either by hand or pipe. The water passes through a sieve, which removes large impurities, then through two filters, which remove

microscopic particles (including nematodes), and finally under an ultraviolet lamp. The ultraviolet light kills bacteria, viruses and worm eggs. It can be activated by the use of an electric battery, by the connection to electricity mains or by using a 75-watt solar panel. Maintenance and management of the unit is simple: if the filters become blocked, they can be easily cleaned by hand, which needs to be done daily.

Heating water for domestic use

Solar thermal capacity for domestic hot water and space heating is growing rapidly. Worldwide, the sector grew by 16 percent in 2003, while in China it grew by 30 percent. Although some developing countries are located in warm or tropical climates where hot water is not of primary importance, in many areas, especially those that are mountainous, there is a considerable demand for hot water. Solar water heaters are especially useful in the tourism sector and the hotel industry, as well as laundries, hospitals and clinics. Where solar water heaters displace electrical ones, they play a significant role in reducing peak electricity demand and reduce the negative environmental impact of fossil fuel use. Appropriate policies and economic incentives need to be put in place to stimulate the spread of this technology.

By 2003 there were about 29 million domestic solar water heaters installed worldwide, 21 million of which were in developing countries. Several million are located in China and India, while Egypt and Turkey have hundreds of thousands of households served by solar water heaters. In Barbados there are over 35,000 solar water heaters installed (33 percent of all households). Each unit saves about 4,000 kWh per year. This represents a considerable foreign exchange savings on the import of diesel fuel for the island, in addition to avoiding carbon emissions. It has been calculated that these solar water heaters replace 30 to 35 MW of additional electric generating capacity that would otherwise have to be installed in Barbados.

The success of solar water heaters in Barbados was supported through various governance mechanisms. A 30 percent consumption tax was put on electric water heaters; furthermore, the cost of electricity is relatively high in Barbados, which is also an incentive. Homeowners can gain concessions on their mortgages by installing solar water heaters. In Australia, each solar water heater with an electricity equivalent of 1 MWh over its lifetime receives between ten and thirty-five green certificates. These certificates have an economic value (US $18 in 2002), since electricity suppliers are obliged to purchase a certain share of electricity from renewable energy sources, which they can prove by presenting a corresponding number of green certificates. In other countries, different means have been used to foster the use of solar water heaters, including direct grants. In Namibia, the government requires solar water heaters to be installed in the construction of all new government housing, while in India, the government has introduced accelerated depreciation for commercial and public applications of solar water heaters.

Part 2. Water for Energy Generation

Hydropower, and small hydropower (SHP) in particular, is recognized as a flexible and affordable renewable energy source. Its role in electricity generation, especially in rapidly developing countries, is crucial. The World Commission on Dams (WCD, 2002) focused attention internationally on the negative environmental and social impacts of large dams, which raised questions about the environmental sustainability of large hydropower projects. However, only about 25 percent of the world's large dams are involved in producing hydropower. The rest were built for other purposes, mainly for irrigation, but also for water storage, for recreation and for assisting in river transport. Conversely, many large hydropower projects are run-of-river projects, which do not necessitate the building of a dam, while the role of small, mini- and micro-hydropower schemes is becoming increasingly important in the energy security of many countries, led by the example of China. It is therefore important to disassociate a discussion of the role of hydropower from the debate over large dams, while not glossing over the environmental and social considerations involved in the choice of technology.

Electricity plays a key role in reducing poverty, promoting economic activities and improving quality of life, health, and education opportunities...

2a. Hydropower in context

Governments have a pressing need to provide, at an affordable price, the convenience and reliability offered by electricity. The role of energy, and electricity in particular, in meeting development targets was discussed in depth in the first edition of the *UN World Water Development Report*. Statistics show that for many developing countries, access to electricity lags behind access to an improved water supply (see **Table 9.5** at the end of the chapter). Although improving access to electricity is not one of the MDGs, it was a target at the Johannesburg Plan of Implementation adopted at the World Summit on Sustainable Development (WSSD) in 2002 (see **Box 9.4**). Electricity plays a key role in reducing poverty, promoting economic activities and improving quality of life, health, and education opportunities, especially for women and children.

Since 1970, as worldwide demand for electricity has steadily increased, governments have met this demand through increasing thermal (gas, oil, coal and nuclear), as well as hydropower generation capacity. Although the share of hydropower in total world energy supply was only 2.2 percent in 2002, hydropower accounted for 19 percent of all electric power generated (see **Figures 9.1** and **9.2**).

Over the same time period, there has been a perceptible increase in the use of other renewable energy sources (geothermal, solar photovoltaics, wind, and combined heat and power[2] [CHP]). **Table 9.2** shows the renewable power capacity in all countries and in developing countries in 2003. Environmental concerns, particularly over climate change and nuclear waste disposal, as well as safety and security of supply, have prompted governments to introduce policies aimed at accelerating the penetration of renewables and CHP (see **Box 9.5**). Total worldwide investment in renewable energy rose from US $6 billion in 1995 to approximately US $22 billion in 2003, and is increasing rapidly.

The economies of scale available to the thermal and hydropower options and the existence of transmission and distribution grids continue to give them a significant cost advantage when compared with renewables. Both the thermal and hydropower options, particularly when used together, offer the load-following capability and reliability demanded by electricity consumers. Subsidies of all types have historically been used worldwide to establish a top-down energy supply system favouring thermal and large hydropower generating plants of ever-increasing capacity. However, both thermal and large hydropower options bring

2. CHP is the simultaneous generation of electric power and steam used for heating.

Part 3. Governance of Energy and Water Resources

China, India and Turkey frequently argue that their electricity requirements for economic growth and social development outweigh the environmental concerns surrounding hydropower...

In the past, some hydropower projects, particularly big reservoirs, have had a negative impact on their immediate surroundings. Damage to the local environment and inadequate provision for those affected in the area have contributed to the hostility shown by some environmental and human rights organizations towards the hydropower industry. The World Commission on Dams attempted to bring the various parties together, although its recommendations were not universally welcomed (WCD, 2000). More recent guidelines published by the International Hydropower Association (IHA) in 2004 have been broadly accepted throughout the large hydropower industry, in particular the core principles of equity, participatory decision-making and accountability.

3a. The continuing debate on large hydropower

IHA argues that equitable sharing of the benefits of any power project requires a careful balance between different stakeholders and interested parties. Hydropower uses renewable water supplies, not finite fossil fuels. In contrast to nuclear power, it leaves no toxic waste to threaten future generations, and in contrast to thermal power, it emits virtually no greenhouse gases. While the vast majority of a project's costs are borne at the start, the benefits continue for 100 years or more.

Furthermore, while any negative effects of a hydropower project are inevitably borne by the local community, the benefits – in reliable electricity supplies – are shared by everyone in the nation or region.

The key to managing changes lies in advance planning and consultation with all interested parties. The IHA Sustainability Guidelines state that hydro developers planning a project should try to minimize the following:

- health dangers, particularly from water-borne diseases or malaria
- loss of homes, farms and other livelihoods
- disruption of community networks and loss of cultural identity
- changes to biodiversity in the affected area.

They should try to maximize the following:

- timely consultation at all levels
- the flow of relevant information to all those affected
- negotiated settlement of disputes
- timely and adequate payment of any compensation.

Where people or communities have to be transferred to new sites, developers should do the following:

- investigate possible alternative ways of doing the project
- ensure adequate consultation with the people to be displaced throughout the project
- guarantee equivalent or improved livelihoods at the new location
- provide better living standards and public health at the new location.

Rapidly developing countries such as China, India and Turkey frequently argue that their electricity requirements for economic growth and social development outweigh the environmental concerns surrounding hydropower, and that support for large hydropower development is a pro-poor policy. This need was recognized in the Johannesburg Plan of Implementation (UN, 2002) where hydropower is included among the 'advanced, cleaner, more efficient, affordable and cost-effective energy technologies' required by developing countries. However, several non-governmental organizations are campaigning to have large hydropower excluded from global efforts to promote renewable energy. Among the arguments advanced for this position are the following:

- including large hydro in renewables initiatives reduces the available funding for new renewable energy technologies
- there is no technology transfer benefit from large hydro, which is a mature technology
- large hydro projects often have major social and ecological impacts
- large reservoirs can emit significant amounts of greenhouse gases from rotting organic matter
- large hydro reservoirs are often rendered non-renewable by sedimentation.

This long-standing debate is still a major issue. Many large hydropower projects necessitate the construction of large dams. These are structures with a long life, which permanently alter the river downstream and affect a significant stretch of the river upstream. They are not, strictly speaking, renewable. However, as discussed in this chapter, there are also very large run-of-river hydropower projects, as well as small, mini and micro-hydropower projects, which are all renewable energy providers. It must also be remembered that the driving force for much new dam construction is irrigation, rather than hydropower generation.

The water/energy nexus can be better understood by distinguishing the issue of large dams from that of hydropower, except in the cases of certain hydropower projects that do require the construction of large new reservoirs. In these specific cases, greater transparency, accountability and oversight of the contractual process to ensure the exposure of corrupt practices are all necessary in order to promote social equity and good governance.

3b. Renewable energy and energy efficiency: Incentives and economic instruments

In the world's developed regions, electricity is delivered to the vast majority of consumers through vertically integrated utility industries based on central power generation. Over the past several decades the efforts of energy policy-makers, utility planners, regulators and generation technology developers have enabled this conventional power generation and supply system to keep pace with rising demand, but with social and environmental impacts that are increasingly considered unacceptable. The inertia within the power supply system – power plants and transmission/distribution systems have lifetimes of several decades – means that this trend will be difficult to change.

However, with a worldwide 30 percent annual growth rate, renewable-based generating capacity is currently increasing faster than the conventional power option. Accelerated interest in renewable energy can be traced to the 'oil crisis' of the 1970s, but a list of environmental concerns headed by global climate change is responsible for the recent surge in interest in clean energy.

In developing countries where affordable power is desperately needed, environmental concerns must be carefully weighed against urgent development needs. As seen earlier in this chapter, governments will be less

responsive to objections to the construction of dams for large hydropower generation or to the deployment of new, greenhouse gas-emitting coal-fired power plants, when their priority is meeting rapidly growing electricity demand. Clearly, the transition to a fully sustainable, global energy supply system needs cooperative and innovative, if not radically new, policy-making.

International and national mechanisms implemented with the Kyoto Protocol

At the international level, the Clean Development Mechanism (CDM) and Joint Implementation (JI) measures established by the Kyoto Protocol seek to provide incentives for the use of low carbon-emitting and renewable energy technologies in developing countries, through the sale of carbon credits arising from clean energy investments. Given its proven track record of decades of successful experience, it is not surprising that hydropower projects are prominent in the current portfolio of CDM and JI projects. Multilateral initiatives establish emission reduction goals and a cooperative means of achieving them. However, they will need to be accompanied by national policies to stimulate a thriving market for renewable energy resources, such as wind, biomass, solar photovoltaics and hydropower as well as for combined heat and power (CHP) generation options. For example, feed-in tariffs oblige utilities to buy renewable electricity from any developer in their service area at tariffs set by government. These are generally a little lower than zthe electricity retail price, facilitating a good return on investment and assuring long-term support. Renewable Portfolio Standards (RPS) require the share of renewable power purchased by a utility to increase yearly to a given percentage. An RPS creates long-term stability and demand that establishes a flourishing renewables-based generation market. Within a given country, regional discrepancies arising from cost and availability of renewable power sources can be levelled out by means of tradable 'renewable energy certificates' (called 'green certificates' in Australia). Feed-in tariffs, RPSs and tradable certificates may need the further support of long-term and stable subsidies, such as investment tax credits and accelerated depreciation (see **Box 9.12**). In effect, renewable power markets need to be driven by a combination of demand- and supply-side measures capable of keeping the costs of electricity retailers and their retail customers at a minimum.

The case of rural electrification

Rural electrification is a special case. The provision of rural electrification through rural cooperatives was employed

Aerial close-up of Tucson Electric Power's cooling towers, Arizona, United States

Table 9.6: continued

	Gross theoretical capability TWh/yr	Technically exploitable capability TWh/yr	Economically exploitable capability TWh/yr
Albania	40	15	6
Austria	75	> 56	56
Belarus	7	3	1
Belgium	1	n.a.	n.a.
Bosnia and Herzogovina	60	24	19
Bulgaria	27	15	12
Croatia	10	9	8
Czech Republic	12	4	–
Denmark	n.a.	n.a.	n.a.
Estonia	2	n.a.	–
Faroe Islands	1	n.a.	n.a.
Finland	48	25	20
France	270	100	70
Germany	120	25	20
Greece	80	15	12
Hungary	7	5	–
Iceland	184	64	40
Ireland	1	1	1
Italy	340	105	65
Latvia	7	6	5
Lithuania	6	2	1
Luxembourg	n.a.	n.a.	n.a.
Macedonia, former Yugoslav Republic	9	6	–
Moldova	2	1	1
Netherlands	1	n.a.	n.a.
Norway	600	200	187
Poland	23	14	7
Portugal	32	25	20
Romania	70	40	30
Serbia and Montenegro	37	27	24
Slovakia	10	7	7
Slovenia	13	9	6
Spain	138	70	41
Sweden	176	130	90
Switzerland	144	41	35
Ukraine	45	24	17
United Kingdom	40	3	1
Total Europe	**2,638**	**> 1,071**	–
Iran, Islamic Republic	176	> 50	50
Iraq	225	90	67
Israel	125	50	–
Jordan	n.a.	n.a.	n.a.
Lebanon	2	1	n.a.
Syrian Arab Republic	5	4	4
Total Middle East	**533**	**> 195**	–
Australia	265	> 30	30
Fiji	3	1	–
French Polynesia	n.a.	n.a.	n.a.
New Caledonia	2	1	n.a.

Table 9.6: continued

	Gross theoretical capability TWh/yr	Technically exploitable capability TWh/yr	Economically exploitable capability TWh/yr
New Zealand	46	37	24
Papua New Guinea	175	49	15
Samoa	n.a.	n.a.	–
Solomon Islands	2	> 1	–
Total Oceania	**493**	**> 119**	–
TOTAL WORLD	**> 40,293**	**> 15,899**	–

n.a. = not applicable due to flat topography

– = information not available

Notes:

1. A quantification of hydropower capability is not available for Comoros, Equatorial Guinea, Mauritania, Réunion, São Tomé and Principe, Guadeloupe, Puerto Rico, St Vincent and the Grenadines, French Guiana, Afghanistan, Korea (Democratic People's Republic) and Palau.

2. As the data available on economically exploitable capability do not cover all countries, regional and global totals are not shown for this category.

Sources: The International Journal on Hydropower and Dams; International Hydropower Association Member Committees, 2003; Hydropower Dams World Atlas 2003.

References and Websites

Martinot, E. 2002. Indicators of investment and capacity for renewable energy. *Renewable Energy in the World.* Vol. Sept/Oct.

NRDC (National Resources Defense Council). 2004. *Energy down the Drain.* New York, NRDC.

UN (United Nations). 2002. Johannesburg Plan of Implementation. www.un.org/esa/sustdev/documents/WSSD_POI_PD/English/WSSD_Planl mpl.pdf

UNECA (United Nations Economic Comission for Africa). 2004. *African Water Development Report.* Addis Ababa, UNECA.

US DOE (United States Department of Energy). 2004. *Improving Pumping System Performance: A Sourcebook for Industry.* Washington DC, US DOE, 2nd edition.

World Bank. 2003. *World Development Indicators.* New York, World Bank.

WRI (World Resources Institute). Climate Analysis Indicators Tool, Washington, DC.

Alliance to Save Energy www.ase.org: www.watergy.org

FAO's AQUASTAT www.fao.org/ag/agl/aglw/aquastat/main/index.stm

International Energy Agency, Energy Statistics: www.iea.org/Textbase/stats/index.asp

International Energy Agency Coal Centre: www.iea-coal.org.uk

International Networking on Small Hydropower: www.inshp.org

International Hydropower Association: www.hydropower.org/

IT Power: www.itpower.co.uk

Naiade solar water purifiers: www.nedapnaiade.com/

Solar water Disinfection (SoDis): www.sodis.ch

UNIDO: www.unido.org/

WCD (World Commission on Dams): www.dams.org

World Resources Institute: Climate Analysis Indicators Tool, Data on Carbon Intensity to Electricity Production from 2002, available online at cait.wri.org/

World Resources Institute: www.wri.org/

SECTION 4

Management Responses and Stewardship

Balancing the increasing competition among the diverse and different water using sectors and the demands of upstream and downstream users – whether within or between countries – is a challenge in watersheds worldwide. Decisions on water allocations have to be made at different scales, based not only on the various demands for water, but taking into account its many values as well.

Though the urgency of many water problems means that effective actions are needed now, water management approaches must also be forward-looking in their ability to deal with changing contexts, such as climate variability and its impact on water-related hazards, namely floods and droughts. The capacity to adapt and to make wise decisions depends upon preparedness, which depends in turn on a sound knowledge base; the complexity of water issues requires a more effective policy framework that builds, maintains, extends and shares our knowledge and uses of water resources, and respects the values we place on them.

Global Map 7: *The Climate Moisture Index Coefficient of Variation*
Global Map 8: *The Water Reuse Index*

Chapter 10 – **Managing Risks: Securing the Gains of Development** (WMO & UN-ISDR)

The climate is changing, thus increasing the occurrence and intensity of water-related natural disasters and creating greater burdens on human and environmental development. Employing an integrated approach, this chapter explores some of the ways of better reducing human vulnerabilities and examines the recent developments in risk reduction strategies.

Chapter 11 – **Sharing Water** (UNESCO)

Increasing competition for water resources can have potentially divisive effects. Mechanisms for cooperation and shared governance among users must be further developed in order to ensure that the resource become a catalyst for cooperation and a medium for deterring political tensions, while encouraging equitable and sustainable development.

Chapter 12 – **Valuing and Charging for Water** (UNDESA)

Water has a range of values that must be recognized in selecting governance strategies. Valuation techniques inform decision-making for water allocation, which promote not only sustainable social, environmental and economic development but also transparency and accountability in governance. This chapter reviews techniques of economic valuation and the use of these tools in water policy development and charging for water services.

Chapter 13 – **Enhancing Knowledge and Capacity** (UNESCO)

The collection, dissemination and exchange of water-related data, information and know-how are imbalanced and, in many cases, deteriorating. It is now more urgent than ever to improve the state of knowledge concerning water-related issues through an effective global network of research, training and data collection and the implementation of more adaptive, informed and participatory approaches at all levels.

Better decision-making, improved planning, effective risk management, innovation in development and environmental protection activities – these are the human activities that can reduce the vulnerability of communities. To this end, risk assessment and disaster reduction should be integral parts of all sustainable development projects and policies.

Kofi Annan, *United Nations Secretary-General*

CHAPTER 10

Managing Risks: Securing the Gains of Development

By

WMO
(World Meteorological Organization)

UN-ISDR
(Inter-Agency Secretariat, United Nations International Strategy for Disaster Reduction)

Left: Coastal destruction in the wake of the 26 December 2004 tsunami in Indonesia

...the causes for disasters need to be analysed so as to guide investment in reconstruction, in particular for infrastructure and land use

The global distribution of water-related disasters shows important regional differences (see **Figure 10.2**), with a large share of events occurring in Asia. **Figure 10.3** offers an overview of the impact of water-related disasters in terms of numbers of deaths and people affected.

To some extent, the increase of water-related disasters shown in **Figure 10.3** can be explained by an increase in reporting activities. Likewise, the number of people affected by disasters and material losses can be attributed to population growth and increasing value of assets. In some cases, however, risk and disaster statistics are still difficult to produce. This is the case for instance when it comes to giving a clear definition of people 'affected' by a disaster, where health, sanitary, social and economic dimensions must be taken into account. Differences are also introduced when comparing developing and developed countries. Statistical difficulties also exist with the qualification of drought-related disasters.

1b. Disaster risk reduction at the international level

Milestone events during the United Nations (UN) International Decade for Natural Disaster Reduction (IDNDR, 1990–2000) and in the Yokohama Strategy and Plan of Action (UN/GA, 1994) have provided policy guidance and tools for the mitigation of natural disasters.

5. For details visit www.mrcmekong.org

6. See the final report of the World Conference on Disaster Reduction (18–22 January 2005, Hyogo, Japan) at www.unisdr.org/wcdr

Based on a review of global disaster risk reduction initiatives, the Secretariat of the International Strategy for Disaster Reduction (ISDR) identified the principal limitations and challenges to the implementation of this strategy and action plan (ISDR, 2004a). These limitations have also become key areas for developing a relevant framework for action in disaster risk reduction for the International Decade 'Water for Life' 2005–2015 and include the following (WCDR, 2005):

- governance: organizational, legal and policy frameworks
- risk identification, assessment, monitoring and early warning
- knowledge management and education
- reduction of underlying risk factors
- preparedness for effective response and recovery.

These points are consistent with the priorities identified in two other major policy documents agreed upon by the international community: the Johannesburg Plan of Implementation (JPoI) and the Millennium Development Goals (MDGs). **Table 10.1** illustrates how the latter are related to risk reduction.

Complementary to the commitment of the international community, many countries have also engaged, bilaterally, regionally and internationally, in cooperative arrangements for water-related disaster risk reduction. This is, for instance, the case in the Mekong River Basin, where in 2001 riparian countries established a Flood Mitigation and Management Plan under the aegis of the Mekong River Commission.[5] In southern Africa, countries of the Southern African Development Community developed a web-based information system to monitor regional conditions when cyclones, floods and droughts occur in the region (see **Chapter 14**).

Strong linkages have been identified between poverty, high social vulnerability to and low capacity to cope with water-related hazards and disasters.[6] The next section discusses how risk management is a key issue of sustainable development.

1c. Linking disaster risk reduction and development planning

Water-related disasters disrupt economic development as well as the social fabric of vulnerable societies. This jeopardizes the accumulated gains in social and economic development and investments in better living conditions and quality of life. Disaster risk reduction policies and measures

Figure 10.2: Distribution of water-related disasters by region, 1990–2004

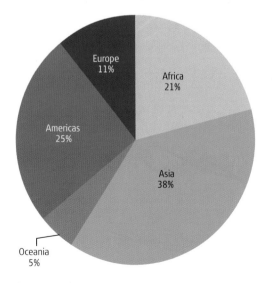

- Europe 11%
- Africa 21%
- Americas 25%
- Asia 38%
- Oceania 5%

Source: Data from OFDA-CRED in Louvain (Belgium) and analysis by PWRI in Tsukuba (Japan), 2005.

Table 10.1: The Millennium Development Goals (MDGs) and disaster risk reduction

Millennium Development Goals (MDGs)	Related risk reduction aspects
MDG 1: Eradicating extreme poverty and hunger	Human vulnerability to natural hazards and poverty are largely codependent. Exposure to hazards plays a critical role in poverty-ridden areas. Hunger reduces individual capacity to cope with stress caused by disasters.
MDG 2: Achieving universal primary education	Educational attainment is a fundamental determinant of human vulnerability and social marginalization. Basic literacy and numeracy enable individuals to become more engaged in their society. Broadening participation in decision-making is key to disaster risk reduction.
MDG 3: Promoting gender equality and empowering women	Facilitating the participation of women and girls in the development process is a key priority. Women across the world play critical roles in shaping development. In some contexts, women may be more exposed to natural hazards. At the same time, women are often more likely than men to participate in communal actions to reduce risk and enhance development.
MDG 4: Reducing child mortality	Children under five years of age are particularly vulnerable to the impacts of environmental hazards, ranging from the everyday risks of inadequate sanitation and drinking water to death and injury as a result of catastrophic events and their aftermath. Post-traumatic psychological disorders are also a major issue.
MDG 5: Improving maternal health	As environmental hazard stress or shock erodes the savings and capacities of households and families, marginal people within these social groups are most at risk. In many cases, it is women, girls or the elderly who are the least entitled to household or family assets. Reducing drains on household assets through risk reduction will contribute to enhancing maternal health.
MDG 6: Combating HIV/AIDS, malaria and other diseases	Interactions between epidemiological status and human vulnerability to subsequent stresses and shocks are well documented. For example, rural populations affected by HIV/AIDS are less able to cope with the stress of drought. Likewise, individuals living with chronic or terminal diseases are more vulnerable to emergency situations.
MDG 7: Ensuring environmental sustainability	Major disasters, or the accumulation of risk from regular and persistent but smaller events, can wipe out any hope of sustainability for urban or rural environments. Again, the equation works both ways. Increasing destruction due to landslides, floods and other disasters related to environmental and land-use patterns are a clear signal that massive challenges remain in achieving this goal.
MDG 8: Developing a global partnership for development	Efforts to enhance sustainable development and reduce human vulnerability to natural hazards are hampered by national debt burdens, terms of international trade, the high price of necessary drugs, lack of access to new technology and new hazards associated with global climate change, among other hurdles. Building a global partnership for development would contribute to disaster risk reduction.

Source: Adapted from UNDP, 2004.

Figure 10.3: Number of dead and affected people in water-related disasters, 1970–2004

Note: The disasters reported in this figure include floods, windstorms, landslides, avalanches, droughts, famines, water-related epidemics and technological water-related disasters (such as traffic accidents due to water). This figure indicates a possible improvement in crisis management, disaster relief and humanitarian activities, while simultaneously illustrating that the number of people living in hazard-prone areas is increasing. The alarming increase of affected people since the start of the twenty-first century is notable: from 2000 to 2004 (four-year data), 1,942 water-related disasters claiming the lives of 427,045 people and more than 1.5 billion affected people were reported in the CRED disaster database.

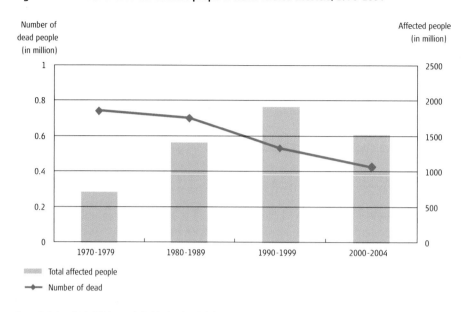

Source: Data from OFDA-CRED in Louvain (Belgium) and analysis done in 2005 by Public Works Research Institute (PWRI) in Tsukuba (Japan).

7. For details, see the Integrated Flood Management concept (IFM) of the World Meteorological Organization-Global Water Partnership (WMO-GWP) Associated Programme for Flood Management (APFM) at www.apfm.info/

8. See, for instance, the activities of the World Conservation Union (IUCN) at iucn.org/themes/wetlands/

9. For more information, visit www.waterandclimate.org/home.asp

need to be designed in such a way that they are consistent with integrated long-term development objectives and implementation plans. Therefore, managing water-related risks is a matter of governance. In particular, post-disaster relief and reconstruction activities need to be improved with the long-term objective of 'building back better'. This means that the causes for disasters need to be analysed so as to guide investment in reconstruction, in particular for infrastructure and land use. Limiting the extent of damage and reducing vulnerability are two interrelated objectives of the risk management cycle (**Figure 10.4**).

There is now international acknowledgement that efforts to reduce disaster risks must be systematically integrated into policies, plans and programmes for sustainable development and poverty reduction (Abramovitz, 2001 in ISDR, 2004a). At the local level, for instance, disaster risk reduction efforts should assist communities not only to recover from disasters but also to move above the poverty line. Land-use planning is another example of integrated policies that can help reduce disaster risk, which should take account of the positive social and economic aspects of flooding, including sediment provision for soil fertility, environmental flow maintenance, and ecosystem maintenance.[7] The value of wetlands for flood protection has also been increasingly recognized as a complement to structural measures.[8]

As part of national and regional plans for sustainable development, risk assessment is needed to anticipate possible impacts of global changes on water resources. It is now widely recognized that climate variability and change have the potential to threaten sustainable development (IPCC, 2001).

A convergence of interests is emerging, and efforts have been made since the 1990s to develop cooperative actions with the objective of integrating climate-related coping strategies into disaster risk reduction and poverty reduction efforts. For instance, the Co-operative Programme on Water and Climate aims to improve the capacity to cope with the impacts of the increasing variability of the world's climate.[9]

However, despite these national and international investments and efforts, limitations still remain in current disaster risk reduction activities.

1d. Limitations in risk reduction: lessons from current practice

A recent study conducted by the World Meteorological Organization (WMO) identified challenge areas in risk management (adapted from WMO, 2004):

▪ Challenge areas related to scientific observations and improved methodologies:

Section 4: MANAGEMENT RESPONSES & STEWARDSHIP

- improving the quantity and accuracy of data in order to map hazards and assess impacts
- making Geographic Information Systems (GIS) more user-friendly
- quantifying uncertainties related to forecasting hydrometeorological extremes
- building up and disseminating knowledge of the effects of climate variability and change
- further developing robust vulnerability assessment methods
- incorporating integrated environmental strategies in risk management.

- Challenge areas related to social and political issues:
  - building risk management frameworks that reflect an integrated approach to risk management
  - promoting the inclusion of risk management aspects in transboundary agreements
  - enhancing public participation in risk management programmes and activities.

Sustainable development, poverty reduction, appropriate governance and disaster risk reduction are interconnected objectives, as reflected by the evolution of risk reduction approaches detailed in the next section.

Figure 10.4: The risk management cycle

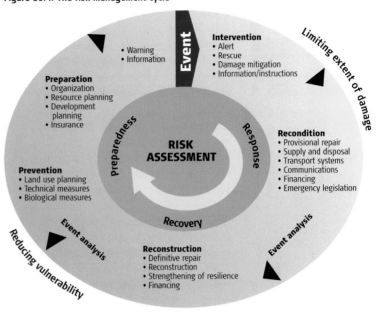

Source: Adapted from Swiss Civil Protection. This mitigation-crisis-rehabilitation cycle shows the challenges of post-disaster reconstruction.

Flooding in Tana River Valley, Kenya, due to extended and unseasonal rain

Part 2. Risk Management Frameworks

The first *UN World Water Development Report* (WWDR1) showed that over the past decade, there has been a shift from crisis management, which was mainly responsive in nature, to proactive risk management and strategies orientated towards disaster prevention. The basic characteristics of these different approaches appear in Table 10.2.

Fighting against rising flood waters in Germany

2a. Risk management over time: From response to integration

In recent years, the understanding of water-related disaster risks has improved, thanks to advances in modelling and forecasting of physical processes, such as climate variability and change, and the progressive inclusion of social and environmental dimensions in assessment (Viljoen et al., 2001). This has been useful in identifying the social and economic factors of disasters, such as the value of assets exposed to hazards, livelihood functions, social vulnerability, coping capacity, cultural dimensions and the role played by the insurance sector (for theory and examples of practice, see Dercon, 2004).

The recognition of the social dimensions of risk and disasters has fostered research and action in developing participatory processes for risk management (WHO, 1989; McDaniels et al., 1999; Parker, 2004; ISDR, 2004a). The objective is that all relevant institutions and stakeholders that are exposed to risk have the opportunity to share their experiences and concerns in the decision-making process (see **Box 10.1** for details).

Such participatory approaches have been implemented in many countries. In the Netherlands, for instance, participatory planning for flood management has been successfully tested (Frijters and Leentvaar, 2001). In France, Germany and Poland, the European Union funded a project involving floodplain communities in the design of a flood information system based on information technologies.[10] In Cambodia, the non-governmental organization Action Against Hunger and the Cambodian Red Cross have developed, since 1998, a community-based project of early warning for Mekong floods (Affeltranger and Lictevout, 2005).

As a support tool to these community-based processes, rapid developments in modern communication technologies can help record and disseminate experience, convey professional knowledge and contribute to decision-making processes. Information and knowledge, both of which are institutional and community-based,[11]

are integral to the design and successful implementation of risk reduction policies (see also **Chapter 13**).

2b. Managing risk-related knowledge and information wisely: Preventing data loss

Water- and risk-related data are needed to support multi-hazard approaches, design risk-related indicators, operate efficient warning systems, develop awareness-raising programmes and enable institutions to adapt to environmental and social changes. Availability of and access to data are therefore essential for hazard analysis and vulnerability assessment (ISDR, 2004a). However, risk-related knowledge and information are often unavailable or missing. Difficulties include a loss of institutional memory and limited access to data and information.

Water- and risk-related data accessibility problems include the following (ISDR, 2004a):

- Data is restricted for presumed security purposes.
- Inadequate cross-sector communication exists about the existence of data.
- Dissemination of information is not considered a priority by the organization.
- Information is maintained in non-standardized formats.
- Existing information is costly to convert into more readily accessible formats.
- Data compilers have not consulted users about their data requirements.
- Information for women's advocacy organizations and other community-based groups is not readily available, and gender-specific data is not consistently gathered or disseminated.

Risk knowledge and know-how can also be lost over time for various reasons, including lack of funding for database maintenance, lack of information-sharing among administrations, loss of institutional memory when civil servants retire or leave office for a job in the private sector. Lost knowledge and know-how include overviews of hydrometeorological processes in river basins, the

---

10. For more information, visit www.ist-osiris.org

11. Institutional knowledge includes the expertise of civil servants; official statistics and databases; and hazard and risk mapping resources. Community-based knowledge includes past flood experience; empirical knowledge; and coping and adaptive capacities.

Table 10.2: Response-based versus prevention-oriented strategies to disaster risk reduction

Response-based strategies (relief)	Emphasis	Integrated strategies (prevention, mitigation and relief)
1. Primary focus on hazards and disaster events		1. Primary focus on vulnerability and risk issues
2. Single, event-based scenarios	**Emphasis**	2. Dynamic, multiple risk issues and development scenarios
3. Basic responsibility to respond to an event		3. Fundamental need to assess, monitor and update exposure to changing conditions
4. Often fixed, location-specific conditions		4. Extended changing and shared regional or local variations
5. Responsibility concentrated in a single authority or agency		5. Involves multiple authorities, interests, actors
6. Command and control, directed operations		6. Situation-specific functions, free association
7. Established hierarchical relationships	**Operations**	7. Shifting, fluid and tangential relationships
8. Often focused on hardware and equipment		8. Dependent on related practices, abilities and knowledge base
9. Dependent on specialized expertise		9. Specialized expertise, squared with public views and priorities
10. Urgent, immediate and short-term periods in outlook, planning, attention, returns	**Time horizons**	10. Comparative, moderate and long-term periods in outlook, planning, values, returns
11. Rapidly changing, dynamic information usage, often conflicting or sensitive		11. Accumulated, historical, layered, updated or comparative use of information
12. Primary, authorized or singular information sources, need for definitive facts		12. Open or public information, multiple, diverse or changing sources, differing perspectives and points of view
13. Directed, 'need to know' basis of information dissemination, availability	**Information use and management**	13. Multiple use, shared exchange, inter-sectoral use of information
14. Operational, or public information based on use of communications		14. Matrix, nodal communication
15. In-out or vertical flows of information		15. Dispersed, lateral flows of information
16. Relates to matters of public security, safety	**Social, political rationale**	16. Matters of public interest, investment and safety

Source: ISDR, 2001.

Left: 2nd wave of the 26 December 2004 tsunami, Sri Lanka

Right: Desertification in Chott El-Djerid, Tunisia

BOX 10.3: **MANUALS FOR COMMUNITY-BASED FLOOD MANAGEMENT: PROJECT IN BANGLADESH, INDIA AND NEPAL**

The Community Approaches to Flood Management project, developed by WMO and its partners, has developed country-wide manuals on community flood management on the basis of information provided by selected flood-prone communities in Bangladesh, India and Nepal. Through field research, including Participatory Rapid Appraisal (PRA), it was first ascertained which activities had been undertaken, individually and collectively, at various stages – before, during and after floods have occurred – with a view to reducing lost lives and destroyed livelihoods and the suffering caused by floods. Once drafted, the manuals were reviewed by the selected communities during workshops and subsequently adopted. This approach, when implemented in selected flood-prone areas, has proven effective at improving the flood management capacity of the communities concerned and reducing their flood vulnerability.

Source: Unpublished project report (as of April 2005), WMO Commission for Hydrology and Water Resources Management.

BOX 10.4: **METHODOLOGY BEHIND THE DISASTER RISK INDEX (DRI)**

A mortality-based index was developed in order to enable comparisons of countries hit by different hazards types, such as droughts versus floods. The other reason for such a choice was that data on mortality is the most complete and the most reliable (the Emergency Disasters Database from CRED was used for this purpose). Other parameters, such as economic losses, number of injured or losses of livelihood, all suffer from either a lack of data or a lack of comparative potential, if not both. The formula used for risk estimation was based on the UN definition of 1979, which states that the risk results from three components: the *hazard occurrence probability*, the *elements at risk* (in this case the population) and their *vulnerability*. By multiplying the frequency of hazards by the population affected, the *physical exposure* was obtained. This figure represents the average number of people affected yearly by a specific hazard. The first task was to find all the requested geophysical data and then model the different hazards in order to obtain the frequency for earthquakes, drought, floods and cyclones for each location on the globe. The model for population distribution, developed by the Center for International Earth Science Information Network, was multiplied by frequency to compute the physical exposure. This already normalized the differences between populations highly affected by a selected hazard and those less frequently affected.

Note: The United Nations Environmental Programme's (UNEP) Global Resource Information Database started a process to update the DRI methodology in April 2005.

Source: UNDP, 2004.[16]

- strengthened credibility across different institutions and interest groups
- increased commitment to help the most vulnerable.[13]

Box 10.2 provides an example of multi-hazard assessment in Costa Rica.

User-based design of warning systems for floods and drought

Designing efficient flood warning systems poses technical, organizational and social challenges: technical constraints include a lack of data, modelling inadequacy and differing flood types, and organizational constraints include weak dissemination of information and institutional deficiencies in the coordination of joint measures for risk management and disaster prevention. Social and cultural limitations include a poor understanding of warning, limited ownership, conflicting information sources and resistance to follow guidance and instructions.

The efficiency of warning systems for water-related disasters was found to be greatly improved by the early involvement of stakeholders in the design of the warning system (McDaniels et al., 1999; Vari, 2004). The objective is to design a warning message that will be most useful to people confronting an impending hazard. Participatory design of warning strategies has been successfully implemented in many developed and developing countries. These approaches aim at involving warning receivers in the various development phases of a warning system, including forms and contents of the message, dissemination channel and options for feedback. (Affeltranger, 2002; Parker, 2004; Affeltranger and Lictevout, 2005). **Box 10.3** provides an example of a community-based approach to flood management.

The development of warning systems for droughts is another challenge for risk managers and water managers. Early warnings of drought help farmers select appropriate crops and irrigation schedules and

13. For more information, see ISDR's Guiding Principles – National Platforms for Disaster Risk Reduction www.unisdr.org/eng/country-inform/docs/Guiding%20Princi ples%20for%20NP.pdf

methods, thus contributing to food security. Timely warning also provides water managers with a chance to allocate available water resources based on rational priority criteria.

Several initiatives have been developed to improve drought-related information management and warning activities. For instance, at the request of twenty-four countries in eastern and southern Africa, WMO established two Drought Monitoring Centres (DMCs), in Nairobi, Kenya (see **Chapter 14**), and Harare, Zimbabwe, in 1989 with financial support from the United Nations Development Programme (UNDP). The main objective of the centres is to contribute to early warning systems and the mitigation of adverse impacts of extreme climatic events on agricultural production.[14]

14. For more information, visit www.drought.unl.edu/monitor/EWS/ch11_Ambenje.pdf

Part 3. Indicators for Risk Management

Indicators are needed to inform the design of disaster risk reduction policies and monitor the implementation and assessment of these policies. Indicators help identify patterns in disaster losses, as well as underlying physical, social or economic trends that influence hazard, vulnerability and risk patterns. Such risk factors include environmental degradation, population growth and the increasing value of assets in flood-prone areas and risk perception. Quantifiable indicators in particular are needed when decisions involve trade-offs between development options with varying degrees of risk.

The development of indicators for water-related risk management is a relatively new field. In water-related risk management, risk-based indicators remain scarce and suffer from limitations in terms of conceptual design, paucity of data and largely insufficient robustness. There is a clear need to further develop indicators for risk management and encourage governments and relevant national and international organizations to provide the necessary data on which these indicators are built. Such data should be of high quality and supplied on a regular basis to enable the development of long-term indicators, especially for monitoring purposes.

Below are three examples of indicators selected to demonstrate their actual or potential applications on global, regional and national scales (see also **Chapter 1**). These indicators are in different testing and application stages. Some are already undergoing a revision of their science base and robustness, underlining the necessity for further research and development on their concepts and applicability.

3a. Disaster Risk Index (DRI)
This index[15] has been developed to help compare disaster-risk country situations, based on a quantitative approach to disaster impacts. Natural hazards assessed by this index include floods, cyclones, earthquakes and droughts. This index allows global ranking on the basis of relative vulnerability of nations (UNDP-BCPR, 2004) (**Box 10.4**).

Indicators used for the DRI aim at grasping the socio-economic dimensions of risks. They include the Human Development Index (HDI), the number of physicians per 1,000 inhabitants, the rate of urban growth, etc. The results showed surprisingly high correlations.[17] This analysis provides a useful and neutral tool for the evaluation of countries facing natural hazard risks. UNDP hopes that this tool will help countries with both high vulnerability and high exposure to adopt more risk reduction measures. **Maps 10.1** and **10.2** and **Figures 10.5** and **10.6** show the DRI graphic results as applied to floods and droughts.

3b. Climate Vulnerability Index (CVI)
Developed for a range of scales (from community to national and regional levels), this indicator links climate variability and change, water availability, and socio-economic factors (Sullivan and Meigh, 2005).[18] The assessment of risk in relation to water resources is strongly dependent on people's vulnerability to water-related hazards. In addition, the uncertainty generated by climate variability and change plays an important role.

The CVI identifies a range of social, economic, environmental and physical factors relevant to vulnerability (see **Table 10.3**) and incorporates them into an integrated index.

15. This index was developed by the United Nations Development Programme's Bureau for Crisis Prevention and Recovery (UNDP/BCPR), based on research done by United Nations Environmental Programme's Global Resource Information Database (UNEP/GRID, Geneva).

16. We acknowledge the contribution of Dr Pascal Peduzzi (UNEP/GRID, Geneva) in the drafting of this section.

17. A web-based interactive tool for comparing countries is provided at: gridca.grid.unep.ch/undp/. The location of frequency and physical exposure can be visualised at: grid.unep.ch/preview

18. For this section, we acknowledge the support of Dr Caroline Sullivan, from the Centre for Ecology and Hydrology (CEH) in the UK.

Part 4. From Frameworks to Policies

The design of a risk management framework is a prerequisite step to the successful development of risk reduction policies.

4a. Risk management frameworks

Risk management frameworks are meant to address the multiple goals of disaster risk reduction in a way that is consistent with the planning of social and economic development. Such frameworks also guide the design of a sound legislation basis, a necessary step for ensuring good governance of risk reduction activities.

Based on an extensive, global review of disaster risk reduction initiatives, the ISDR Secretariat designed a framework for disaster risk reduction, which provides a design concept for the development of risk management policies. The framework shows that treating interrelated issues such as 'knowledge development', 'political commitment' and 'application of risk reduction measures', involves a wide range of public policy issues (see **Figure 10.8** for details and **Chapter 14**).

The elements presented in the ISDR framework also advocate the development of a solid institutional background for disaster risk reduction policies.

21. Much of this section has been adapted from Plate, 2002.

4b. Risk management: A matter of legislation and policy

The legal basis for risk reduction policies is critical for transparent decision-making and allocating public funding for disaster mitigation. Examples include legislation, land-use planning regulations, building codes, inter-administration cooperation and operation rules for reservoirs. In some cases, the adoption of a new law on water-related disaster risk reduction has been fostered by the occurrence of a disaster or by a noticeable change in the natural environment. Under these circumstances, a new law concerning countermeasures against flood damages in urban areas was enacted in Japan in June 2003 (see **Figure 10.9** for details).

Disaster risk reduction policies also need to be consistent with existing policies in other sectors that have risk-related components (see **Table 10.5** for details).

4c. Example of practice: Flood risk management

Flood risk management[21] includes the planning of natural, technical or social systems, in order to reduce flood risk. Risk management therefore involves the value system of a given society, because it aims at balancing the desired state of the environment and the demands placed on it, while managing where trade-offs are best made.

Risk management actually takes place on three different levels: the operational level (see **Figure 10.10**), which is associated with the operation of existing systems; the project planning level, which is used when a new project or a revision of an existing project is planned (see **Figure 10.11**); and the project design level, which is embedded into the second level and describes the process of reaching an optimal solution for the project.

In the operation of an existing flood protection system, risk management involves a series of actions including the process of risk analysis, which provides the basis for long-term management decisions for the flood protection system. Continuous improvement of the system requires a reassessment of the existing risks and an evaluation of the hazards, making use of state-of-the-art data, information and assessment tools.

Table 10.5: Public policies with water-related risk components

Public policy	Risk-related aspect or impact
Development planning	▓ Social and economic activities
	▓ Poverty reduction
Land-use planning	▓ Urban sprawl in flood-prone areas
	▓ Exposure of the most vulnerable groups
Water resources management	▓ Upstream/downstream flow of water
	▓ Environmental flow management
	▓ Drought warning and management
Agriculture and forestry	▓ Erosion and sedimentation
	▓ Concentration time of river basin
Civil defence and the military	▓ Relief response capacity
	▓ Warning and crisis communication
Public health	▓ Emergency relief response capacity
	▓ Water-borne disease management
Education	▓ Awareness-raising campaigns
	▓ Learning self-protective behaviours
	▓ Academic research and staff training
Diplomacy	▓ Cooperation for water sharing
	▓ Exchange of data for forecast/warning
	▓ International basin management

Note: This table is indicative and should be adapted to the characteristics of regional, national and local situations.

Figure 10.8: Framework for disaster risk reduction

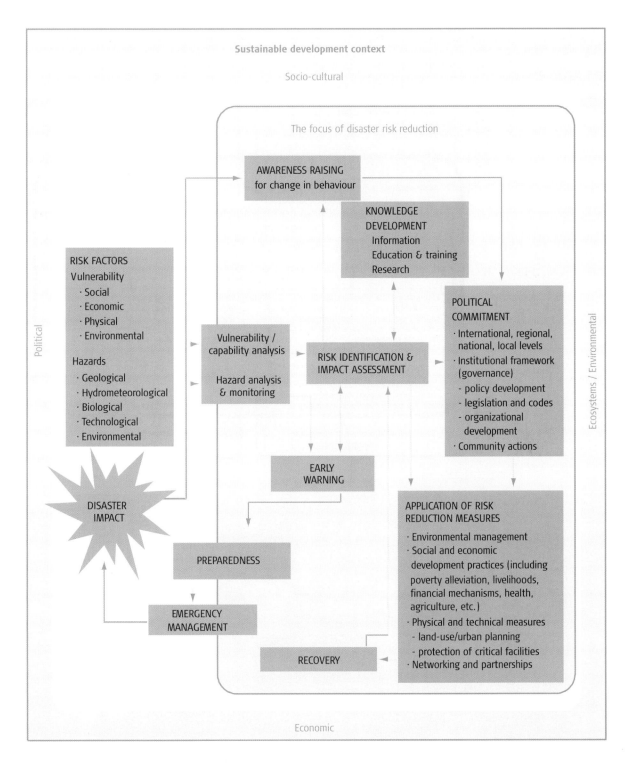

Source: ISDR, 2004a.

...in some cases the adoption of a new law has been fostered by the occurrence of disaster

The project planning aspect of risk management is summarized in **Figure 10.11**. This figure basically consists of two parts: risk assessment, which yields the basis for decisions on which solution to use, and the implementation phase, which involves a great deal of activities ranging from the fundamental decision to move forward to the studied complexity design and construction.

Figure 10.9: Framework of the Designated Urban River Inundation Prevention Act (Japan, 2003)

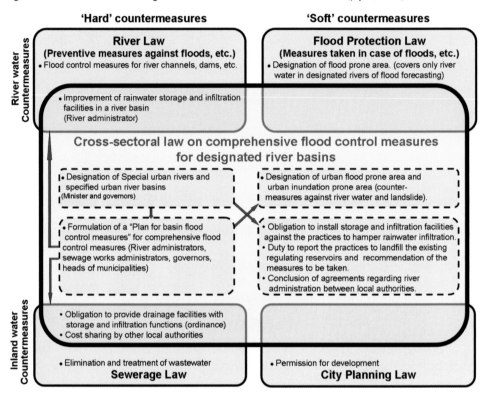

'Hard' countermeasures | **'Soft' countermeasures**

River water Countermeasures

River Law
(Preventive measures against floods, etc.)
• Flood control measures for river channels, dams, etc.

Flood Protection Law
(Measures taken in case of floods, etc.)
• Designation of flood prone area. (covers only river water in designated rivers of flood forecasting)

• Improvement of rainwater storage and infiltration facilities in a river basin (River administrator)

Cross-sectoral law on comprehensive flood control measures for designated river basins

• Designation of Special urban rivers and specified urban river basins (Minister and governors)

• Designation of urban flood prone area and urban inundation prone area (countermeasures against river water and landslide).

• Formulation of a "Plan for basin flood control measures" for comprehensive flood control measures (River administrators, sewage works administrators, governors, heads of municipalities)

• Obligation to install storage and infiltration facilities against the practices to hamper rainwater infiltration.
• Duty to report the practices to landfill the existing regulating reservoirs and recommendation of the measures to be taken.
• Conclusion of agreements regarding river administration between local authorities.

Inland water Countermeasures

• Obligation to provide drainage facilities with storage and infiltration functions (ordinance)
• Cost sharing by other local authorities

• Elimination and treatment of wastewater
Sewerage Law

• Permission for development
City Planning Law

Source: Ministry of Land, Infrastructure and Transport (MLIT), Japan. Graphic provided by PWRI Institute (Tsukuba, Japan).

Note: The central box in this graphic figures the logical connections existing between the new law and the existing laws (River, Flood Protection, Sewerage and City Planning).

Section 4: MANAGEMENT RESPONSES & STEWARDSHIP

Figure 10.10: Risk management at the operational level

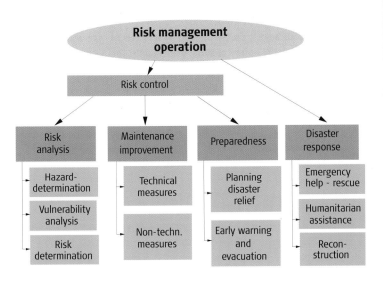

Source: Plate, 2002.

Figure 10.11: Risk management at the project planning level

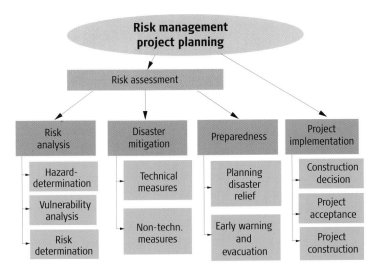

Note: Although not appearing in this graphic, a 'public participation' dimension is needed at all levels. Involving stakeholders in project planning is essential to the social ownership of the process.

Source: Plate, 2002.

Left: Floating market, Mekong Delta, Viet Nam

Above: The Indonesian coast, between Banda Aceh and Meulaboh, after the earthquake and tsunami of 26 December 2004

Below: Inundated houses during a flood in New Bethlehem, Pennsylvania, United States

*Floating market, Mekong
Delta, Viet Nam*

Part 5. Strategies for the Future

**The future of disaster risk reduction depends heavily on the capacity of societies to cope with changes
in the nature of water-related hazards, and in the nature of social vulnerability. This section therefore
advocates flexibility in the design and implementation of disaster risk reduction policies and activities.**

5a. Climate variability and change: Consequences for risk reduction

Climate variability and change are natural trends aggravated
by the emission of natural and man-made greenhouse
gases. The International Panel on Climate Change (IPCC)
has noted that 'regional changes in climate have already
affected hydrological systems and terrestrial and marine
ecosystems', and that 'the rising socio-economic costs
related to weather damage and to these regional variations
suggest increasing vulnerability to climate change'. This in
turn is projected to 'increase threats to human health,
particularly among lower-income populations and within
tropical and subtropical countries' (IPCC, 2001).[22]

Inhabitants of small islands and low-lying coastal areas
are particularly at risk of severe social and economic
effects from rising sea-levels, storm surges and
tsunamis.[23] There are also severe threats to the
freshwater resources on many of these islands, due
to climate variability and change.

It is now widely recognized that climate change poses a
major threat to sustainable development. The extreme
vulnerability of certain societies to present and future
climate risks necessitates integrating climate change
issues in the planning of social and economic
development. As disaster reduction has been recognized
as a developmental issue, a convergence of interests to
better manage risks related to climate and disasters for
sustainable development is emerging. **Box 10.5** provides
an example of climate change impacts and governmental
response in Uganda.

Disaster risk reduction and uncertainty

Dealing with uncertainty in water-related risk management
is not a new topic. Both natural and social scientists, as
well as decision-makers, risk managers and water
managers, have been dealing with this issue for decades.
However, the challenge is to devise disaster risk reduction
policies and strategies that can be adapted to uncertain
changes in the environment, which are influencing both
natural processes (e.g. global warming) and social systems
(e.g. demographic pressure).

For instance, and in addition to limitations in forecasting
accuracy, climate variability and change are additional
sources of uncertainty for decision-makers and risk
managers, potentially reducing the effectiveness of risk
reduction measures. Limitations also include inaccurate
hazard mapping, biased land-use planning and inefficient
warning systems.

In addition to increased investments in natural and social
science research, a way to reduce uncertainty is to
improve the information exchange between the climate
and risk management communities. This is, for instance,
the aim of the Disaster Reduction and Climate Change
(DR+CC) Infolink, an initiative that stimulates linkages and
information exchanges between the disaster reduction
and climate change communities.[24]

5b. Advocating adaptive risk reduction strategies

As explained above, the issue of climate variability
and change needs to be treated as a cross-cutting
issue related to governance issues including the
following topics:

- climate variability change: changing rainfall and hazard
  patterns (frequency, magnitude, etc.)
- land degradation: deforestation, erosion, sedimentation
  in rivers, landslides
- migration and demographic pressure, uncontrolled
  urbanization
- poverty: loss of livelihoods, financial capacity for
  rehabilitation, illness, weakness, health
- loss of knowledge: migration to hazard-prone areas,
  lack of risk-related experience
- governance: failing States, corruption, political
  fragmentation, etc.

In a context of potentially increased uncertainty,
successful disaster risk reduction strategies need to be
adaptive, stressing, for instance, resilience to changes in
the recurrence periods and duration of floods and
droughts, in terms of exposure to water-related risks and
to changes in patterns of social vulnerability.

22. For additional information,
    IPCC, 2001; findings of the
    World Water Agenda;
    MunichRe Topics Geo Annual
    Review 2003; 10 Year Review
    process of Barbados Plan of
    Action for SIDS, etc.

23. For more information on
    tsunamis, visit
    www.tsunamiwave.info
    On the 2004 Indian Ocean
    Tsunami Warning and
    Mitigation System, visit
    ioc3.unesco.org/indotsunami/
    and see **Chapter 1**.

24. For details, see
    www.unisdr.org/eng/risk-
    reduction/climate-change/
    rd-cch-infolink1-03-
    eng.htm#n1

BOX 10.5: CLIMATE CHANGE AND DISASTER PREPAREDNESS IN UGANDA

Climate in Uganda, particularly rainfall, has been erratic since the early 1990s (see **Chapter 14**). The incidence, duration and amount of rainfall have all exhibited abnormal departures from long-term means. While rainfall in some years was far short of long-term means, thereby causing droughts, in other years it was excessive and produced catastrophic floods. The heaviest rains in recent years were recorded in 1994 and were associated with the El Niño phenomenon. This led to sharp rises in lake levels, widespread flooding, washing away of roads and bridges, extensive soil erosion and landslides. In Lake Kyoga, rising water levels caused the detachment of previously firmly anchored floating papyrus swamps, which in turn caused a near total blockage in the lake. The blockage caused a further rise in lake levels and led to partial inundation of marginal homesteads and farmlands, the spread of water-borne diseases and the disruption of economic activities around the lake shores. In order to respond to these risks, the Government designed a National Strategy for Disaster Preparedness and Management. This strategy aims at creating an integrated and multi-sectoral strategy to address these threats.

Source: Uganda National Water Development Report, 2004 from the World Water Assessment Programme, March 2005, Personal Communication.

BOX 10.6: PROJECTED IMPACTS OF CLIMATE CHANGE IN THE RHINE RIVER BASIN

■ Water supply: Demand for irrigation water will increase, which may lead to critical supply conditions in summer months. Drinking water supply may be constrained during summer months due to extreme low flows and reduced aquifer recharge.

■ Floods: Winter peak floods in alpine rivers will increase, but major changes in the flood condition of small catchments in the middle hill section of the Rhine are not anticipated using the present distribution of precipitation patterns. In the main stem of the Rhine River, an increased risk of winter floods is anticipated. Based on a design period of 1,250 years, the design flood may increase by 5 to 8 percent by the year 2050 in the lower stretch of the Rhine River.

■ Low flows: More frequent low flows have negative impacts on inland navigation, energy supply and the ecology of wetlands along the Rhine River. Use of processed water for industrial purposes and cooling water for thermal power plants will be constrained due to low flows and limits on warming up the river water. Low flows have a direct impact on the costs of shipping on the river.

■ Natural disasters: Due to a shift of the 0°C isothermal line in the Alps, an increased frequency of mudflows and slope failures is expected, which can cause dangerous flash floods.

■ Winter tourism in the Alps: By the year 2020 the decrease of winter sport potential in the Swiss Alps will be dramatic. In addition, it is expected that cumulated losses in income generation from winter tourism will be in the range from 1.8 to 2.3 billion Swiss francs (US $1.4 to 1.8 billion) by 2030–2050.

Source: Grabs, 1997.

All aspects of water-related risk management need to be considered in an adaptive perspective:

■ Adaptive risk reduction can be achieved through a society's capacity to devise new legislation and revise institutional integration accordingly. For instance, new public and private partners can be introduced into the National Platforms for disaster reduction.

■ A better response to changing conditions also requires a more flexible decision-making process. This can be the case for the chains of command and response from the forecasting services down to civil defence agencies and local instructions for the public. These objectives clearly require improved access to and circulation of information for decision-makers and other key players.

■ A capacity to anticipate changes in risk and disaster patterns requires a further development of risk-related indicators to monitor environmental and social changes.

A scenario-based study of hydrological impacts of climate change is also an important option for introducing flexibility in risk reduction policies and actions. See **Box 10.6** for an example on the Rhine River Basin.

5c. Vulnerability assessment: An insight into human security

Kofi Annan (2005) has recently stated that 'Human Security can no longer be understood in purely military terms. Rather, it must encompass economic development, social justice, environmental protection,

...climate variability and change are additional sources of uncertainty for decision-makers and risk managers...

Section 4: MANAGEMENT RESPONSES & STEWARDSHIP

BOX 10.7: COMMUNITY RISK ASSESSMENT BASED ON VULNERABILITY AND RESILIENCE

■ **Contextual aspects:** analysis of current and predicted demographics, recent hazard events, economic conditions, political structures and issues, geophysical location, environmental conditions, access/distribution of information and traditional knowledge, community involvement, organizations and management capacity, linkages with other regional/national bodies, critical infrastructures and systems

■ **Highly vulnerable social groups:** infants, children, elderly, economically disadvantaged, intellectually, psychologically and physically disabled, single-parent families, new immigrants and visitors, socially/physically isolated, seriously ill, poorly sheltered

■ **Identifying basic social needs/values:** sustaining life, physical and mental well-being, safety and security, home/shelter, food and water, sanitary facilities, social links, information, sustaining livelihoods, maintaining social values/ethics

■ **Increasing capacities/reducing vulnerability:** positive economic and social trends, access to productive livelihoods, sound family and social structures, good governance, established regional/national networks, participatory community structures and management, suitable physical and service infrastructures, local plans and arrangements, financial and material resources reservation, shared community values/goals, environmental resilience

■ **Practical assessment methods:** constructive frameworks and data sources including local experts, focus groups, census data, surveys and questionnaires, outreach programmes, historical records, maps, environmental profiles.

Source: ISDR, 2004a.

Figure 10.12: Pressure and Release (PAR) model in vulnerability analysis

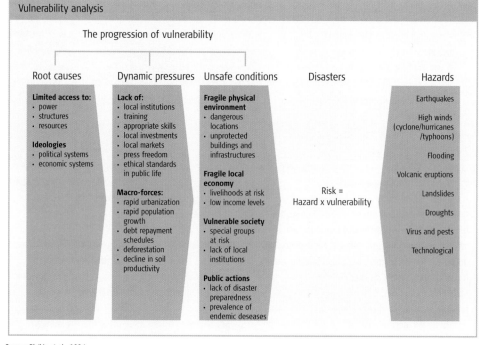

Note: 'Hazards' are the natural or man-made physical processing threatening social systems. In some cases (e.g. land degradation and landslides), hazards, characteristics are influenced by social practices. Besides, vulnerability level differs depending on social groups. For instance, some of these have been pushed to settle in marginal, hazard-prone areas, therefore increasing their exposure to hazards

Source: Blaikie et al., 1994.

democratization, disarmament, and respect for human rights and the rule of law'. Safeguarding human security requires a new approach for a better understanding of many interrelated social, political, economic, technological and environmental variables. These dimensions of human security are also key factors that influence the severity of impact generated by environmental deterioration and hydrometeorological extreme events.

Vulnerability is recognized as a central concept of human security and risk management. One definition of vulnerability is 'the conditions determined by physical, social, economic, and environmental factors or processes, which increase the susceptibility of a community to the impact of hazards' (ISDR, 2004a). In a wider perspective, however, the definition and effective assessment of vulnerability need to include more dynamic elements, such as social processes of exposure and responses to natural disasters.

Conceptual frameworks and models that provide a basis for vulnerability analysis in relation to specific hazards

have been developed. These models link dynamic processes at different scales and access to resources with vulnerability conditions. The Pressure and Release (PAR) model (see **Figure 10.12**) provides a good basis for the analysis and further identification of specific vulnerable conditions (Blaikie et al., 1994).

The basis for the PAR model is that a disaster is at the intersection of two opposing forces (Wisner et al., 1994): those processes generating vulnerability on one side, and the natural hazard event (or sometimes a slowly unfolding natural process) on the other.

In a risk management framework, vulnerability is also treated as a matter of scale, because individual vulnerability can be very different from vulnerability at the scale of communities (see **Box 10.7**), municipalities, regions or nations. Likewise, vulnerability is goal-specific as it involves activities such as knowledge management, awareness raising, risk perception, warning systems and communication mechanisms. Both features advocate for a strong community-based approach when designing, implementing and assessing disaster risk reduction strategies.

New Orleans residents walking through flood water in search of gasoline after the passing of hurricane Katrina in August 2005

Part 6. The Way Forward

The six key messages identified at the beginning of the chapter are specifically aimed at decision-makers, risk managers and water managers. The importance of establishing an integrated risk management policy has been stressed throughout the chapter, with the need to seek a sturdy framework from which implementation plans can stem. The World Conference on Disaster Reduction organized by UN/ISDR in Kobe, Japan, in January 2005 was of particular importance in providing a venue for reviewing disaster risk reduction strategy and its primary output, the Hyogo Framework for Action, proposes building a new strategy for the next ten years.

The Indonesian coast, between Banda Aceh and Meulaboh, after the earthquake and tsunami of 26 December 2004

6a. The Hyogo Framework for Action 2005–15

The World Conference on Disaster Reduction (WCDR), held in January 2005 in Kobe, Japan, provided essential recommendations to decision-makers and risk managers. Although it dealt with all kinds of natural hazards, its framework provides very relevant guidance for water-related disaster risk reduction.

National delegates to the WCDR and international organizations both agreed on the following key challenge areas for developing a relevant framework for action for the International Decade 'Water for Life' 2005–15 (ISDR, 2005):

■ governance: organizational, legal and policy frameworks; public participation
■ risk identification, assessment, monitoring and early warning
■ knowledge management and education
■ reducing underlying risk factors
■ preparedness for effective response and recovery.

WCDR participants also recognized the need to enhance international and regional cooperation, as well as assistance in the field of disaster risk reduction, by the following means for advanced international and regional cooperation in disaster risk reduction (ISDR, 2005):

25. Revised Version Oct 2005.

BOX 10.8: HIGHLIGHTS OF THE HYOGO FRAMEWORK FOR ACTION 2005–2015

- Ensure that the reduction of disaster risk from hydrometeorological events is a national and a local priority. An IWRM approach is needed, together with a strong institutional basis for implementation: national institutional and legislative frameworks, resources, community participation.

- Identify, assess and monitor hydro-meteorological disaster risk and enhance early warning: national and local risk assessments, early warning systems, capacity

building, regional and emerging risks. Improve regional and international cooperation for hazard assessment and data sharing.

- Use knowledge, innovation and education to build a culture of safety and resilience at all levels: information management and exchange, education and training, research, public awareness. Foster applied research in technical and social aspects of hydro-meteorological hazards, risks and disasters.

- Reduce the underlying risk factors: environmental and natural resources management; social and economic development practices, water resources management and development, land-use planning and other technical measures.

- Strengthen disaster preparedness for effective response at all levels.

Source: ISDR, 2005.

- transfer of knowledge, technology and expertise to enhance capacity building for disaster risk reduction
- sharing of research findings, lessons learned and best practices
- compilation of information on disaster risk and impact at all scales in a way that can inform sustainable development and disaster risk reduction
- appropriate support to enhance governance for disaster risk reduction, for awareness-raising initiatives and for capacity-development measures at all levels in order to improve the disaster resilience of developing countries
- consideration of the impact of disasters on the debt sustainability of heavily indebted countries
- financial assistance to reduce existing risks and avoid the generation of new risks.

The Hyogo Framework for Action 2005–2015 sets a useful road map for the design of improved risk management frameworks and implementation plans. Finally, and in view of the practical implementation of the recommendations made above, WCDR identified key actions to improve disaster risk reduction. See **Box 10.8** for details, from a water-related disaster perspective.

6b. Conclusions
The future of living with water-related risks lies in the capability of societies to anticipate and adapt to changes occurring in their natural and social environment.

Improved management of risk-related knowledge and information is therefore a first and necessary step in that direction. There is a need to support further investment in data collection and analysis and modelling capacities,

as well as in indicator development. Indicators are essential to identifying and monitoring underlying trends in disasters, hazards, vulnerability and risk.

It is necessary that risk-related knowledge be made available to decision-makers, risk managers and water managers. Access to information is vital for the design of comprehensive risk management frameworks. Integrated policies for risk reduction need a sound governance framework, which includes a good legislation basis and efficient cooperation among the various administrations and institutions involved.

Disaster risk reduction is a key component of IWRM and sustainable development. Consequently, disaster risk reduction objectives need to be integrated into social and economic development planning. Moreover, risk reduction policies need to be consistent with other risk-oriented policies of different organizational entities such as different ministries or line departments and agencies. Risk assessment is therefore an important step on the route to sustainable development. At the local level, the involvement of stakeholders in the design, implementation and assessment of policies must be ensured.

Global processes, such as climate variability and change, increase the level of uncertainty for both water-related physical processes and the social processes of exposure to hazards, vulnerability and adaptation to change. Again, theoretical and applied research in the natural and social sciences needs to receive additional financial support with the purpose of improving our understanding of the physical and social processes leading to increased vulnerability. Climate variability and change is a strong incentive for advocating more adaptive policies for disaster risk reduction.

The main points raised in this chapter also show explicit links to challenge areas – and related chapters – of the *World Water Development Report*:

First, the need to incorporate disaster risk planning into national policies for socio-economic development confirms the governance dimension of risk management (see **Chapter 2**). This dimension is itself related to vulnerability assessment for human settlements – in particular when it comes to marginal communities and smaller social groups.

Second, managing the aftermath of water-related disasters requires continued investment in epidemiology and public health, as well as in water and sanitation development (see **Chapter 6**). Providing these resources to water users should however integrate features of the water cycle. These include: ecosystem functions, pollution and consequences of climate variability and change (see **Chapters 4 and 5**). In particular, managing risks cannot

be separated from food security issues, such as livelihood functions of riverine environments (see **Chapter 7**).

Third, controversies related to water resources development such as hydropower, show that the management of water-related risks is related to the broader debate on energy security, policies and technical choices (see **Chapters 8** and **9**). This dimension is particularly acute on transboundary river basins, where risk management very much depends on the institutional choices made for sharing water resources and conflict avoidance (see **Chapter 11**).

These various, interrelated dimensions of risk management all point to the common issue of knowledge management. Despite an increasing volume of environmental data produced worldwide, technologies for analysing water-related information remain insufficient – especially in developing countries, where information exchange remains very low. One of the key challenges related to risk management is the adequate sharing of water-related data and information, both within and among countries.

Access to information is vital for the design of comprehensive risk management frameworks

Water is not a commercial product like any other, but rather a heritage that must be protected, defended and treated as such.

European Commission Water Framework Directive

CHAPTER 11

Sharing Water

By

UNESCO
(United Nations Educational, Scientific and Cultural Organization)

Geothermal power plant with bathers enjoying geothermally-heated water, Blue Lagoon, Iceland

Key messages:

The emerging water culture is about sharing water: integrated water resources managements (IWRM) looks for a more effective and equitable management of the resource through increased cooperation. Bringing together institutions leading with surface water and aquifer resources, calling for new legislative agreements all over the world, increasing public participation and exploring alternative dispute resolutions are all part of the process.

Above: A man-made entrance to an underground aquifer in Quintana Roo, Mexico

Right: Itaipu dam and hydro-electricity power station on the river Parana, Brazil / Paraguay

Below: Tea plantation in Kerala, India

■ Sharing water resources constitutes a major part of integrated water resources management (IWRM).

■ There is a need to further expand special indicators for measuring efficient, effective and equitable water sharing.

■ Increasing complexity and interdependence regionally, nationally and internationally requires new approaches to shared water systems.

■ There is a need for developing new knowledge and new capabilities in order to understand aquifers and the difficulties of underground boundaries that are difficult to define.

■ There is a need to concentrate on the implementation of mechanisms for conflict avoidance and conflict management.

Section 4: MANAGEMENT RESPONSES & STEWARDSHIP

Part 1. Towards Integration and Cooperation

The comprehensiveness of water resource planning and sharing has been the subject of much controversy and debate. It has been widely recognized that in order to maximize the benefits from any water resource project, a more systematic analysis of the broader environment is needed. In addition to a broadening of traditional management approaches, there needs to be increased sensitivity to decision-making that involves multi-purpose actions and multi-user considerations.

A proposed framework for sharing water would mean taking the following issues into account:

- natural conditions (e.g. aridity and global changes)
- variety of uses (irrigation, hydropower, flood control, municipal uses, water quality, effluent control, etc.)
- various sources of supply (surface water, groundwater and mixed sources)
- upstream/downstream considerations
- socio-demographic conditions (population composition and growth, urbanization, industrialization, etc.).

The mismatch between political boundaries and natural river basins has become a focal point for the difficulties of joint planning, allocation of costs and benefits, advantages of scale and other integrated water management issues and is usually referred to as transboundary (the terms transnational, trans-state and international have also been used), which refers to any water system that transcends administrative or political boundaries, which often do not coincide with river basins' or watersheds' natural boundaries (see **Chapter 4**).

The time lag between the implementation and impact of management decisions – sometimes measured in decades – significantly reduces the power of contemporary water resource institutions. Efforts to implement more integrated shared water resources management are confronted with continuous changes in values, structural transformations in society and environment, as well as climatic anomalies and other exogenous shifts. These transformations have created a context of complexity, turbulence and vulnerability. The emerging water sharing paradigm attempts to bring together the above concerns with cross-cutting sustainability criteria, such as social equity, economic efficiency and environmental integrity.

Access to adequate water is becoming a highly contested issue, which is further complicated by traditional values

and customs, cultural and religious considerations, historical factors and geographical variations. As for sharing the resources of an aquifer system, in which upstream-downstream relationships do not apply, current thinking is moving away from 'equitable utilization', a remarkably vague notion, given the predominance of slow responding storage overflows, towards ensuring the sound functioning and integrity of the aquifer system.[1]

1a. Setting the context

Sharing water is essential to meeting the goals of equity, efficiency and environmental integrity and answering the more complex questions that stem from broader challenges, such as the issue of overall security. Water sharing mechanisms (i.e. new institutional arrangements) help us adapt to these challenges through structural changes (specific organizations, joint engineering structures, etc.) and more resilient political institutions.

In 2002, UNESCO and the Organization of American States (OAS) launched the International Shared Aquifer Resource Management (ISARM) project for the Americas, which organized three workshops, in 2003, 2004 and 2005, to present the data gathered on transboundary groundwater in North, Central and South America and highlight the need to follow up on this cooperative project. The UNESCO-IHP ISARM project initiated transboundary aquifer resources inventories, covering the Americas (sixty-five aquifers; see **Map 11.1** and **Table 11.1**) and Africa (thirty-eight aquifers) as well as a recent update including the Balkan countries (forty-seven aquifers) and plans to extend coverage to Asia and the Pacific.[2]
Table 11.1 provides detailed information on shared aquifers located in Central and South America. To date, the UNESCO-ISARM project has inventoried over 150 shared aquifer systems with boundaries that do not correspond to those of surface basins. Progress in the consolidation of these newly created inventories has resulted in unprecedented development in global transboundary aquifer resources assessment.

Efforts to implement more integrated shared water resources management are confronted with continuous changes in values

---

1. The integrity of an aquifer can be destroyed if, for example, saline intrusion invades to such an extent that the aquifer system ceases functioning and cannot be effectively rejuvenated.

2. A publication on the achievements of the project is under preparation. Maps for these regions can be found on the CD-ROM accompanying the book and at www.unesco.org/water/wwap

BOX 11.1: SHARED AQUIFERS BETWEEN ARGENTINA, BOLIVIA AND PARAGUAY

The Yrenda-Toba-Tarijeño aquifer system occupies about 300,000 square kilometres (km²), located mostly in the Gran Chaco Americano region. Its recharge zone, located in Argentina and Bolivia, determines groundwater flow towards the east and crosses national boundaries, emerging in low-lying lands and draining into a series of streams that discharge into the Paraguayan-Argentine Chaco and eventually into the Parana River in Paraguay.

The livelihood of the 1 million indigenous people in the region is closely linked to the aquifer's surface area. Increasing pressure on scarce water resources, poor land quality and soil degradation is causing alarm. The natural water quality transition (fresh in Bolivia, to brackish and saline in Paraguay and Argentina) may be changing.

There are many pressures on the land in the region, which have arisen from the expansion of poorly planned mechanized agriculture, which has in turn led to land degradation, the decline of wetlands and the deterioration of water quality. Increased rain intensity from anticipated climate change could trigger erosion, and re-sedimentation in recharge zones could inhibit aquifer infiltration from stream beds. Due to poor awareness and divergent regulations, current aquifer management by institutions in the sharing countries is inadequate. Therefore, coordination for the long-term management and protection of the recharge zones, as well as the discharge zones, is lacking.

A case study by the UNESCO International Shared Aquifer Resource Management Programme (UNESCO-ISARM) is part of a Plata Basin project financed by Global Environment Facility (GEF). The case study's activities focus on raising awareness of the aquifer system, as well as ensuring the sustainability of its resources, the lifeline of the local population and the aquifer-dependent environment. The project will help further develop engaged and strengthened institutions that practise sound aquifer management and offer educational and technical support to the community.

Source: www.isarm.net.

High altitude landscape at the border between Argentina and Bolivia

Part 2. Water and Geopolitics

Given the interdependencies of water resource uses, spatial variations and surface water and groundwater, as well as upstream and downstream differentiations, the need to develop mechanisms for the sustainable sharing of water is obvious. Attention to environmental security exemplifies the growing regional and global environmental concerns that could also lead to new forms of conflict.

2a. Trends in geopolitical developments

History shows few outright transboundary water-related conflicts. Although strong competition does occasionally occur between users, such as in the Tigris-Euphrates Basin, in the Jordan Basin and the Paraná-La Plata Basin (see **Box 11.2** for an example in southern India), there is an increasing trend towards inter-state collaboration (as in the case of the Nile), as well as cooperation through increased public participation, non-governmental organizations (NGOs), the common search for alternative water sources and the collaborative spirit of international water conferences, arbitration mechanisms and mediating agents (see **Box 11.3**). Efforts like the Division of Early Warning and Assessment (DEWA), UNESCO's From Potential Conflict to Cooperation Potential (PCCP) and ISARM have been developing case studies on the management of transboundary water resources, illustrating the impressive range of examples of water as a catalyst for peace and cooperative capacity-building. Many programmes – financed through the International Waters focus area of the Global Environment Facility (GEF) in Eastern Europe – are working together to develop cooperative frameworks and encourage the development and implementation of policies that support the equitable use of water and the sound functioning of other water-related natural resources.

BOX 11.2: CAUVERY RIVER DISPUTE IN SOUTHERN INDIA

In India, the federal government plays a mediating role in river water disputes. The Inter-State Water Disputes Act of 1956 requires the government to encourage states to settle disputes through dialogue. If that does not work, a tribunal is to be constituted. After a hearing, the tribunal makes a binding judgement.

The Cauvery Basin in southern India has 75,000 square kilometres (km²) of area spread over four riparian states: Karnataka, Kerala, Tamil Nadu and Pondichery. The basin is mainly drained by the 780 km-long, rain-fed, perennial Cauvery River, which flows from west to east into the Bay of Bengal. In addition to being a major source of irrigation and hydroelectric power, the Cauvery River is an important water supply source for Bangalore, a centre for information technology and the software industry.

When a dam project was developed by the upstream state of Mysore (now in Kerala), two agreements were made (in 1892 and in 1924) detailing how the river waters were to be shared. The agreement was open for review once it expired, but no agreement has been reached between the two main riparians, Kerala and Tamil Nadu, since the 1970s. A tribunal was constituted in 1990, and an interim judgement was passed in 1991. The tribunal is expected to make its final decision soon.

The dispute is based on the fact that the demand for irrigation far exceeds the irrigation potential of the river. In drought years, this leads to a flash-point. The monsoon pattern is peculiar: the southwest monsoon brings rains to the upstream areas in June and July. The downstream and delta regions depend mainly on the weaker northeast monsoon (September-October). In the Cauvery Delta in Tamil Nadu, three crops are grown annually, but the summer crop depends on the timely release of waters from upstream areas. However, upstream farmers argue that it is unfair to be forced to share their water in summer when demand for water is at its highest. The downstream farmers argue that historically they have grown three crops and hence, their livelihoods crucially depend on maintaining the sharing scenario as accepted in the 1924 agreement.

There have been attempts to promote citizen efforts towards conciliation through people-to-people dialogues, and most recently, to form a 'Cauvery family'. Such efforts should help in encouraging informed dialogue and building trust. Collective action theory suggests that it is possible for riparian states to voluntarily reach self-enforcing agreements, provided the costs and benefits are considered in a transparent manner and sustainable development priorities are given primacy.

water used for the production of export commodities on the global market can contribute significantly to the changes in local and regional water systems (**Box 11.6**). It has been noted, for example, that since Japan consumes large quantities of American cereals and soybeans, it might be suggested that this in turn leads to the mining of aquifers (Ogallala, for example) and further water use of rivers in North America. **Map 11.2** shows national water footprints around the world. The concept

Below: Iguazu Falls, Brazil

of virtual water was first defined by Allan (2003) as the 'water embedded in commodities'. In terms of global trade, not only does it raise awareness about water interdependencies, but it can also serve as a means for improving water efficiency (see **Map 11.3** on water savings around the globe and **Map 11.4** on net virtual water imports). In addition, it can be an indicator of sharing water, as well as a sign of contributing to water security in water-poor regions.

BOX 11.6: VIRTUAL WATER AND THE WATER FOOTPRINT

International virtual water flows

The International trade of commodities implies flows of virtual water over large distances, where virtual water should be understood as the volume of water required to produce a commodity. Virtual water flows between nations can be estimated from statistics on international product trade and estimates of the virtual water content of products. The global volume of virtual water flows related to the international trade in commodities is 1.6 trillion m³/yr. About 80 percent of these virtual water flows relate to the trade in agricultural products, while the remainder is related to industrial product trade. An estimated 16 percent of global water use is not for producing domestically consumed products, but rather products for export. With the increasing globalization of trade, global water inter-dependencies and overseas externalities are likely to increase. At the same time, the liberalization

of trade creates opportunities to increase global water use efficiency (see **Chapter 12**).

Globally, water is saved if agricultural products are traded from regions with high water productivity to those with low water productivity. At present, if importing countries produced all imported agricultural products domestically, they would require 1.6 trillion m³ of water per year; however, the products are being produced with only 1.2 trillion m³/yr in the exporting countries, saving global water resources by 352 billion m³/yr.

The water footprint

The water footprint shows the extent and locations of water use in relation to consumption. The water footprint of a country is defined as the volume of water needed for the production of the goods and services consumed by the inhabitants of the country. The internal water footprint is the volume

of water used from domestic water resources, whereas the external water footprint is the water used in other countries. Water footprints of individuals or nations can be estimated by multiplying the volumes of goods consumed by their respective water requirement. The US appears to have an average water footprint of 2,480 cubic metres per capita per year (m³/cap/yr), while China has an average footprint of 700 m³/cap/yr. The global average water footprint is 1,240 m³/cap/yr. The four major factors that determine the water footprint of a country are volume of consumption (related to the gross national income); consumption patterns (e.g. high versus low meat consumption); climate (growth conditions); and agricultural practice (water use efficiency).

Sources: Chapagain and Hoekstra, 2004; Chapagain, et al., 2005.

Map 11.3: Water savings around the world

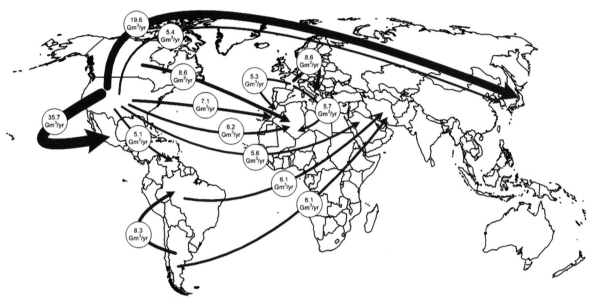

Global water saving = 352 x 10⁹ m³/yr

Note: Global water savings (>5.0 Gm³/yr) associated with international trade of agricultural products. Period 1997-2001. The arrows represent the trade flows. The numbers show the global water savings, calculated as the trade volume (ton/yr) multiplied by the difference between water requirement (m³/ton) in the importing country and water requirement (m³/ton) in the exporting country. Global water savings occur if an exporting country requires less water per ton of product than an importing country.

Source: Chapagain, et al., 2005.

Map 11.4: Net virtual water imports around the world

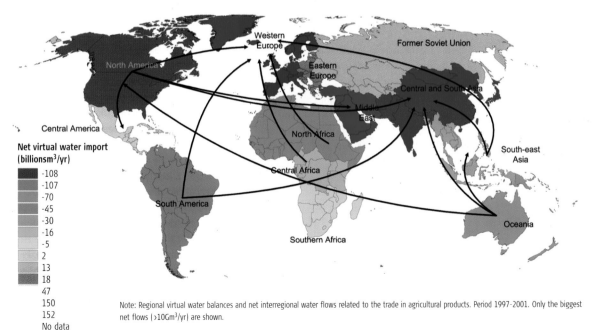

Note: Regional virtual water balances and net interregional water flows related to the trade in agricultural products. Period 1997-2001. Only the biggest net flows (>10Gm³/yr) are shown.

Source: Chapagain and Hoekstra, 2004.

Nowadays people know the price of everything and the value of nothing.

Oscar Wilde

CHAPTER 12

Valuing and Charging for Water

By

UNDESA
*(UN Department of
Economic and Social
Affairs)*

Key messages:

Because of the unique characteristics and socio-cultural importance of water, attempts to value water, or more specifically water services, in monetary terms is both difficult and, to some people, inappropriate. Nevertheless, economic valuation – the process of attaching a monetary metric to water services – is an increasingly important tool for policy-makers and planners faced with difficult decisions regarding the allocation and development of freshwater resources. With market prices unable to capture the full spectrum of costs and benefits associated with water services, economists have developed special techniques to estimate water's non-market values. Two important occasions when these tools are employed are assessments of alternative government strategies and tariff-setting. In this chapter, we examine valuation tools, explain how they are used, and explore underlying social, economic and environmental principles that condition their application. Finally we look at the emerging issues including private-sector participation, 'virtual water' trade, and payments for environmental services, which are playing an ever more prominent role in the debate on the allocation and development of scarce freshwater resources.

Top to bottom:

Men and women bathing in the Ganges, India
above: Irrigated paddies, Viet Nam

Women washing clothes at the Ralwala spring in Siaya district, Kenya. The spring serves 30 households

Public water pump in Amboseli Reserve, Kenya below: Public water pump in Amboseli Reserve, Kenyaenya

■ Given its unique, life-sustaining properties and multiple roles, water embodies a bundle of social, cultural, environmental and economic values. All of these must be taken into consideration in the selection of water-related policies or programmes if the goals of integrated water resources management (IWRM) are to be realized.

■ Public policy analysis employing economic valuation provide a rational and systematic means of assessing and weighing the outcomes of different water policies options and initiatives and can assist stakeholders, planners and policy-makers to understand the trade-offs associated with different governance options.

■ Charging for water services – household, commercial, industrial and agricultural – requires, firstly, consensus on the underlying principles and objectives (e.g. full cost recovery, protecting the needs of the poor and the marginalized, etc.); secondly, a thorough, systematic analysis of all costs and perceived benefits; and thirdly, a tariff structure that endeavours to maximize governance objectives within prevailing socio-economic conditions.

■ Public-private partnerships, though not appropriate to all situations, can play a significant role in developing cost-efficient water service systems. Government authorities, however, must be open to a variety of initiatives, including local enterprise, public-private partnerships, community participation and water markets, and must take an active regulatory role in ensuring that societal goals are met with regard to social equity and environmental sustainability – as well as economic efficiency.

■ There is a great need not only for planners and policy-makers who understand the advantages and limitations of economic valuation techniques and their potential role in informing decisions regarding water resources management, but also for technicians who can clearly express these concepts, utilize these tools, and assist stakeholders in expressing their values and preferences. In this way, economic valuation can contribute more fully to information sharing and transparency, all of which are important for good governance.

Part 1. Understanding the Multi-faceted Value of Water

Water is vital for all life on this planet, but is also essential for food production, many manufacturing processes, hydropower generation, and the service sector. The value of water varies for different users depending on the ability to pay, the use to which the water will be put, access to alternative supplies, and the variety of social, cultural and environmental values associated with the resource. Acknowledging the totality and interdependence of water-related values important to stakeholders and water users is critical to realizing Integrated Water Resources Management (IWRM). Understanding the distinction between the *value* of water – determined by its socio-cultural significance and the broad spectrum of direct and indirect benefits it provides – the *price* of water, as charged to consumers, and the *cost* of water as derived from the expense of providing water to consumers, is a critical first step to understanding the role of economic valuation in water governance and management.

The Dublin principle[1] to treat water as an economic good follows a growing consensus on the need to maximize benefits across a range of water uses. Still, the importance of ensuring equitable access and meeting the needs of the poor and disadvantaged members of society is widely recognized. How to finance this task remains a key challenge. While higher-income countries move toward systems of water tariffs based on full cost recovery and metered service, low-income countries struggle to cover basic operating costs and, for the most part, still tolerate various systems of subsidies as many users are unwilling or unable to pay for water services. According to the World Bank, pro-poor policies relying on cross-subsidization have created an inefficient and unsustainable water services sector with serious impacts on the environment in many countries. Similarly, the 'polluter pays' principle, like the 'user pays' principle, although broadly accepted, suffers from poor enforcement due to a weak governance environment. While some countries favour decentralization and management transfer as a way to relieve cost burdens, others see private sector participation as a means of achieving better services and improved cost recovery. Pricing or tariff-setting is widely supported in the financial community both to raise the needed investment capital and to curb inefficient use. None of these options are without problems.

Difficulties associated with decentralization often stem from political weakness and lack of institutional capacity at the local level. Half-hearted support by national and international organizations for community-driven development of water services has also been a problem in some areas. Private sector involvement, often touted

as a key to solving financial problems in this sector, remains limited in many areas while the transfer of management models from one region to another has met with mixed results. Pricing, expected to serve a variety of objectives, including cost recovery, more prudent use of water, distributive justice and assured supplies for poor, has generally led to rising prices and a decline in water use in some countries. Many would argue that the poor would be better served by more focused tariff systems, which would be gradually introduced and underpinned by a minimal level of free service, or complimentary vouchers for water service rather than cross-subsidization.

Although economic valuation is recognized by many as an important tool in water management and substantial efforts have already been made in clarifying concepts associated with this technique, valuing water remains a controversial issue. Many stakeholders still feel that economic valuation is incapable of fully capturing the many social, cultural and environmental values of water. However, the variety of innovative initiatives attempted worldwide illustrates an increasing sensitivity to local needs and a growing understanding that the development and management of water resources must be a shared responsibility.

Although economic valuation is recognized by many as an important tool in water management... valuing water remains a controversial issue

1. See Chapter 1 for definition.

Part 2. The Socio-cultural Context

We speak of a crisis in water management because in many places the available freshwater is insufficient to meet all demands. As discussed in previous chapters, demand for water is increasing because, despite falling fertility rates in many countries, the world's population continues to increase while freshwater water supplies remain constant. Meanwhile, economic growth in many countries, especially in India and China, has increased disposable income and instigated lifestyle changes that have often meant increased water consumption. Agriculture and industry, also growing in response to these changes, require water for production, processing and transport, while electric utilities look increasingly to hydropower to meet 'clean' energy demands. Urbanization, a seemingly unstoppable trend worldwide, intensifies the pressure.

As the competition for water resources accelerates, one becomes increasingly aware of water uses in different areas. The essential value of water is universally recognized: without water there is no life. For many ecosystems, such as rivers, lakes and wetlands, freshwater is the defining element. The utility of water as a raw material, as a solvent, and as a source of kinetic energy has long been recognized. The role of water in

---

BOX 12.1 THE HIGH COST OF BOTTLED WATER

Over the last decade, sales of bottled water have increased dramatically to become what is estimated to be a US $100 billion industry (Gleick et al., 2004). From 1999 to 2004, global bottled water consumption grew from approximately 26 billion gallons to over 40 billion gallons (IBWA, 2005). In several cities of the developing world, demand for bottled water often stems from the fact that the municipal water supplies – if available at all – fail to meet basic criteria for drinking water quality. But companies manufacturing bottled water are also generating large revenues in developed countries. Bottled water sales in the United States in 2004 – higher than in any other country – totalled over US $9 billion for 6.8 billion gallons of water, that is, enough water to meet the annual physiological needs of a population the size of Cambodia (IBWA, 2005). Countries in the top ten list of bottled water consumers include Mexico, China, Brazil, Italy, Germany, France, Indonesia, Spain and India.

When asked why they are willing to pay so much for bottled water when they have access to tap water, consumers often list concerns about the safety of tap water as a major reason for preferring bottled water (NRDC, 1999). While

most companies market this product on the basis that it is safer than tap water, various studies indicate that bottled water regulations are in fact inadequate to ensure purity or safety. The World Health Organization (WHO, 2000) warns that bottled water can actually have a greater bacterial count than municipal water. In many countries, the manufacturers themselves are responsible for product sampling and safety testing. In the United States, for example, the standards by which bottled water is graded (regulated by the Food and Drug Administration) are actually lower than those for tap water (regulated by the Environmental Protection Agency) (Gleick et al., 2004).

The explosive increase in bottled water sales raises important questions related not only to health, but also to the social and environmental implications of the phenomenon. It remains to be seen, for example, how the growth of this industry will affect the extension and upkeep of municipal water services upon which the poor depend. In fact, those most likely to need alternative, clean water sources are also those least likely to be able to afford the high cost of bottled water. In China, where roughly 70 percent of rivers and lakes are polluted, the

largest demand for bottled water comes from city dwellers, for in rural areas people are too poor to pay for this alternative (Yardley, 2005).

Most water bottles are meant to be recyclable. However, only 20 percent of polyethylene terephthalate (PET), the substance used for water bottles, is actually recycled (Gleick et al., 2004). In Greece, it is estimated that 1 billion plastic drinking water bottles are thrown away each year (BBC, 2005). In addition, the PET manufacturing process releases harmful chemical emissions that compromise air quality.

Where safe tap water is temporarily unavailable, bottled water can provide an effective short-term solution for meeting a population's needs. But as noted above, the massive growth in sales of bottled water worldwide comes at a cost. A better appreciation of how people value water may help us understand how the bottled water phenomenon is impacting society's health, economic and environmental goals.

Sources: BBC, 2005; Gleick et al., 2004; IBWA, 2005; NRDC, 1999; WHO, 2000; Yardley, 2005.

BOX 12.2: VALUING WATER, VALUING WOMEN

In most, if not all, developing countries, collecting water for the family is women's work. While water for drinking and cooking must be carried home, dishes, clothes and often children may be carried to the water source for washing. Women and girls are often seen queuing with their water pots at all-too-scarce taps, then walking long distances home balancing them on their heads or hips. If the water is contaminated and a family member falls ill, it is often the woman who must care for them. Children in particular are vulnerable. In parts of the world where AIDS is rampant, individuals with weakened immune systems also easily fall prey to pathogens in the water supply.

The low status of women in many societies means that their contribution – in terms of the time and energy spent, for example, in fetching water – is considered to be of little value. In economic terms, the opportunity cost[2] of their labour is perceived as near zero. Where

women have been given access to education and to money-making work, such as handicrafts production, and are permitted to sell their products and to earn income for the family, their social as well as financial position improved dramatically.

Attitudes toward water-collecting can also shift. The time women spend collecting water, especially when simple and readily available technological alternatives exist, looks very different and far more costly to the family and

society as a whole, when women have income-earning opportunities. Thus, investments made to improve access to safe drinking water are both a reflection of the value placed on water for human well-being and the value accorded women. Providing regular and dependable access to safe drinking water is one way of improving the position of women as well as society as a whole.

Source: UNICEF/WHO, 2004.

human health is, of course, critical. Recently we have seen the growth in bottled water consumption, which although a necessity in some cases, is also a growing trend in places where safe and inexpensive water is readily available on tap (see **Box 12.1**).

As a physical, emotional and cultural life-giving element, water must be considered as more than just an economic resource. Sharing water is an ethical imperative as well as an expression of human identity and solidarity (see **Chapter 11**). Accordingly, the high value placed on water can be found in the cosmologies and religions and the tangible and intangible heritage of the world's various cultures. The unique place water holds in human life has ensured it an elevated social and cultural position, as witnessed by the key role water plays in the rituals of all major faiths. The proposition that water is a human right alongside the increasing competition between water users has resulted in water becoming a political issue in many regions (see **Chapter 2**). The amount of time spent in collecting water – a task mainly performed by women and children – is increasing in many areas. Water supply

must, therefore, also be viewed as a social issue and, more specifically, a gender issue (see **Box 12.2**).

Restored interest in ethnic and cultural heritage in many societies around the world has lead to a revival of numerous traditional rituals, festivals and social customs, many of which feature water as a key element. Thus, the tradition of social bathing endures, for example, in Turkey and Japan. Water sports too play an important role; currently nearly one-third of Olympic sports use water, snow or ice. Many archaeological sites – the Roman aqueducts, the Angkor ruins, the Ifugao and Inca terraces, among others – are monuments to ancient societies' ingenuity in water engineering. Listing these historic sites on the roster of World Heritage protected cultural properties is in effect formal recognition of the high value that the international community accords these locations (see **Map 12.1**).

Water splashing at a festival in the Dai ethnic Minority Village, China

---

2. Opportunity cost is defined as the maximum worth of a good or input among possible alternative uses (OMB, 1992).

BOX 12.5 BENEFITS VERSUS COSTS OF IMPROVED WATER AND SANITATION SERVICES

Adoption of the Millennium Development Goals (MDGs) that deal with extending the availability of water and sanitation services has prompted interest in assessing the net economic benefits of such programmes. Hutton and Haller (2004) evaluated five different scenarios with different levels of intervention for seventeen World Health Organization (WHO) sub-regions. The five levels of intervention were:

1. Water improvements required to meet the MDG for water supply (halving by 2015 the proportion of those without safe drinking water).
2. Water improvements to meet the water MGD for water supply *plus* the MDG for sanitation (halving by 2015 the proportion of those without access to adequate sanitation).
3. Increasing access to improved water and sanitation for everyone.

4. Providing disinfectant at point-of-use over and above increasing access to improved water supply and sanitation.
5. Providing regulated piped water supply in house and sewerage connection with partial sewerage connection for everyone.

Costs were determined to be the annualized equivalent of the full capital cost of the intervention. Benefits were measured in terms of several variables: the time saving associated with

estimated benefit-cost ratios for selected regions. Economic benefits were found to greatly exceed the costs for all interventions, particularly level (4), a result that was robust for all regions and under alternative intervention scenarios.

Source: Hutton and Haller, 2004.
www.who.int/water_sanitation_health/
wsh0404.pdf

WHO Sub-Region	Population (million)	Benefit-cost ratio by intervention level				
		1	2	3	4	5
Sub-Saharan Africa (E)	481	11.50	12.54	11.71	15.02	4.84
Americas (D)	93	10.01	10.21	10.59	13.77	3.88
Europe (C)	223	6.03	3.40	6.55	5.82	1.27
South East Asia (D)	1689	7.81	3.16	7.88	9.41	2.90
Western Pacific (B)	1488	5.24	3.36	6.63	7.89	1.93

Note: The parenthetical letters identify WHO sub-regions as classified by epidemiological (health risk) indicators. See source for definitions.

Part 4. Charging for Water Services

For both municipal and irrigation water services in developing countries, performance, efficiency and conditions of water delivery systems tend to fall far short of normal standards. Many people, but mostly the poor, lack access to safe water supplies and/or sanitation facilities, and for many others, the only access may be via water vendors or public latrines. Often over one-third of water transmission is lost to leakages or to unregulated access. The World Water Council's report 'Financing Water for All' (commonly known as the Camdessus Report), addressed the issue of mustering financial resources to meet internationally agreed water supply and sanitation goals, concluding that currently available sources will be insufficient to maintain and expand coverage (Winpenny, 2003). As the financing of water services is becoming ever more urgent, recovering costs is seen to be central to improving the conditions of water services. In this context, charging for water services is increasingly being promoted as an appropriate response.

An increasingly important aspect of water governance is the regulation of water quality

Criteria applied to tariff-setting

Multiple criteria influence policy decisions on how to finance water services and how much revenue to collect from beneficiaries (cf. Herrington, 1987, 1999; Hanemann, 1997). In addition to the goals of safe and affordable water for all and maximum net social benefits, two key criteria are:

- **financial sustainability**, requiring the collection of sufficient revenue to meet present and future financial obligations, that is, operating costs as well as the capital costs of facilities and infrastructure, and the

- **user pays principle**, which holds that consumers should pay an amount equivalent to the burden of their consumption on society. This implies that charges should attempt to recover full costs, including not only operation, maintenance and capital replacement, but taking into account foregone benefits (opportunity costs), as well as any externalities (damages to third parties) (see **Figure 12.1**).

Other characteristics important in the successful implementation of any charging plan are:

- **simplicity**, which means that the selected tariff plan should be open, understandable and straightforward with users able to see how usage patterns affect the amount payable

- **transparency**, enabling consumers to understand how their own tariffs and those of other user classes are set, and

- **predictability**, permitting customers to reasonably anticipate and plan for their water-related expenses.

These criteria often come into conflict. For example, assuring that the less fortunate members of society are charged an affordable rate is likely to clash with both the user pays principle (recovering full costs) and maximizing net social benefits (pricing at marginal social cost). As shown in **Figure 12.1**, tariff-setting must balance both cost and value considerations as the upper level of charges is limited by user willingness to pay. Resolving the conflicts of rate-setting is inherently a political process. Any assessment of the various charging options must consider carefully the incidence of all costs and benefits, if charging is to be equitable as well as efficient.

Structuring user charges

For most marketed goods and services, units are obvious and the price per unit is easily understood. The case of water tends to be more complex. Water users may pay only a charge for access to the delivery network, but not for water itself. Charges may include a fixed periodic (e.g. monthly) access fee as well as a variable charge based on volume used. Many utilities require an initial connection fee. Hence, there is no single 'price'. In general the tariff structure for water services can be described in two dimensions: form and level.

The form refers to if and how the charge relates to the quantity used, while the level refers to the proportion of the cost of service to be recovered from users. Flat rates are more or less independent of the quantity used or may be linked to the projected level of use, according to, say, the number of family members or size of pipe connection. Conversely, charges may vary directly with the quantity of water used. Rate structures are changing because of the falling costs of metering, the increasing tendency to define water as a commodity (rather than a

BOX 12.6: IRRIGATION MANAGEMENT TRANSFER (IMT) AS A COST RECOVERY TOOL

Many developing countries (aided by international donors) have in the past several decades invested large sums in irrigation systems with the expectation of increasing agricultural productivity and improving incomes for poor farmers. It was assumed that most such schemes would be economically and financially self-sufficient under reasonable management. However, most developing countries have not implemented charging programmes to recover actual operating and maintenance costs, let alone to pay for the capital costs of the investments. As governments have been unable or unwilling to adopt cost-recovery policies that keep pace with inflation or the need for periodic system rehabilitation, they have found that budgetary demands of the irrigation sector increasingly compete with other public needs. Policy reforms to transfer more of the irrigation costs to water users have come as

part of a package called 'Irrigation Management Transfer' (IMT). These programmes assume that farmer management of public irrigation systems would make the system more responsive to members, and thereby encourage water users to be more receptive to paying costs. Expectations were that local control would not only improve the cost-effectiveness but by transferring costs to users reduce costs to the public exchequer. Results of such reforms have been, at best, mixed. While IMT programmes have been somewhat successful in more developed countries (US, New Zealand and Mexico), elsewhere the results are less promising. In many cases, charges to farmers did increase, but farmer-managed systems have tended to under-invest, thus necessitating public rescue. Little evidence of an overall increase in agricultural productivity or farm incomes has been observed. In large systems with

many smallholders, costs of administration and revenue collection are necessarily high, and the users have ended up with lower productivity and income. In some cases, the systems have collapsed. The conclusion seems to be that IMT can work in cases where irrigation is essential to high-performing agriculture, and farmers are not too numerous, better educated and behave as businessmen. Furthermore, the cost of operating and administering the irrigation system must represent a modest proportion of the increment in farmers' income expected from irrigation. Where the system serves numerous, small farms producing low-value staple crops (such as in the rice-producing regions of Asia), in terms of cost recovery, system efficiency and productivity, IMT has not produced the expected results.

Source: Shah et al., 2002.

expected net returns to water. With subsidies to irrigation capitalized into higher land prices, governments find that levying higher user charges may not only depress farm income, but risk imposing significant capital losses on landowners. Nevertheless, many countries are moving toward collecting a larger proportion of irrigation costs from farmers. As part of a larger reform and decentralization effort, this trend aims not only to reduce public subsidies, but also to increase efficiency and the responsiveness of irrigation delivery. Such policies, often called irrigation management transfer (IMT), seek to shift the administration of all or part of irrigation water delivery to associations of water users, thus sharing the responsibility of water management. **Box 12.6** reviews the experience in various developing countries for transferring responsibility for irrigation water delivery to user groups.

4c. Charging for discharge of industrial effluent

An increasingly important aspect of water governance is the regulation of water quality. Water's solvent properties and widespread availability provide both producers and consumers with an inexpensive means of waste disposal. With public expectations of near zero effluent discharge, policy-makers face a paradoxical situation with regard to water use and quality. In many countries minimum waste

disposal would be enormously expensive, even impossible, unless some important industries were closed altogether. Assessing the costs and benefits in such cases demands careful consideration of the relative effectiveness and desirability of the alternatives, not only from an economic perspective, but also in terms of the distribution of costs and benefits, the ease of monitoring and enforcement, and industry flexibility, among other factors. Although direct regulation has been the main tool of water quality management in the past, water pollution is increasingly being addressed by decentralized systems of incentives and disincentives, such as effluent charges (see **Chapter 8**).

The effluent charge, also called an emissions or pollution tax and essentially a fee levied on each unit of contaminant discharged, is based on the principle of 'polluter pays'. Initially this principle was intended to 'suggest' to governments that they should refrain from subsidizing investments required to comply with pollution-control regulations. A more recent interpretation holds that emission charges should be set so that the costs, or the economic value, of the damages inflicted by polluters on third parties are borne by the polluters themselves, in effect 'internalizing' the previously externalized costs of production. With the unit charge set to rise with

Figure 12.2: Actual and planned water pollution charges in the River Narva and Lake Peipsi Catchment, 1993–2005

Legend:
- BOD7
- Suspended solids
- Ntot
- Ptot
- Phenols
- Oil products

Y-axis: Charge (EEK/t)
X-axis: 1993, 1994, 1995, 1996, 1997, 1998, 1999, 2000, 2001, 2002, 2003, 2004, 2005

Note: EEK/t is Estonian Kroon per ton. 1 Estonian Kroon (EEK) = 0.06390 Euro (2005).

Source: Environmental Information Center, Tallinn, Estonia.

increased levels of discharge, polluters may respond as they choose, that is, reduce effluent or pay the charges. Firms facing low pollution reduction costs relative to the charges imposed would presumably move to reduce discharges. Others might find it cheaper to pay the tax than to make the necessary pollution control expenditures. Such charges should provide incentives for pollution discharge to be reduced by the least cost methods available. All firms would find it in their interest to seek changes in processes, technologies and/or in discharge treatments that reduce the cost of coping with the problem of residuals disposal.

Criticisms have come from all sides but most prominently from polluters, who complain of potential impacts on profits and hence, over the longer term, on net worth and share value. Public officials, on the other hand, are concerned producers may be forced into reducing output and employment with corresponding negative effects on tax revenues. From the viewpoint of regulatory agencies, effluent charges present challenges of monitoring and enforcement. Environmental groups object to effluent charges on the grounds that they convert the environment into a commodity. Surveys of pollution control strategies in OECD nations show that environmental charges for the most part were not applied to induce less polluting behaviour nor to compensate damaged parties, but to fund specific environmental expenditures. Despite all criticism, effluent charges for water pollution management are seeing increasing application (see **Figure 12.2**).

Chemical outflow, Germany

BOX 12.8: THE 'WATER WAR' IN COCHABAMBA, BOLIVIA

The city of Cochabamba, Bolivia, the third-largest city in Bolivia, has a chronic water shortage. A sprawling city of 800,000 people, whose population has exploded during the last decades with immigrant workers from the countryside, it has many poor neighbourhoods lacking connection to municipal water supplies. In recent years, residents in peri-urban areas pushed for workable community initiatives with the help of foreign aid. Small-scale water companies built electric pumps to access well water and distribute it throughout these neighbourhoods, at a total cost of US $2 to US $5 per month. In 1997, conditions on the World Bank US $600 million loan for debt relief included the privatization of the water supply in Cochabamba, and in 1999, a private operator was granted a 40-year

concession contract to rehabilitate and operate the municipal water supply system, as well as the smaller ones. The contract provided for exclusive rights to all the water in the city, including the aquifers used by the water cooperatives. Billing and metering was implemented, with the cost of these services, as well as of connections, being reflected in the tariffs.

Within weeks of taking control of the city's water supply, prices were raised to unaffordable levels, effectively leaving the poor in marginal areas without access to any water as they were no longer permitted to draw water from their community wells. Workers living on the local minimum wage of US $60 per month suddenly had to pay US $15 for the water bill. In 2000, a

coalition of workers, farmers and environmental groups, 'Coalition for Defence of Water and Life', organized a general strike and massive protests in opposition of the rate hikes. Bolivians blocked highways, and the city was shut down. Police forces and the military were sent to take control of the city, and martial law was declared. As protests grew stronger despite being suppressed, the private operator withdrew from the city and the government rescinded the concession contract. This experience led the government to reconsider private sector participation, and to enact a law granting legal recognition to traditional communal practices, under which small independent water systems shall be protected.

Source: Finnegan, 2002.

allocate ownership rights and responsibilities for investments and management differently.

In larger-scale initiatives private corporations can also partner with local governments and NGOs. NGOs can provide local governments with information on the specific needs of poor areas, which then can be better addressed in negotiating concession contracts, for example, by defining specific connection targets or obligations for expansion into peri-urban areas. NGOs and communities can also participate in tariff collection on behalf of the private utility in exchange for deferred payment of connection fees. Likewise, municipal governments can facilitate connections by, for example, waiving the land title requirements for slum dwellers. To reduce connection costs, NGOs can help by providing transportation and materials, while the community contributes labour, for instance carrying pipes, digging trenches and laying lines (Franceys and Weitz, 2003). As described in **Box 12.9**, researchers have discovered such innovative approaches in Manila in the Philippines.

The value of public-private partnerships

Both the value and economic valuation of water are important in assessing water supply and sanitation alternatives. While privatization may not be suitable in all cases, neither are underfinanced public utilities a sustainable solution given burgeoning water demand.

Likewise, the global replication of community-driven arrangements is not viable on a large-scale. Experience with both public and private delivery of water services over the past decade has taught us that ownership of water infrastructure, whether public or private, has no significant effect on efficiency nor on the selection of the public versus private sector as service provider (Estache and Rossi, 2002; Wallsten and Kosec, 2005). Indeed, ownership has proved less significant than governance, and thus a good institutional climate is important, not only for private sector investment, but for the transfer of relevant technical knowledge and management skills (Estache and Kouassi, 2002; Bitrán and Valenzuela, 2003). Similarly, institutional mechanisms that enable various degrees of engagement by consumers must be put in place in order for efficiency-oriented water supply schemes to be successful. Ultimately, the decision as to whether to involve the private sector, civil society and government is political and influences the kinds of governance mechanisms needed to ensure efficient and equitable service.

Provided that mechanisms to ensure affordable access by those without ability to pay are put into place, the potential economic and social benefits of improved access to water services are great. In addition to the considerable health benefits gained from connection to the official

BOX 12.9: TARGETING THE POOR THROUGH GRASSROOTS MECHANISMS IN MANILA, THE PHILIPPINES

In 1997, a twenty-five-year concession contract for water supply and sewerage in the city of Metro Manila, Philippines, was granted to two companies: Manila Water Company to supply the east side, and Maynilad Water Services to provide the west side of the city, with an aim at having spare capacity in case of failures. In order to increase access to the poor, the concession agreement provided for public standpipes for every 475 customers in 'depressed' areas. Instead of implementing this conventional solution, both companies have devised innovative approaches to extend service to poor areas.

Manila Water has a programme which relaxes some application requirements in order to enable water connections for poor customers. Group taps are designed for every two to five households where users get together to apply for a single connection. The group is given a 'mother meter' and thus, share the cost of their

usage. Each group chooses a representative, who is in charge of collecting and paying the bill to Manila Water. Besides group taps, Manila Water has a programme of community-managed water connections whereby a metered master connection is provided, and a community association acts as water distributor through individual or shared connections, which allows local residents to manage water according to their needs.

Maynilad Water Services favours individual to shared connections. Under its 'Water for the Community' programme, the land title requirement for connections is waived and payment of connection fees is deferred over a period of six to twelve months, and in some cases twenty-four months. NGOs were crucial in providing information to the private utilities, as well as in information campaigns aimed at community mobilization. They helped with the provision of materials while the community

contributed labour for carrying pipes into the city, which helped decrease connection costs. The number of connections has increased dramatically, and poor consumers, who now pay less for water than under their previous informal supply arrangements, are able to enjoy the same kind of services provided to other sectors of society.

In specific focus group discussions, several residents stated that connecting to the urban water supply had greatly decreased their water bills. In the Liwang Area of Manila, one resident related that, after being hooked up to the network, her monthly bills came to on average between 25 and 50 pesos per month, in contrast with 40 pesos per day spent on informal water vendors. Another resident, who used to pay a flat fee of 300 pesos per month to a neighbour with access to the system, now pays 60 pesos per month for a larger amount of water.

Source: Franceys and Weitz, 2003.

---

network, poor people freed from the burden of water collection can expect to have more time to engage in productive poverty-alleviating pursuits. Similarly, the public sector can expect to benefit from a reduction in unaccounted-for water losses, enabling them to price water more efficiently and potentially reduce subsidy mechanisms. Finally, participation of all kinds, from information-sharing, to consultation in PSP arrangements, to having a voice in decision-making and management in public-private community partnerships, is crucial for the long-term success of improved water supply and sanitation.

The choice of public-private partnership depends on the political, institutional, social and cultural features of the area where the service is to be provided. An assessment of the capability of governments to provide service in the target areas plus an analysis of the costs and benefits of different options and associated tariffs – including their potential impact on different sectors of society – will enable policymakers to make more informed choices as to which management tool can provide water services that best meet the societal goals of equity, efficiency and environmental sustainability.

5b. Virtual water trade

Virtual water, a concept that emerged more than a decade ago, is defined as the volume of water required to produce a given commodity or service. Allan proposed the term 'virtual water' to describe a phenomenon he observed in countries of the Middle East. They were using imports in the form of water-intensive products, such as food, to create a 'virtual' inflow of water as a means of relieving pressure on scarce domestic water resources (Allan, 1997). Several Middle Eastern nations, most notably Jordan and Israel, have altered their trade and development policies to promote the import of water-intensive products, generally agricultural crops, and the export of crops of high water productivity, that is, high income per unit of water consumed in production (Hofwegen, 2003). The adoption of such policies, in effect, recognizes the value of water.

As Allan (1997) noted, 'It requires about 1000 cubic metres of water to produce a ton of grain. If the ton of grain is conveyed to … [an] economy short of freshwater and/or soil water, then that economy is spared the economic, and more importantly the political stress of

Wetlands in Amboseli Reserve, Kenya. These wetlands are fed by the Kilimanjaro mountain glaciers

Knowledge has to shuttle between the local and the global level, taking account of the retroactive effect of the global on the particular.

Edgar Morin

CHAPTER 13

Enhancing Knowledge and Capacity

By

UNESCO-IHE
(Institute for Water Education)

Madhukari Ganokendra (People's Centre), in Rajapur village, western Bangladesh, holds monthly meetings to discuss primary school attendance and other important issues for the community to take action

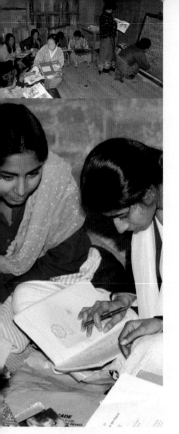

Key messages:

Financial investments made in the last decades in the water sector have often failed to bring about the expected outcomes, largely due to lack of attention given to enhancing knowledge and capacity. While infrastructure is needed, it is doomed to deteriorate if not properly maintained by adequate human resources and institutional capacity within an enabling environment. In a time of climate change and declining hydrological data collection systems, all countries need to take seriously the threat to their water resources and invest in capacity development.

- Self-assessments of knowledge and capacity needs are urgently required to assist water resources managers in all challenge areas in setting priorities, identifying gaps and improving the effectiveness with which they can respond to a continuously changing environment.

- It is essential that the knowledge base of capacity development be enhanced through case studies, best practices, twinning organizations and shared experiences and that the capabilities of national statistical agencies to deal with water sector data be improved.

- Increased access to education at all levels through information and communication technologies is a cornerstone for development, and efforts to broaden individual capacities through education should be actively pursued.

- Knowledge requires continuous investment to enable society to adapt to an uncertain future generated by climate change. In particular, increased investments in the hydrological data network and remote sensing are needed to provide the information necessary for modelling future scenarios.

- The capacity of water management institutions should be increased to ensure that they have a clear mandate, an effective organizational system, and improved decision support through lessons learned and indigenous knowledge.

An education programme provides free of cost relevant life skills ranging from reading, writing, simple calculating to tailoring, furniture making, etc. to out of school youth and adults in Bhutan Katha public school provides an education to 5–16 years olds in Govinpuri slums, south Delhi, India

Section 4: MANAGEMENT RESPONSES & STEWARDSHIP

Part 1. Assessing Knowledge and Capacity

Spurred by the Millennium Development Goals (MDGs), many nations are now intensifying their actions to improve water services and infrastructure development. Over the past two decades, developing countries have invested hundreds of billions of dollars in water services and water resources, a substantial portion of which has failed to bring about the desired outcomes and impacts. The operations assessments by the development banks and other donors attribute this in many cases to inadequate knowledge bases and weak capacities.

As our understanding of the interactions between water management and society develops, it becomes increasingly evident that the past focus on developing infrastructure has overlooked the need for a strong knowledge base and capacity to plan, manage and use that infrastructure and enable proper governance of the water sector. Today, there is a growing consensus that knowledge and capacity in the water sector is a primary condition for sustainable development and management of water services.

Knowledge development and accessibility lie at the heart of this concern. Knowledge takes a variety of forms: as databases; as the competence to integrate and interpret data and create meaningful information that can inform decisions; as capacity to generate new data and information, to identify gaps, to learn from past experiences and to explore the future; and educational and dissemination mechanisms. A knowledge system extends well beyond data pertaining to physical and technical parameters. Involving civil society and increased community participation foster a greater understanding of the interactions of the complex social and environmental processes involved in water management, which enables the rethinking of approaches to effective water development.

The knowledge base is made up of databases, documents, models, procedures, tools and products. It also includes knowledge that may not be explicitly available because it is contextual, cultural and relates to skills, heuristics, experience and natural talents (such as local or indigenous knowledge). This implicit knowledge leads the way for capacity-to-act or a competence to solve problems, but describing and communicating such implicit knowledge remains challenging (Snowden, 2003).

The support of a strong knowledge base can greatly improve capacity development and spur the kind of informed decision-making that drives policy directives, which enable

local institutions to be better equipped to direct their own self-sufficient and sustainable futures in the face of change. As such, research, assessment, know-how and communication are not simply components of a development initiative that compete with other components: they are primary targets in any effort towards effective and sustainable development in water-related sectors.

1a. From knowledge to capacity development

Capacity development is the process by which individuals, organizations, institutions and societies develop abilities (individually and collectively) to perform functions, solve problems and set and achieve objectives (UNDP, 1997; Lopes and Theisohn, 2003). A country's capacity to address water-related issues is not just the sum total of individual capacities, but rather a broad holistic view of the central concerns of management, namely how to resolve conflict, manage change and institutional pluralism, enhance coordination, foster communication, and ensure that data and information are collected, analysed and shared. This involves not only individual capacities (human resources), but also the effectiveness, flexibility and adaptability of organizational processes (institutional capacity) and an enabling and stimulating management framework (the enabling environment). These three levels of capacity development are presented in **Figure 13.1** with its associated activities, outputs and goals. A detailed description of these three levels is included in Part 3 of this chapter.

Sustainable development increasingly requires countries to have the capacity to put in place effective knowledge generation and learning mechanisms. This capacity-to-learn or 'adaptive capacity' is the potential or capability of a system to adjust or change its characteristics or behaviour, so as to better cope with existing and future stresses. More specifically, adaptive capacity refers to 'the ability of a socio-ecological system to cope with novelty without losing options for the future' (Folke et al., 2002)

The knowledge base is seen to be of a higher order than a database... it relates to how such collected explicit knowledge on the world's water resources and their use is archived and analysed

In order to achieve sustained progress, knowledge building and capacity development must be viewed as development objectives in and of themselves...

Figure 13.1: Capacity development: Levels, activities, outputs and goals

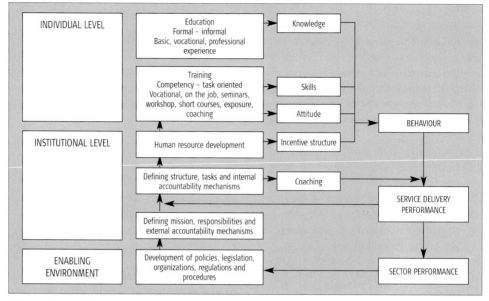

Source: van Hofwegen, 2004.

and 'is an aspect of resilience that reflects learning, flexibility to experiment and adopt novel solutions, and development of generalized responses to broad classes of challenges' (Walker et al., 2002). There is a need therefore to build into capacity development a concern that individuals have the skills to innovate when faced with a non-standard problem and a structural flexibility that does not penalize, but rather rewards and capitalizes on such innovation.

A new paradigm for water development has begun to emerge. It stresses the importance of country ownership and shifts the focus from passive knowledge transfer (e.g., from the North to the South) to knowledge acquisition and integration within the developing countries themselves. It does this by supporting home-grown processes for knowledge development – often using existing local and indigenous capacities – while also specifically including local participatory processes. In order to achieve sustained progress, knowledge building and capacity development must be viewed as specific development objectives, which command their own resources, management attention and evaluation standards, much along the lines of gender, poverty or environmental issues (Morgan, 2000).

The concept of capacity development implies that improved water services delivery and sustainable development are to be achieved as much through

improving the enabling environment, the institutional frameworks and human resources as through the technocratic approach of investments in infrastructure. Capacities must be developed at all three levels while acknowledging that these layers of capacity are mutually interdependent – if one is pursued in isolation, development still remains skewed and inefficient (Fukuda-Parr et al., 2002). The right combination of actions depends on the local situation, which calls for extensive prior analysis and priority setting, for instance, by region or by river catchment (Alaerts et al., 1999).

1b. Identifying socio-economic benefits

While high-income countries have been able to couple large investments in infrastructure with human and institutional knowledge building many middle- and low-income nations lag behind in their ability to adapt to the ever-increasing pace of change in a complex world (Alaerts et al., 1999). Industrialized countries, for example, can afford to invest in better understanding and preparedness for the effects of climate change. Middle-income countries are generally characterized as having built sufficient infrastructure assets to provide adequate water services and prepare for the 'conventional' larger water-related risks such as floods. They may still however lack the necessary institutional and human knowledge base that is needed to reap a greater benefit from water resources development for more sustainable growth. Lower-income countries typically have not yet been able to invest in a minimum stock of water infrastructure, and often do not have the capacity to govern and manage these investments effectively once they are made. They thus have a strong incentive to invest their scarce resources in infrastructure that brings rapid returns. However, past experience shows that heavily investing in infrastructure without enhancing existing local capacities can result in dilapidated infrastructure, exasperated water problems and increased debt.

Even though there exists in the world at large the know-how and knowledge to solve many, if not most, of the world's pressing water problems, this knowledge is often slow to make an impact. National governments, often with overburdened and underpaid staff, possess only limited capability to acquire and interpret that knowledge, and turn it into practical action and realistic proposals. Vested interests often prevent the adoption of new approaches, and staff are forced to respond to short-term priorities.

While it is agreed that good governance and management require local government involvement, the devolution of responsibility for managing a range of water services from national to lower levels further raises the need to strengthen capacities. This is because local-government staff tend to have benefited less from proper education than their colleagues in central-government agencies, and because the local administrative procedures are even less geared to appreciate the value of sound knowledge. Similarly, better governance hinges on users and communities that are informed and have the capacity to access and use information with which they can hold government accountable.

Each country needs a development strategy that recognizes the balance between knowledge, capacity and infrastructure in order to adopt the most suitable governance strategy and utilize its water resources in line with sustainable development. Such a development strategy must acknowledge that radical social, environmental and technological changes are taking place at an increasing rate. As discussed throughout this Report, these include the burgeoning population growth in lower-income countries, the global consequences of climate change, the pervasive influences of globalization and the exponential growth in Internet-based communication.

The ability to predict the trends, measures and potential consequences of such complex systems depends on our capacity to understand and integrate information and knowledge, as well as on our assessment of the effectiveness of the knowledge economy both of which are fuelled by the new information and communication technologies (ICTs) that facilitate the collection, storage and sharing of data and information globally.

More than ever before, our increasingly interconnected world can enable more societies to identify opportunities and means for determining their own path to sustainable development. However, while the communication of lessons learned, and the sharing of experiences have allowed the international community to better articulate the objectives of water management in various sectors, the knowledge base and the development of capacity to implement and effectively achieve these objectives remain very much 'work in progress'. Major constraints include the large sizes of the funds required to build these knowledge bases and capacity; the low sense of urgency at political levels; and, perhaps most importantly, the fact that people must first recognize the value of better knowledge and capacity, and that capacity-building is inevitably a long-term and continuous process.[1]

Yet because of the complexities faced in turning the social and economic benefits of research and development into knowledge generation and building capacity, economic returns are often overlooked, and there remains a strong reluctance to invest the necessary resources as a sustained initiative (see **Box 13.1**). Understanding and appreciating the need to change the approach to water development is the first step in overcoming deficiencies. The private sector has long since recognized the difficulties involved in designing and managing programmes of intentional change in corporations, and it has accepted occasional failures as normal episodes on a learning curve, spurring efforts to master change as a process (Pasmore, 1994; Senge et al., 1999; Kotter and Cohen, 2002). The response from development agencies, in contrast, has typically been to minimize risks and boost the apparent benefits to be achieved (Morgan et al., 2005). Without further intensive efforts to understand the dynamics of the complex processes of institutional change in international development, initiatives to enhance knowledge and capacity will fail to be properly targeted and will not produce the desired outcomes. Indeed, compared with other sectors, the water sector has been slow to seek out and internalize knowledge from other sectors, affecting issues such as climate change, and to investigate more deeply the longer-term scenarios needed for proper governance.

...the devolution of responsibility for management of a range of water services from national to lower levels further raises the need to strengthen capacities...

1. These long-term goals are gradually becoming recognized, and development banks like the World Bank, the Inter-American Development Bank, the Asian Development Bank, the African Development Bank and the international donor community are providing increasing support for capacity-building.

Map 13.1: WMO'S World Hydrological Cycle Observing System (WHYCOS)

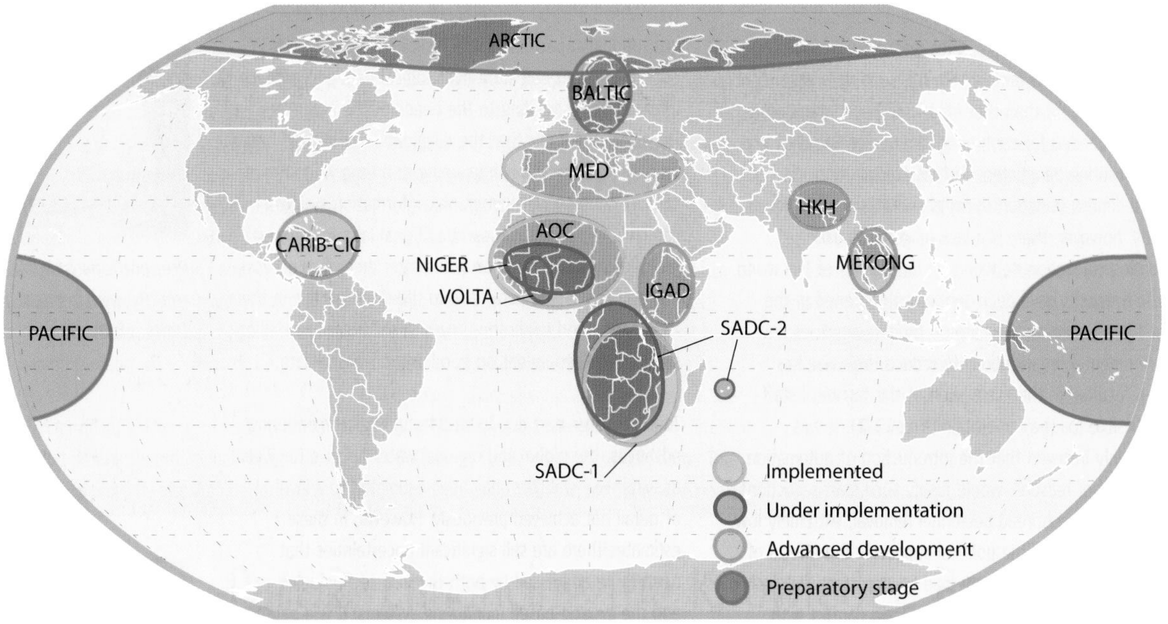

Note: The WHYCOS programme is implemented through various regional HYCOS components, as shown in the coloured areas of the map above. Each component concerns either a transboundary basin or a community of countries. As for 2006, three components have been implemented:

- MED-HYCOS (Mediterranean see medhycos.mpl.ird.fr/ for more details)
- AOC-HYCOS (West and Central Africa see aochycos.ird.ne/ for more details)
- SADC-HYCOS (South African Development Community).

Moreover, three components are still under implementation (in blue):

- Niger-HYCOS
- Volta-HYCOS
- SADC-2HYCOS.

The main activities of each project include updating the observing network, developing regional databases (see www.r-hydronet.sr.unh.edu/), establishing websites for easy data access and dissemination, and training personnel. Data collected through the HYCOS components also contribute to a better understanding of the global water cycle and its variability.

Source: WMO-WHYCOS, 2005.

India is regarded as a world leader in using satellite data techniques for managing its natural resources and supporting rural development

Remote sensing

In recent years, water resources management has benefited from the powerful assessment tools provided by remote sensing. Since the Rio Declaration on Environment and Development in 1992, a number of major developments have occurred. Over 100 new satellite sensors for sustainable development have been put into operation, and advanced warning for extreme storms and floods has increased in some instances to over 100 hours (UNESCAP, 2003). Remote sensing is used for the provision of simple qualitative observations, the mapping/detecting features of hydrological importance and the direct estimation of hydrological parameters and water quality (see **Box 13.3**).

India is regarded as a world leader in using satellite data techniques for managing its natural resources and supporting rural development. However, most countries, including relatively developed ones, do not yet use these techniques on a day-to-day basis to support decision-making in water resources management. Because of this, the United Nations (UN) has made the enhancement of the capacity of countries to use and benefit from remote-sensing technologies a key focus for many space-related activities (UN, 2004). Of particular note is the TIGER Initiative led by the European Space Agency (ESA) in partnership with the United Nations Educational, Scientific and Cultural Organization (UNESCO), the United Nations Office for Outer Space Affairs (UNOOSA) and others, which

---

BOX 13.3: **ADVANCES IN THE PRACTICAL USE OF SATELLITE REMOTE SENSING FOR WATER RESOURCES** .

Considerable improvements in the assessment of hydrological parameters for water resources management have been made during the last two decades using remote sensing from satellites (Schultz and Engman, 2000). Using a combination of radar and thermal sensors from weather satellites, the accuracy of precipitation estimates for crop forecasting, flooding and river flows over large areas and basins has improved considerably, as has the extent of snow cover and water equivalents. In addition, satellite data provide a unique means of assessing separately the actual evaporation over different areas, such as river basins, irrigated areas and wetlands, using the surface energy balance equation. This has led to methods for determining crop water efficiencies, water use by groundwater irrigation, and wetland water requirements. Another important hydrological parameter that is

monitored using active or passive radar is the moisture of the uppermost soil layer.

Important progress has also been made in surveying the land surface. The Shuttle Radar mission has made freely available a worldwide coverage of digital terrain models, required for example, by rainfall-runoff modelling. Satellites, through radar altimetry, are now surveying water levels in lakes and large rivers within a few centimetres accuracy. This is particularly important for remote water bodies. Satellite images with resolution of 1 or 2 metres can be purchased, enabling the rapid preparation of maps through digital photogrammetry and showing terrain heights of floodplains or coastal areas, which are required for assessing flood risks and the propagation of floods. Land subsidence, often due to groundwater extraction,

can also be measured with high precision by radar interferometry.

Imaging spectrometry (or hyperspectral remote sensing) provides information about the water quality of optically deep-water bodies. The first operational applications from airborne platforms were reported in the 1990s, and the first imaging spectrometry satellites were launched in 2000. The most successfully monitored water quality parameters are chlorophyll, a blue-green (or cyannobacterial) pigment, total suspended matter, vertical light attenuation coefficient and turbidity. The technique can be used in coastal waters for the assessment of the health of coral reefs and for bathymetric mapping.

Sources: Schultz and Engman, 2000; Dekker et al., 2001.

BOX 13.4: **TIGER INITIATIVE: IMPROVING WATER SYSTEMS OBSERVATION IN AFRICA**

Established in 2003, the European Space Agency's (ESA) TIGER Initiative aims to make earth observation services more accessible for developing countries, with particular focus on Africa. In 2005, there were four separate ESA projects operating under the TIGER umbrella:

■ GlobWetland: provides land cover and land-use change maps on fifteen African wetland sites to support reporting obligations for the Ramsar Convention on Wetlands.

■ Global Monitoring for Food Security (GMFS): maintains a continental-scale overview of sub-Saharan Africa in order to produce sub-national and selected high-resolution crop production forecasts.

■ Epidemio: uses satellites to provide environmental information in the service of epidemiology, including the charting of water bodies in order to prepare malaria risk maps.

■ Aquifer: generates land-use cover and land-use change charts, digital terrain maps, soil moisture

mapping and subsidence monitoring, so that new aquifers can be identified and existing aquifers exploited in a sustainable manner.

The Envisat environmental satellite and European Remote Sensing satellite data are freely available for African hydrology research. TIGER also enhances capacities in space technologies in African regions, while supporting its integration within the user's traditional working procedures to improve the sustainability of water resources management.

Sources: ESA, 2004; earth.esa.int/tiger/

---

aims to provide earth observation data, capacity-building and technical support services for IWRM in developing countries with a particular focus on Africa (**Box 13.4**).

The advantages of remote sensing lie in its ability to map conditions across regional, continental and even global scales on a repetitive basis at a relatively low cost compared to ground-based monitoring. The coupling

of biophysical, socio-economic, hydrometric and remote sensing data with modelling now leads to the emergence of valuable new information on water stress at global, regional and local levels (see **Box 13.5**). The United States National Aeronautics and Space Administration (NASA) and ESA plan to launch special water management and hydrology-related satellites (see, for example, Alsdorf and Rodriguez, 2005), optimized for

Networks of all kinds, representing all sectors, such as professional associations, are powerful tools for knowledge sharing and distribution

Map 13.2: The Knowledge Index, 2005

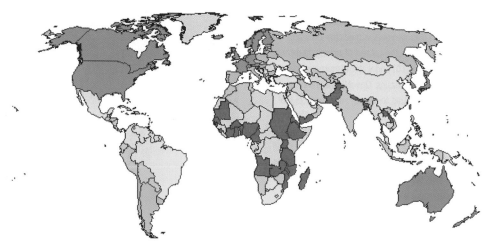

Map Legend (0 is the lowest score and 10 is the maximum score)

0 <= KI <= 2	2 < KI <= 4	4 < KI <= 6	6 < KI <= 8	8 < KI <= 10	No data

Note: The Knowledge Index (KI) benchmarks a country's position vis-à-vis others in the global knowledge base. It is the average of the performance of a country or region in three knowledge economy pillars (education, innovation and information and communications technology) and is calculated considering the following variables: adult literacy rate, secondary enrolment, tertiary enrolment, researchers in research and development per million population, patent applications per million population, scientific and technical journal articles per million population, telephones per 1,000 people, computers per 1,000 people, and Internet users per 10,000 people.

Source: World Bank Institute, 2005.

Arsenic Removal Family Filter being set up in a Bangladeshi home

(DWD) established a Management Information System for the water sector in 1998 in order to improve management and facilitate decision-making processes. With the purpose of monitoring financial and physical activities, it has since produced a series of design reports that currently constitute the archives for the sector, and it has developed data collection procedures that are used in all the districts of the country. Data are collected, processed and shared with other stakeholders through reports, Intranet and the DWD website.[8]

However, despite considerable progress in recent years, access to ICTs remains unequally distributed. There are, for example, more computers in Brazil, more fixed line telephones in Italy, more mobile phones in Japan and more Internet users in France, than in the whole continent of Africa. Yet the population of Africa and the needs of its people greatly exceed those of these other countries (ITU, 2004). In response, the World Bank Institute's Knowledge for Development Programme has developed a user-friendly tool designed to assist decision-makers in understanding and benchmarking their strengths and weaknesses in terms of their ability to compete in the global knowledge economy. While not specific to water-related fields, the Knowledge

Assessment Methodology uses a series of relevant and widely available measures that can allow for a preliminary country comparison and the identification of strengths and weaknesses in order to focus policy attention or future investments in making the transition to the knowledge economy. The assessment tool is available online.[9] The state of the global knowledge economy, weighted by population, is presented in **Map 13.2**.

The language barrier and quality assurance and control

Today, due to the ever-increasing speed with which technology can collect, store and disseminate data, we are possibly encountering for the first time a situation in which human individuals and their capacities are the primary bottleneck in the chain of information processing, making people the limiting factor for further understanding (Maurer, 2003). Knowledge has to be presented in a way that people can assimilate it. One barrier is that information and knowledge on water management and water use often uses terminology that only academicians, theoreticians and technical people can understand, or worse, in a language foreign to the end user. Language barriers constitute a critical obstacle to local information for literacy and education as well as a level playing field in the global digital knowledge

8. See www.dwd.co.ug

9. www.worldbank.org/kam

economy. This is unfortunate, considering the potential value that this knowledge could contribute to alleviating the water crisis by increasing public engagement in the process.

With roughly 7,000 living languages in the world (Gordon, 2005), participatory approaches to water management immediately become more complex. SIL International, for example, works to develop community-level capacities to enable communities to carry out their own research, translation, and production of literature in their native tongue. In addition, with more than 90 percent of Internet content today existing in just twelve languages, UNESCO's Initiative B@bel[10] uses ICTs to support linguistic and cultural diversity, protect and preserve languages in danger of disappearing and facilitate access to this important communication medium. To further facilitate the use of software products and websites across multiple platforms, languages and countries, the Unicode Consortium has developed a standardized computer language.[11] This could support the increasing trend in the development and use of online water information networks that can provide another means of surmounting the language barrier. This is particularly appropriate for the translation of technical terms that are peculiar to water development.[12]

Another major problem that arises in using information or knowledge from elsewhere is assuring its quality. Information or knowledge can originate from a reputable source, such as a peer-reviewed journal or the website of a trusted organization, but this hardly accounts for the majority of information found on the Internet. Almost anyone can put anything online. In doing so, they bypass many of the benefits of traditional publications – issuance by an authoritative source, editorial or peer review, evaluation by experts, etc. Quality is still a matter of trust by the recipient in the trustworthiness of the supplier. Third-party confirmation of any information and knowledge is generally recognized as one of the best ways of assuring quality. Responsibility for the use and application of the data provided remains largely in the hands of the user, who has to rely on his or her education and experience to exercise discernment. Networking and involvement in professional associations largely stimulate quality assurance through continuous peer review, as in the case, for example, of the peer-reviewed web-based information service provided by FAO's International Programme for Technology and Research in Irrigation and Drainage (IPTRID).[13]

Knowledge networks

Networks of all kinds, representing all sectors, such as professional associations, are powerful tools for knowledge sharing and distribution. They offer a framework for resource optimization and knowledge combination, saving valuable financial and time resources, in addition to providing an excellent platform for peer discussions (see **Box 13.7**).

Networks for capacity-building in integrated water management are a relatively new phenomenon. The advantages of networking for scaling up capacity-building to reach the MDGs are gaining recognition in the international water community. The advantages are predominantly in providing a more coherent and coordinated approach to capacity-building, increased impact, relevance and sustainability from working with local institutions, improved sharing of knowledge and expertise and a platform for cross-disciplinary and cross-regional discussions.

There are more computers in Brazil, more fixed line telephones in Italy, more mobile phones in Japan and more Internet users in France, than in the whole continent of Africa

10. See www.unesco.org/ webworld/multilingualism for more details.

11. See www.unicode.org/ standard/whatisunicode.html for more details.

12. See water.usgs.gov/wsc/ glossary.html, for example.

13. See www.fao.org/iptrid for more details.

BOX 13.7: **FARMNET – FARMER INFORMATION NETWORK FOR RURAL DEVELOPMENT**

Since the early 1990s, the UN Food and Agriculture Organization (FAO) has assisted in the development of networks among rural farmers and supported intermediary organizations using ICTs and conventional communication media for capacity development. Operated by farmers, these FarmNets disseminate locally relevant information that is needed to improve livelihoods. FAO adopted a participatory approach to performing the preliminary assessment of needs and then provided the electronic network designs, some basic equipment, logistical support, coordination, technical backstopping and training to local extension and farm organization personnel. The impact of FarmNet has been significant. Transmitting price and market information through computer-based networks cost 40 percent less than using traditional extension methods. In one case, by using the market information provided by the network, a farmer association was able to sell cotton for US $82 per metric quintal as opposed to US $72, which was the price local buyers were trying to impose. Vegetable producers reported that the information on meteorological conditions informed them of climatic conditions faced by competitors in other regions and countries. This enabled them to plan their irrigation strategies and market their produce more successfully.

Source: FAO, 2000.

BOX 13.11: THE NEED FOR GENDER BALANCE

Women produce between 60 and 80 percent of the food in most developing countries and provide up to 90 percent of the rural poor's food intake. Women are major stakeholders in all development issues related to water. Yet they often remain on the periphery of management decisions and planning for water resources.

To overcome this deficiency, an inter-agency Task Force on Gender and Water was inaugurated to work towards the implementation of gender-sensitive water and sanitation

activities. In addition, the Gender and Water Alliance (GWA) was established at the World Water Forum in 2000.

The GWA has developed a training methodology geared towards building capacity to mainstream gender equity in integrated water resources management. The Vice Ministry of Basic Services and the Ministry of Agriculture of Bolivia have undertaken gender audits in both institutions, turning this unique research and analytical initiative into a 'learning by doing gender'

experience. Although the audits indicated that the approach to gender equity is not reflected in sector policies – nor is the impact of programmes and projects on local women and men systematized with feedback to decision-making levels – issues related to gender responsiveness are becoming increasingly important.

Sources: See www.un.org/esa/sustdev/sdissues/water/Interagency_activities.htm#taskforce_water for more information; UN, 2003a; Arce, 2005; www.genderandwateralliance.org

Mid-career professionals receive on-the-job training by local experts in Indonesia

salaries, lack of equipment, demoralized environment and the bureaucratically inefficient management. As it turned out, the trained personnel stayed in the public sector but were underperforming because 'the opportunity to use office hours and equipment to significantly augment official salaries through private-income earning activities provided a major incentive to stay in the civil service' (Cohen and Wheeler, 1997). The institution's performance therefore suffered not from a lack of skilled human resources, but from lack of incentives coupled with poor accountability and management structure.

Sound demand-driven research on water-related issues enhances the ability for more rational decision-making on costs, impacts, and benefits of alternative policy options and institutional arrangements. Investing in research and development and its associated infrastructure, equipment and human resources means that conventional approaches to recurring problems can be challenged and new ways of addressing local engineering, social, economic and environmental issues may begin to flourish.

3c. Creating an enabling environment

The enabling environment consists of the broader political, policy, legal, regulatory and administrative frameworks that set the boundary conditions for the execution of the organizational and operational functions of the agencies and institutions entrusted with the development and management of water resources and services. A truly enabling environment is created primarily by policies that focus on sustainable development, consider water as a social and economic good, and are supported by legal and financial frameworks that ensure the policies are

implemented. A proper enabling framework will also emphasize the need for sector agencies to continuously improve their performance, through knowledge creation and acquisition, and through reform. For a broader sector reform to run its course, governments must be able to rely on realistic fiscal and monetary policies in the water sector, including adequate cost-recovery mechanisms, and transparent and equitable judicial systems (van Hofwegen and Jaspers, 1999). Civil society has an important role in developing the enabling environment. Well-informed civil groups and the media can enhance the awareness of the public at large of the need for particular actions, and can at the same time provide the information that empowers and motivates them to change their attitudes (social learning).

As a consequence of their decentralization policies, many governments such as Indonesia and Pakistan are now discussing and facilitating the possibilities of sub-sovereign financing and decentralized funding. Enhancing availability and access to finance especially is an essential element of the institutional capacity and was identified as one of the main recommendations of the Camdessus Panel, an initiative of the World Water Council, the Global Water Partnership and the Secretariat of the 3rd World Water Forum (Winpenny and Camdessus, 2003). To support the investment requirements at sub-sovereign level, various innovative initiatives and financing mechanisms have been recommended and some of them have been launched. These initiatives enhance the amount of financing available as they mobilize local capital markets by provision of guarantees for especially local political and currency risks and they enable financing at sub-sovereign level. Some of them,

BOX 13.12: INITIATIVES TO ENHANCE ACCESS TO FINANCE AT SUB-SOVEREIGN LEVEL

The Municipal Fund that was established in May 2003 is a joint World Bank/International Finance Corporation (IFC) initiative to invest in projects at the state and municipal level - without taking sovereign guarantees.

The Department and International Development (DFID)/World Bank Global Partnership on Output-Based Aid (OBA) provides a strategy for supporting the delivery of basic services where policy concerns justify the use of public funding to complement or replace user fees. OBA approaches utilize targeted subsidies that are performance-based and paid largely after the delivery of specified outputs (e.g. water supply connections) and mobilize private capital and management. The most common form of OBA is subsidizing water supply connections for the poor. Some other initiatives are the European Union Water Facility for the African, Caribbean and Pacific Countries (ACP-EUWF) and the Asian Development Bank Water for All initiative.

Source: Spicer, 2005; Veevers-Carter, 2005; van Hofwegen, 2005; www.ifc.org/municipalfund

like Output Based Aid and ADB-Water for All initiatives, focus particularly on reaching the poor (see **Box 13.12**).

Capacity development is dependent on the government's political will to change the existing policy, legal, management and economic frameworks and to implement reforms, as well as on the introduction of new governance systems and the familiarization of decision-makers and implementers with improved ways of managing water. This implies that capacity development actions have to include the political, social, economic and administrative dimensions of systems that may affect management of water resources and delivery of water services. This can go as far as the inclusion of policies in relation to organization of government, delegation of authority, career planning, salary and reward systems within the civil service and the creation of incentive mechanisms to enhance effective governance. It also implies development of policies that enhance access to finance for development and management of water infrastructure and services.

Until now capacity development has often been focused at the level of new utility management, communities or basin and water users associations. However, the decentralization and management transfer policies in many countries add a new dimension to capacity development: the development of new regulatory and governance systems at the decentralized levels. Unfortunately, the changing roles of government are not always accompanied with the associated capacity development and incentive systems required to effectuate the change. This is often due to a combination of a lack of knowledge on the implementation of these new roles, inherent resistance to innovation and a lack of appreciation of local capacity, knowledge and experience.

It follows that an important aspect of good governance in stimulating capacity development is related to research and education. Governments have to provide incentives and mechanisms that stimulate education and research institutions to address the real societal issues and demand. This can be done through applied-oriented research funds and through activation of professional, commercial, civil society and political institutions in the development of education and research programmes. The European Union has provided instruments through its fifth and sixth framework programmes that support the development of such linkages in society and among education and research institutions.

A country may even have to modify its national laws and regulations to enable education institutions to adjust their curriculum in response to demands from society. One such example is the new law on higher education in Indonesia (2003). This law has opened up the possibility to include private education institutions with their linkages to professional organizations and the private sector. Moreover, the accreditation system has been changed from pre-approval of the curricula to post-approval by an accreditation board. This is a big step towards the development of dynamic and society responsive education and research environment.

Similarly, supply-oriented programmes for education and training of water user associations and community organizations have to be changed into demand-driven programmes with a menu structured delivery system of training services where the communities or user organizations can match their needs and priorities. This will facilitate a better assimilation of new knowledge and put it into practice more quickly.

National and international meetings are another way of providing a platform for local authorities, politicians, water

...retention rates of trained individuals were much higher than expected for the perceivably low salaries, lack of equipment, demoralized environment and the bureaucratically inefficient management

UNEP GEMS/Water Programme: www.gemswater.org
US National Academies' Water Information Centre: water.nationalacademies.org
Water and Sanitation International Benchmarking Network (IBNET): www.ib-net.org
Water and Sanitation Programme: www.wsp.org
Water Research Network: water.nml.uib.no/
WCA infoNET: www.wca-infonet.org

Some international water networks and professional associations
American Institute of Hydrology (AIH): www.aihydro.org/
Freshwater Action Network: www.freshwateraction.net
International Association of Hydraulic Engineering and Research (IAHR): www.iahr.org/
International Association of Hydrogeologists (IAH): www.iah.org/
International Association of Hydrological Sciences (IAHS): www.cig.ensmp.fr/~iahs/
International Commission on Irrigation and Drainage (ICID): www.icid.org
International Network of Basin Organizations: www.inbo-news.org/
International Water Association (IWA): www.iawq.org.uk/
International Water Resources Association: www.iwra.siu.edu/
International Waters Learning Exchange and Resource Network (IW:LEARN): www.iwlearn.org/
Latin American Network for Water Education and Training (LA WETnet): www.la-wetnet.org/
Nile Basin Capacity-Building Network for River Engineering (NBCBN-RE): www.nbcbn.com
Streams of Knowledge: www.streams.net
Water Environment Federation (WEF): www.wef.org/
WaterNet: www.waternetonline.ihe.nl/
World Meteorological Organization – World Hydrological Cycle Observing System (WHYCOS): www.wmo.ch/web/homs/projects/whycos.html
For additional professional associations see www.unesco.org/water/water_links/Type_of_Organization/Professional_Organizations/

Environmental & Water Resources Institute (EWRI): www.ewrinstitute.org/
Global Development Learning Network (GLDN): www.gdln.org
International Water Management Institute (IWMI): www.iwmi.cgiar.org and www.iwmidsp.org/iwmi/info/main.asp
Research Institute for Development (IRD): www.ird.fr

Some international institutions for water education and research
UNESCO Centre for Water Hazard and Risk Management: www.unesco.pwri.go.jp/
UNESCO-IHE Institute for Water Education: www.unesco-ihe.org
Water Virtual Learning Centre: www.inweh.unu.edu/inweh/Training/WVLC.htm
For additional information on institutions for water-related training, education and research, visit www.unesco.org/water/water_links/Type_of_Organization/
Educational_Training_and_Research_Institutions/.

SECTION 5
Sharing Responsibilities

Local-level actions and on-the-ground insights are the starting point of the global strategy to improve the overall quality and quantity of the world's water resources. Lessons learned — successes and failures — are invaluable sources of information and, if properly shared, will help us to solve some of the world's most pressing freshwater-related problems.

Improving water management and stewardship means meeting basic needs, reducing vulnerabilities, improving and securing access to water and empowering the poverty-stricken to manage the water upon which they depend.

Chapter 14 – **Case Studies: Moving Towards an Integrated Approach**

These 16 case studies from around the world examine water resource challenges and provide valuable on-the-ground insights into the facets of the water crisis and different management responses: The Autonomous Community of the Basque Country (Spain), Danube River Basin (Albania, Austria, Bosnia-Herzogovina, Bulgaria, Croatia, the Czech Republic, Germany, Hungary, the Former Yugoslav Republic of Macedonia, Moldova, Poland, Romania, Serbia and Montenegro, Slovak Republic, Slovenia, Switzerland, Ukraine), Ethiopia, France, Japan, Kenya, Lake Peipsi (Estonia, Russian Federation), Lake Titicaca (Bolivia, Peru), Mali, the State of Mexico, Mongolia (Tuul Basin), La Plata Basin (Argentina, Bolivia, Brazil, Paraguay, Uruguay), South Africa, Sri Lanka, Thailand, Uganda.

Chapter 15 – **Conclusions and Recommendations for Action**

Drawing on the essential points and key messages presented throughout the Report, this chapter weaves together a set of conclusions and recommendations to guide future action and enhance the sustainable use, productivity and management of the world's increasingly scarce and polluted freshwater resources.

Water links us to our neighbour in a way more profound and complex than any other.

John Thomson

CHAPTER 14
Case Studies

14

implemented to mitigate the negative effects of droughts and floods. However, experience has shown that defensive action against water-related hazards alone is insufficient. The action programme, recently adopted by the members of the International Commission for the Protection of the Danube River, recognizes floods as a natural part of the hydrologic cycle and emphasizes the need to be cautious when planning development activities in flood-risk areas and manage risk through a basin approach, with the participation of governments, municipalities and stakeholders. Within the framework of the programme, which primarily refers to United Nations Economic Commission for Europe (UNECE) Guidelines on Sustainable Flood Prevention and adopts EU Best Practices on Flood Prevention, Protection and Mitigation, conservation and improvement of water-related ecosystems are a high priority, since wetlands act as a buffer against floods, thereby reducing their intensity.

In several regions, both surface and groundwater resources are under varying levels of stress due to growing population and continuing industrialization. In many instances, water resources are not utilized in a sustainable manner. In the State of Mexico, it is estimated that groundwater resources are used at twice their rate of natural recharge which causes land subsidence up to 40 centimetres (cm) per year due to the shrinking of aquifers as water is drawn out and leads to the disruption of water and sanitation infrastructure and increases vulnerability to floods.

Droughts are also a part of the water cycle and take place with varying frequency and severity. The outcomes of our case studies show how drought aggravates the level of poverty and famine, especially in Africa. In Ethiopia, one of the poorest countries in the world, there have been about thirty major drought episodes over the past nine centuries, thirteen of which were severe at the national scale and put millions of Ethiopians in dire need for basic food assistance. Even countries with abundant rainfall are prone to droughts. In Sri Lanka, twenty-three droughts were reported between 1947 and 1992, severely disrupting the Sri Lankan economy. During the 2001 drought, for example, the country faced power cuts for up to eight hours per day. In 2004, over fifty thousand hectares of crops were damaged, and the government had to appeal for assistance to provide food rations for approximately one million people for a six-month period. Flood and drought forecasting systems are necessary to take precautionary measures and to reduce the socio-economic impacts of such natural disasters. However, lack of funding or limited funding slows down the effective implementation of such systems. Consequently, flood-warning systems are missing in a great number of flood-prone basins. Flood-forecasting models in Sri Lanka fail to simulate real-life situations due to the poor mathematical algorithms employed. In Kenya, disaster management has not been viewed as an integral part of development planning, and water-related disasters were responded to in an ad hoc manner whenever they occurred. As a result, the variation in rainfall has had a significant effect on rainfed agriculture, upon which Kenya's economy heavily relies.

Climatic variations affect livelihoods of urban and rural dwellers. For example, in the Lake Titicaca Basin (Peru and Bolivia), glaciers, which are the major source of water for drinking and irrigation, are receding and reducing volumetrically. This trend will spell disaster for small and medium-scale irrigation, causing an increase in water prices, possibly aggravating poverty and triggering social movements.

BOX 14.1: THE EUROPEAN UNION WATER FRAMEWORK DIRECTIVE

Abundant and clean water is a given for most of the people living in the European Union (EU). However, many human activities put a pressure on both water quality and quantity. Polluted water from industry, agriculture and household use causes damage to the environment and affects the health of those using the same water resources. The EU Water Framework Directive (WFD) came into force on 22 December 2000 and aims to establish a framework for the protection of surface and groundwater, as well as coastal waters.

This directive requires all inland and coastal waters to reach 'good status'[1] by 2015. The definition of the good water status includes the chemical composition of water and the ecological elements. In order to reach this goal, a river basin structure is established within which certain environmental targets are set. The most important aspects of the WFD is that it calls for sustainable development, requires the adoption of integrated river basin management and links and coordinates all previous water policies, such as the directives on urban waste water treatment, nitrates, bathing or drinking water into a common framework. Finally, the integration of water policy with other major EU policies (like agriculture, hydropower and navigation, for example) is a prerequisite for successful protection of the aquatic environment.

In 2009, measurement programmes will be established in each river basin district for delivering environmental objectives (article 11). The first river basin management plan for each river basin district, including environmental objectives for each body of surface or groundwater and summaries of programmes of measures (article 13) will also be published.

Recognizing that water management must respond to local conditions and needs, the WFD, has strong public information and consultation components that encourage all interested parties to become involved in the production, reviewing and updating of river basin management plans.

1. The values of the biological quality elements for the surface water body type show low levels of distortion resulting from human activity, but deviate only slightly from those normally associated with the surface water body type under undisturbed conditions.

Source: EC, 2000.

The importance of Integrated Water Resources Management (IWRM) is becoming increasingly recognized throughout the world and the legislative and regulatory frameworks needed for putting IWRM tools into use are being created and revised. The involvement of stakeholders is encouraged through the establishment of community councils and river basin organizations, which share the responsibility of water management with national institutions. However, the World Summit on Sustainable Development (WSSD) target for the preparation of IWRM and efficiency plans in all countries by 2005 has not been fully met. Furthermore, although water management laws, policies, programmes and regulations do exist, their enforcement and implementation remain problematic. Implementation has proven to be particularly difficult in cases where there has been little public involvement. Hence, facilitating the participation of water users and stakeholders in the management and allocation of water resources remains an important challenge.

The major problem plaguing many of our case study partners is the lack of coordination between institutions and agencies responsible for drafting and implementing policy. This is especially critical for multi-state

countries, such as Mexico where decisions taken at the federal level need to be implemented at the state level. In the State of Mexico, the legal framework has been revised to allow the creation of the Secretariat of Water, Public Works and Infrastructure for Development (SAOPID), which is single-handedly responsible for preparing and implementing State policy guidelines concerning public works and infrastructure development. This secretariat, which reports back to National Water Commission at the federal level, is the first of its kind in Mexico.

Lastly, and perhaps most importantly, the case studies demonstrate that where gross inadequacies exist in the provision of water and sanitation facilities, a lack of financial and human resources capacity can clearly be seen. Human resources capacity is not only essential to the implementation of policies and programmes, but to the proposal of innovative solutions overall. Furthermore, a lack of synergy and an unclear division of responsibility among institutions often exacerbates these problems and inhibits reforms from reaching the local level. Until these issues can be addressed, they will likely remain the most outstanding problems challenging the water sector of developing countries in the near future.

1. The Autonomous Community of the Basque Country

The Autonomous Community of the Basque Country (ACB) is one of seventeen autonomous bodies in Spain. It is densely populated, with 5 percent of the overall population of Spain (over 2 million people) living in 1.4 percent, or 7,234 square kilometres (km^2), of the total surface area of Spain (EUStat, 2005). Accordingly, the population density was 292 inhabitants per km^2 as of 2003. The surface area of exclusive internal basins is around 2,200 km^2 with a population density of over 600 inhabitants per km^2.

The ACB is a highly mountainous territory located across the western end of the Pyrenees and the eastern part of the Cantabrian Mountains. The Cantabrian-Mediterranean water divide formed by mountain ranges of modest altitude (1,000 to 1,600 m) divides the territory. A great portion of the ACB lies in the Bay of Biscay-Mediterranean watershed. However, on both sides of this basin, there are a series of small catchments, generally characterized by a high level of rainfall and extremely uneven terrain. Rainfall is abundant throughout the ACB, with an annual average of over 1,000 mm and a long-term variability of about 20 percent. Despite its relatively constant levels of rainfall, the region has experienced serious flooding and a number of droughts. The region's rugged surface conditions and high rainfall have prompted ACB to establish an extremely dense hydro-meteorological monitoring network, with over 330 control stations currently in operation.

Urban settlements are the biggest user of water resources. In fact, 72 percent of the overall water demand is utilized for urban consumption, whereas 14 percent is utilized by industry, and the remaining 14 percent

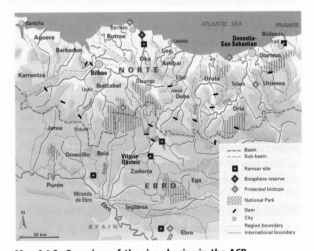

Map 14.2: Overview of the river basins in the ACB
Source: Prepared for the World Water Assessment Programme by AFDEC, 2006.

is used by agriculture. Although non-consumptive demands like hydroelectric energy production and aquaculture exert considerable local pressure on the movement of water in the region, these activities do not constitute an important part of the regional economy.

In parallel to industrial and urban development, the quality of the region's water resources and aquatic ecosystems has constantly degraded. In response to this situation, a network with 360 operational sampling points has been set up in order to survey the environmental

8. Lake Titicaca Basin

The Lake Titicaca Basin is composed of four major basins: Lake Titicaca, Desaguadero River, Lake Poopó and Coipasa Salt Lake. These four basins form the TDPS System, the main element being Lake Titicaca, the largest lake in South America and the highest navigable lake in the world. The TDPS System stretches approximately 140,000 km^2 and is located between 3,600 and 4,500 m.a.s.l.

Poverty and conflict: Persistent challenges

The initial case study report presented in WWDR1 (see **CD-ROM**) concluded that poverty was the most critical social problem in the TDPS system, affecting both rural and urban populations and undermining attempts to implement solutions to various problems. Unfortunately, in the past three years, no significant progress has been made to improve the situation.

In January 2005, the inhabitants of El Alto, Bolivia (located near La Paz), the main city of the TDPS System with 800,000 inhabitants (Instituto Nacional de Estadistica, 2005), protested the contract with Aguas del Illimani (Waters of Illimani), a subsidiary of French Suez Lyonnaisse des Eaux that was running a thirty-year concession for the water and sewage services in La Paz and El Alto. A week of civil disturbances finally came to an end with the resignation of the Constitutional President of Bolivia and the government's unilateral decision to end the water concession with Aguas del Illimani. The political transitions occurring in some Latin American countries since the 1980s have further added to the complexity of finding a solution to poverty. Peru was among the first Latin American countries to shift to a democratic regime. However, an increasingly authoritarian regime led to public outrage and caused the president to flee the country in 2000.

These events can be linked to structural poverty (see WWDR1 for more information), which stems from the combination of several socio-economic factors. Some of these factors are land property fragmentation (causing the under-utilization of land resources and thus low productivity) and indigenous cultural patterns leading to social exclusion. The effects of these factors are more pronounced in rural areas. Consequently, migration to urban settlements becomes the only choice for the rural poor, who hope to find better living conditions and mostly end up in crowded degraded districts. These migrants, the inhabitants of the Bolivian urban TDPS System, were the real actors of the social upheaval that took place in October 2003.

The impact of climate change on glaciers

During dry seasons, glaciers are the main source of drinking and irrigation water for many urban dwellers and farmers living in Peru and Bolivia. However, the climate variability and associated changes in ambient temperatures have started affecting the tropical glaciers of the region. The loss in volume of these unique tropical glaciers is alarming, and continuing melting trends will translate

Map 14.9: Overview of the Lake Titicaca Basin
Source: Prepared for the World Water Assessment Programme by AFDEC, 2006.

into drought for thousands of people. **Figure 14.1** illustrates the impact of climate change on the availability of water resources in the TDPS System.

The consequences of glacial melting for local populations are serious. Acting as reservoirs, glaciers regulate stream flow and diminish seasonal discharge variation. This effect is vital, especially between September and November, when ice melting (and water demand) is at its maximum. Discharges in glacier basins are important during those months, since the flows of other rivers in the Altiplano Basins reach minimum levels.

To counterbalance the negative effects of glacial melting, more dams and reservoirs will have to be constructed, increasing the cost of the water supply to Andean cities. It can be expected that the additional cost will be transferred to urban users by means of tariff increases, particularly in El Alto and La Paz, where the urban water supply is under private administration. Judging from recent social movements, any tariff increase would likely trigger potential conflicts, particularly in the poorest areas of El Alto. The additional costs of flow regulation in glacier basins could also be hard to afford for small and medium-sized irrigation systems, rendering rural poor more vulnerable.

Conclusion

Poverty remains the underlying cause of many social problems experienced by both rural and urban populations. Since the first WWAP case study was conducted in 2003, there has unfortunately been no improvement in living conditions. The poor are still struggling to meet the most basic of food and water needs. The expectation of better living conditions tempts young people to migrate to the cities; however, most of these people find themselves living in degraded crowded informal settlements, which lack even the most basic of utilities. The poor, even if they have physical access to water and health services, can only marginally take advantage of them due to poverty. In this context, the water-related problems of basin countries cannot be isolated; they must be addressed within the greater social framework. Better management of these countries' land, water and gas resources is the only means to break the vicious circle of poverty.

Figure 14.1: Areal and volumetric variation of the Chacaltaya Glacier

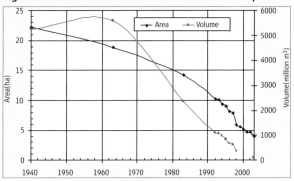

The data collected in the TDPS System shows the receding trend of tropical glaciers. Between 1991 and 2003, Zongo and Chacaltaya glaciers suffered both areal and volumetric losses. In fact, the accumulated mass balance, expressed as water depth, was -11.02 m for Zongo and -15.06 m for Chacaltaya. Chacaltaya glacier, a small glacier located at a medium altitude, lost 97 percent of its mass between 1960 and 2003 and is expected to disappear completely by 2010. This figure clearly shows that the receding trend started in the 1960s and has accelerated in the last twenty years.

9. Mali

Located in the heart of western Africa, Mali has a surface area of 1,241,000 km², over 50 percent of which is located in the Sahara Desert. More than 1,000 km away from the sea, the country is completely landlocked. Mali's location means that the country's climate can sometimes be quite unpredictable: years of abundant rainfall and years of extreme drought.

Three climatic groups can be discerned: arid desert in the northern region, arid to semi-arid in the centre and savannah in the south. The Sahara region, in the northwest tip of Mali, covers up to 57 percent of the national territory with an arid and semi-arid desert climate (rainfall usually does not exceed 200 mm per year). At its centre, the country's climate is characterized by the Sahel, encompassing about 18 percent of the land. The humid rainy season (June to October) usually brings between 200 and 700 mm of rainfall per year. The Niger River is an important part of this region, as the annual flooding of the river makes the surrounding land fertile for agricultural production. In the southern region of Mali, the rainy season generally brings over 1,200 mm of rain per year. This region and climate covers approximately 25 percent of the country. It is by far the most fertile area, where the majority of the population resides and where most agricultural activities take place.

Despite its northern desert, Mali has a number of important water resources. Two major rivers – the Niger River and the Senegal River – run through Mali. These two rivers constitute the majority of Mali's perennial surface water resources, providing the country with 56 billion m³ of water. Important non-perennial surface waters are estimated at a volume 15 billion m³. Mali also has seventeen large lakes situated near

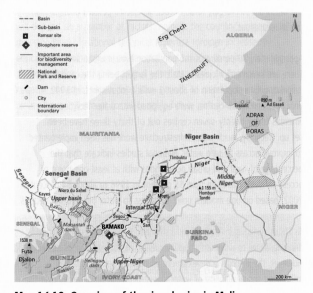

Map 14.10: Overview of the river basins in Mali

Source: Prepared for the World Water Assessment Programme by AFDEC, 2006.

the Niger River, and renewable groundwater resources from aquifers have been assessed at 66 billion m³. The volume of renewable water resources per capita per year is 10,000 m³.

However, these water resources are geographically dispersed and not always available when needed, greatly limiting their exploitation and economic development: overall, only 0.2 percent of Mali's potential water resources is put into use. Furthermore, the country has had many droughts in the past, compounding problems of water shortage issues.

BOX 14.8: TRANSBOUNDARY WATER RESOURCES IN MONGOLIA

There are about 210 rivers flowing through Mongolia into Russia and China. Mongolia aims for international cooperation concerning the equitable utilization of transboundary waters with its neighbours. The first international agreement on transboundary water resources was between the governments of Mongolia and the USSR in 1974 on the use of water and protection of the Selenge River Basin, which plays an important role for the economic and industrial development of both countries. The agreement made between the governments of Mongolia and the Russian Federation in 1995 on the protection of transboundary water resources focuses on over 100 small rivers and streams located in the western part of the country. In general, the drainage basins of transboundary rivers between Mongolia and the Russian Federation cover about 31.4 percent of the Mongolia's territory.

In 1994, an agreement was signed between China and Mongolia on the protection of transboundary water resources concerning Lake Buir, the Kherlen, Bulgan, Khalkh rivers, and eighty-seven small lakes and rivers located near the border. Transboundary water resources shared with China include surface water bodies in Dornod, Khovd, and Bayan-Ulgii provinces and groundwater resources in Gobi-Altai, Umnugobi, Bayankhongor, Sukhbaatar and Dornogobi provinces.

---

programme into the secondary school curriculum. However, due to the competing interests of different sectors and a lack of incentives for environmental protection, the rate of implementation of rules and regulations has been weak (MFA, 2004).

Challenges to well-being and development

Average per capita water consumption in Mongolia is very low. The average water consumption of populations living in yurt (the traditional tent-like structures used by nomads) districts of big settlements is around 10 litres per person per day, far from being enough to meet sanitary requirements. There are 10,000 cases of diarrhoea every year in Mongolia and almost 70 percent of these cases occur in Ulan Bator. Dysentery and hepatitis are also common. These infections stem from a lack of access to safe water and sanitation infrastructure.

Water for food

Nomadic livestock husbandry has long been the dominant economic activity in Mongolia. This sector employs 47 percent of the total population, produces 34.6 percent of agricultural gross production and accounts for 30 percent of the country's exports. Until recently, crop production was not considered a significant economic activity in Mongolia. Intensive land cultivation only began in 1958. Currently, about 130 million ha of land is used for agriculture. Almost 98 percent of this surface area is utilized as pastureland whereas farmland occupies less than 1 percent (806,000 ha) of this land (UNEP, 2002). As of 2000, agriculture employed 48 percent of the total work force, made up about 35 percent of Mongolia's GDP and 30 percent of total export products. Until 1990, crop production was sufficient to surpass the total domestic demand for flour, and surpluses of flour, potatoes and vegetables were exported. However, after the collapse of Soviet Union, both cropping area and yield have declined, due to a lack of funding and technical and managerial problems. Today, wheat production satisfies only 50 percent of domestic demand, and potato and vegetable production barely meets 40 percent of demand. Yet irrigation continues to be the most water-demanding sector. Approximately 43 percent of annual water abstraction is used for agriculture.

In recent years, climate changes have caused groundwater levels to fall, which has resulted in the drying up of some wells and springs (NSO, 2000). This has a great impact on animal herders living in remote areas of Mongolia. Consequently, the risk of livestock losses during the dry periods has increased enormously, and pastures near abundant water sources have become overused. The increasing number of livestock (from 25 million in 1990 to 30 million in 2000) clearly indicates that the problem is likely to get worse.

Water and industry

The mining industry contributes approximately 20 percent of national GDP and accounts for over 50 percent of overall exports. While mining is the largest industry in Mongolia, traditional industries such as fur and leather processing have also caused water pollution and affected ecosystems. Industrial water demand corresponds to 26 percent of annual supply. This rate of utilization is expected to increase in parallel to economic growth: since the 1990s, many new enterprises have been established, but environmental problems have increased due to lack of adequate environmental precautions.

Water and energy

Mongolia experiences an extremely cold climate for eight months of the year, making energy for heat generation crucial for survival. The large geographical area of the country and its low population density makes the provision of energy services a very difficult task. Wood and coal are commonly used for heating and cooking purposes. During the last decade, however, deforestation caused by firewood production has become one of the most serious and urgent environmental concerns in the country. Currently, only about 8 percent of Mongolia's territory (mostly in the north) is covered by forest. Using coal and wood for heat generation leads to serious air pollution.

People living in steppe, Gobi and desert areas face serious fuel shortages. The government of Mongolia has given top priority to developing the energy sector as the main electricity grid covers only 30 percent of the total land area, supplying power to about 1 million people.

Mongolia's hydropower potential is stagnant, due to a lack of funds for the implementation of large-scale hydropower projects. Currently, hydroelectricity is produced at five small hydropower plants in the western region of Mongolia.

Risk management and responses

The central and northern parts of the country are prone to floods during the periods of heavy rain. The inhabitants of yurt settlements are the most affected, as they are usually located in flood-prone areas. Floods cause greater economic damages when they take place in densely populated areas. For example, in July 1966, the water level of the Tuul River increased by 3 m. This flooded the industrial region of Ulan Bator, claiming the lives of 130 people and causing US $7.5 million in economic damages (UNEP, 2002).

Due to low average rainfall, drought is very common, especially in the desert-steppe zone of country, where droughts up to three consecutive years have been recorded. The biggest impact of drought is definitely on the agriculture sector, including animal husbandry. For example, in the central and southern regions of the country, droughts are frequently observed during the first stage of the growing period (UNEP, 2002). As a result, crop cultivation is becoming more and more dependent on large-scale irrigation schemes.

Unfortunately, neither flood nor drought prevention measures are organized in a systematic manner. In the case of floods, communities lack the advantage of early warning systems. Furthermore, there is a definite lack of public awareness.

Water resources management

The Government recognizes that conservation of water resources is of primary importance for the long-term development of the economy. This is reflected in the terms of reference of the National Water Programme, which aims to ensure sustainable development of the country by the efficient use and protection of water resources. In 2000, the National Water Committee (NWC) was established with the purpose of coordinating and monitoring the National Water Programme's implementation. It serves as the coordinating body of a number of ministries and local governments. However, there are no resources allocated for the realization of the National Water Programme. Furthermore, no specific milestones were identified. As a result, the NWC struggles to coordinate the actions of several ministries within the fragmented management scheme of water sector.

The legislative and regulatory framework for the use of water resources is in place and updated when necessary. For example, the Water Law, which was adopted in 1995, was amended in 2004 to integrate river basin management practices (including the establishment of enhanced water resources information systems, the development of river basins management plans and the establishment of river basin organizations) with the goal of better utilizing water resources while protecting ecosystems. The Water Law also recognizes the economic value of water, requires capacity-building in the water sector, focuses on the decentralization of water management, puts forward the need for environmental impact assessments and sets new penalties for violating water legislation. However, the provisions of the law are vague and open to interpretations by different sectors. Furthermore, although the newly amended law foresees provisions for IWRM, public involvement at the local level is missing. Therefore, developed policies and programmes lack any public ownership. Facilitating the involvement of water users and stakeholders in managing the allocation of water resources remains a challenge.

Water-related policies and programmes developed at the national level often do not reach the local level. Policy implementation and monitoring mechanisms are also strained. At the institutional level, financial and human resource capacity is limited. The coordination of numerous institutions at national and local levels is missing, and the division of responsibility is not clear. Due to financial limits, laws and regulations are not adequately enforced.

Ulan Bator and the surrounding settlements located upstream of the Tuul River Basin are the biggest water users. However, no management plan currently exists for the water resources of the Tuul River Basin.

Mongolia's pricing policy is decentralized; local authorities are entitled to set up and revise the water tariffs. Although in theory, the Mongolian Government gives priority to the interests and water needs of the poor and marginalized, in practice, the current pricing scheme has become pro-industry and pro-wealthy due to weak regulations. Water tariffs for the mining industry are about US $0.006 per 1,000 L, whereas small businesses pay about US $0.48 per 1,000 L (eighty times more). For metered apartment users, a fixed rate of between US $1.5 and $7.5 per month is charged per inhabitant. The rate for yurt consumers, similar to small businesses, is eighty-four times higher than for industries and mining companies. As a result, those with the lowest income pay the highest and consume the least.

Conclusion

After the fall of the Soviet Union, Mongolia has been going through a profound economic and political transition period. Poverty is on the rise, only a limited portion of the population has access to safe water, sanitation facilities are poor, the quality of water resources are decaying, water-related diseases are common, and health services are out of reach for the poor. These problems are further accentuated by water scarcity, a

16. Uganda

Situated southeast of Uganda is Lake Victoria, the principal source of the White Nile and the second largest freshwater lake in the world. Uganda's rivers and lakes, including wetlands, cover about 18 percent of the total surface area of the country.

Lake Victoria is very significant for the Ugandan economy, since it is the source of almost all of the country's hydropower and provides the domestic and industrial water supply for the three biggest towns in Uganda: Kampala, Jinja and Entebbe. It is also an important location for the fishery and horticulture industries. Additionally, the lake serves as a key transport link between Uganda, Kenya and Tanzania.

Uganda's total annual renewable water resources are estimated to be 66 km³. With an annual average of 2,800 m³ of water available per capita, Uganda is better off than many other African countries. However, rapid population growth, increased urbanization and industrialization, uncontrolled environmental degradation and pollution are placing increasing pressure on the utilization of freshwater resources.

Water and Ecosystems

With 13 percent of its total surface area covered by wetlands, Uganda is very rich in biodiversity. In spite of the existence of national policies and laws for the conservation of ecosystems, there has recently been an observed decline in aquatic biodiversity in most of Uganda's water bodies. This has mainly been attributed to destructive fishing habits, increasing eutrophication as a result of pollution, degradation of riparian watersheds and deforestation (see **Chapter 5** for a discussion of the alarming loss of biodiversity in Lake Victoria).

Rural areas

The percentage of rural inhabitants with access to improved sanitation increased from 68 percent in 1991 to 85 percent in 2002. However, access to clean and safe water is still far from universal (see **Chapter 6**). In 2003, only 59 percent of rural inhabitants had such access. Frequently, people have to collect water from distant locations. This burden falls mainly on women and children, who are the most vulnerable members of society. The long distances they travel significantly reduce their productive time and subsequent contribution to the economic development of the country. Furthermore, the amount of water that can generally be collected is insufficient to meet drinking, cooking and hygiene needs. According to National Surveys conducted in 1996 and 1999, average rural per capita water consumption was found to be about 13 litres per day. Though the sanitation coverage has increased significantly, in some rural areas, basic sanitation still remains elusive, due to poverty and low hygiene and sanitation awareness.

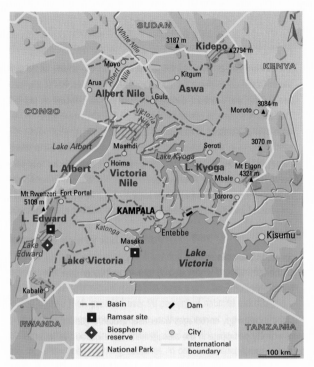

Map 14.17: Overview of the river basins in Uganda
Source: Prepared for the World Water Assessment Programme by AFDEC, 2006.

Urban settlements

In Uganda, urban areas are defined as settlements with over 5,000 inhabitants. Towns of 5,000 to 15,000 inhabitants are classified as small, and those with more than 15,000 inhabitants as large. Based on these criteria, there were 106 small towns and 43 large towns in Uganda in 2004. The current urban population is estimated to be 3.7 million out of a total population of 25 million. The urban population has been growing faster than that in rural areas – the overall population growth rate is 3.4 percent, while that in urban areas is 4.1 percent. The percentage of the population residing in urban areas increased from 12 percent in 1993 to 14 percent in 2003. National urban water coverage is an estimated 65 percent, up from 54 percent in 2000. The sanitation coverage is equally low, 65 percent.

Cost recovery

The current tariff structure of Ugandan water resource systems is aimed towards covering only operation and maintenance costs. Full cost recovery (operation and maintenance, depreciation and investment) would require a significant increase in tariffs. Therefore, major investments in system improvement and extension are financed separately through grants from the Government and international donors. The collection efficiency of revenues, although variable, is about 79 percent on average. Although funding levels are increasing, significant investment is still required to raise the safe water and sanitation coverage to meet the national targets and MDGs.

Water and health

Low access to clean water has had many health implications in Uganda. According to a study carried out in 2002, diarrhoea alone accounted for approximately 19 percent of infant mortalities in the country. Furthermore, statistics from the Ministry of Health indicate that malaria is the leading cause of child morbidity. Approximately 70,000 to 100,000 children in Uganda die every year from malaria. This represents 30 percent of the country's child mortality rates (between the ages of 2 and 4), and accounts for 23 percent of total disability-adjusted life years (DALYs) lost and 25 percent of all instances of illness in Uganda. Estimates from the Ministry of Health indicate that the average expenditure on malaria-related treatments are as high as US $300 million annually. AIDS is the leading cause of death for people between the ages of 15 and 49 and is responsible for 12 percent of all annual deaths (see **Chapter 6**).

Food security

The total potential irrigable area in Uganda is approximately 202,000 ha (FAO, 1995). However, a recent study by JICA (2004) revealed that about 14,000 ha of the potential irrigable area is under official irrigation and 6,000 ha under unofficial irrigation, particularly for rice production. The total amount of water used for irrigation is 12 km^3 per year, whereas the annual total renewable water resources are 66 km^3. These figures reveal the high potential for irrigated agriculture in Uganda. Currently, most of Uganda's agriculture is rainfed and thus more vulnerable during climatic variations. Food shortages and nutritional deficiencies are common in many parts of the country: 40 percent of deaths among children in Uganda are due to malnutrition. According to the 2002 Uganda Population and Housing Census, the country's annual population growth rate was 3.4 percent, while the annual growth rate of food production was only about 1.5 percent. If food production levels do not increase, food shortages will become more acute in the near future.

Livestock production is concentrated along 'the cattle corridor' which runs southwest to northeast across Uganda, encompassing twenty-nine districts. Animal husbandry is a considerable source of income. It represents 7.5 percent of the GDP and 17 percent of the agricultural GDP. However, water scarcity in the cattle corridor reduces productivity and triggers conflict among herders.

Fisheries also contribute to food security in Uganda and are crucial to populations living along rivers, lakes and islands as well as the disadvantaged rural poor. Current annual fish consumption is estimated to be 10 kg per capita. In the past, Uganda's fishing industry boasted over 300 endemic fish species, but unsustainable fishing practices and a deterioration in the quality of local water bodies have greatly reduced the number of commercial fish species. Today, only twenty-three remain. The Ugandan Government is also promoting aquaculture to boost fisheries production to better meet the increasing fish demand in both the domestic and international markets (see **Chapter 5**).

Poverty

As of 2002, close to 40 percent of Uganda's population lives below the poverty line, giving Uganda a rank of 142 out of 162 countries in terms of poverty. Poverty reduction has been a leading objective of Uganda's development strategy since the early 1990s. The Government, in its combat against poverty, prepared a Poverty Eradication Action Plan (PEAP) in 1997. The plan, which has been revised twice, employs a multi-sectoral approach that takes into consideration the multi-dimensional nature of poverty and the inter-linkages between influencing factors. In this regard, the government is making continuous efforts for development in the areas of agricultural modernization, land management, rural credit and microfinance, rural electrification, primary health care, primary education and water supply and sanitation. Of all these, perhaps the PEAP's most critical intervention is the modernization of agriculture. Considering that the agricultural sector employs 82 percent of Uganda's labour force and is the mainstay of the economy, these efforts have the potential of improving the living standards of most Ugandans. Furthermore, through the Plan for the Modernisation of

---

BOX 14.12: THE IMPACT OF RISING TEMPERATURES

The continent of Africa's temperature has risen by 0.5°C in the past century. The five warmest years in Africa's recorded history all occurred after 1988. Recent studies have shown that the glaciers and ice fields on Rwenzoris, one of a few of permanently ice-capped mountains in Africa, have decreased markedly both in number and size and that the greatest rate of shrinkage has been after 1990.

Malaria has for long been the leading cause of illness in Uganda and accounted for almost 39 percent of all mortality cases in 2002. Today, malaria incidences in the highlands (1,500 to 1,800 m a.s.l.) are thirty times higher than at the beginning of the twentieth century. Rising temperatures in addition to heavy El Niño rains, local climate changes arising from wetland drainage, population growth and human migrations are thought to be some of the most important factors contributing to this increase.

Rising temperatures will have a detrimental effect on the agriculture sector of Uganda. For example, if the current trend continues, a further 2°C rise in temperature would lead to an 85 percent shrinkage in the area suitable for growing rubusta coffee, which constitutes a significant portion of Uganda's export (see **Chapters 4 and 10** for discussions on climate change).

Infraestructura para el Desarrollo). 2005. *Damages Caused by the Overexploitation of Aquifers in the State of Mexico, Mexico.* Mexico City. 2005.

CAEM (Comisión de Agua del Estado de México. 2005. *Atlas de Inundaciones No. 11.*

—— 2004a. *Prontuario de Información Hidráulica del Estado de México.* Mexico City.

—— 2004b. *Situación Actual y expectativas del Subsector Agua y Saneamiento en el Estado de México.* Mexico City.

CNA (Comisión Nacional del Agua). 2004. *Estadísticas del Agua en México.* Mexico City.

11. Mongolia

Unless otherwise noted, all information is from the preliminary version of the Mongolia Case Study Report.

Altansukh, N. 1995. *Country Report to the FAO International Techincal Conference on Plant Genetic Resources.* Ulan Bator, National Plant Genetic Resources Research and extension Programme.

Myagmarjav, B and Davaa, G. (eds). 1999. *Surface waters of Mongolia.* Ulan Bator (in Mongolian).

UNEP (United Nations Environment Programme). 2002. *State of the Environment, Mongolia.* Ulan Bator, UNDP.

NSO (National Statistical Office). 2000. *Child and Development Survey.* Ulan Bator.

MFA (Ministry of Foreign Affairs). 2004. *Millennium Development Goals: The 2004 National Report on the Status of Implementation in Mongolia.* Ulan Bator.

12. La Plata River Basin

Unless otherwise noted, all information is from the executive summary of the La Plata River Basin Case Study Report.

Bucher, E. and Huszar, P. 1995. Critical Environmental Costs of the Paraná-Paraguay Waterway Project in South America. *Ecological Economics,* Vol. 15, No. 1, pp. 3-9.

Gottgens, J., Fortney, R., Meyer, J, Perry, J. and Rood, B. 1998. The Case of the Paraguay-Paraná Waterway (Hidrovía) and its Impact on the Pantanal of Brazil: A Summary Report to the Society of Wetlands Scientists. *Wetlands Bulletin* pp. 12-18.

Petrella, F. and Ayuso, A. 1996. *The Paraguay-Paraná Waterway: Towards Convergence with the Plata Regime, a Personal Approach.* Proceedings of an International Conference, Harvard University, David Rockefeller Center for Latin American Studies, Cambridge, Massachusetts, 3-4 April 1996.

13. South Africa

All information is from the preliminary version of the South Africa Case Study Report.

14. Sri Lanka

Unless otherwise noted, all information is from the executive summary of Sri Lanka Case Study Report.

UN (United Nations). 2002. Sri Lanka Country Profile. *The 2002 Country Profiles Series.* World Summit on Sustainable Development, Johannesburg, 2002.

Ministry of Social Welfare. 2004. *Request for Drought Relief Assistance, Initial Assessment of Emergency Requirement (Revised).* Colombo.

15. Thailand

Unless otherwise noted, all information is from the executive summary of the Thailand National Case Study Report.

ICEM (International Centre for Environmental Management). 2003. Review of protected areas and development in the Lower Mekong River Region, Indooroopilly, Queensland, Australia.

Ahuja, V., Bidani, B., Ferreira, F. and Walton, M. 1997. *Everyone's Miracle? Revisiting Poverty and Inequality in East Asia.* New York, World Bank.

FAO (Food and Agriculture Organization). 2000. Irrigation water use per country in the year 2000, *Aquastat 2000.* www.fao.org/ag/agl/aglw/aquastat/water_use/index.stm

Mekong River Commission:www.mrcmekong.org/

16. Uganda

All information is from the preliminary version of the Uganda Case Study Report.

All know the way, but few actually walk it.

Bodhidharma, 6th Century

CHAPTER 15

Conclusions and Recommendations

Flooded slum on the edge of Pasig River, Manila, Philippines

Maps

Figures

Photography

The World Water Assessment Programme would like to thank Bastien Affeltranger, the Ankara Fotoğraf Sanatçıları Derneği (AFSAD), Yann Arthus-Bertrand, the Australian Water Partnership, Robert Bos, Thomas Cluzel, Deanna Donovan, FAO, Richard Franceys, the GAP Bölge Kalkınma İdaresi Başkanlığı Arşivi (GAP-BKİ), the Ministry of Water and Agriculture of Kenya, IFAD, Christian Lambrechts, ICHARM, Alexander Otte, José María Sanz de Galdeano Equiza, Andras Szöllösi-Nagy, the Secretariat of Water, Public Works and Infrastructure for Development of the Government of the State of Mexico (SAOPID), Surapol Pattanee, UNESCO, UNESCO-IHE, UN-HABITAT, UNHCR and Sajith Wijesuriya for generously providing photographs.

cover
© SAOPID Mexico
© UNESCO – Andes / CZAP / ASA
© UNESCO – I. Forbes
© Sven Torfinn / Panos
© UNESCO – J. W. Thorsell
© Yann Arthus-Bertrand/La Terre vue du Ciel
© Surapol Pattanee
© Chris Stowers / Panos
© Australian Water Partnership

Front matter
IV: © Wim Van Cappellen / Still Pictures
VI: © Thomas Cluzel
VII: © Thoma Cluzel

SECTION 1
ii: © Thomas Cluzel
1: © Yann Arthus-Bertrand/La Terre vue du Ciel, © Sean Sprague / Still Pictures, © Yann Arthus-Bertrand/La Terre vue du Ciel

Chapter 01
8: © Ron Giling / Still Pictures
9: ©UN-HABITAT
10: © UNHCR/D. Shrestha
12: © UNESCO
13: © Mark Edwards / Still Pictures
16: © UNESCO – O. Brendan
17: © AFSAD / Selim Aytac
19: © Thomas Cluzel
20: © UNESCO
21: © Yann Arthus-Bertrand/La Terre vue du Ciel
27: © UNESCO - Evan Schneider
29: © UNESCO – Ines Forbes
34: © UNESCO – Niamh Burke
40: © Chris Stowers / Panos

Chapter 2
42: © Sean Sprague / Still Pictures
44: © Yann Arthus-Bertrand/La Terre vue du Ciel © Richard Franceys, © Mark Edwards / Still Pictures
45: © Julio Etchart / Still Pictures

52: © Thomas Cluzel
53: © Jorgen Schytte / Still Pictures
54: © Sean Sprague / Still Pictures
60: © Ton Koene / Still Pictures
74: © UNESCO / O. Brendan
77: © Hartmut Schwarzbach / Still Pictures
80: © Dirk R Frans / Still Pictures
81: © UNESCO / O. Brendan
83: © Thomas Cluzel

Chapter 3
86: © Ron Giling / Still Pictures
88: © UNESCO – Alexis Vorontzoff, © UN-HABITAT, © UN-HABITAT
89: © John Maier, Jr / Still Pictures
93: © Yann Arthus-Bertrand/La Terre vue du Ciel
94: © Andras Szöllösi-Nagy
96: © Andras Szöllösi-Nagy
97: © Mikkel Ostergaard / Panos
99: © Neil Cooper / Still Pictures
103: © UNESCO - Alexis Vorontzoff
105: © UN-HABITAT, © UN-HABITAT
107: © UNHCR/D. Shrestha
108: © UN-HABITAT
111: © Alexander Otte, © Alexander Otte / Veolia, © UNESCO – Dominique Roger

SECTION2
114: © Voltchev/UNEP / Still Pictures

Chapter 4
120: © Thomas Cluzel, © FAO/17287/ J. Holmes, © Mitchell Rogers/UNEP / Still Pictures
123: © Manit Larpluechai / UNEP / Still Pictures
125: © Thomas Cluzel
127: © UNESCO – A. de Crepy
136: © Yann Arthus-Bertrand/La Terre vue du Ciel
142: © Thomas Cluzel
143: © UNESCO – G. Boccardi
146: © UNESCO - A. Wheeler
147: © Ron Giling / Still Pictures
157: © AFSAD / Serpil Yıldız

Chapter 5
158: C Johnson /WWI / Still Pictures
160: © SOAPID Mexico, © UNESCO - I. Forbes, © Yann Arthus-Bertrand/La Terre vue du Ciel
161: © FAO/17121/M. Marzot
163: © C. Zöckler
164: © Nicolas Granier / Still Pictures
166: © SAOPID Mexico, © Sajith Wijesuriya
167: © SAOPID Mexico
168: © UNESCO – I. Forbes
171: © UNESCO
173: © Paul Glendell / Still Pictures
175: © Sajith Wijesuriya
184: © UNESCO – E. Timpe
191: © Alexander Otte/Veolia
192: © Christopher Uglow/UNEP / Still Pictures
197: © UNESCO – Peter Coles

SECTION 3
198: © Marcia Zoet / UNEP / Still Pictures

Chapter 6
202: © Julio Etchart / Still Pictures
204: © UN-HABITAT, © Andras Szöllösi-Nagy, © Shehzad Noorani / Still Pictures
205: © FAO/19526/G. Bizzarri
208: © UNESCO – O. Brendan
210: © Yann Arthus-Bertrand/La Terre vue du Ciel
212: © Jorgen Schytte / Still Pictures
221: © Jorgen Schytte / Still Pictures
223: © UNESCO – Dominique Roger
225: © UNESCO - Henry Bernard
227: © UNESCO/IHE – Fred Kruis
235: © Jacob Silberberg / Panos
236: © Robert Bos
241: © Mark Edwards / Still Pictures

Chapter 7
242: © UNEP/Still Pictures
244: © FAO/17346/R. Faidutti, © Mark Edwards / Still Pictures, © Yann Arthus-Bertrand/La Terre vue du Ciel, FAO/18992/R. Faidutti

245: © Glen Christian / Still Pictures
247: © SAOPID Mexico
248: © FAO/17268/ C. Sanchez
250: © FAO/15157/A. Conti
252: © FAO/17343/R. Faidutti
254: © AFSAD / Serpil Yıldız
255: © FAO/22404/ R. Faidutti, © Jinda Uthaipanumas/UNEP / Still Pictures
256: © FAO/22375/R. Messori
257: © FAO/19756/G. Bizzarri
259: © FAO/17086/M. Marzot
261: © Peter Frischmuth / Still Pictures
262: © Jeremy Horner/Panos
263: © Yann Arthus-Bertrand/La Terre vue du Ciel
264: © Joerg Boethling / Still Pictures
265: © Julio Etchart / Still Pictures
270: ©Alexander Otte/Veolia
271: ©Alexander Otte/Veolia, © FAO/13504/I. de Borhegyi

Chapter 8
274: © Jim Wark / Still Pictures
276: © UNESCO / I. Forbes, © MARK EDWARDS / Still Pictures
277: © Agence de l'eau Artois Picardie
279: © Adrian Arbib / Still Pictures, © Ron Giling / Still Pictures
284: © Agence de l'eau Artois Picardie
288: © UNESCO – Dominique Roger
290: © Jochen Tack / Still Pictures
292: © William Campbell / Still Pictures
294: © Yu Qiu/UNEP / Still Pictures
299: © Agence de l'eau Artois Picardie
300: © Agence de l'eau Artois Picardie

Chapter 9
304: © William Campbell / Still Pictures
306: © UNESCO, © Sean Sprague / Panos
307: © Yann Arthus-Bertrand/La Terre vue du Ciel
308: © Martin Bond / Still Pictures
309: © Sean Sprague / Still Pictures
310: © Jorgen Schytte / Still Pictures